GEORGE GISSING: A CRITICAL BIOGRAPHY

JACOB KORG

GEORGE GISSING:

A CRITICAL BIOGRAPHY

University of Washington Press
Seattle · 1963

⌐√

The end-paper design is from Tallis' view
of Tottenham Court Road from north to
south, circa 1838, reprinted from London's
Old Latin Quarter, by E. Beresford Chancel-
lor.

THIS BOOK IS PUBLISHED WITH THE ASSISTANCE
OF A GRANT FROM THE FORD FOUNDATION.

ACKNOWLEDGMENTS

For permission to quote from manuscripts, I am indebted to Mr. A. C. Gissing, to the Yale University Library, and to the Henry W. and Albert A. Berg Collection of the New York Public Library as owner of original documents, for access to its Gissing materials and its consent to publication. Permission to quote from manuscripts in the Carl H. Pforzheimer Library has been granted by the Carl and Lily Pforzheimer Foundation, Inc. Quotations from *Demos* are published by permission of E. P. Dutton and Company. I am indebted to Professor Susan H. Nobbe and the late Professor Angus Burrell, both of Columbia University, for guidance in preliminary work leading to this book. For assistance in locating materials, I should like to thank Mr. George Matthew Adams, Dr. John D. Gordan, Miss Eleanor L. Nicholes, Miss Marjorie G. Wynne, and staff members of the Huntington Library. I am indebted to Mme. Denise le Mallier and M. Pierre Coustillas for a number of important facts.

This book was prepared with the support of the Research Fund of the Graduate School of the University of Washington and is published with the aid of a grant from the Agnes Anderson Fund.

CONTENTS

LIST OF ILLUSTRATIONS

GEORGE
GISSING:
A CRITICAL
BIOGRAPHY

I

FROM WAKEFIELD TO LONDON

I

O N THE evening of July 21, 1880, Frederic Harrison stayed up long past his usual bedtime to read a novel sent to him by an unknown author. It was a savagely realistic account of life in the slums of London, the story of an orphan boy who gains friends among the poor and grows up, in spite of poverty and abuse, into a thoughtful and talented young man. Although Harrison felt that the novel's treatment of "prostitutes, thieves, and debauchees" verged on impropriety, he was stirred by its confrontation of the social evils and ethical dilemmas to which he had devoted his own career as a social reformer. The next day, in the first flush of his enthusiasm, and without giving himself a chance to finish the novel, he wrote to the author. "There can be no doubt as to the power of your book," he began. "It will take rank amongst the works of great rank of these years. . . . I especially hate the so-called realism of Zola. . . . Your book therefore goes against all my sympathies in art, so that my admiration for its imaginative power is wrung from me. . . . There are scenes, I am sure, which can hold their ground with the first things in modern fiction." [1] The book which won this praise from the reluctant Harrison was *Workers in the Dawn*. It was the first novel of a young man of twenty-two named George Gissing.

The novelist was soon invited to dinner, and Harrison found him to be a tall, shy man whose serious dignity of manner made him seem older than his years. His face was pale, sensitive, delicate in feature, and touched with freckles. He wore a drooping, full mus-

3

tache, and his flowing, wavy, reddish-brown hair was combed straight back from his high forehead. His light blue eyes, deep-set under a prominent brow, might already have begun to acquire the piercing, agonized look that they had in later years. His face was always grave, and it sometimes bore an unconscious expression of deep sadness which contrasted with the neat waxing of his mustache, the conventional stiffness of his collar, and the vigor of his walk. Harrison liked the young writer, and, learning that he was poor and in need, made a cause of him. He invited him to visit often, wrote on his behalf to a number of literary men, including John Morley, then editor of the *Pall Mall Gazette*, and recommended him to friends as a private tutor. Toward the end of the year he engaged him to teach his two oldest sons, who were being educated at home.

The new tutor was an immediate success. At the first lesson he introduced himself to his pupils with a grave smile, turned their names of Austin and Bernard into comic Latin, and made warm friends of them. He seemed full of resources for making the lessons more vivid and enjoyable. He could talk about Greece and Rome with a fiery enthusiasm that carried over to such dull subjects as Roman history. The boys found him as playful and energetic as themselves on occasion. He could see the amusing side of common things and bring it forward with gentle irony. Often his humor and laughter became so uproarious that their father, hearing the noise, came in from the next room to join in the joke.

In public, however, Gissing's boisterous good humor melted away, and he became shy and self-conscious. "Gissing at parties was an unforgettable spectacle of misery," reports Austin Harrison. "He would sit in a corner of the room, crouched together like a wet bird, silent and strangely watchful." [2] The music played at these parties made a profound impression on him, and he was visibly moved as he listened. He could whistle very skillfully himself, in a low, soft style. The boys often made him repeat a favorite melody, "Twickenham Ferry," after their lesson was over. Gissing had his own odd way of keeping order in the schoolroom. When the boys misbehaved, he simply stared at them with his sad and tortured eyes until their own shame had corrected them. Then he laughed and continued the lesson.

Because they loved to hear the discussions between their tutor and their serious, dogmatic father, the boys often adopted the ruse of delaying their lessons so long that Gissing had to stay for lunch. Harrison was then in his fifties and in the middle of his career as a militant liberal. He had intended to become a clergyman as a young man, but his dissatisfaction with the church's general incompetence and indifference to social problems led him to revolt against his Evangelical upbringing. After holding a fellowship at Wadham College, Oxford, from 1854 to 1856, he decided not to take orders and instead entered legal practice in London. He read Comte under the influence of Richard Congreve, one of the first English Positivists, became a Radical, and entered upon his lifelong work of attacking mid-Victorian prejudices with typical mid-Victorian earnestness and depth of conviction.

Harrison described himself as "a humble follower of Comte, Mill, Spencer and Darwin." [3] A firm Positivist, he felt that the rapidly developing sciences had profound implications for political and social life and might serve as the source of a new ethical ideal. Although he was sympathetic with the 1848 revolutions and the Paris Commune of 1870, he advocated reform rather than revolution in England. Popular education, improved working conditions, and liberal labor legislation were among his interests. By the time Gissing came to know him, he had achieved a considerable public reputation as the author of two books and many articles, a member of two Royal commissions, a supporter of striking laborers, and a leading figure in the small English Positivist Society of which he was soon to become president. *Workers in the Dawn* must have interested him because of its treatment of such problems as poverty, working conditions, and labor politics, and because its heroine, after a long quest, adopted Positivism as her personal religion.

All this, no doubt, led Harrison to expect in the author an enthusiasm for reform comparable to his own. But Gissing was concerned, he found, not with reform, but with fact; not with the abstractions of theory, but with the particularities of art. He felt that the moral and spiritual destruction wrought by poverty lay beyond the scope of political remedies. To Harrison, who was accustomed to dealing with practical matters, Gissing seemed to lack ethical sense. He despised the ignorance and brutality of the poor whose way of life he had so vividly captured in his novel, and he wrote about them, it seemed to Harrison, simply to feed the pessimism he perversely enjoyed. Harrison, who hated pessimism, could not abide the casual nihilism of this otherwise congenial young man. He did his best to instill some of his own reforming spirit into him, but Gissing refused to be converted. "I must wallow and describe," he insisted. Thus, at the luncheons the Harrison boys enjoyed so much they saw the earnest advocate of the common people, armed with the ideals of science and progress, facing the detached, and no doubt slightly cynical, exponent of the interests of art and culture. It was not the first time Harrison had tried to convince an author of his responsibility toward social reform. In 1866 he had proposed to his friend and fellow Positivist, George Eliot, that she write a poetic drama illustrating the advantages of a society run on Comtian principles. And in the following year, by writing a vigorous rejoinder to Matthew Arnold's *Cornhill* article, "Culture and Its Enemies," he had forced Arnold to state his defence of culture more fully in the series of essays that became *Culture and Anarchy*.

Harrison, who had stiffly warned Gissing that he was less interested in literature than in the character and integrity of authors, began to learn some unpleasant things about his protégé as time went by. For one thing, he was impractical. His career as a writer for magazines, inaugurated under Harrison's sponsorship, did not prosper; Harrison was critical of his style, and Gissing said that he found the work "degrading." After writing two pieces on socialism for the *Pall Mall Gazette*, he gave up journalism, and in spite of Harrison's advice to take some regular position appropriate to his abilities he returned to earning his living by tutoring while working on another novel after hours. Harrison's respect for Gissing survived these disagreements, but it soon had to face a far more serious test. One day a man who had known Gissing when he was a student at Owens College in Manchester saw him at Harrison's house and let it be known that he had been arrested for stealing from the college common room when he was an undergraduate. He had been dismissed from the college in disgrace and had been tried, convicted, and sentenced to a term in prison.

There followed, says Austin Harrison, "a long morning's explanation." Gissing must have been completely honest with his protector in this discussion. He undoubtedly admitted his crime, explaining that he had committed it only because he had hoped to save the girl he loved from prostitution with the money it brought him.

Later he had married her, and he now lived with her in poor lodgings, carrying on a bitter daily struggle against her illness, drunkenness, and irresponsibility. Harrison might easily have applied his severe moral standards to Gissing's past behavior and dismissed him. Instead he heard his confession sympathetically, acknowledged that he had gone through terrible trials for so young a man, and maintained an unchanged relationship with him.

II

The pathetic and shocking life story Harrison heard from Gissing began in a perfectly ordinary way. The novelist's father, Thomas Waller Gissing, was a chemist, whose shop stood in the market place of the town of Wakefield in Yorkshire. George Robert Gissing was born in the rooms over the shop on November 22, 1857, the oldest in a family that was to consist of three brothers and two sisters. The house, which is still standing in a busy part of Wakefield, is now called 30 Westgate. It is a straight-fronted brick structure of three stories, and Thomas Gissing's pharmaceutical business is still carried on in the ground-floor shop by a modest branch of the Boots chain of chemist's shops. The novelist's father was a religious skeptic with pacifist leanings, a man of active mind. He had a knowledge of botany and wrote a study of the ferns of the locality, *The Ferns and Fern Allies of Wakefield and Its Neighborhood,* a little green-bound book of twenty-four pages, illustrated with drawings and published by R. Micklethwaite, Journal and Examiner Office, Wakefield, in 1863. Two of Thomas Gissing's enthusiasms were Dürer and Tennyson. He often read poetry aloud, taught little George to recite "Break, Break, Break," and called his attention to a vivid line from "The Passing of Arthur." Certain of his blind spots puzzled his son when he later came to think about them. For example, in spite of his interest in natural science, he had no notion of applied science, and did not realize that a steam engine ran by mechanical action. He was so ignorant of classical languages that he did not know that Greek and Latin poetry lacked rhyme.

This last deficiency seemed fairly serious to young George, whose bookish tastes flourished in the literate, if unsophisticated, environment of his home. The household was well supplied with books;

Gissing once made a list of the ones he owned which included, in addition to a number of the usual boys' favorites of the time, seven novels by Cooper, some by Scott, *Robinson Crusoe*, a volume of Wordsworth, Praed's poems, and Lemprière's *Classical Dictionary*. The family also possessed a large volume of Hogarth's etchings, framed portraits of Dickens and Tennyson, and a number of Dickens' novels. Dickens was at the height of his fame during Gissing's boyhood; the first book Gissing remembered reading all the way through was *The Old Curiosity Shop*. Every one of these early cultural impressions had a lasting influence upon Gissing's interests and his work as a writer, but none aroused his imagination so powerfully as his study of Greek and Latin authors at Harrison's Back Lane School. It is clear that, before he left Wakefield at the age of thirteen, Gissing had already developed the passionate interest in classical literature that absorbed him throughout his life, amounting at times to a kind of mania.

Even as a child Gissing regarded himself as the mentor and guardian of his two younger brothers, Algernon and William, and his two younger sisters, Ellen and Margaret. When his father died in December, 1870, just after Gissing had turned thirteen, he felt that serious responsibilities toward his brothers and sisters had fallen to him, and in later years his sense of duty toward them persisted. Three lively caricatures of himself and his brothers, drawn when he was fourteen, give some interesting insights into the boy's mind and reveal the emergence of some of the most characteristic traits of his maturity. The first of the drawings shows Algernon, untidily clad, seated at a piano whose rack holds a sheet of music inscribed "Potherb waltz." The walls of the room are dotted with posters referring to Algernon's interest in catching newts, and on the floor lies a pole with a net at the end. Beneath the caption "My library" stands an open volume named *Martin Rattler*, a popular adventure story for boys by Ballantyne, while under the table lies a neglected book with the title *Lives of Great Men*. The drawing is accompanied by some verses which reflect the poet's serious nature and show that he recommended good literature and art and disapproved of such idle activities as chasing newts and gathering pot herbs.

The caricature of William shows him with a hammer raised high over his head, standing trouserless at a table on which is a box labeled "Tools." Toys and tools litter the floor. In the corner is a

chest of medicine bottles—Will must already have been sickly—
and over a chair are draped his trousers. Posters on the wall allude
to his interest in building things: "Model Boats," "How to make a
steam engine," "5 ft. plank for sixpence." *Martin Rattler* is the first
name on a scroll headed "List of Books." The verses beneath the
picture describe Will's activities as a waste of time and speak in
favor of "instructive, useful books."

The third drawing, a self-caricature which has been described by
Ellen Gissing, is most revealing of all.

My brother represents himself as a hideous, round-backed figure sitting on a
high stool, and leaning over a very small table on which a large volume is
open entitled "Ossian." Near to him, on the floor, is a pot of jam with a
spoon sticking out of it; a bill is hanging on the wall which says "Reduction
in price, Apricot—5/—p. pot." On the same wall hang other notices: one,
"Excursion to Roman Road," another, "Vote for no walks." A bunch of
keys is hanging on a nail with the words "non tangendum" attached. A
ragged-looking volume, entitled "Martin Rattler" hangs on the wall, with
the words above "For the fire." In the room stands an easel bearing an unfinished picture, and at the foot are laid a pallet and paint brushes. Near to
these is a tall pile of books, the bottom one of which is very large and la-
belled "Hogarth." On the wall near-by hangs a scroll inscribed with the
word "Perseverance.". . . The inscription "Perseverance," placed near these
books, is significant as referring to the extraordinary persistence which, even
at that early age, characterized his reading and studies in general.[4]

Although there are no explanatory verses with this drawing, its details are transparently suggestive. Gissing's boyhood appetite for
jam was to develop into the hearty and indiscriminate eating habits
of his manhood. The reference to the "Roman Road" is probably
an allusion to his interest in Latin literature. He must have condemned *Martin Rattler*, which was favored by his brothers, for
its mealymouthed optimism; in later life he always preferred to take
the serious view. He was very fond of the volume of Hogarth which
appears in the caricature, sometimes copying or imitating the pictures in his own drawing. Qualities like Hogarth's irony and exactness of detail are characteristic of Gissing's fiction and his lasting
curiosity about the poor and their lives may well have been stirred
for the first time by Hogarth's art.

Perhaps the most significant detail of all is the motto on the scroll.
Overwork was Gissing's most settled habit. Both as a student and
later in life, as a writer, he spent enormous stretches of time at his

desk, stubbornly wrestling with the distractions and sterility of mind that seemed to beset him. Although his most painful efforts were often least productive, he seems to have derived a perverse satisfaction from application alone. Gissing probably suffered from some sort of psychological compulsion, subconsciously regarding his work sessions as acts of penitence which were doubly effective when they were futile.

This compulsiveness, combined with great natural intelligence, enabled Gissing to achieve brilliant results as a student. His qualities are displayed in some school exercises which survive. One of the earliest of these, a long narrative poem in the meter of Byron's "Destruction of Sennacherib," called "The Battle of Roncesvalles," is impressive for its length, complexity, language, and meter, and for its evidence of the poet's knowledge of his subject. "A Description of and critical dissertation upon Fingal, a poem of Ossian" consists of a summary, lists of names and epithets, and some remarks about the customs revealed in the poem. An essay called "John Milton," written when Gissing was fourteen, and copied in a large copperplate hand, contains apt and fresh observations about the poet, including the statement that he did not give way to melancholy, though he had good reason to. "Poetry," Gissing says, "is one of the great, and perhaps the greatest instrument of the education and enlightenment of the general public. . . . In many poems there is a great deal more truth than in many histories. . . ." In a lifetime devoted to literature, Gissing never changed this view that it should enlighten by telling the truth. An eighteen-page essay entitled "The English Novel of the Eighteenth Century," probably written several years later at Owens College, begins with a review of medieval narratives and then deals with Richardson, Fielding, Smollett, and Sterne. The opinions expressed are perfectly standard, but they are obviously based on a thorough firsthand knowledge of the material.

Gissing's intense concentration on his studies was partly due to his realization that, as a poor youth, he would have to make his own way academically. It was possible for a really gifted student to go very far by means of scholarships, and Gissing was well equipped for the competitive examinations that led to them. He began to show his mettle at Lindow Grove School, a Quaker establishment at Alderley Edge, Cheshire, where he and his brothers were sent after his father's death. A series of his letters written to a friend named Bowes in 1872 and 1873 bristles with references to exhibitions, prizes, and examinations. While carrying on simultaneous programs of study for various examinations and academic competitions, he limited himself to five and one-half hours of sleep a night, read Shakespeare through three times, and declined an invitation to the theater because the thought of the study time he was missing would make him writhe in his seat throughout the performance.

He agreed that he was already behaving like "a man who had an object in life," and recommended to Bowes, who had academic ambitions of his own, the motto on the books he had won as school prizes, *Arduus ad solem.* One year he won so many prizes, some of them in scientific subjects, that he had to take them home in a cab, although, as he wrote to Bowes, he had not done as well as the year before. When he sat for the Oxford Local Examination in 1872, he achieved the highest grade in the entire country, and he won exhibitions in German, Greek, and Latin that carried free tuition for three sessions at Owens College in Manchester.

Owens College, which had been founded in 1852, was primarily a scientific institution, but Gissing was able to specialize in the humanities there. In his first year he won a poetry prize with "Ravenna," a poetic history of the capital of Byzantine Italy in twenty-one dignified and sonorous Spenserian stanzas. Although it is an interesting expression of the love for antiquity which appears in *By the Ionian Sea* and *Veranilda,* "Ravenna," like all of the poetry Gissing wrote from time to time, is conventional and undistinguished. In 1874–75 he took the matriculation examination of the University of London, for which he had been preparing intensively for more than a year, and matriculated as B.A. with high honors, winning exhibitions in Latin and English.

By 1876 Gissing, having accumulated an impressive number of academic distinctions, seemed ready to move on to the University of London and begin a scholarly career. But his promising development was suddenly and tragically interrupted. Books, money, and coats were missed from the common and locker rooms at Owens College where the students left their belongings. A detective who was hired caught the student responsible for these thefts by hiding himself in the room. That student was Gissing. The father of one of his schoolmates and some other people of Manchester seem to have combined to assume responsibility for him and give him aid; a post as a clerk was found for him in Liverpool, and he was supplied with some money which he used to sail to America, arriving in Boston in the autumn of 1876. Thus, at the age of nineteen, he had to abandon all thoughts of taking his degree, following a university career, and leading a normal life in England.

An explanation of the events leading up to this catastrophe must have formed an important part of the conversation between Gissing and Harrison that took place some six years later. What actually happened remains obscure, though the general outline is depressingly clear. Gissing was living alone in sprawling, industrial Manchester, in a loneliness very different from the warm atmosphere of his boyhood home in Wakefield, or that of the school at Alderley Edge, where he had his two brothers for company. Loneliness made him unhappy, but his reticence and studious habits prevented him from making friends easily. The result was that he somehow met and fell in love with a young prostitute, a girl a year younger than himself named Marianne Helen Harrison. He showed her picture to Morley Roberts, a school friend who has left the only firsthand account of these incidents, and told him that he was going to marry her.

It is easy to imagine the mixture of idealism, naïveté, and infatuation that made up Gissing's devotion to "Nell," as he always called her. Years later, long after she was dead, he copied into a notebook the historian Lecky's comment about the social role of the prostitute: "She remains, while creeds and civilizations rise and fall, the eternal priestess of humanity, blasted for the sins of the people." [5] Gissing regarded Helen as a victim of society, and he undertook the mission of redeeming her. In an attempt to supply her with a respectable way of making a living, he bought her a sewing machine. He gave her money and gifts, even selling a watch left him by his father. But he soon found that he could not provide enough for her needs, for, as subsequent events clearly show, the facts were that Helen was addicted to drink and had turned to prostitution to get money for it. Gissing had innocently plunged himself into a hopeless struggle with character, a bitter experience which he later used as material for some of the most vivid scenes of *Workers in the Dawn*.

Tyrannized by the fear that Helen would revert to her old habits,

Gissing gave her whatever he had. When that was gone he turned, in despair, to rifling the common room at Owens College and making off with his schoolmates' possessions.

Gissing's crime cannot be explained as the result of youthful irresponsibility, for he seems never to have been too young to be dutiful and conscientious. The sense of duty instilled by his upbringing in the puritanical environment of a north-of-England manufacturing town had been reinforced by his success in the conservative atmosphere of his schools. He was certainly no hypocrite. He took Victorian propriety seriously, and he earnestly tried to make himself an example for his younger brothers and sisters. Even minor breaches of conduct tortured him with remorse, and he was capable of suffering agonies over imagined faults. Yet his crime did not represent a sudden shattering of his youthful inhibitions. Gissing never became the sort of person who consciously acts upon pure desire. He would have examined his motives closely, using all the ingenuity of his fine student's intellect to rationalize the conduct into which he was being forced.

The time itself encouraged moral originality. As a thoughtful youth and a wide reader, Gissing was aware that established ethical doctrines were being deeply probed by the blade of scientific inquiry, and that science seemed to suggest the possibility of a systematic code of morality based on its own principles. A vigorous rationalism, captained by such agnostics as Leslie Stephen, Thomas Henry Huxley, John Stuart Mill, and Herbert Spencer, clashed with intuitive religion, attacking especially its three most crucial doctrines, the existence of God, the literal accuracy of the Bible, and the immortality of the soul. All the old spiritual convictions seemed open to question and subject to revision. Throughout Victorian literature the crumbling of religious belief was a common subject. As early as 1855, in Mrs. Gaskell's *North and South*, a clergyman who loses his faith appears in fiction, and the theme could still stir up controversy in 1888, when Mrs. Humphry Ward's *Robert Elsmere* described the undermining of a devout young minister's belief by the formidable Biblical criticism of a rationalist scholar.

But if God and the Bible no longer commanded absolute allegiance, what was there for man to serve? The answer to this question had been clearly given about the middle of the century by

Positivism, Auguste Comte's "Religion of Humanity," and it was an answer that grew increasingly popular with clever young men. Winwood Reade's *Martyrdom of Man* (1872), a quasi-scientific history of religion which won great popularity in its time, declared:

Those who desire to worship their Creator must worship him through mankind. Such, it is plain, is the scheme of Nature. We are placed under secondary laws, and these we must obey. To develop to the utmost our genius and our love, that is the only true religion. . . . to cherish the divinity within us, to be faithful to the intellect, to educate those powers which have been entrusted to our charge and to employ them in the service of humanity, that is all we can do.[6]

When the hero of Samuel Butler's *The Way of All Flesh* (1903) escapes the tyrannous influence of his clerical father for the first time and wonders what authority he ought to obey, a voice within him seems to say:

Obey *me*, your true self, and things will go tolerably well with you, but only listen to that outward and visible husk of yours which is called your father, and I will rend you in pieces even unto the third and fourth generation as one who has hated God; for I, Ernest, am the God who made you![7]

Expressing another typical agnostic view of morality, Henry Maudsley wrote, in an article entitled "Materialism and Its Lessons," which appeared in the *Fortnightly Review* in 1879, that moral laws were not handed down by divine revelation but were products of social evolution. Materialism, said Maudsley, enjoins men to follow the Golden Rule on the ground that "it is the true scientific function, and at the same time the highest development of the individual, to promote the well-being of the social organization—that is, to make life subserve the good of his kind." [8]

Gissing came to agnostic principles early and held to them, with some modifications, until his death. But, as his novel *Born in Exile* shows, he learned that the principles of free thought, excellent as they may be in themselves, are peculiarly vulnerable to the corruption of personal desire. The hero of his novel, Godwin Peak, is moved by ambition to conclude that dishonesty is justified in the name of self-fulfillment. His conflicts of thought and feeling are described in great detail; Gissing had reason to know them well, for they had once been his own. "Peak," he wrote to a friend, "is myself

—one phase of myself." [9] Like his own character, and like those other representative figures, Dostoevsky's Raskolnikov and Turgenev's Bazarov, the youthful Gissing was betrayed by the sophistry of unconscious self-interest as he strove toward the radiant nineteenth-century ideal of a rational, humanistic morality.

III

The period of disgrace following Gissing's dismissal from Owens College was also a period of silence. Nothing is mentioned in his books, his letters, or his diary of his arrest, imprisonment, or clerkship in Liverpool. The Gissing we rejoin through the medium of his letters in Boston in October, 1876, appears to have entirely forgotten his grim experiences. He has enjoyed the rough weather of his recent Atlantic crossing, and is now occupied with equally enjoyable observation of the people and customs of his new country. He is not in need, but is living comfortably in a small boardinghouse at 71 Bartlett Street where he is impressed by the excellence and quantity of the food. His curiosity is extremely active, and his letters are full of odd facts about America, which he discusses in a buoyant and zestful mood. He approves of the air of democracy, the splendor of the railway cars, and the general bustle of American life, and constantly draws comparisons unfavorable to England. The presidential election of 1876, whose results were both contested and delayed, produced an atmosphere of excitement that he finds exhilarating. He is impressed by the huge sizes and numbers he finds everywhere, reporting with awe that the *Boston Herald* on election day printed 232,000 copies, which weighed fourteen tons. He is fascinated by a new invention called the "Telephone" and by a stereopticon used to report election results. He is delighted by the free Boston library system; everybody about him reads and he himself sits in the library reading George Sand's novels one after another. Even the weather, which is bitterly cold, agrees with him. "Altogether Boston is a splendid place. I should be very sorry ever to leave it for good." [10]

It was at this cheerful time of his life, in the bracing and open atmosphere of the New World, that Gissing appears to have first tried to earn his living as a writer. He had brought a letter of introduction to William Lloyd Garrison and hoped, through his influence, to connect himself with the *Atlantic Monthly*, then edited by William Dean Howells. He also met Professor Francis J. Child of Harvard, who gave him a glimpse of the notes for his important edition of early English ballads. While in Boston, Gissing wrote that he was working on an article on Burns and Heine, and that he had submitted a piece entitled "Sketches of Life in an English Manufacturing Town" to a periodical. Neither of these was published or heard of again.

In the meantime he looked for something practical to do and succeeded in obtaining a position as teacher of English, French, and German at the high school in nearby Waltham, Massachusetts. Everything about his work pleased him. He was interviewed by a local reporter on his arrival and took this as a mark of respect. He found his classes attentive and obedient, and one of his students remembered him in later life as a successful and enthusiastic teacher.

It is hard to say why Gissing left Waltham, where he appears to have been in his natural element. The fact remains, however, that about the first of March, 1877, he arrived in Chicago after a long, uncomfortable, and pointless journey. H. G. Wells, in his *Experiment in Autobiography* (1934) vividly described the hazards to health and self-respect that young masters risked at country schools in England; perhaps, like Wells, Gissing found himself overworked, underpaid, isolated, and confronted with bleak prospects, and was inclined to escape at the first opportunity. On the other hand, it is true that more than once in his life he abandoned a secure situation for a doubtful and unpromising one. He was not the kind of person who was strengthened by adversity; on the contrary, he was easily demoralized by obstacles. But it is not too much to say that he was also afraid of success. He was already firmly convinced of "the native malignity of matter," to use one of his favorite phrases, and prosperity would have conflicted with the pessimism and sense of injustice that seem to have been parts of his nature. It is difficult to go further than this in accounting for the peculiar self-defeating and self-tormenting quality as obvious in his books as in his actions, or for his departure from Waltham so soon after his cheerful arrival.

If he sought hardship, he found it immediately. The ironic account which the writer Whelpdale gives in *New Grub Street* of his travels in America fits in very well with what is known of Gissing's own experiences, and may be taken as a passage of autobiography. The desire for adventure and the search for material to write about drew Whelpdale first to America and then to Chicago. Arriving in Chicago almost penniless, he spent most of his money for a week's board and lodging and tried to earn more by approaching a newspaper editor. The editor had no work to offer an inexperienced young man, but seemed willing to accept a short story. Whelpdale bought writing materials and busied himself in producing the required article under the most adverse conditions.

Impossible to write in my bedroom, the temperature was below zero; there was no choice but to sit down in the common room. . . . A dozen men were gathered about the fire, smoking, talking, quarrelling. Favourable conditions, you see, for literary effort. But the story had to be written, and write it I did, sitting there at the end of a deal table; I finished it in less than a couple of days, a good long story, enough to fill three columns of the huge paper. I stand amazed at my power of concentration as often as I think of it! [11]

In this way Gissing wrote his first published work, an alarmingly autobiographical short story entitled "The Sins of the Fathers," which appeared in the *Chicago Tribune* of March 10, 1877. It tells of a meeting between a poor girl and a young man in the streets of a city in northern England. The man, Leonard Vincent, falls in love with the girl and sends her to live with his father while he goes to New England where he becomes a schoolteacher. In time, learning that Laura has died, he marries a pretty student and settles down in America. But it soon appears that Laura's death is only a fiction plotted by Leonard's disapproving father, who has disrupted their correspondence by sending her a forged letter in which Leonard retracts his love. As a result, she leaves his house, and the father is sure she will never be heard of again. However, she goes to America, where Leonard recognizes her in the chorus at a theater. He talks to her, explaining that he is now married and can no longer love her, and the story ends as the unhappy girl, overcome by despair, wraps her arms around him and pulls him into a river during a snowstorm. Thus, reflects the author in conclusion, are the children compelled to pay for the sins of the fathers.

It is certainly a poor story, but the opening passage, a description of Laura weeping on the pavement of a squalid street, has some of the restrained power characteristic of Gissing's later descriptions of poverty. He made use again of some of the episodes of this little tale in *The Unclassed* and other novels. There is far more incident than a story of its length should have, and much of it is told in a rapid, summary style without detail, so that its effect is diffuse. The initial situation shows that Gissing intuitively reached directly into his own experience for his fictional material, although he departed from it in later stages of the plot. He seemed to be exploring his own feelings toward Helen when he said, of Leonard's attitude toward the girl he has saved from the streets:

The truth was that from the first his love had contained far more of mere compassion and self-complacency than he could imagine or would have been willing to admit. Very soon after leaving England he had confessed to himself the wish that Laura had been intellectually more of a companion for him.[12]

Gissing remained in Chicago for about four months, supporting himself by writing short stories for newspapers. He was able to place one or two stories nearly every two weeks with the *Tribune*, the *Evening Post*, or the *Journal*. Three of the nine stories attributed to him, a Poesque trilogy, are unlike his later work. The others, however, have interesting suggestions of his later style and plots. "Joseph Yates' Temptation," which appeared in the *Evening Post* on June 2, is a grim story of starving people trying to make the best of a penniless Christmas. The plot situation, in which a clerk finds himself compelled to take a hundred-pound check home over the weekend, appears again in *A Life's Morning*. Very different from Gissing's mature work is "Brownie," an eerie tale of murder and revenge in the countryside, not unlike Hardy's tales in its atmosphere and description of nature.

The friendly *Chicago Tribune* editor who had accepted Gissing's stories gave very little for them, but what he paid kept the new author from actually starving for a few weeks. At the end of that time Gissing's tenuous connection with the *Chicago Tribune* ceased, and he left the city. "The Sins of the Fathers" had been pirated by a newspaper published in Troy, New York, and a mixture of innocence and desperation drew him there in the hope that the editor of the paper would give him something to do. It was, of course, a foolish hope, and Gissing's unworldliness led him to the situation that has made him a celebrated case among starving authors. For a certain period of time during his stay in Troy, variously reported as lasting two and five days, he lived on peanuts bought by the handful from a street vendor. It was the lowest imaginable level of poverty.

A fortunate chance lifted him to a somewhat higher estate when he found employment as an assistant to a traveling photographer. After wandering with this man through many New England towns, Gissing returned to Boston in September, 1877, and took ship for Liverpool. Before leaving America, however, he achieved one more small success as a writer of short stories. A little tale entitled "An English Coast-Picture" and signed "G. R. Gresham" appeared in the July, 1877, number of *Appleton's Journal*, a periodical published in New York. A very slender love story whose setting is the Northumberland coast where Gissing spent his holidays as a boy, it is pitiably weak in plot, but has a respectable description of the gull-haunted Farne Islands.

Gissing's picaresque American adventures did little to change him from the introverted, bookish boy he had been at school and college. In spite of his frequent encounters with the edge of starvation he managed to do some reading and some thinking, and to keep a record of both. This record survives, in the form of a small, worn, pocket-sized notebook with the elaborately curving initials "G.R.G." inscribed in ink on the cover, and it shows that his intellectual activity continued through his travels. He read widely and copied quotations from all sorts of sources: George Sand, Tocqueville, Musset, Goethe, the letters of Dürer, Arnold, George Eliot, and Shelley. He composed aphorisms expressing enlightened commonplaces. For example: "An unmarried woman living outwardly with a single man is worthy of more respect than one who is married." Among the miscellany of notes, quotations, and addresses is clear evidence that he often had his mind on fiction. Here and there brief outline plots are jotted down. Like Henry James, Gissing made a habit of scribbling lists of likely names for future use in stories. Many of these are cacophonous and Dickensian: "Funk, Philander Griggs, Gorbutt, Goggin, Flipp, Dryfuss, Debeer, Pendeysan, Patwin, Scroggie." One of the names in this notebook, "Widdowson," appears years later in *The Odd Women*. Also recorded in the American notebook is a list of "Books on London Streets," which shows the direction his thoughts were taking.

The fourteenth chapter of *Workers in the Dawn* gives so circumstantial an account of its heroine's visit to Germany, referring to details of the topography of Tübingen and to certain features of the university system, that early writers on Gissing were led to believe that he had made a detour to Germany on his way from England to America. Austin Harrison even offers a sketch of the intellectual development he supposedly underwent while he lived in Jena studying philosophy. Actually, Gissing went directly home, for the last two entries of an itinerary noted on the flyleaf of the American notebook read: "Boston, Sept/77. Liverpool Oct 3/77." The eyewitness details that misled his biographers had been supplied by his German friend, Eduard Bertz, who collaborated with him in writing the chapter by providing an outline for it.

IV

When Gissing arrived in London, probably for the first time, in the autumn of 1877, it was a city of four million whose older districts had deteriorated into extensive areas of slums. Faced with the need to live as economically as possible, Gissing found his way into the picturesque but run-down region near the southern end of Tottenham Court Road, where he rented the mean lodgings described in *The Private Papers of Henry Ryecroft*. The address of the house was 22 Colville Place, and Gissing lived there between January and September, 1878. He moved often in the next few years, to various addresses in Bloomsbury, Islington, and Canning Town, but was rarely able to afford anything better than a single hall bedroom in a squalid lodginghouse. While he was comparatively indifferent to his own discomfort, the hardships of the poor Londoners he saw about him made him aware for the first time of the terrible degradation that might befall the human condition. He dated his real education from this time. ". . . my early years in London were a time of extraordinary mental growth, of great spiritual activity," he wrote some years later. "There it was that I acquired my intense perception of the characteristics of poor life in London." [13]

He saw whole families about him living in single rooms for which they paid an exorbitant weekly rental. They owned little or nothing of what they used, and were at the mercy of landladies hardened in their trade who supplied cleaning, a certain amount of service by dullard housemaids, and occasional meals. Vermin, dirt, drunkenness, violence, and profanity were common; open doors, crowding, and thin partitions made privacy impossible. Young people found it difficult to meet their friends under pleasant conditions and all but impossible to visit with members of the opposite sex. Love affairs, quarrels, tearful reunions, and the other crucial emotional episodes of daily life took place in streets and parks rather than at home. Family relationships were chaotic and unstable; children were neglected and abused, and desertion was frequent among married people. At night these dens became dangerous, for their halls and stairs sheltered homeless people who came in from the streets.

Living under conditions like these, Gissing began a period of persistent literary labor that was to last almost without interruption for eleven years. He was still very young, a month short of twenty, and very poor. *The Private Papers of Henry Ryecroft* gives a good idea of the life he led in London's dreary "Latin Quarter." The accounts of Ryecroft's moving from a dismal attic to a dismal cellar for the sake of saving a few pennies in rent, going without dinner in order to buy a beloved book, and gazing hungrily at pies and puddings steaming in a shopwindow are probably autobiographical. Like Ryecroft, Gissing considered himself lucky to be several shillings above destitution. He seems to have taken the view that his poverty was a test of character, and on these terms he almost enjoyed the squalor he was compelled to live in. Making a small living by tutoring whatever pupils came his way, he went about in ragged clothing, took his dinners at humble coffee shops, and communed with Greek and Latin authors. In the seclusion of small and hideous rooms let by the week, where he proudly set his gleaming Owens College prizes on whatever shelves were available, he began to write.

He sometimes went to the British Museum for the sake of the warmth in the reading room or to work unsuccessfully on magazine articles, but his main occupation was writing a novel. On February 28, hardly four months after his arrival in England, he wrote to his brother Algernon, "I am getting on with my novel which I hope to be drawing to a conclusion in a little more than a month." [14] In those years he wrote swiftly, exulting in the energy that welled up in him when he had succeeded in earning enough to free himself from worrying about money for a few hours. The process of creation led him into a different and exciting world, and helped him to forget the squalor of his life.

In the meantime, he can hardly have been as desperately poor as Ryecroft reports himself to have been. There is no doubt that he lived in poverty and spent many precious hours tutoring for the sake of a few shillings. But he was looking forward to receiving on his twenty-first birthday, November 22, 1878, a share of a trust fund left by his father. Even after the money, which came to about five hundred pounds, was actually his, he continued to give lessons and live in much the same way. Part of this money may have been used to pay a debt contracted in America for which Gissing had left some of his belongings as security. The debt was paid about the first of May, probably by a loan against his share of the trust fund. By June of the following year his inheritance had been reduced to three hundred pounds, and Gissing was seriously considering investing this amount in a house where he could live and take in lodgers. It continued to dwindle for another year until he spent what remained of it on the publication of *Workers in the Dawn*.

Nor was Gissing's life in London the solitary one described in the Ryecroft papers. Some time before September, 1878, when he wrote to Algernon that "we" were moving from the address in Colville Place, Helen had come to live with him, and they were married in October, 1879. Hence, if he lived alone at all during this period, it was for less than a year. Gissing's motives in linking himself to Helen again have been given all sorts of curious interpretations, but it is most probable that, like his counterpart in *Workers in the Dawn*, he loved her and hoped to reclaim her. At first the two faced poverty bravely together, even resorting to vegetarianism for a time to save money. Once Gissing discovered an Egyptian lentil which made a thick and nourishing soup; he and Helen adopted it as a staple of their diet, and it was enthusiastically recommended to Algernon; but in later years, Gissing, who was a meat eater at heart, had only bitter words for vegetarianism in general and lentils in particular.

He had relatives in Paddington whom he visited, though he soon found the company of these working-class people tiresome and wrote to Algernon that his intercourse with them would have to come to an end. His brothers came to stay with him occasionally, and he took an eager provincial's interest in theaters, meetings, and public affairs. He went to see Irving in his famous performance in "The Bells," and, with an uncle from Paddington, witnessed a disorderly meeting of workingmen in Hyde Park in February of 1878. In the same month he went to watch the wedding of Eleanor Locker and Tennyson's son at Westminster Abbey on the chance that he might catch sight of the poet.

Early in January, 1879, he made the acquaintance of Eduard Bertz, a young German of intellectual tastes four years his senior who became one of the two intimate friends of his London years. The two were said to have met through an advertisement Bertz placed in a newspaper, an action Gissing introduced into *The Unclassed* as a means of bringing Waymark and Casti together. Bertz, who had been an active socialist when he was a university student, was an exile from Bismarck's Germany. He resembled Gissing in being studious, poor, lonely, and interested in literature. An unsuccessful attempt on Bertz's part to teach at a girls' school no doubt provided Gissing with material for the figure of Eggers, the genial and ineffectual Swiss schoolmaster of *The Unclassed*. Bertz was even more incompetent in practical affairs than Gissing, but the two profited from the moral support they exchanged with each other. He played a significant part in Gissing's life, not only because of the companionship he provided while he lived in London, but also through the long correspondence the two maintained from the time of Bertz's return to Germany until Gissing's death. In later years Bertz became a man of letters like Gissing, though with a somewhat different emphasis; he was managing editor of a periodical, *Die Deutsche Presse*, and an active journalist, and he produced a number of novels, miscellaneous works, and critical studies, including two on Walt Whitman. He promoted Gissing's literary interests in Germany by finding translators for his books and publishing critical articles about him. During the last sixteen years of his life, Gissing corresponded with Bertz about once a month. In these letters he discussed his travels, his literary opinions, his professional problems, his moods, and many other topics very fully, so that they form an important record of his activities and ideas.

On November 9, 1878, Gissing wrote to Algernon about Auguste Comte's *Cours de philosophie positive* with an enthusiasm which suggested that he had just read it for the first time. Comte's philosophy of Positivism was to play a vital part in the genesis of his first novel, as he declared in the letter accompanying the copy of *Workers in the Dawn* which he sent to Harrison in 1880. Gissing had, somewhat belatedly, come under the influence of one of the most significant currents of nineteenth-century thought, the philosophy of science. Positivism sought to classify religion out of existence by declaring that of the three ages of knowledge, the eras of theological certainty and metaphysical speculation were over, and that a time when men would limit themselves to the acquisition of verifiable knowledge through scientific means was at hand. The human faculties, said Comte, are incapable of solving the problems of essences and first causes and the other mysteries involved in the conception of God. Man must therefore accept the fact that he will always be ignorant of ultimate reality, and should devote himself to gathering practical knowledge which will serve to promote his well-being.

Gissing frequently said in his later years that he had never had any religious belief, and it is more than likely, as we have seen, that Comte's ideas fell on the ground of a mind thoroughly prepared for them by skepticism. Some four months after writing the letter about Comte, Gissing was ready to address an audience on the subject of religion. In March of 1879 he prepared for his performance by hearing a lecture on "Dogma and Science," which attacked "the parsons," and by gathering material from such books as Lecky's *History of European Morals* and *Rise and Influence of Rationalism in Europe,* Draper's *Conflict between Science and Religion,* and Huxley's *Lay Sermons.* The latter pleased him, and he admiringly quoted its definition of liberal education, apparently agreeing with Huxley that it included a knowledge of science. His own lecture, "Faith and Reason," was delivered on March 23 in Paddington before a workingmen's club of which his uncle was a member. It was well received, and Gissing was invited to speak again in a larger hall. He planned to talk on "The State Church from a Rationalist Point of View," but this second lecture was never given, and his

GEORGE GISSING in 1895

GABRIELLE FLEURY GISSING,
*about 1904. The dog, "Bijou," was
greatly attached to Gissing*

COURTESY OF
MADAME DENISE LE MALLIER

EDUARD BERTZ *in 1895*

COURTESY OF
MADAME DENISE LE MALLIER

career as a platform orator on religion came to an end after his first flight.

Gissing continued to look after his family in spite of his busy life in London. His brother Algernon, who wanted to be admitted to the bar, was preparing for his B.A. examinations, and Gissing took as active a part in his studies as he could through the medium of the mail. It was the beginning of a long and curious process of education by letters. Gissing gave Algernon detailed advice, told him what subjects to concentrate on, sent some of his old notes, and even made extracts for him from books in the British Museum. The gratifying result was that Algernon passed his examinations with a first class. Gissing also corresponded with William, whose health gave considerable concern, and who sometimes engaged his brother in intellectual skirmishes on matters of religion and politics, forcing Gissing to state his position with great clarity and exactness.

Although Gissing took every opportunity of earning a little money and was soon tutoring four pupils, the novel was ultimately finished and sent to a publisher. It was probably sent to many more than one, in fact, for on July 24, 1878, Gissing wrote to Algernon, with a characteristic blend of pessimism and determination: "The publishers respectfully decline the honour of publishing my novel. Just what I anticipated. The next must be better." [15] Nothing is known directly of this first unsuccessful novel, which was consigned to obscurity without a title. However, judging from some questions in Gissing's letters to Algernon about the legal aspects of lurid episodes involving murder and gunplay, it could not have been a serious effort. Almost two years of poverty, useless labor, and disappointment could not overcome his determination to write, for he set to work immediately on another long novel, which was to become *Workers in the Dawn*.

During these years he drifted constantly from one disreputable lodginghouse to another, seldom remaining in one place for more than a few months. In September of 1878 he found a very attractive set of two rooms, but since the rent of fifteen shillings was more than he could pay he was forced to move into a single room in Gower Place for which he paid 6/6. In the same month he took a position as a temporary clerk at St. John's Hospital, a charitable institution for the treatment of skin diseases. He haunted the bookshops as usual, but was so poor that he would have been unable to buy a bargain if he had found one.[16]

Whatever illusions may have possessed Gissing when he took Helen back must have been quickly dispelled, for by November of 1879 he had learned enough about her to write the powerfully circumstantial account of a marriage like his own that appears in *Workers in the Dawn*. Helen was continually ill. At different times she had neuralgia, "rheumatics," an abscess of the arm, an eye condition necessitating an operation, and, most sinister of all, mysterious convulsions followed by comas. The constant medical expenses caused by her sicknesses sometimes reduced Gissing to despair. The single room which was usually the best he could afford must have served as her sickroom as well as his writing room.

But Helen had worse faults than poor health. She was not merely ignorant, but foolish, willful, and disobedient as well. When he was not distressed at her illnesses, Gissing was repelled and distracted by her vulgar friends, her foolish conversation, and her slovenly habits. Worst of all, however, were her alcoholism and the problems it created. Morley Roberts, who saw Gissing often after 1880, has described his situation:

. . . they were turned out of one lodging after the other, for even the poorest places, it seems, could hardly stand a woman of her character in the house. I fear it was not only that she drank, but at intervals she deserted him and went back, for the sake of more drink, and for the sake of money with which he was unable to supply her, to her old melancholy trade. And yet she returned again with tears, and he took her in, doing his best for her.[17]

Although he was Gissing's oldest friend, Roberts was never allowed to see Helen. During an evening Roberts spent at Gissing's lodgings, his host was constantly called to the next room to attend to his wife, who, he said, was ill. Ultimately he had to ask Roberts to leave, and later, when he knew him better, told him what he already knew perfectly well, that Helen had been too drunk to be seen. The effects of a life like this upon the exceptionally sensitive Gissing can be imagined. It is clear that the indefinite allusions to miseries and burdens that are found so often in his letters to Algernon refer to Helen and the troubles she brought upon him.

If the novel that had failed in 1878 really was a potboiler, Gissing undertook a very different project in his second attempt at fiction. In a letter written to Algernon soon after the death of their brother

Will, in the spring of 1880 and about three months after he had succeeded in arranging for the publication of *Workers in the Dawn*, Gissing expressed some of the feeling of moral responsibility that now began to motivate his writing. He did not believe in a future life, he said in meditating on Will's death. Nevertheless, he believed that men could achieve what he called "subjective immortality."

The immortality of man consists in this reflection—that not a word we utter, not a thought we think, not a battle we win, not a temptation we yield to, but has, and *must* have, influence upon those living in contact with us, and from them, like the circles spreading in a pool, extends to the whole future human race. Therefore is it of vast importance to me whether I set an example of an ignorant and foolish man, or of one bent upon using his faculties to the utmost.[18]

In his second novel, inspired by this Comtian sense of mission, he made serious use of his gifts to write a strong and honest portrayal of the poverty he saw about him in the slums, feeling that in doing this he was bringing to light for the first time the manners of a submerged social class which had never been treated realistically. A poem he wrote at the age of fourteen shows that Gissing had seen industrial poverty in Yorkshire as a boy. The lines strangely anticipate his voyage to America. They are called "On Leaving England."

> Breezes, fill the swelling canvas!
>   Billows, bear us from the land!
> Far away from yonder island,
>   Yon' low-lying, sea-beat strand.
>
> Nay, don't turn to gaze upon it,
>   'Tis not worth another look;
> Never sigh at parting from it,
>   'Tis not worth the breath it took.
>
> Who would grieve to leave a country
>   Choked with smoke and swamped with rain?
> 'Gainst the fogs which rest upon it
>   Sun and breezes strive in vain.
>
> Look upon the glorious ocean,
>   Forward to the glorious West,
> Far away from smoke and trouble,
>   *There* is pleasure, *there* is rest.
>
> We will climb the lofty mountains,
>   Far above the valleys fair,

Up beyond the clouds around them,
Till we stop for want of air.

Then when we can see around us,
Sun above and clouds below,
When we cool our burning foreheads
In the everlasting snow;

Then we'll think of one low island
In the smoke and vapour roll'd
Think of struggling, toil-worn creatures,
And we'll grudge them not their gold.[19]

But after the "glorious West" had failed to fulfill his expectations, the spectacle of the slums of London asserted an irresistible claim upon him. At first he called the novel *Far Far Away*, an allusion to a song that occurs in it, but he eventually adopted the resounding title of *Workers in the Dawn*. "It is," he wrote, "a novel . . . of social questions and the principal characters are earnest young people striving for improvement in, as it were, the dawn of a new phase of our civilization." [20] He stated his aims formally in a letter written to Algernon soon after the novel appeared:

The book in the first place is not a novel in the generally-accepted sense of the word, but a very strong (possibly *too* plain spoken) attack upon certain features of our present religious and social life which to *me* appear highly condemnable. First and foremost, I attack the criminal negligence of governments which spend their time over matters of relatively no importance, to the neglect of the terrible social evils which should have been long since sternly grappled with. Herein I am a mouthpiece of the advanced Radical party. . . . It is *not* a book for women and children, but for thinking and struggling *men*.[21]

V

The mission Gissing undertook was a timely one, for the economic depression of the 1870's was making "social questions" desperately important by intensifying conditions that had been with England since the early days of the Industrial Revolution. The rapid rise of manufacturing at the beginning of the nineteenth century had created a large class of urban workers whose ordinary standard of living was deep poverty. Periodic fluctuations in trade could cause unemployment so serious that it resulted in death by starvation or exposure. In the thirties a recession of this kind made the poor a national problem. A new Poor Law was followed by investigations, factory reforms, and reports on working and living conditions, and by the Chartist agitations, which sometimes led to serious violence. The worst hardships of the poor were alleviated by the relative prosperity of the fifties, and ceased to weigh so heavily on the conscience of the nation, although the huge hard core of poverty persisted.

By 1878 far-flung economic developments, both in England and overseas, had caused a depression. The completion of the railways, the rise of industrial competition in Germany and the United States, and the discovery of new processes in steel manufacturing that made the old ones obsolete were some of the causes for the reduction of Britain's exports from 256 million pounds in 1872 to 192 million pounds in 1879 and the rise of unemployment from 1 to 12 per cent. Industrial poverty had once been a result of increased manufacturing, but it was now being intensified by the contraction in trade. It grew in good times and bad; and, while it was not worse than it had been in the thirties, it had shown itself, after almost a century of attempted reforms, to be a far tougher, grimmer, and more durable opponent than the first industrial reformers had taken it to be.

The tradition of social-protest literature which Gissing renewed in *Workers in the Dawn* had arisen in response to the worst period of poverty, the thirties. Firsthand information about conditions was made available in reports of Parliamentary commissions on factory reform and sanitation, in Carlyle's passionate condemnation of industrialism, *Past and Present* (1843), in Friedrich Engels' *Condition of the Working-Class in England in 1844*, and in Henry Mayhew's *London Labour and the London Poor* (1861). Mayhew, whose work is of particular interest, visited and interviewed hawkers, scavengers, prostitutes, thieves, and other members of the lowest social class, and compiled a clear and intimate report on their way of life. His book is full of humane feeling but free of the strident indignation characteristic of most protest literature. It has an interesting connection with Dickens' *Oliver Twist* (1837–39), for Mayhew's account of the methods used by pickpockets corresponds exactly with Dickens' description of Fagin's gang.

Between 1845 and 1860 social conditions furnished a whole

school of humanitarian novelists with material for arousing the indignation of the public. Disraeli's *Sybil* (1845), Mrs. Gaskell's
Mary Barton (1848) and *North and South* (1855), Kingsley's
Yeast (1848) and *Alton Locke* (1850), and Dickens' *Hard Times*
(1854) were typical of the many novels that gave vivid impressions
of the lives of the poor and dramatized the suffering, crime, and social antagonisms produced by poverty. The reforming spirit expressed in these works was characteristically religious, romantic, or
conservative. Carlyle and Disraeli were hostile to political liberalism, Kingsley and the Christian Socialists based their program on
the religious principle of brotherly love, and Mrs. Gaskell felt that
help for the poor must come from the upper classes. Mrs. Browning's famous poem, "The Cry of the Children," may be regarded as
the keynote of this period of protest; it sought simply to arouse the
feelings with accounts of the horrors of poverty, and its primary
appeal was to the heart.

When conditions improved in the middle of the century, protest
literature tapered off. After 1860 there were no important social
novels, with the notable exception of *Our Mutual Friend* (1864–
65). The depression of the seventies revived many of the old questions, however, and a new wave of protest broke forth. During Gissing's early years in London a powerful, though not necessarily
violent, spirit of revolution was in the air, and the reform literature
of the eighties, responding to recent scientific, philosophical, and
political developments, had a sharp new edge. The vague and sentimental humanitarianism of the middle of the century was sup-
planted by a scientific purposefulness that entered social reform
through the work of Robert Owen, Comte, and Herbert Spencer.
Beatrice Webb, whose work as a social investigator made her one
of the leaders of the new reform, accounted for the shift in this way:

There was the current belief in the scientific method, in that intellectual
synthesis of observation and experiment, hypothesis and verification, by
means of which alone all mundane problems were to be solved. And added
to this belief in science was the consciousness of a new motive; the trans-
ference of the emotion of self-sacrifice from God to man.[22]

The new attitude taught that the lot of the common man must
be improved, not merely relieved. Its outlook was secular rather
than religious, for science and agnosticism had taught that there
was likely to be no afterlife in which suffering on earth would be

rewarded and that man must look to himself for help. It was now clear that appeals to the sympathy of the rich could not produce more than sporadic philanthropies which were quickly swallowed in the gulf of the needs they were meant to satisfy.

A new science of humanity, or sociology, seemed to promise that principles for the ordering of society on a rational basis could be developed by empiric methods. A new breed of scientific investigators, motivated by a desire to discover useful information as well as by sympathy, now set busily to work on systematic sociological projects. Beatrice Webb, for example, trained herself for this new profession and brought to light significant facts about housing and the exploitation of workers on the London docks. The Fabian Society, in its famous tracts, published information on pauperism, housing, municipal administration, and many other subjects, allowing the facts to speak for themselves.

In spite of its scientific tone, the new reform literature did not lack emotional urgency. One of the most influential books of the time was Henry George's *Progress and Poverty* (1882), which gave, in a fiery and eloquent style, a penetrating analysis of conditions and a simple, radical remedy for them. While Marx had denounced the capitalist as the villain of the economic tragedy, George denounced the landlord and suggested that his power be taken away from him by the expedient of a single expropriative tax on land. Although George's principles never gained significant acceptance, his book seemed to release dormant reforming energies and was responsible, according to Sidney Webb, for the rise of socialism. Another impetus to the cause of reform was provided by *The Bitter Cry of Outcast London,* a penny pamphlet written by the Reverend Andrew Mearns and issued by the London Congregational Union in October, 1883. It declared, in tones of powerful indignation, that the efforts being made to help the poor were insufficient. It gave the most horrifying details of squalor, immorality, overwork, and privation, setting the style for the frank and perceptive reporting that was soon to become commonplace in reform literature.

The climax and, in many ways, the summation of the work of the social investigators was Charles Booth's *Life and Labour of the People in London,* which corresponds to the work of Mayhew in an earlier period. In 1886 Booth started a project of investigation whose results he began to publish in 1889. Ultimately he produced seventeen volumes of factual and descriptive material on the daily lives, occupations, and religious state of the working people of London. Booth's London is the same London Gissing knew, and his details corroborate the accuracy of Gissing's realism much as Mayhew's work corroborates Dickens. Booth himself recognized the accuracy of Gissing's work as social history, for he named *Demos* as one of the few novels that gave trustworthy information about the lives of the poor.

By writing with furious energy, Gissing completed *Workers in the Dawn* in about a year, in spite of poverty and pupils. Some of the credit for this novel belongs to Bertz, for he encouraged Gissing when his confidence flagged, gave him details about Germany for it, and when it was finished sat listening for five days from morning till night as Gissing read it aloud to him. The novel was first submitted to a publisher in November, 1879. Although it is now clear that Gissing's book anticipated an approaching return to social themes in the novel and other forms of literature, it came too early to profit from the interest aroused by W. H. White's Mark Rutherford books, *Progress and Poverty*, and *The Bitter Cry of Outcast London*. It was rejected by a number of publishers, including Chatto and Windus, Smith and Elder, Sampson, Low, and C. Kegan Paul. Gissing refused to be discouraged. While the manuscript was making its depressing tour of publishers' offices he turned out some short stories and wrote, "I am now setting to work at another long novel." [23]

Finally, he entered into an agreement with Remington and Company to publish his novel at his own expense and to pay £125, which was no doubt all that was left of his father's trust fund, for the cost of publication. The contract provided that the author pay fifty pounds on signing the agreement, forty pounds when the first two volumes were printed, and thirty-five pounds when publication was completed. This sum covered the production of exactly 277 copies. The three-volume set was to be priced at a guinea, and the author was to receive two-thirds of the profits after the deduction of advertising expenses. The novel emerged from the press in May, 1880, and Gissing waited hopefully for the reviews. "If I am ignored," he wrote, "I must think very seriously of some mechanical day-labour." [24]

Workers in the Dawn was intended to be both a novel of social protest and a drama of ideas. Its structure shows no originality, for Gissing uncritically accepted the conventions of the Victorian novel with its main and subordinate plots, numerous characters, wide social range, variety of incident, thorough exposition, and mixture of narrative styles and interests; but he did achieve something new in his intimate, realistic treatment of slum life. He was following the program, later described by Waymark in *The Unclassed*, of "digging deeper" into the customs of the poor. By describing their ordinary activities instead of limiting himself to moments of crisis and sensation as the earlier social novelists had tended to do, he succeeded in capturing the texture of their daily lives. Gissing had a genuine talent for such mundane particulars as the outrageous wit of a cheap-Jack, the tricks of a spurious beggar, the conversations of the respectable poor, and the shoddy ostentation of lower-middle-class homes. It was this capacity for sustaining interest in the essentially uninteresting that struck Henry James and led him to grant Gissing the mild virtue of "saturation." Unfortunately, it was part of his method to invest his careful observations with interpolations of sarcasm, indignation, sympathy, and revulsion that jostle each other incongruously, and the result is an unsettling alternation of objective description and strident commentary. When the commentary is set aside, however, the passages about the Blatherwick household, Christmas at the Pettindunds', and the figures of Carrie Mitchell, Ned Quirk, and Michael Rumball are seen to be as accurate and pragmatic as the reports of social investigators.

Workers in the Dawn tells most of the life story of Arthur Golding, a young man with artistic gifts who feels called upon to take up arms against the social conditions of the slums where he has been bred. Circumstances shuttle him back and forth between working-class friends and political reform on the one hand, and the studio of his wealthy art teacher and a life of art on the other, until, at a decisive point, he commits himself to radicalism. Sympathy leads him to befriend and then to marry the poor and disreputable Carrie Mitchell, and his radical principles lead him to make an attempt to reform and educate her. When his wife fails to respond and abandons him, Golding turns to Helen Norman, a refined and intellectual girl who teaches him to seek fulfillment in art rather than revolution. Their relationship ends, in spite of their love, when Helen learns that Golding is married. In the course of his unsuccessful search for a meaningful way of life, Golding encounters most of the social remedies of his day, and rejects them. Toward the end of the novel, he experiences a short period of Wordsworthian calm in watching the stormy sea during an Atlantic crossing, but the ultimate wisdom he learns after arriving in America is suicide, and the story closes melodramatically as he leaps into Niagara Falls with Helen's name on his lips.

During the first part of the novel, while the main characters are children and much of the action takes place in London slums, a Dickenslike atmosphere prevails. Golding as a wandering and neglected waif, a cruel cockney, sprightly lower-class characters, Christmas kindness among the poor, and satire at the expense of a foolish clergyman all suggest counterparts in Dickens' work. However, as the story progresses, with Golding trying to choose between art and social reform, Helen Norman actively seeking a philosophy of life and choosing Positivism, and other characters experiencing moral crises, it becomes clear that Gissing is attempting the psychological analysis typical of the generation of novelists after Dickens. Like George Eliot and Meredith, he conducts his story with the expectation that the interest will arise from the spiritual development of his characters. His protagonists, like those of George Eliot, are idealists bent on testing their philosophies in action. As a result, the narrative leans heavily upon character analysis and exposition of thought. However, these were skills Gissing had yet to learn; all the accounts of mental and emotional life, with the exception of some of Golding's reactions to Carrie, are stiff, lifeless, and unsuccessful.

Because he felt that it was more important to infuse a "personal" quality into his work than to strive for an impression of objectivity, Gissing did not hesitate to comment on his story, sometimes even couching his remarks in the first person. A similar intention, perhaps, led him to make use of his own experiences without much disguise. Helen Norman's intellectual development, Golding's trip to America, and the marriage between Golding and Carrie Mitchell are among the most prominent autobiographical elements in the novel. Gissing said, in his reply to Harrison's first letter, that he had never known a Helen Norman, but it is perfectly clear that he knew a Carrie Mitchell, and that the exceptionally convincing narrative of Golding's unhappy marriage is based on Gissing's experiences with Helen Harrison. It was drawn from life as directly as any fiction ever has been, for he wrote it while he and Helen were sharing cramped lodgings, so that he composed with his original actually before him.

Gissing detected regrettable weaknesses when he read the proofs of his novel. Mrs. Harrison later commented that there was enough material in it for six novels, and there are enough beginner's faults for six novels as well. The language of both the dialogue and the narration is stiff and literary. The two main characters are naïvely idealized; Gissing is found saying, in perfect seriousness, that Golding has a heart "throbbing with generous sympathy with all that is most beautiful in the world of nature or imagination," [25] and that the youthful Helen Norman is "on fire with noble thoughts." [26] The plot, although it has impressive range and vigor, is sprawling, awkward, weakly motivated, and full of coincidence. A shallow sansculottism mars the vivid descriptions of slum life, and the satire directed against religion is too facile and exaggerated to be effective.

VI

The real subject of *Workers in the Dawn* is the effort of Victorian civilization to reform itself. Poverty is merely the most obvious symptom of its disorder and the extreme test of the philosophies professed by the characters. In this first novel Gissing initiated the pessimistic double task carried out by his novels as a whole: an examination of the evils of society and a systematic rejection of the remedies suggested for them. *Workers in the Dawn* deals with social philosophies covering the whole range of Victorian opinion, from the patrician indifference of the wealthy Gresham to the fanatical republicanism of the depraved Pether, and finds them all inadequate.

Positivism occupies a conspicuous place in this trial of ideas. It is personified by Helen Norman, a clergyman's daughter who loses her religious faith through a reading of Strauss's *Leben Jesu* and goes to Germany to search for another belief. After a study of the Church fathers and the German idealist philosophers, she turns to Darwin, Schopenhauer, Comte, and Shelley, and goes back to England to do social work among the poor in the name of the Religion of Humanity. In undergoing this intellectual change, Helen Norman represents the movement of nineteenth-century thought from the religious ideals of the earlier part of the century to the secular and scientific ones of its later years. Ultimately her new philosophy proves inadequate. She finds that the poor do not respond to her kindness, that the money she gives them goes for drink, and that her devotion and hard work produce no improvement. The cold intellectual doctrines that have made religious faith impossible for her have left her lonely and unsatisfied, and she dies in an exile she has sought as an escape from her failures in social work and in love.

Helen Norman's disappointing experiences among the poor and Arthur Golding's futile effort to educate and reform his wife are negations of one of the underlying tenets of Victorian liberalism, the principle of perfectibility. The familiar doctrine that schooling and material improvements could raise the poor from their ignorance and debasement had deep roots in English philosophic thought, for its origin was Locke's theory that, except for a few fundamental ideas, the content of the mind is drawn from experience of the external world, and that man can therefore be molded by education and environment. Similarly, William Godwin, in *Political Justice* (1793), repudiated the idea that judgment was innate, and declared that the responses mistakenly called instinctive were really learned. He contended that children normally came into the world with equal capacities, and that education and environment accounted for the differences that developed in them.

The same principle was held by Jeremy Bentham, who sought in his *Principles of Morals and Legislation* (1789) to show how conduct could be influenced by "sanctions" imposed by society, and by Robert Owen, who found that people could be entirely reformed by external influences. "Train any population rationally," said Owen flatly, "and they will be rational." [27] In the philosophical radicalism of his youth, John Stuart Mill believed that education could improve men's minds indefinitely. Later, in *Utilitarianism* (1863), he asserted that conscience and social feeling, the bases of good conduct, were not inborn, but acquired. A partial retreat from the principle of perfectibility on Mill's part is perceptible in the 1852 edition of *Political Economy* and "Chapters on Socialism" (1879), in which he admits that the standard of education necessary for the communal organization of society is difficult, though not impossible, to achieve. Nevertheless, the doctrine of environment acquired great political importance toward the end of the century, after it had been strengthened by Darwinism; it remained an integral part of liberal programs like those of the Fabians and Socialists, and it was the basis of the reforms in education and housing which were put through in the seventies and eighties. In taking issue with this principle, Gissing was swimming against the tide of the radicalism he professed to support.

Workers in the Dawn is also critical of whatever spiritual remedies might be offered by conventional religion. Orlando Whiffle, the self-important and heartless curate, is a merciless caricature. Mr. Tollady, whose views are sympathetically presented, denounces organized religion in vigorous terms. But Gissing's ultimate verdict is far more temperate. He offers a likable clergyman in the character of Mr. Heatherley, who has been chosen by Helen Norman as her guide in social work with the understanding that he will not try to convert her. When, after her disillusioning experiences with the poor, she allows him to state his religious principles to her, she is surprised to find how inoffensive they seem. In the light of her own disappointment with Positivist ideas, religion seems a forgivable error, but the sad truth is that it offers no hope for social improvement.

Another approach to the problem of poverty is represented by Arthur Golding's Radical club. In a brief sketch Gissing describes the type of organization to which it belongs—a group of workingmen banded together in the name of egalitarian principles who looked forward to bringing the French Revolution to England and establishing a republic. Gissing is sympathetic enough with those aspects of the movement which stress self-help for the poor, but he does not approve of its program of social reform. Arthur ultimately leaves the club, not because he feels free of the social responsibilities it imposes, but because he thinks he is better suited for carrying on its work in another way. In actuality, he is torn between the rival claims of art and social reform. This was a conflict which interested Gissing deeply, for it was responsible for one of his most tormenting divisions of mind, and although he offers a solution for it in his novel he was never able to make that solution work for himself.

One of the most persistent themes in Victorian literature is the sense of responsibility for the condition of the poor, which haunted the minds of sensitive and educated men of the leisure classes. Louis Cazamian has said, "Le 'remords social' est né en Angleterre vers 1840; il ne meurt plus." [28] One of the classic contemporary expressions of this feeling, Tennyson's "Palace of Art," plays a part in *Workers in the Dawn* by leading Arthur Golding to weigh the importance of his artistic talent. The poem tells how the poet's soul builds a secluded "ivory tower" furnished with sensuous delights and reminders of art and history where it means to pursue its pleasures. But vague and sinister horrors invade the palace from the forsaken humanity outside it, and the soul leaves her elegant retreat, saying:

> Yet pull not down my palace towers, that are
>   So lightly, beautifully built;
> Perchance I may return with others there
>   When I have purged my guilt.

The soul's guilt is the same sense of something gone wrong in the bleak, joyless scene of nineteenth-century industrial civilization that forced Ruskin to drop his writing on esthetics and turn to political economy, provided Carlyle with his most thunderous themes, made William Morris an active socialist, and monopolized the interest of young intellectuals like those who made up the Fabian Society. Explaining why he had begun to write on social questions, Ruskin said in the first letter of *Fors Clavigera*:

For my own part, I will put up with this state of things, passively, not an hour longer. I am not an unselfish person, nor an Evangelical one; I have no particular pleasure in doing good. . . . But I simply can not paint, nor read, nor look at minerals, nor do anything else that I like, and the very light of the morning sky . . . has become hateful to me, because of the misery I know of, and see signs of, where I know it not, which no imagination can interpret too bitterly.[29]

It was this widespread and profound sense of moral responsibility, said Beatrice Webb, that motivated the reform movement in which she participated. In the face of emotions like these, art could not flourish in its own right.

The hero of Gissing's novel has been trapped in this typical Victorian dilemma since boyhood. Mr. Tollady urges him to use his talent as a painter in the manner of Hogarth to depict the abuses of society, but Arthur feels unequal to this course. After his revolutionary fervor dies down, he is attracted to art again but cannot reconcile this attraction with his feeling that he must continue to help the poor. The solution for his problem is offered by Helen Norman, who turns him in the direction taken by many important Victorians. Arnold and William Morris, for example, sought to win for art, or, to use Arnold's broader term, "culture," a legitimate place in the social structure by claiming that it exercised a formative influence upon character and intellect. Art, Helen tells Arthur, has a much more profound effect upon civilization than direct social action, for it forms the spirit of which social institutions are merely the embodiment. In becoming a "pure artist," she argues, Arthur will be doing far more to serve society than in undertaking philanthropic or political activities.

Helen has included Shelley in her studies, and what she is doing here, in effect, is trying to persuade Arthur that "poets are the unacknowledged legislators of the world." The logic behind this famous assertion supported the view that social reform could best be achieved by spiritual, rather than material, ends:

A man to be greatly good, must imagine intensely and comprehensively; he must put himself in the place of another and of many others; the pains and pleasures of his species must become his own. The great instrument of the moral good is the imagination; and poetry administers to the effect by acting upon the cause.[30]

On the other hand, says Shelley, it is wrong for the poet to preach moral doctrine directly, for morals are no more than temporary social expedients. The poet must instead consult his intuition and seek to express the divine element in his own nature in undistorted form. Helen tells Arthur, ". . . nothing in this world is more useful than the *beautiful*, nothing works so powerfully for the ultimate benefit of mankind. . . . Genius has always had, and always will have, laws to itself, laws not applicable to the mass of mankind. . . ."[31] This belief in the ultimate social value of art enables Arthur to accept with resignation the reproaches of a fellow radical who feels that he has betrayed the movement by leaving it.

The Shelleyan principle of imagination with its corollary of artistic independence is one of the two positive opinions offered in *Workers in the Dawn*. The other is a philosophy of conditional determinism expounded by Mr. Tollady. Ultimate destinies, says

Mr. Tollady, are fixed. Human beings do not have the power to choose their fate, but they do have the limited power of choosing the manner in which their fate shall be fulfilled. They are free to meet the inevitable with honor, courage, and nobility, and whatever satisfaction they seek must be derived from their behavior in the face of historical events which are predetermined. For that reason, people should not be held responsible for the ultimate consequences of their actions, which are really beyond their control, but should be judged instead according to the spirit in which their actions are performed. Martyrs who died for their religions, says Mr. Tollady, may have been mistaken in devoting themselves to superstitious beliefs, but their beliefs were only accidents of history; their true value for humanity lies in the examples of courage and devotion they furnished, and for that reason the anticlerical Mr. Tollady remembers them with as much pride as any pious believer.

These two convictions were a small harvest to rescue from the pessimism of *Workers in the Dawn*, but they were the more valuable to Gissing for that reason. He never felt the need to submit them to a fictional test again but made them parts of his method and outlook. Fragmentary, and even illogical, they did not offer enough material for constructing a coherent philosophy, though Gissing, inspired by the synthesizing example of Positivism, was eager to lay his hands on such a philosophy. In a letter to Algernon written while *Workers in the Dawn* was in the press he gave a very creditable summary of Positivist views, concluding:

So the Positivist Philosophy bids us keep our eyes on science, to do our best to collect all the results of human knowledge, and deduce therefrom a scheme of *the history of the world*, and from an intimate knowledge of the past to discern a number of general rules which shall enable us in a certain sense to predict the future, and so to lead our political, social and individual lives more in consonance with reason. . . . Consistency is *always* admirable in itself and more than ever when it is displayed in a cause whose end is the elevation of humanity.[32]

He had not succeeded, however, in eliminating the inconsistencies of his own social views. In his indignation on behalf of the poor, his recognition of the effects of environment, his insistence on personal liberty, and his belief in the efficacy of scientific methods, Gissing was a liberal of the school of Bentham, Owen, and Mill; yet he could not accept the egalitarian reform measures that followed from their theories. On the contrary, he shared with Carlyle a profound distrust of democracy, and he echoed, in a somewhat altered and much vaguer form, Carlyle's faith in the elect. Like Victorian England itself, he hovered between the two social philosophies that can be roughly attributed to Bentham and Burke. On the central question of democratic reform, the ability of the masses to govern themselves, Mill himself remained undecided. In the early editions of his *Principles of Political Economy*, which first appeared in 1848, he took the view that the spirit of brotherhood required for the communization of property was beyond the capacity of human nature; but in the third edition, in 1852, he ventured the proposition that communism was practical, although it required as a condition of its success a thorough cultivation of public spirit on the part of the workers. Gissing felt that so radical a change was beyond the power of mere education. After reading Edward Bellamy's *Looking Backward* in 1889 he wrote to Bertz: "The ingenuity of the man in working out details is most remarkable and plausible. But I feel—as you do—that these men postulate too great a change in human nature." [33]

He had learned this pessimism during his first years in London and recorded his lesson in *Workers in the Dawn*. His disillusionment with the potentialities of human nature is reflected in an anecdote he told Roberts about the incident that formed the basis for a short descriptive piece, called "On Battersea Bridge," which he contributed to a London newspaper. One evening, while he was standing on the bridge admiring the Thames gleaming with glorious colors in the sunset, he noticed a workman near him enjoying the spectacle and was delighted to think that the poor man was able to respond to the beauty of the scene. But the man turned to him with the remark, "Throws up an 'eap of mud, don't she?" A fictional version of this incident appears in *Workers in the Dawn* as one of Arthur's last discouraging attempts to educate Carrie. He calls her attention to a beautiful sunset, but her reply is, "It's almost as pretty as the theaytre, isn't it?"

Gissing's first novel thus included an exploration of the London slums that brought the newly converted Comtist and radical idealist face to face with truths he would rather have ignored. As a result, when Frederic Harrison impatiently prodded him for some statement of principles and some positive views about social reform, Gissing had none to offer, for his views and his principles were already being undermined by the tormenting actuality reflected in his novel.

II

THE PALACE OF ART

I

GISSING celebrated the publication of *Workers in the Dawn* by taking Helen to Hastings for a late June holiday. In spite of the amusement the change provided, he took the cares of authorship with him and wrote from Hastings that the publisher, Remington, was not advertising his book properly. Next time, said Gissing, he would take his work elsewhere. The fact was that, after straining every nerve to write and publish the novel, Gissing found that only forty-nine copies were sold in the first three months, and, when the publisher sent him a check for his share of the first year's sale after the cost of advertising had been deducted, the amount came to sixteen shillings. He seized, for encouragement, upon the fact that his book had been included in Mudie's selected list, but that was only a small light in the darkness. The reviews were not enthusiastic. The *Athenaeum*, which gave the novel an unusually long paragraph, praised the telling use of detail but criticized Gissing for singling out so easy an object of attack as Mr. Whiffle, the ridiculous clergyman. The anonymous reviewer disapproved of what he took to be Gissing's radicalism. He wrote:

Some people think the social difficulties of over-population and pauperism may be redressed by rousing the passions of the poor, and others that religion may be usefully replaced by an amalgam of Schopenhauer, Comte and Shelley. To both of these opinions our author is an enthusiastic subscriber.[1]

The opinions expressed by the novel as a whole are, of course, nearly the opposite of these. The *Athenaeum* review contained the

43

first of the many misinterpretations Gissing's social opinions were to suffer at the hands of reviewers. The *Spectator* conceded that *Workers in the Dawn* was a powerful work of fiction, but its anticlericalism led the reviewer to add that Gissing was guilty of a prejudiced presentation of life and character. The truth of the book, he said was "unquestionable"; its remedies, however, were "Quixotic."

Disappointed but not demoralized by these reactions, Gissing took the step of sending a copy of his book to Harrison, explaining in a stiffly phrased letter that, although the reviewers had evaluated it as a novel of ideas, and had neglected its esthetic qualities, he could not give up hope for it. He added that he now wrote to Harrison in gratitude because he had learned about Comte, whose ideas had inspired his novel, from Harrison's writings. After Harrison's letter of July 22, in which reserve and enthusiasm were mingled, Gissing replied with one of the most revealing letters he ever wrote. He was sufficiently humble about the faults of his novel; he said distinctly, in answer to Harrison's expression of distaste for Zola, that he had never read Zola's work and that the qualities of *Workers in the Dawn* resulted from his own reactions to the life of the poor. In the first part of his career, Gissing often had to defend himself against charges that he was a social reformer rather than an artist, but his letter shows that, for him at least, moral indignation and imaginative insight could be fused into a single psychic experience. He wrote that, after walking through the slums,

. . . I have involuntarily stood still and asked myself—what then is the meaning of those strange words, Morality, Decency, Intelligence, which I have somewhere heard? . . . here they mean nothing, nay, their presence would be the intrusion of an utterly incongruous element. —And I have undergone a strange interval of feeling, in which the absence of all that mankind esteems good and lofty seemed to me quite normal and natural.[2]

Strongly impressed by the cultural gap between the classes, he wrote his novel in order to penetrate the "realms of darkness" and to dramatize the spiritual dangers run by sensitive people who undertook missions of social reform. As for the satirical treatment of religion, "I have never, since first I reasoned on such things, known one moment of enthusiasm for, one instant of belief in, the dogmas of religion." Positivism, he wrote, has been his only resource, and he is glad that he has been spared the struggle of freeing himself from "the bondage of creeds." [3]

Within a week after reading *Workers in the Dawn*, Gissing wrote to Algernon, Harrison sent letters to *"eight* literary friends" recommending him. One of these was John Morley, who, it was reported, persuaded Matthew Arnold to read Gissing's novel and also asked Gissing for contributions to the *Pall Mall Gazette*. It was natural for Gissing to respond to this encouragement by transferring his hopes to Harrison and his circle.

Two articles on socialism, written with Bertz's help and published in the *Pall Mall Gazette* in the early part of September, 1880, show Gissing to have been sympathetic, at that time, with the rational approach to social reform advocated by responsible socialists and by the Positivists. Morley also asked Gissing to use his talent for description in writing "some sketches of eccentric life," and Gissing seems to have enjoyed the prospect of prowling about the streets disguised in workman's clothing in search of material. No descriptive articles appeared, although some years later in *Thyrza* Gissing did make use of his impressions of a large public-house party he visited on one of these expeditions.

Early in November he went to a meeting of the Positivist Society at the Harrisons', where he met some eminent members and formally joined the organization himself. Not long afterwards he began to tutor the Harrison boys, and early in the following year he was recommended to Vernon Lushington, a former Secretary of the Admiralty, who hired him to tutor his four girls.

In this way began a strange double life. Almost every day Gissing left the cramped misery of his room, where his sick and drunken wife awaited him, to appear at fashionable homes, both as tutor and guest. The contrast sometimes led to amusing situations. One lady who could not keep her servants asked Gissing how he managed his butler, and Gissing coolly replied that he preferred a maid. More often, however, the conditions of his life made him so unhappy that he could not bear to write to his brother about his feelings, only saying that he wished he had a relative nearby to whom he could look for sympathy. Something of an improvement came at the end of February, 1881, when he moved to the West End for the sake of living closer to his pupils and saving traveling time. His new quarters at 55 Wornington Road had two rooms, and one of them was used as a study. This, together with the time he saved, made it possible for him to continue writing. For in spite of all difficulties and disappointments, his writing did continue. The novel begun before *Workers in the Dawn* had been accepted for publication had lain untouched for several months, but it was already half finished, and Gissing now felt that he would be able to go back to it.

His relationship with Harrison led to welcome opportunities for earning money by tutoring, but these involved incursions into his writing time. He gradually increased his clientele, until in March of 1882 he was occupied from nine to six with ten pupils, most of them children of wealthy families. His subjects were generally Latin and Greek, but when he was forced to discuss some field in which he was not prepared, like English history, or a new Latin text, he enjoyed the chance for study. The number of pupils and the hours he gave to private teaching of this sort diminished as time went on, but it was years before he felt able to give it up entirely.

Another chance of making money came to him through Harrison and the Positivist Society in November, 1880, when Gissing received a note from a fellow Positivist, Professor Edward Spencer Beesly, inviting him to write a quarterly article on English affairs to be printed in translation in the Russian periodical *Le Messager de l'Europe*, which was published once a month in St. Petersburg. At first he was happy to accept this offer, for he was paid eight pounds for each article. However, he prepared his contributions with his usual conscientiousness, gleaning social and political material from the press and keeping himself scrupulously informed about current matters, so that each one took him about a month of hard work. The first was sent off to Russia in January, 1881. Gissing received copies of the magazine, which he described as "a fine-looking periodical, about the size of the *Nineteenth Century*," [4] but the only part of it that he could read was the English initials "G.R.G." following his article. This work brought in a much-needed thirty-two pounds a year, but it involved labor that Gissing soon found intolerable, and by October of 1882 he was writing to Algernon that he was "struggling bitterly with the old foe, the Russian article." [5]

As an indirect result of the publication of *Workers in the Dawn*, Gissing renewed the acquaintance of a college friend who was ultimately to become his first biographer, Morley Roberts. The two had not met since Gissing had left Owens College, but Roberts, seeing the name of his old schoolmate in the advertisements for *Workers in the Dawn*, wrote to him through the publisher. At Gissing's death, Roberts ranked as his closest and oldest friend. He had literary interests and was a prolific author and journalist, but as a vigorous, robust, Bohemian personality whose energies sometimes involved him with the police and often carried him off to distant parts of the empire and to America in search of fortune and adventure, he had little in common with Gissing. He was certainly less able to sympathize with Gissing than to criticize his deficiencies, but he was a sincere and congenial friend whose company Gissing enjoyed. The two frequently met in each other's shabby rooms to pass the time in animated literary discussions of the kind that take place between Reardon and Biffen in *New Grub Street*. Roberts was awed by Gissing's profound knowledge of the classics, but he was also impatient with his pedantry, timidity, and impracticality.

Roberts' biography of Gissing, *The Private Life of Henry Maitland*, was badly received when it was published in 1912 and has always been regarded with distrust because the names in it are disguised. Roberts makes many errors of judgment, an almost inevitable result of the difference between his temperament and Gissing's. In addition, his book is rambling, unsystematic, and digressive. Nevertheless, it gives invaluable personal impressions and many facts, however inaccurately narrated, that would not otherwise be known. Although he often quotes from letters written to him by Gissing, Roberts never does so without making some deliberate minor change in the wording of the passage. His reason for doing this and for disguising the names was probably to forestall legal action on the grounds of unauthorized quotation or libel. He certainly did not intend to conceal anything, for he gave many direct clues, and no one seems to have been in any doubt whatever as to the real identity of "Henry Maitland" or most of the other thinly disguised personages in the book.

When he moved to Wornington Road in February of 1881, Gissing was forced to borrow ten pounds from his mother, although his poverty was no longer as acute as it had been a year or two earlier, for he was soon to be earning forty-five shillings a week through his pupils alone. The trouble was that Helen's illnesses constantly produced doctor's bills, raising his expenses to three pounds a week. In spite of money troubles and pupils, however, he locked himself into the second room every evening after his day's teaching was done and wrote busily.

When he was writing *Workers in the Dawn* he rose early, spent an hour thinking of his work and then wrote from nine until two, finishing a whole chapter of three thousand words or more. Now, however, he no longer felt the creative urge that had carried him through his first book and was content with half a chapter written in the evening. His obstacles multiplied. He became prey to indigestion, especially in bad weather. Helen's actions and illnesses disrupted his peace of mind. One day in April, 1881, for example, she had a fit in a nearby chemist's shop and had to be carried home through the streets. Incidents like these, combined with his constant struggle to earn a living, cast him into a profound depression. He was jealous of every moment taken from his writing. When a grandfather who lived in London complained of being neglected, Gissing was distressed, but insisted that he could not spare a precious evening in listening to the old man's conversation. As for leaving him alone with Helen, that was impossible. She could no more entertain a visitor, said Gissing, than his writing chair. The chair would, in fact, be preferable, for its silence was better than Helen's foolish and offensive remarks.

In May one of the hazards of life in cheap lodgings spoiled their enjoyment of the pleasant pair of rooms in Wornington Road; a dead rat was found in the water pipes. Early in August they moved to 15 Gower Place. Gissing's letters to Algernon at this time are often full of complaint: "I struggle with absolute anguish for a couple of hours of freedom every day, and can only obtain the semblance of whole-hearted application. To say that I am like a man toiling up a hill with a frightful burden upon his back is absolutely no figure of speech with me; often, very often, I am on the point of stumbling and going no further." [6]

But there were expressions of resolution too, and the new novel progressed steadily through 1881. "I know very well," he once wrote to Algernon, "that this alone is my true work, and it shall not be sacrificed to whatever exigencies." [7] He had to do without Bertz's support, for his friend had become a member of the group which Tom Hughes sent to Tennessee to establish the model community he called Rugby. Bertz was out of England from July of 1881 until June of 1883.

Gissing now began to tell Algernon some of the details of his life with Helen, and it is clear that similar facts lay behind the vague allusions to "conditions" in earlier letters. In the middle of January, 1882, after having been hospitalized for one of her many disorders, Helen came home prematurely, and insisted on going out to do some marketing the next day. The result was another fit, this time in a chandler's shop. It was followed by a faint, which took place in the street while she was on her way home. She was taken to a hospital, where the doctors were mystified by her condition, as they had always been. Gissing was greatly disturbed, both by the public commotion these attacks caused, and by his own fear. He described the seizure as convulsions followed by periods of unconsciousness, and they may well have been caused by Helen's addiction to alcohol, which must by now have become chronic. She was often overcome in public places, and although Gissing forbade her to go out she disobeyed him and had to be locked in. Their relations had become hopeless. She continually deceived him, even conspiring with the servants. Once, for example, Gissing reported that when he had asked a maid to sell some old newspapers for him, Helen told her to say that they had brought a lower price, and cheated him of the difference. With the money she secretly bought liquor.

He now felt clearly that his only hope of continuing his work lay in ridding himself of his wife. After her attack in January, 1882, he made arrangements for her to stay at an invalids' home in Battersea kept by two kindly old ladies. Helen begged not to be sent there, for it meant that she would be unable to obtain drink, but Gissing stood firm against her entreaties. He felt that it would be folly to give in to her, and he decided, furthermore, that once he had succeeded in sending her away he would never have her back. Her protests grew so violent and her melancholy so profound that Gissing was afraid she would go insane. She even threatened, he wrote, to become a Roman Catholic. She promised to reform, but Gissing realized that he could not trust her when he found a bottle of gin among her belongings. A few days later he succeeded, in spite of her resistance, in getting her to the lodging in Battersea. He told himself that she was mad and that her lunacy freed him from the responsibility of living with her. The invalids' home was a heavy additional expense, but he felt that his new freedom was well worth its cost.

He immediately began to make up for lost time, and in his solitary evenings wrote busily at the novel that he was to call *Mrs. Grundy's Enemies*. He shared his quarters with a big black tomcat named Grimmy Shaw whose way of devouring fishheads and then sleeping in the middle of his study table presented the toiling author with a spectacle of enviable contentment. During the day he was occupied with pupils from nine to six but found time for companionship. Algernon visited him in March, and the two went to see the famous elephant, Jumbo. On Mondays and Fridays he lunched with the Harrisons and was sometimes their dinner guest as well. When he stayed at home, he was often joined by Morley Roberts, who has described how they spent hours in lively literary conversation, interrupting their talk to create a miscellaneous and substantial stew in a pot cooked at the fire. In June Gissing saw "Frou-Frou," played by Sarah Bernhardt and a visiting French company. At about this time, the Harrisons, who were planning to spend September in Normandy, suggested to Gissing that he accompany them at their expense in order to give the boys lessons during the holiday. Gissing was greatly excited by this proposal and began to make plans to free himself from pupils for the month, but when September came the invitation had to be withdrawn because of an illness of Mrs. Harrison.

In the middle of June the comparative equanimity that Gissing was now enjoying was shattered again by Helen. She had somehow escaped from her captivity in Battersea and was now living with friends who sent Gissing abusive letters, accusing him of mistreating her. One day she caused so serious a disturbance that the police were called, and he was summoned to court to take charge of her. He now had to find the police officer who had arrested her, and he complained that the affair disrupted his work.

In spite of all this, *Mrs. Grundy's Enemies* was completed at the beginning of September, 1882, and a new novel was begun before it had been sent to a publisher. In the same month Gissing moved to 17 Oakley Crescent, Chelsea, where he was to stay for almost two years, ending the troublesome wandering from one squalid lodging to another that had characterized his London life. Before the end of the month, Smith, Elder returned *Mrs. Grundy's Enemies* with a note saying that it was too "painful" and that it would not attract the kind of reader who subscribed to Mudie's circulating library. Gissing greeted this verdict with contempt, and sent the manuscript off to another publisher.

In the meantime, Helen had been taken to the hospital again, this time for an eye operation. Instead of coming home afterward, however, she had gone to the house of another patient, and was being cared for there. Apparently her presence soon grew unwelcome, for in October, 1882, Gissing received a telegram asking him to come and take her away at once. He and Helen were now together again with equal unwillingness on both sides. Finding it impossible to keep Helen at home, even though she could not see, Gissing had to hire a woman to accompany her when she went out, at the troublesome expense of a shilling a day.

The harsh experiences of these years were teaching him to modify his faith that society could be transformed by rational means. For a time at least, he seems to have persisted in believing that particular cases did not nullify the validity of generalizations derived in a rational manner. In February of 1881 he wrote that although he felt Positivism could satisfy emotional needs usually associated with religion, he preferred to stress its intellectual aspects. In January, as the newest of Harrison's converts, he had begun to date his letters according to the Positivist calendar, which, as he explained to Algernon, numbered the years from the year before the French Revolution. In six months, however, he returned to the conventional way of dating letters, and in less than two years the conditions of his life brought him to the pessimistic conclusions implied in *Workers in the Dawn*.

He formulated his new ideas in an article entitled "Hope of Pessimism," which was completed in October, 1882, but never submitted for publication because Gissing felt that it would not be accepted anywhere, and that if it were he would be embarrassed by Harrison's reaction to it. In this remarkable document, Gissing subjects the philosophy of nineteenth-century Radicalism, which he calls "Agnostic Optimism," to a critique based on standards drawn from Schopenhauer. It is a unique performance, beginning with the Victorian scientism of Mill, Comte, Darwin, and Spencer, and advancing to the twentieth-century pessimism of Camus, Orwell, and Aldous Huxley. Gissing argues that it is a mistake to believe, as the Comtists did, that science can eliminate "the metaphysical instinct," for even after people have been educated out of their religious ideas, they will still think in religious terms unconsciously. Further, science itself, when it has gone as far as possible in revealing the secrets of nature, will ultimately confront the unknowable, thus inspiring a sense of wonder that can only result in a return to mysticism. It can give no better knowledge of the nature of the universe than can conventional religion. When the scientist and the Philistine are on their deathbeds, both will be forced to acknowledge the futility of their beliefs, says Gissing, coining one of his best phrases, by "the convincing metaphysics of death."

If "Agnostic Optimism" succeeded, however, the society it would produce would be intolerable. Optimism, says Gissing, is an expression of the will to survive, "egotism under another name," and it encourages the vices of competition. Also, it is opposed to reason and to realism, for the facts that life is unhappy and human nature radically evil are self-evident. In spite of its long struggle for improvement, the human race can never achieve absolute knowledge and is destined, one day, for extinction. With an inverted logic that recalls Camus' "Myth of Sisyphus," Gissing argues toward the close of his essay that an awareness of these tragic facts can serve as the basis for a new conception of virtue. Men must realize "the pathos of the human lot," must face each other with "compassion," must make mutual sympathy a duty. "We are shipmates tossed on the ocean of eternity," he says, "and one fate awaits us all." Gissing seems to be anticipating certain phases of Huxley's *Brave New World* and Orwell's *1984* when he says that the ultimate result of such a view of life would be the elimination of egotism, together with its concomitants, the will to live and the procreative impulse. Finally, ". . . a childless race will dedicate its breath to the eternal silence, and Mercy will have redeemed the world."

The long, twenty-eight-page manuscript, written in passionate and ironic prose, is a key both to Gissing's convictions and to the many problems of his novels. It explains why his social novels so consistently reject not only reform, but even the possibility of reform. His opinion that the order of the universe is intrinsically evil and that human idealism can do little to change that fact is expressed in his novels through the failures of such genuinely well-intentioned social reformers as Helen Norman. His way of relating political democracy to competition and its vices in later novels such as *In the Year of Jubilee* recalls his view that "Agnostic Optimism" is merely a ratification of the process of evolutionary conflict within the social order.

"Hope of Pessimism" is a manifestation of that independence of mind which irritated Gissing's friends and kept him at odds with his age. It shows that his thoughts could go beyond the intellectual commitments of his time, to deal sensitively and imaginatively with issues that still lay beyond the horizon. Having honestly followed the premises dictated by his experiences and prejudices to their logical, if eccentric conclusions, he was no longer a militant of the Religion of Humanity or a "mouthpiece of the advanced Radical party," as he had once called himself. Gissing felt some satisfaction with his essay, for in the same letter of October 6, 1882, in which he told Algernon about "Hope of Pessimism," he said that he felt more inclined to state his social ideas as speculations than to embody them in fiction.

The day after Christmas, 1882, Gissing wrote joyfully to Algernon that the firm of Bentley and Company had accepted *Mrs. Grundy's Enemies.* What matter if their price was fifty pounds, hardly more than a token payment? To the eager young author the chance of having his work published seemed reward enough in itself. Besides, the fifty pounds, little as it would seem to an established writer, was by no means unwelcome. As it turned out, however, Gissing's joy was premature. While the book was in proof the objectionable material that had led Smith and Elder to refuse it attracted the attention of the new publisher, and Gissing was asked to change certain scenes and dialogue. He consulted Harrison, who had by now become his confidant and adviser on legal and literary matters. Harrison thought that Gissing ought to make the required concessions. Gissing disagreed, but, after a lively discussion of the issues involved, he gave way, chafing under the necessity of compromising with "prejudices" and determining to take revenge on the "namby-pamby public" by means of a satirical novel and an article on morality in fiction.

In the meantime, George Bentley asked Evelyn Abbott, a historian and fellow of Balliol College who had acted as a literary adviser to his firm, to read the novel and mark passages for omission and revision. By March, Abbott, working with the proofs of the first two volumes and the manuscript of the third, had completed his task. There the matter rested for nearly a year. As late as February of 1884 Gissing was still waiting to hear of the publication of *Mrs. Grundy's Enemies*. At last, in August, he wrote to Algernon that he had received a moralizing letter from Bentley about the novel. Gissing spent the next six weeks revising it, and returned it in the middle of October, 1884. In spite of the revisions of Abbott and Gissing, however, the novel was never published, and the manuscript and proofs have been lost.

Judging from Abbott's comments about it in his letters to Bentley, *Mrs. Grundy's Enemies* reflected Gissing's continued interest in the poor, although his sympathetic attitude was changing. The realities of London were making it impossible for him to preserve whatever illusions he may have brought from Wakefield and Dickens about the potentialities of the poor. His radical idealism must have weakened quickly when he heard his own principles declared at restless and sometimes violent street meetings, for such scenes aroused in him a profound distrust of crowds. He had always feared and hated large groups of people, as a poem written when he was a boy shows.[8] This aversion asserts itself whenever he describes crowds in his novels. He felt them to be uncontrollable herds, capable of unlimited violence, in which human individuality was swamped by numbers. He could hardly continue for very long to be an advocate of democratic socialism when he feared the multitude and abhorred the possibility of mass action. One of the consequences of this prejudice was a pronounced dislike of theaters and plays, which he associated with crowds. Although he went to plays often enough, he looked upon them as attempts to pander to low public tastes. For this reason he disliked Dickens' dramatic flair and, in spite of his admiration for Ibsen, regretted that he had chosen to express himself in the form of plays. The spectacle of the poor swarming out on the May Bank Holiday of 1882 to waste their freedom in crowded discomfort at the seashore or in the parks filled him with disgust. It was a sight that never failed to make him think and one that he often described in novels and short stories.

The trouble was, he wrote to his sister Margaret, that people did not enjoy periods of leisure often enough to learn to make use of them. "What we want is a general shortening of working hours all the year round, so that, for instance, all labour would be over at 4 o'clock in the afternoon." [9] However, such a thing could not come to pass while society continued to grub so hard for money.

All the world's work—all that is really necessary for the health and comfort and even luxury of mankind—could be performed in three or four hours of each day. . . . Every man has to fight for a living with his neighbour, and the grocer who keeps his shop open till half an hour after midnight has an advantage over him who closes at twelve. Work in itself is *not an end; only a means;* but we nowadays make it an end, and three-fourths of the world cannot understand anything else.[10]

II

The events of the time reported in the newspapers convinced Gissing that he was living in a materialist society which had no nobility of spirit. Reports of athletic feats reminded him of the lack of attention paid to matters of intellect. When many thousands of pounds were spent to erect an ornamental statue of a griffin in Fleet Street, and it was then found that the griffin interfered with traffic, Gissing saw in the ugliness of the statue and the wasteful muddle of the whole affair typical reflections of the period's state of mind. Reading of a man who gave twenty thousand pounds to the Congregational Church, Gissing attributed the action to social ambition and an appetite for display and wished such sums could be contributed to humanitarian ends. The thought of all this money reminded him that London was unable to raise enough to establish a free library of the kind he had seen in America. "Our age," he wrote to Algernon, ". . . is thoroughly empty, mean, wind-baggish, and the mass of people care so little to find employment in intellectual matters that they are driven to all manner of wild physical excesses for the sake of excitement." [11] At the death of Carlyle in 1881 he reflected, as every generation does, that the giants of the time were going, leaving no great men to take their places, and envisioned the coming of an age democratized into mediocrity.

Still, London offered some pleasures he could enjoy. In February of 1883 he went to see an exhibition of pictures by Dante Gabriel Rossetti, and he wrote to his sisters about the Gilbert and Sullivan operas, including the current "Iolanthe," which he had seen. In spite of his aversion to the theater, Gissing seldom missed a new opera at the Savoy, and he felt a great interest in W. S. Gilbert and his work. Characteristically, he tempered the charming illusions of art and music with the harshness of reality by going for a long stroll in the East End on one day in the same month and taking note of the life he saw there.

Since he had jettisoned Positivism and concluded that much of the world's suffering was due to frenzied industrial competition, it was natural that he should find something attractive in the economic doctrines of Ruskin. In a letter of May, 1883, he recommended *Unto This Last* to his sister Margaret, as much for its thought as for its style, and admitted that he went very far in agreeing with it.

The first of the works on economics that occupied the later part of Ruskin's career, *Unto This Last* had first appeared in 1860 as a series of essays in *The Cornhill*. It attacked the principles of "political economy" because they ignored emotions, which Ruskin felt should be recognized as subtle and active economic forces. In the problems of production and distribution, he said, human and spiritual values ought to take precedence over mere volume of goods. His most ambitious move was an attack on orthodox conceptions of value. Mill had said that the measure of a product's value was its usefulness, and Ricardo had equated value with the labor of production, but Ruskin, drawing upon his own experience as an art critic, pointed out that these strictly material definitions failed to measure the value of works of art. Denying the common economic principles with more eloquence than logic, Ruskin declared that the value of a manufactured article, like the value of a great painting, was inherent. The end of production should be that of serving human beings; its object should be "mouth-gain," not "money-gain." Even prices, said Ruskin, are subject to the operation of human values, for they depend partly on the purchaser's desire for articles on sale.

Gissing did not approve of the practical suggestions for workshops, government schools, unemployment relief, and other social measures set forth in the preface of *Unto This Last*. But Ruskin's attempt to humanize the most established principles of a materialistic age, his distrust of democracy and egalitarianism, and his insistence that real social advances could come only through indi-

Demos.

Chapter I.

Stanbury Hill, remote but two hours' walk from a region blackened with mine & factory & furnace, shows with its western slope a fair green valley, a land of meadows & orchard, untouched by poisonous ath. At its foot lies the village of Wanley; the opposite side of the hollow is clad with native wood, rising for more than a mile the bank of a shallow stream, a tributary of Severn. Wanley consists in main of one long street; the houses are stone-built, with mullioned windows, here & there showing a picturesque gable or a quaint old chimney. The oldest buildings are four cottages which stand at the ... of the street; once upon a time they formed the country residence of the abbots of Belwick. The ... of that name still claims for its ruined self a portion of earth's surface, but, as it had the misfortune to be erected above the thickest coal-seam in England, its walls are blackened with the ... of collieries & shaken by the strain of mighty engines. Climb Stanbury Hill at nightfall, &, ... eastward; you behold, far off a dusky ruddiness in the sky, like the last of an angry sunset; with ..., you can catch glimpses of little tongues of flame, leaping & quivering on the horizon. That is Belwick. The good abbots, who were wont to come out in the summer time to Wanley, would be at a loss to recognize their consecrated home in these sooty relics. Belwick, with its hundreds & its fire-vomiting blast-furnaces, would to their eyes more nearly resemble a certain igneous ... of which they thought much in their sojourn upon earth, & which we may assure ourselves ... dream not of in the quietness of their last long sleep.

A large house, which stands aloof from the village & a little above it, is Wanley Manor. The ... history tells us that Wanley was given in the fifteenth century by that same religious foundation ..., at the dissolution of monasteries, the manor passed into the hands of Queen Catherine. The ... is half-timbered; from the height above, it looks old & peaceful amid its immemorial ... Towards the end of the eighteenth century it became the home of a family named Eldon, the estate ... the greater part of the valley below. But an Eldon who came into possession when William IV ... king brought the fortunes of the house to a low ebb, & his son, seeking to improve matters by ... his prejudices & entering upon commercial speculation, in the end left a widow & two boys ... little more to live upon than the income which arose from Mrs. Eldon's settlements. The manor was, ... after this, purchased by a Mr. Mutimer, a Belwick ironmaster; but Mrs. Eldon & her boys still ... the house, ... in consequence of certain events which ... will shortly be narrated. ... would have mourned their departure; they were the aristocracy of the neighbourhood, & to have ... by a name which no one knew, a name connected only with blast-furnaces, would have.

First page of the manuscript of Demos

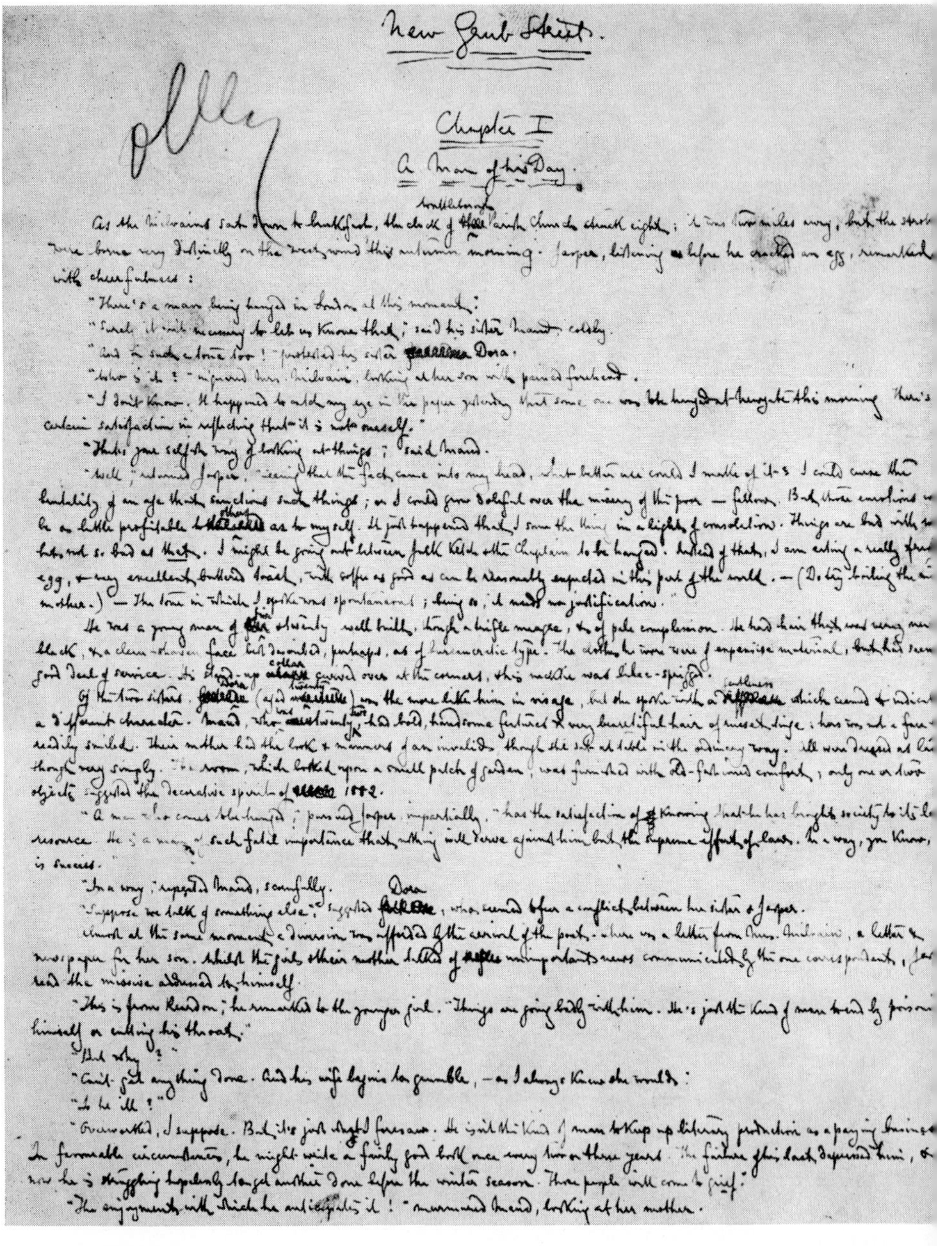
New Grub Street.

Chapter I

A Man of his Day.

As the Milvains sat down to breakfast, the clock of Wattleborough parish church struck eight; it was two miles away, but the strokes were borne very distinctly on the west wind this autumn morning. Jasper, listening as before he cracked an egg, remarked with cheerfulness:

"There's a man being hanged in London at this moment."

"Surely it isn't necessary to let us know that," said his sister Maud, coldly.

"And in such a tone too!" protested his sister Dora.

"Who is it?" inquired Mrs. Milvain, looking at her son with pained forehead.

"I don't know. It happened to catch my eye in the paper yesterday that some one was to be hanged at Newgate this morning. There's a certain satisfaction in reflecting that it is not myself."

"That's your selfish way of looking at things," said Maud.

"Well," returned Jasper, "seeing that the fact came into my head, what better use could I make of it? I could curse the brutality of an age that sanctions such things; or I could grow doleful over the misery of the poor fellow. But those emotions w… be as little profitable to others as to myself. It just happened that I saw the thing in a light of consolation. Things are bad with m… but not so bad as that. I might be going out between Jack Ketch and the Chaplain to be hanged. Instead of that, I am eating a really fre… egg, and very excellent buttered toast, with coffee as good as can be reasonably expected in this part of the world. — (Do try boiling the c… mother.) — The tone in which I spoke was spontaneous; being so, it needs no justification."

He was a young man of five-and-twenty, well built, though a trifle meagre, and of pale complexion. He had hair that was very ne… black, and a clean-shaven face best described, perhaps, as of Lucianic type. The clothes he wore were of expensive material, but had seen … good deal of service. His stand-up collar curved over at the corners, his necktie was lilac-sprigged.

Of the two sisters, Dora (aged twenty) was the more like him in visage, but she spoke with a gentleness which seemed to indica… a different character. Maud, who was two-and-twenty, had bold, handsome features, and very beautiful hair of russet tinge; hers was not a face … readily smiled. Their mother had the look and manners of an invalid, though she sat at table in the ordinary way. All were dressed as la… though very simply. The room, which looked upon a small patch of garden, was furnished with old-fashioned comfort; only one or two objects suggested the decorative spirit of 1882.

"A man who comes to be hanged," pursued Jasper, impartially, "has the satisfaction of knowing that he has brought society to its la… resource. He is a man of such fatal importance that nothing will serve against him but the supreme effort of law. In a way, you know, is success."

"In a way," repeated Maud, scornfully.

"Suppose we talk of something else," suggested Dora, who seemed to fear a conflict between her sister and Jasper.

Almost at the same moment a diversion was afforded by the arrival of the post: there was a letter for Mrs. Milvain, a letter and newspaper for her son. Whilst the girls and their mother talked of unimportant news communicated by the one correspondent, Jas… read the missive addressed to himself.

"This is from Reardon," he remarked to the younger girl. "Things are going badly with him. He's just the kind of man to end by poison… himself or cutting his throat."

"But why?"

"Can't get anything done. And his wife begins to grumble, — as I always knew she would."

"Is he ill?"

"Overworked, I suppose. But it's just what I foresaw. He isn't the kind of man to keep up literary production as a paying busine… In favourable circumstances, he might write a fairly good book once every two or three years. The failure of his last depressed him, and now he is struggling hopelessly to get another done before the winter season. Those people will come to grief."

"The enjoyment with which he anticipates it!" murmured Maud, looking at her mother.

First page of the manuscript of New Grub Street

COURTESY BERG COLLECTION, NEW YORK PUBLIC LIBRARY

vidual improvement were all attractive to Gissing. In particular, he sympathized with Ruskin's view that art and art values deserved a central position in society. "His worship of Beauty I look upon as essentially valuable," he wrote. And he said in the same letter, ". . . I am growing to feel, that the only thing known to us of absolute value is artistic perfection. The ravings of fanaticism— justifiable or not—pass away; but the works of the artist, work in what material he will, remain, sources of health to the world." [12]

Although his social ideas were changing, Gissing's agnosticism remained firm. Bertz had recently returned from America, after suffering considerable hardship at Tom Hughes's experimental farm in Tennessee, which had failed and gone into bankruptcy. Late in the summer of 1883 he was struck by a new form of idealism, suddenly joined the Blue Ribbon Army and the YMCA, and began to frequent Salvation Army revival meetings. Gissing found this behavior "shocking" in an intelligent man, and asserted that there was no chance that he would go the same way. Reviewing his beliefs in a letter to his sister Margaret written at about the same time, he wrote that he did not think the senses were capable of apprehending absolute truth, and that this incapacity bound him to respect, though not to share, her religious convictions.

In very deed, I can prove absolutely, nothing whatever. Am surrounded by infinite darkness, and live my little life by the light of such poor tapers as the sun, moon and stars. But I earnestly beg of you to understand that this position is compatible with the extremest reverence. If you tell me you believe that the light has been brought to you, by means of a certain revelation, I cannot possibly say you are wrong. I could only do so if my own senses were final arbiters of truth. All I can say is that I am so constituted that I *cannot* put faith in the light you hold to me; it appears to me an artificial reflection of man's hopes. My position with regard to the universe is that of Carlyle in the wonderful chapter of "Sartor" called "Natural Supernaturalism." [13]

Gissing continued to hold himself responsible for the education of his sisters and his brother. His letters to Ellen and Margaret exalt the ideal of the educated woman, suggest reading and methods of study, and call their attention to topics of the day. In the fall of 1883 his education of Algernon took a new turn. The latter had qualified himself as a solicitor and begun practice in Wakefield, but he apparently found little use for his training except that of advising Gissing about points of law involved in the plots of his novels. In September of 1883, however, when he sent Gissing a copy of a letter he had written to a Wakefield newspaper, Gissing praised it extravagantly, saying it showed that Algernon had writing talent and urging him to try his hand. He mentioned the kind of subject he felt would suit Algernon—social material—and, although he recommended the essays of W. H. Mallock as models, he reminded him that it was important to be original.

Gissing had taken Helen back in October of 1882, but she probably did not stay with him very long. He seems to have enjoyed freedom for both work and leisure during most of 1883, and by autumn of that year Helen was certainly living elsewhere, for in September a policeman called to inform Gissing that she had again become involved in a street disturbance. Although she was the plaintiff in a case in which she charged two men with assault, things seemed likely to go against her. The policeman told Gissing that she was known as a drunkard and a person of bad character. The disturbance had taken place at one-thirty in the morning, and so many of Helen's faults of character seemed likely to emerge in the case that, as the policeman apparently suggested to Gissing, it would be easy to provide evidence to serve as grounds for divorce. Gissing was eager to follow the suggestion, but he feared that the legal proceedings might be beyond his means and, as he always did in such emergencies, consulted Harrison.

Harrison advised immediate legal action, and offered to lend Gissing the money for it. Encouraged by the hope of freeing himself, Gissing told himself that the worst of the distress Helen had caused him was over. He had sent her a pound a week when they were separated, and he intended to continue this allowance when the proposed divorce was effected, provided Helen met such requirements as living where he asked her to. Haste was important, and he asked Algernon to recommend a London barrister, impressing on him the extreme importance of the affair. By the middle of October he was consulting an attorney named Poole, who was optimistic but suggested that Gissing gather more evidence. Accordingly, he engaged a policeman for a weekly fee to watch Helen's movements. After a couple of weeks, however, no new evidence had been secured, and toward the end of November Poole advised Gissing to give up hope of a divorce. There is no doubt that he was greatly disappointed, but he wrote to Algernon that it made little difference. He would have continued to send Helen money in any event, and as far as moral questions were concerned, he felt himself free of convention. Helen remained his wife, but he never saw her again until after she was dead.

III

While awaiting the publication of *Mrs. Grundy's Enemies*, Gissing took advantage of his relationship with George Bentley to submit some of his work to Bentley's periodical, *Temple Bar*. A poem called simply "Song," the only verse Gissing seems to have published in his lifetime, appeared in the number of November, 1883; it is a sentimental Swinburnian effusion, written, according to Gissing's confession, in seven minutes. This acceptance seems to have suggested the possibility of earning some much-needed money by trying *Temple Bar* with short stories, and he succeeded in placing two, which were published early in 1884. The first, "The Four Silverpennys," is little more than a bagatelle, though it shows an original hand, which tells of a lonely man who searches for someone of his own unusual name to designate as his heir. The second, entitled "Phoebe," has a number of characteristic elements: a sympathetic English *grisette* finds in her room a large sum of money left by its eccentric former lodger, but she does not know how to make use of it, and it is eventually stolen by an ungrateful beggarwoman whom she shelters for the night.

Gissing was, as always, occupied with a novel of his own, but he took time in October and November of 1883 to continue Algernon's literary education. In October, he covered three pages of a letter with the outline of a short novel for Algernon to try his talent on. It was a story about a love affair between two young people who meet under the auspices of an unconventional elderly lady but are prevented from marrying by the disapproval of the girl's parents. Compelled to wait until the girl is of age, they spend a year apart, then return to their patroness and are married. Gissing later used this plot, with some improvements, at the end of *Thyrza*, and he felt that as it stood it might be worked into a marketable short novel. He sent it to Algernon with many suggestions about characterization, warnings against possible mistakes, and even a title—"Pastures New." He also offered to send a chapter outline if it should be needed.

The pupil went busily to work and early in November submitted a first chapter which his master returned with detailed criticism. Although Gissing wisely limited his suggestions to matters of craft, and adapted them to the talents of his pupil, his advice to Algernon gives some excellent insights into his own methods. He recommended that the chapter in question begin with a description, and that didactic passages be omitted. He warned against the faultless character and advised Algernon to give more details and to introduce the facts obliquely, with the accompaniment of satire or humor, but without comment. It was extremely important to keep the plot simple and to command a firm grasp of the characters; publishers paid more attention to the larger aspects of plot and character than to style. He ended by asking Algernon to rewrite the chapter according to his suggestions and send it to him again. He suggested that Algernon read the newspapers for ideas and observe people carefully for characteristics and opinions that might be useful. He regarded Scott as a "dangerous model" because he introduced long discursive passages and did not attempt the psychological realism necessary in the newer fiction; but he recommended George Eliot for her structure, transitions, and conversations. The slow pace of his own plot-developments is partly explained by his rule that each chapter should have its own incident, and should move the story along one step. He pointed out Hardy's practice of keeping his people busy with small actions, a device that has much to do with the quiet atmosphere of his later novels: ". . . it is astonishing how much interest can attach to the paltriest affairs if only they be vividly presented. Nay, it is often better to trust to the trivial." [14]

The letters of late 1883 are the beginning of a painstaking pedagogy that continued long after the novels of country life Algernon learned to write by these methods began to achieve publication. After 1888 the two brothers pursued parallel careers as novelists; Gissing occasionally wondered whether they were interfering with each other's interests; their work was certainly dissimilar, and Algernon never succeeded in establishing a reputation. Even after Algernon had begun to publish prolifically he still found his older brother's guidance necessary. Gissing discussed possible titles with him, sent lists of corrections and suggestions after reading each of his books, helped him through difficulties with publishers, told him where he might place his novels when he met with rejections, and recommended that he try A. P. Watt, the agent, when one of his books could not find a publisher.

Though Algernon wrote fluently and published much, his work brought such small prices that it never promised to provide him with a livelihood. He never entered a profession, though law and the church suggested themselves to him at various times, but seems to have spent his life in inexpensive country cottages with his wife and child, scribbling his inoffensive and unprofitable novels, and wondering what to do. Gissing was continually concerned about him. At one difficult juncture he warned that he ought not to continue with his efforts to make a living by literature, saying that writing was "a waste of life," "destruction in the prime of manhood," and "slow suicide." But Algernon persisted, and his novels kept appearing for years after Gissing's death.

Toward the end of 1883 Gissing completed *The Unclassed*, and after sending it to Chapman and Hall, promptly began a new novel which was to be written at the rate of half a chapter a day. His life had now settled into a checkerboard pattern. The squares were novels, and hardly a day elapsed between the end of his work on one and the beginning of the next. It took him just half a year to pass from one square to another, so regular was his production. The regularity is deceptive, however, for Gissing was not a calm and methodical workman like Trollope, who could work by his watch and be sure of turning out a certain number of words of marketable fiction hour by hour. He worshiped prolific heroes like Dickens and Scott and tried to emulate them, but, in spite of his capacity for long hours and patient planning, every other quality he possessed was against him. He was self-critical, unsure of himself, easily disturbed by noisy neighbors or changes of routine or bad weather, and prey to sudden fits of sterility and reversals of judgment.

Although he had enjoyed writing at first, it soon became an agonizing struggle for him. He often had to make a number of attempts, sometimes as many as ten or a dozen, all recorded with anguish in his diary, before he could progress with the beginning of a novel. Even then he was not sure of himself; frequently he saw his way clearly only when the first volume was completed, and then went back to begin over. One day in 1888 he recorded an experience "familiar enough and horribly distressing." He was on his way home from a public meeting when, ". . . of a sudden, like the snapping of a cord, I became aware that the plot of my story, as arranged for the next few days, would not do. Sat late brooding, and had a troubled night." [15] The difficulty of writing increased as time went on, and he found himself more dependent on notes and more concerned with matters of style. Every chapter of *The Nether World*, he said, was rewritten a number of times. More than once he completed a whole novel, only to lay it aside as unsatisfactory. He was bitter about this wasted time, for he wrote for bread and felt hunger watching every stroke of his pen jealously. But he also felt that these failures were valuable training and an inevitable part of his work. Even when he once spent three hours impotently struggling with twelve lines and had to give up in despair, he felt that it was all for the best.

The Unclassed, like *Mrs. Grundy's Enemies*, offered a challenge to the standards of propriety observed by Victorian publishers. Bentley rejected it on the ground that its sympathetic portrayal of a prostitute would mislead the young, and, when it was submitted to Chapman and Hall, the reader, who spoke to Gissing personally, expressed enthusiasm but asked him to delete a scene in which the heroine goes for a moonlight swim and to revise the last volume. Gissing was willing to accept these recommendations, not only because he needed money, but also because he was impressed by his critic. This conference was reported a few years later:

Mr. Gissing did not know the reader's name, but was amazed by the extraordinary familiarity which he showed with all the details of the story, using no paper. He went over these details, suggesting all sorts of alterations, and leaving Mr. Gissing impressed with the conviction that he knew the story far better than the writer did himself.[16]

He completed the revisions in a single desperate week's work, and at the end of February, 1884, had the double satisfaction of feeling that he had improved his book and of having it accepted for what was supposed to be immediate publication. Two weeks later he managed to trap the elusive reader in Henrietta Street and to reach a final agreement with him. His payment was the incredibly small sum of thirty pounds, but he was so accustomed to genuine failure that he was probably grateful for this small success. He had still heard nothing from Bentley about *Mrs. Grundy's Enemies* and feared that an embarrassing situation would arise if it were published after *The Unclassed*. Chapman and Hall's man had promised to send his check promptly, and Gissing was bitter when it did not arrive on time. Publication of the book also proceeded slowly, and he waited impatiently through May, his annoyance at the delay interfering with his work. In addition, the house in Chelsea where he had lived for a comparatively long period now grew too noisy, and he moved to a single room at 62 Milton Street near Regents Park, where he could take his daily walk and enjoy the Sunday band concerts.

In April, 1884, Bertz left England. His aimless and unfortunate ventures as a schoolmaster, a utopian, and an evangelist had been crowned at last by a minor success when a boys' book entitled *The French Prisoners*, which he had written, was accepted by Macmillan. Bertz himself had been too discouraged to submit the book to a publisher, but Gissing did it for him, and the twenty-five pounds it earned enabled Bertz to go back to Germany.

After reading a story sent for criticism by Algernon in May of 1884, Gissing decided that his brother's talents were not congenial to the realism characteristic of current literature, and he advised him not to try fiction after all. His proper medium, said Gissing, seemed to be the "Ruskin" essay. Algernon was now reading Comte, at Gissing's suggestion, and the latter offered to send some relevant pamphlets, no doubt left over from his Positivist days.

Just before *The Unclassed* emerged from the press in the middle of June, Gissing learned that the astute reader had been none other than George Meredith. Meredith did his work for Chapman and Hall anonymously, coming in from his home in the country only at the beginning of the week. The discovery of Gissing's talent was one of the services to literature he quietly performed in his capacity as a reader, for he was the first to accept one of Gissing's books on professional terms. Harrison promised to write to Meredith on Gissing's behalf, though Gissing feared Harrison would not like *The Unclassed* when he read it. His kindness to Gissing had persisted, in spite of Gissing's flirtations with impropriety. He was a strong-minded man who consistently disapproved of Gissing's social views, yet their arguments seem to have been conducted in an atmosphere of tolerance, and he never ceased to invite Gissing to much-needed meals, help him with advice, keep his secrets, and recommend him to useful people.

IV

The Unclassed is primarily a novel of love and character, though it is heavily charged with social awareness. In it Gissing addresses himself to the proposition that art and decency can be pursued by exiling oneself from modern industrial society instead of trying to reform it. The hero, Osmond Waymark, who enters the story through an advertisement reading "Wanted, human companionship," is a young novelist, a schoolmaster and a former radical, who is learned, poor, talkative, unrecognized, and, in fact, very much like Gissing himself. Having passed through the phase of social responsibility experienced by Arthur Golding, he is no longer occupied with seeking a creed, but is simply trying to earn his living without yielding to society's distorted moral standards. He has grown so indifferent to questions of social justice that he prefers working as a rent collector in the miserable slum neighborhoods of Elm Court and Litany Lane to teaching. The main plot of *The Unclassed* is concerned with Waymark's choice between two girls who represent contrasting spiritual alternatives. Maud Enderby, the daughter of a disgraced clergyman, accepts him at first but ultimately enters a convent in obedience to an inward call. He then turns to Ida Starr, who has risen from poverty and prostitution to become a practical, self-sufficient, altruistic woman, a counterbalance to the dreamy and religious Maud.

Waymark, Ida, and Waymark's friend, Julian Casti, are "the unclassed," young Bohemians of unconventional moral standards who are willing to let society go its way but find that the disorders generated by poverty and false morality intrude upon the separate lives they propose to lead. In the course of the story, Waymark is robbed of his rents by a pauper and left bound and gagged; Ida is falsely accused of theft by Casti's proletarian wife and sent to prison; and her uncle, the landlord Woodstock, dies of a disease caught in his own slums, giving Waymark occasion to think, "The slums have avenged themselves. . . ." Social evils exercise moral claims too, for Waymark gives money to a needy prostitute, and Ida renovates her uncle's slums and takes poor children on outings where they are given nourishing food and taught good habits like washing and reading. Though these social problems are not really central to the action, Gissing's bold confrontation of them, and the unconventional attitudes of his characters, were sufficiently alarming to attract attention in 1884. Gissing once heard that the novel had been banned from the lending library in a provincial town.

So many of the minor details of the novel are drawn from Gissing's own immediate experiences that they cast doubt upon his ability to find other sources of material. Waymark, like Gissing, has the advantage of a small patrimony, publishes his novel at his own expense, and has once delivered a lecture attacking religion; Woodstock owns a book of Hogarth's pictures as the Gissing family in Wakefield did, and even the name of Ida Starr's cat is the same as that of Gissing's, Grim. There are, however, more significant autobiographical elements as well. Gissing very curiously used the opportunity presented by Waymark's conversations with Casti to set forth an *apologia* for his own novel and to state some of the principles it followed. Waymark says that the writer should not express moral doctrine but should approach life with detachment, as material for his art. In his own work he promises a stern realism, not in the interest of arousing reform sentiment but for the sake of artistic truthfulness. He says:

The fact is, the novel of every-day life is getting worn out. We must dig deeper, get to untouched social strata. Dickens felt this, but he had not the courage to face his subjects; his monthly numbers had to lie on the family tea-table. Not *virginibus puerisque* will be my book, I assure you, but for men and women who like to look beneath the surface, and who understand that only as artistic material has human life any significance. . . . The artist is the only sane man.[17]

When Casti objects that Waymark, in spite of his doctrine that art should be independent of morality, still writes about social evils, Waymark replies with Taine's theory that "Every strong individuality is more or less the expression of its age. This direction may be imposed upon me; for all that, I understand why I pursue it."[18] The modern artist, he explains, must deal with misery because misery is the dominant element of his time. Unstated, but implicit in Waymark's observations, is Gissing's feeling that the esthetic theories of Ruskin, Morris, and Arnold had established a satisfactory bridge between pure art and the improvement of society. "I would make a chief point," he wrote to Algernon, "of the necessary union between beauty in life and social reform." [19]

The Unclassed, like *Workers in the Dawn*, betrays Gissing's preoccupation with Helen as a victim of society, but it has no single personage like Carrie Mitchell who is patterned upon her. Instead her characteristics are divided between the two figures of Ida Starr and Harriet Casti. Ida's account of her girlhood as an orphaned waif and a household slave in low lodginghouses may have been suggested by Helen's tales of her life; but Ida is, unlike Helen, intelligent, dignified, compassionate, and eminently capable of rising to a higher station. The ailing, malevolent Harriet, however, is a realistic representation of Helen; one detail, her way of interrupting her husband's conversations with visitors by tapping on the wall to call him into the next room, closely resembles an instance of "Mrs. Maitland's" behavior given by Roberts, but even without this and other parallels the convincing quality of the characterization leaves little room for doubt that it is based upon intimate experience.

Technically, *The Unclassed* represents a considerable advance over *Workers in the Dawn*. Though he is still awkward at managing the ample proportions of the three-volume novel, Gissing is fairly successful in fixing his attention upon a group of central characters. Esthetic idealism, now relegated to the position of a spiritual failing in a figure of secondary importance (Maud Enderby) no longer prevents him from achieving some significant characterizations, and the result is that Waymark and Ida Starr are far more human than Golding and Helen Norman. *The Unclassed* presents many features that came to be typical of Gissing's novels. Julian Casti, though he does not occupy the role of the protagonist, is a good representative of the tormented and ineffectual man who is the characteristic Gissing hero. The hearty man-to-man conversations about literature, classical languages, and the deplorable state of the contemporary world that take place between Casti and Waymark are the forerunners of many such scenes in later novels. Waymark himself is the first instance of that type of young man, "well-educated, fairly bred, *but without money*," which Gissing later described as his characteristic contribution to fiction.

Like nearly all of Gissing's social novels, *The Unclassed* fails to adopt a coherent attitude toward social problems. Having introduced the horrors of slum life through descriptions of Elm Court and Litany Lane, it offers no better remedy for them than the private philanthropies of Ida Starr. But the value of even this remedy is undercut when Waymark declares that he has "not a spark of social enthusiasm," and when Ida herself realizes that her devotion to a good cause is no substitute for Waymark's love. The question of whether "the unclassed" can withstand the corrupting effects of society is bypassed, for both of the main characters are ultimately enriched by Woodstock's will, thus becoming free to detach themselves from social problems and to find happiness within conventional limits. Perhaps the novel's failure to resolve this issue is due to the revision Meredith insisted upon, for it would have been very like Gissing to end by showing the lovers separated, their lives blighted by destructive social forces.

The provocative subject matter and opinions of *The Unclassed* aroused much criticism, and Gissing felt again, as he had after the publication of *Workers in the Dawn*, that his readers were ignoring the artistic aspects of his novel for the sake of attacking the opinions expressed by the characters. The *Athenaeum* reviewer declared that preaching was out of place in a novel. Algernon was critical, and he must have been much surprised when Gissing denied that Waymark's opinions were his own, for he had read them, expressed in nearly the same language, in letters Gissing had written to him. Harrison took violent issue with Waymark's nihilistic views, calling them "mere moral dynamite." In June, 1884, he and Gissing had a conversation about the book that became so sharp that Gissing wrote later to apologize and to admit, in a revealing moment of self-analysis, that his rebellious tendencies often led him to antagonize his best friends.

As for the element of protest in his novel, said Gissing, it was mild in comparison with the work of Balzac, Turgenev, and Dumas. "And, I repeat, it is not a social essay, but a study of a certain group of human beings. Of course I am responsible for the selection, but for nothing more." [20] But since it is the purpose of objective realism to allow its material to create its own effect, Gissing was obviously as responsible for the effect of his novel as for its subject. As he should have known, the incidental descriptions of Elm Court and

Litany Lane, and the actions of Slimy and Harriet Casti, are far more forceful than the parts of the novel devoted to the love story and character development. The poor, evoking in Gissing a curious blend of guilt and indignation, called forth his strongest powers. He told himself that such feelings had nothing to do with the mission of the artist, but he could not suppress them. As a result, his books had a didactic quality he was unwilling to recognize and, to judge from his many statements about the nature of art, neither intended nor approved. The trouble was that he had not succeeded in solving for himself the dilemma of art and social reform as he had solved it for Arthur Golding in *Workers in the Dawn*. In spite of his theory that art should be answerable only to itself, the sense of moral responsibility abroad in his time, made keener by his experiences with Helen, took control of him. The impulse to reform and the impulse to create were both vigorously at work in him, but they contended tirelessly with each other, creating a conflict in which the purposes of each were, to some extent, defeated.

Although it is tempting to speculate on what Gissing might have done if he had been free in spirit to devote himself to the "worship of Beauty," the fact appears to be that, however he might have rationalized the intrusion of social concerns into his work, they were an inevitable and fundamental component of it. His own unhappy life, his observation of the social injustice of Helen's fate, and his awareness of the abuses of industrial civilization forced him to participate in the social protest of his time. The Shelleyan theory does not exempt the artist from social responsibility; on the contrary, it puts him at the source of the spiritual forces that mold society. Perhaps it was this aspect of the doctrine that enabled Gissing to feel that his novels, heavily weighted as they were with social concerns, could still be regarded as purely artistic productions.

No one, not even Bertz or Algernon, agreed with him. The reviewers found his novels both didactic and inconclusive and were sometimes aroused by them to declare that novelists had no business to toy with morality. One of them, commenting on Gissing's later novel, *The Nether World*, pointed clearly to his division of mind:

It is difficult to discover whether he hoped to add to that sort of fiction which has at times been more successful than Blue-books or societies in calling attention to evils crying for remedy or whether . . . the author chose his subject in something like an artistic spirit. . . . His work does not show the energy either of an artist or of an enthusiast. . . .[21]

The conflict between esthetic and moral intentions that is so clear in *The Unclassed* continued to embarrass Gissing. He had to make the choice anew with every novel, and yet the choice was never really made. It may be that one of the reasons why he found it so painful to reread his books in later years was the realization that he had failed to achieve the objectivity for which he had struggled so hard. He did not hesitate to spin out fine-sounding theories in his letters to Algernon and to defend himself against critics who regarded him as a moralizing or political novelist. But he seems to have profited from the unpleasant reaction to *The Unclassed*, for some time later, in criticizing a story of Algernon's suggestively titled "Sewage Farm," he warned against shrill protest. It was much better, he said, to approach social abuses with surface calm, allowing the reader to infer one's indignation from occasional touches of irony.

V

In the months after *The Unclassed* was published, Gissing's mode of life underwent a transformation which he himself found strange. He began to be invited to social gatherings at the fashionable homes of the children he tutored, and these in turn led to other invitations, so that he was soon too busy to find time for his writing. In August of 1884 he spent two weeks with the Harrisons in the Lake Country, where he climbed Helvellyn with Austin and Bernard and toured the countryside near Grasmere associated with Wordsworth. Early in September he went on a weekend visit to a family named Gaussen who had a large country house in Gloucestershire. He came as a tutor to examine the children, but, at the warm invitation of Mrs. Gaussen, stayed as a guest. It was a highly enjoyable visit. Gissing's hostess was a well-traveled woman who had been born in India, "one of the most delightful women imaginable"; she had once known W. S. Gilbert, spoke both Hindustani and Armenian, and at the time of Gissing's visit was entertaining two Armenian ladies. The Gaussens were a horsy county family without much interest in intellectual matters, but Gissing seems to have been impressed by their comfortable style of living and their intimacy with titled people. To judge from his lively and good-humored account of the visit, he talked incessantly, amused everyone, and saw all the sights, including William Morris' house at nearby Kelmscott. Mrs. Gaussen's son soon became a pupil of his, and she herself cultivated Gissing eagerly in the next few years. Toward the end of 1884 he became a regular guest at dinner parties, private concerts, and musical Sundays, where he saw something of the wealth and leisure he had always admired at a distance. In November he even went to the expense of having some dress suits made. He drew the line, however, at tennis parties.

His new upper-class friendships were at first a welcome change from his loneliness and provided him with material for his later novels. But they troubled him too, for he now began to learn the dreadful truth that he was at heart not a rebel at all but the most conventional of Victorians, who loved good manners, pleasant surroundings, and cultivated conversation and envied the easy urbanity of the people he was meeting. "Yes, there is very much to be said for civilization," he wrote, "if one is in a position to enjoy it." [22] He could not enjoy it because, as he later showed in *Isabel Clarendon, Demos*, and *Born in Exile*, a man who tried to gain acceptance in a class higher than his own met many unexpected hazards and experienced strange inner conflict. Gissing could not enter into friendships without reservation, for the dreadful secrets of the Owens College episode and Nell haunted him. He was a provincial of obscure education who had not yet offset his deficiencies of birth and breeding with any notable achievement. When he brought his sister Ellen to spend a week with the Gaussens in the spring of 1885, it was an uneasy occasion. Gissing had to send her detailed instructions about dress and behavior, preparing her elaborately and self-consciously, as though for a visit of state. He was too poor to be more than an inferior in the homes where he dined, and he had to tell acquaintances who wanted to know him better that he had no address.

There was another reason for his lack of social success that corresponded to the cause of his comparative failure thus far as a writer. He loved company, but he abhorred the artificiality of large social occasions, and could not bear to make phrases or strike attentive poses. In the same way, he wanted fame desperately, and knew that a reputation as a successful author would compensate for everything else, enabling him to meet fashionable people as an equal, but he could not bring himself to make the compromises with principle necessary for achieving popularity. Each of the novels he had written so far had fallen foul of the proprieties, caused offense, or prompted editors to demand revisions in the interest of discretion. Neither cultivated society nor the publishers would accept him on his own terms. Ultimately, after a period of gregariousness, he found polite social intercourse tiresome and refused all invitations, returning to his old solitude.

His attitude toward his writing underwent a parallel change. Embittered by his failure to gain recognition, he now felt that art itself, regardless of its acceptance by society, was the ultimate source of value, and he adopted the role of the lonely and unrewarded acolyte of art. He had always admired futile heroism, as one of his boyhood poems, "The Battle of Hastings," shows.

> They faced the foe like heroes,
>   They fought but fought in vain;
> The bravest and the noblest
>   Are numbered with the slain.[23]

A letter written to Algernon in the summer of 1883 expresses an attitude of detachment very different from the involvement in politics, programs, and systems that filled his letters of 1881 and 1882:

Philosophy has done all it can for me, and now scarcely interests me any more. My attitude henceforth is that of the artist pure and simple. The world is for me a collection of phenomena, which are to be studied and reproduced artistically. In the midst of the most serious complications of life, I find myself suddenly possessed with a great calm, withdrawn as it were from the immediate interests of the moment, and able to regard everything as a picture. I watch and observe myself just as much as others. The impulse to regard every juncture as a "situation" becomes stronger and stronger. In the midst of desperate misfortune I can pause to make a note for future use, and the afflictions of others are to me materials for observation. . . . Brutal and egotistic it would be called by most people. What has that to do with me, if it is a fact? [24]

He seems to have been only faintly aware of the connection between his painful social experiences and his faith that art was the source of "absolute value," a connection that is implied in a letter of 1884 in which he wrote:

When I am able to summon any enthusiasm at all, it is only for ART—how I laughed the other day on recalling your amazement at my theories of Art for Art's sake! Well, I cannot get beyond it. Human life has little interest to me, on the whole—save as material for artistic presentation. I can get savage over social iniquities, but even then my rage at once takes the direction of planning revenge in artistic work.[25]

Although he used a currently fashionable phrase to describe it, Gissing's philosophy of art had little to do with the estheticism of Pater, Moore, and Wilde, for it was based, not on the doctrine that sensation is the ultimate reality, but on a belief in the special perceptive powers of the artist. Whatever the egotistic or even narcissistic origin of Gissing's policy of "Art for Art's sake" may have been, the doctrine of the autonomy of art enabled him to resist alternatives offered by journalism, radicalism, and the propaganda novel.

III

ESCAPE FROM THE SLUMS

I

ECAUSE Mrs. Gaussen had "threatened" to visit him, and his old room at 62 Milton Street was too "disreputable" for guests, Gissing moved to better quarters toward the end of 1884, signing a three-year lease for a small flat in a "block" not far from the Marylebone Road near Regents Park. He had spent his years in London drifting from one unsatisfactory lodging to another, sometimes at intervals of only a few months, but his new address, 7K Cornwall Residences, was to remain his home for the next six years. The rented or leased flat was then a relatively new development, and Gissing, delighted with the privacy and convenience it afforded in comparison with furnished lodgings taken by the week, predicted that the system would spread. He was especially pleased with his neighbors, who were respectable and well behaved. Apartment 7K consisted of two rooms and a kitchen, where Gissing could cook his own meals, and where, shortly after taking possession, he discovered the virtues of canned soup. Morley Roberts has described 7K as sufficiently depressing, for its windows overlooked the yards of the city's underground railway, and the hissing of the trains at the Baker Street Station could be heard, but it was the best London home Gissing had had up to that time. The building was still standing in 1952, and while it was ugly and simple, it was by no means a slum. Austin Harrison refers to this flat as the place in back of Madame Tussaud's which showed that Gissing was no longer in dreadful poverty. At about Christmastime Gissing moved in with his books, papers, pipes, and tobacco, and after hiring a woman to char for him, settled down in comfort and seclusion. He was able to give Herculean stretches of time to his writing, and to make a living of sorts from a smaller number of regular pupils.

In January of 1885 Gissing crossed swords with *Punch* on the question of frankness in fiction. The *Pall Mall Gazette* had published a letter of his fixing the responsibility for the inferior quality of novels on the novelists themselves, who, according to Gissing's charge, allowed fear of offending public taste to influence their work. "It is a hard thing to say," he wrote, "but Thackeray, when he knowingly wrote below the demands of his art to conciliate Mrs. Grundy betrayed his trust; and the same thing is being done by our living novelists every day." Thackeray had said in his introduction to *Pendennis* that it had been impossible since Fielding's time to portray "a man" fully, and Gissing, no doubt still mindful of the fate of *Mrs. Grundy's Enemies*, attacked him and novelists in general for truckling to prudery. "Let novelists be true to their artistic conscience," he counseled, "and the public taste will come round." [1]

It was the irreverent allusion to Thackeray, who had been one of its first comic writers, that aroused *Punch* to reply to Gissing's admirable challenge to convention. An age which found "the humour of Fielding" to be "contradictory" confidently thought it saw the real motives behind any demand for greater liberty in the treatment of "delicate" subjects, and *Punch* felt free to drub Gissing mercilessly and tastelessly.

All the world knows what that preface meant, save and except GISSING, who thinks that THACKERAY'S artistic conscience suggested Dirt, and his art demanded it, but that he was afraid of losing money by it!! Had he but been true to his conscience and his tastes, his receipts would have gone up in time, for GISSING would have bought his books. . . . As for our living novelists, they are disgusting GISSING by "doing the same every day." Well, they are, GISSING; and speaking with some knowledge of them, we do not altogether regret it. We regret that GISSING cannot get the reading he likes except by going back to more conscientious days. . . . Praised be the gods for thy foulness, GISSING! but also that, as we fondly hope, there are not very many like thee.[2]

The *Punch* writer's knowledge of contemporary novelists did not, by his own admission, include the fact that Gissing was one himself. Gissing assured Algernon that having his name and opinions thus abused on the first page of *Punch* had not disturbed him in any way. The incident is of some importance in illustrating a state of public opinion that made it impossible to publish *Mrs. Grundy's Enemies* and surrounded the publication of nearly every vigorous treatment of social life with a question of propriety. Gissing returned to the attack in *The Emancipated*, and the whole controversy became more general when Henry Vizetelly was sent to jail in 1888 for publishing translations of Zola's novels, and when Hardy's *Tess of the D'Urbervilles* appeared in 1891.

Gissing's new quarters enabled him to work more comfortably, although the projects that occupied the first six months of 1885— a novel called *The Graven Image* and a play entitled *Madcaps*— remained unfinished. He still spent all day tutoring and snatched some hours from the night to turn out six of his large, closely written pages, but in the middle of the year he effected a deliberate change in his writing habits. He freed himself from all his pupils except one, a boy named Walter Grahame, who came in the morning, and devoted himself to his writing for the rest of the day. He first planned what he was going to do and then wrote it out, continuing from two in the afternoon until eight or ten o'clock at night. Sometimes he wrote for as long as nine hours a day. "When I am intensely occupied with fiction," he wrote to his sister, "the problems in hand fatigue my brain through the hours of sleep. I cannot get rid of them." [3]

He immersed himself, not only in work, but also in the massive intellectual application he enjoyed as a kind of sport. Inside the cover of a diary that he began to keep in 1887, he made the following notation:

July–Sept 1885, Wrote "Isabel Clarendon"
Sept–Nov   "   Wrote "A Life's Morning"
Dec–March 1885–6 Wrote "Demos"
During the same months, I first studied Italian, and read through the whole of the Divina Commedia. —Also, it should be noted, I earned my living by teaching, which generally took all morning.[4]

This record of industry astounded him when it caught his eye a few years afterward, and it is probably wrong in at least one respect, for *Isabel Clarendon* seems to have been begun in October, 1884. He always read widely in several languages, and his friend Bertz had stimulated in him an interest in foreign writers that ultimately made him better acquainted with Continental literature than any of his contemporaries among the novelists.

Not long after moving into 7K he sent his sister Ellen some advice about a program of reading which tells something of his own range.

Homer, Aeschylus, Sophocles, Euripides among the Greeks: Virgil, Catullus, Horace, among the Latins: in Italian, Dante and Boccaccio: in Spanish, Don Quixote: in German, Goethe, Jean Paul, Heine: in French, Molière, George Sand, Balzac, De Musset: in English, Chaucer, Spenser, Shakespeare, Milton, Keats, Browning and Scott. These are the indispensables. I rejoice to say I can read them all in the original, except Cervantes, and I hope to take up Spanish next year, just for that purpose.[5]

This list does not cover the scope of his reading entirely, of course. It omits, for example, the German philosophers such as Kant and Schopenhauer and less "indispensable" authors such as Dickens and Dumas. Gissing was devoted to the Greek and Latin classics, and they continued, in spite of his other occupations, to be almost an obsession with him. Roberts was both awed and irritated at the importance Gissing attributed to fine points of Greek scansion, and H. G. Wells thought that Gissing's classical education had made him something of a pedant. Gissing's favorite of all books was Gibbon, and his favorite historical period was that of the later Roman Empire, when the classical civilization was being colored by other cultures. Although he was indifferent to organized religion, he studied the early Christian sects because of their connection with Roman history. He read French and German with ease, usually finishing a novel in these languages in a single day, and he now undertook Italian, applying himself to such good effect that he was able to read Dante and to carry on conversations when he visited Italy. He did not fulfill his ambition to read Cervantes in the original, however, until just before his death.

Gissing's stern monastic regime had serious effects on his spirits. He suffered from loneliness and monotony and at one point was ready to go back to America. This was the sort of existence that earned him a reputation as a recluse. The legend that Gissing once spoke to nobody but his landlady for a period of weeks is supported by this remark from a letter to Algernon written in the summer of 1885: "For three weeks I have not opened my lips, except in entering a shop or in speaking to my servant. I find it difficult to talk even to that amount, one gets unused to the sound of one's own voice." [6] But he found this sort of life unbearable. He tried to divert himself with Dante and with Crabb Robinson's *Reminiscences,* and he spared himself the time for a visit with the Harrisons in the country. His reward came in October, when he could look back at the two novels he had completed in less than a year.

Gissing's devotion to classics of all languages did not prevent him from keeping up with such rivals and contemporaries as Walter Besant, Hardy, Meredith, and Daudet; and, after Turgenev had died, he secured six of his novels in German translation. This proved to have some effect on his own work, for *Isabel Clarendon,* his next effort after *The Unclassed,* was a departure in the direction of Turgenev.

It was originally to be called "The Lady of Knightswell." Gissing always found titles troublesome, and was continually escaping disaster by a hair. "Far, Far Away," the original title of his first novel, was practically meaningless, and entirely unsuitable for the book. *Workers in the Dawn* was handsome and sonorous, but its relevance was far from clear to most readers. He once planned to write a novel about characters who fail to gain their ends, and to call it "Will-o-the Wisp." This led him into an amusing perplexity, for he realized that it should be "Wills-o-the Wisp," which he found "awkward." *The Unclassed* has many virtues as a title; it is challenging and ironic, and it arouses a piquant echo of the French *déclassé.* Its difficulty is that it applies to the people in the novel only in a special sense which Gissing found it necessary to explain. "The Lady of Knightswell" would have been perfectly satisfactory as a title for a book intended to be "inoffensive," and it is more difficult than usual to understand Gissing's motives for making the change. Isabel Clarendon is not the chief character, and her surname is that of her uncongenial husband who has been dead for some time when the novel opens.

II

Unlike Gissing's first novels, the two books written in 1885, *Isabel Clarendon* and *A Life's Morning,* are not concerned with poverty, London slums, or social problems. In his earlier books Gissing had often approached upper-class characters with a certain amount of criticism and hostility. He once wrote to his sister Margaret in tones of ironic surprise that he found the aristocracy whose children he tutored no better than other people. Reviewers thought they saw in his novels signs of unfamiliarity with the lives of gentle folk, and were led to believe that Gissing was a working-class novelist. Gissing, armed with his new experiences with the Harrisons, the Gaussens, and others, was enough of a snob to be anxious to refute this suspicion. One reason that has been given for his radical change of subject matter at this time is the influence of Meredith. *Isabel Clarendon* was written expressly for Meredith, who had accepted *The Unclassed* for Chapman and Hall with praise, and who was, as a result, promptly offered Gissing's next book. Meredith suggested that it be recast for publication in two volumes instead of three, and Gissing had to devote some months in the middle of 1885 to this unwelcome task before Chapman and Hall accepted it. In spite of all these indications, and the fact that Gissing admired Meredith's work, a more likely inspiration for *Isabel Clarendon* seems to have been Turgenev.

When allowances are made for the setting and social class of the characters, *Isabel Clarendon* has no resemblance to Meredith's novels. It is not comic, even in the philosophical Meredithian sense, it is little occupied with manners, and it takes a very different view of character from Meredith's. The chief personage, Bernard Kingcote, is a self-oppressed, introspective ex-medical student who falls in love with the refined widow for whom the book was named. He objects to her social activities, however, and his jealousy becomes open when he sees her in the company of other men. After a period of brooding and self-torment he finds himself attracted to the more modest but less superficial charms of Isabel's ward. Kingcote is the first of the self-defeating, self-tormenting characters who were to become typical of Gissing's books, and he closely resembles the sort of Turgenev hero exemplified by Rudin. The milieu of country house and garden that is the scene of most of the action resembles a number of Turgenev's stories, including *Liza*, and the character of Ada Warren has a suggestive resemblance to Liza herself. Finally, the incident in which Kingcote sees Isabel walking hand-in-hand in a garden with another man, and his emotional reaction to this, have a counterpart in the scene from *Diary of a Superfluous Man* in which Tchulkaturin hears his beloved accept the proposal of a rival.

Although *Isabel Clarendon* was a deliberate attempt on Gissing's part to purge his work of its *Tendenzroman* character by writing about aristocratic country scenes where poverty and social evils never appear, his old concerns filtered into the story. One of the steps that lead Kingcote to realize the frivolity of Isabel's kind of life is his return to London to rescue his widowed sister from the poor lodgings where she and her children have been staying. Not long afterward, he makes the decision that he prefers to give happiness rather than to seek it for himself. On the whole, however, Gissing was successful this time in preventing social criticism from usurping an undue amount of interest. But he was successful in little else. The novel contains an unusual number of underdeveloped minor issues and characters only slightly related to the main progress of events. The chief plot is ill-defined and rambling. Kingcote's rejection of Isabel and his strongly suggested acceptance of Ada Warren depend both on his own emotional development and that of Ada. But the development of these characters is irregular, obscure, and unmotivated. Kingcote's ultimate preference for Ada is no doubt supposed to reflect somehow the spiritual progress that enables him to be content at the end with a humble position in a bookshop, but this idea, in spite of much effort, is only dimly worked out. The valuable parts of the book are Kingcote's reactions to the commercialism of London, to the social success of Isabel, and to other aspects of life that make him feel alien. These, however, were not enough to save it, some years later, from Gissing's opinion that it was too weak to be revised for another edition.

Unsuccessful though it was, *Isabel Clarendon* served as a rehearsal for some future projects. In writing it Gissing was testing his ability to break away from the kind of novel that capitalized on the injustices of the poor, and to deal with the social class to which he returned, with greater success, in *The Emancipated* and *The Whirlpool*. It was also his first attempt to deal with qualified defeat, the kind of conclusion that offers the acceptance of modest goals and a low station in life as a triumph over ambitious feelings; this motif appears again in his last completed novel, *Will Warburton*.

Even after it had been shortened to two volumes, *Isabel Claren-*

don was not accepted for publication without delay. The only payment he received for it was fifteen pounds. By the time he received the proofs, Gissing had another novel well under way, and it was finished so quickly that the two books appeared destined for simultaneous publication.

Written in only three months, and sent out with trepidation, *A Life's Morning* (which at first had the title "Emily") was accepted with enthusiasm by Smith, Elder, and Company's reader, James Payn. Like *Isabel Clarendon*, it was an effort on Gissing's part to detach himself from social problems, for it has no poor, earnest, autobiographical hero and no passionate advocacy or denial of social theories. Unlike *Isabel*, however, it provided Gissing with opportunities for exercising some of his mature talents and expressing some of his favorite ideas. Its heroine, Emily Hood, is Gissing's first moderate success in the mode of mature character-analysis practiced by George Eliot, Meredith, and James. For the first time, Gissing achieves in this novel a well-realized, plausible study of the thought processes of a complicated and principled mind. It is interesting to observe that he accomplished this advance through the same esthetic idealism that impairs the characterization of *Workers in the Dawn* and *The Unclassed*. Instead of merely insisting that esthetic experience produced spiritual benefits, as he had in his earlier novels, he undertook to examine the effects of this belief on the thoughts of a girl who accepts it as a practical doctrine. The result is a creditable portrayal of his heroine's development as she moves from the conviction that beauty is the supreme good, through a number of emotional crises, to the realization that her "religion of beauty" is an illusion based upon ignorance of the problems of life.

Emily Hood, a poor but cultivated girl from a north of England town (a fictional version of Gissing's native Wakefield), is genuinely intellectual and lacks none of the sensitivity and moral scruple that the Victorians associated with refined womanhood. While serving as a governess in the country home of a wealthy family, she becomes engaged to her employer's son, Wilfrid Athel. During a visit to her home, she is subjected to the demands of her father's passion-ridden employer, Dagworthy, who has learned that her father has committed a theft, and threatens to expose him unless she agrees to marriage. The unhappy Mr. Hood resolves her dilemma by putting an end to his life. Emily then turns her lover, Wilfrid, away, partly out of sympathy for her father, partly as a spiritual discipline. Only many years later, when they have lost their youth, do the lovers become reunited and marry, a happy ending introduced, according to Roberts, at the insistence of Payn. The original ending must have shown Emily, submitting to the coercion exercised by guilt upon an idealistic nature, renouncing her lover and her hopes for happiness. In the final version, she realizes that her renunciation was a hysterical act, withdraws it, and marries Wilfrid after all, belying what was apparently Gissing's original intention, that of portraying a sacrifice made in the name of an austere personal morality. Emily's story forms a sequence of spiritual developments that is logical without being banal. By comparison, the character shifts in Gissing's earlier novels seem heavily manipulated. It is safe to fix *A Life's Morning* as the point at which he achieved the power of translating moral and spiritual issues into the medium of character.

There are two other simpler, but no less impressive instances of characterization in the novel: James Hood, Emily's father, and Richard Dagworthy, his employer. Hood, a toiling middle-aged clerk whose self-respect has been destroyed by years of poverty and drudgery, stumbles unintentionally into a crime. After finding a ten-pound note among the pages of an old ledger, he is compelled to go on an errand before he is able to return it. He loses his hat in the train and has to spend part of the money in a neighboring town in order to buy a new one. Once the note has been exchanged, he finds himself spending more and more of it, until he abandons his original intention of giving the money back. Even before the full consequences of his act overtake him, he suffers severely. His gradually changing intentions, accesses of guilt and fear, and his ultimate feeling that he has cut himself off from his daughter form a series of authentic psychological developments. In the shorter episode of Mr. Hood's tragedy Gissing achieved a union of plot and doctrine which he had been attempting since *Workers in the Dawn*, and which he remained unable to perfect in the novel as a whole. Mr. Hood's story expresses two of Gissing's favorite ideas. It demonstrates that even the smallest compromise with honor leads to disaster, and that poverty destroys the moral sense.

Although he could be severely critical of the excesses of Victorian propriety, Gissing's moral standards were very much like those of the ordinary middle-class Victorian liberal. He felt that human nature was capable of following a course of right conduct without the support of systematic belief. Victorians might disagree about religion or economic reform, but society as a whole accepted the Kantian doctrine that morality was a self-validating principle which everyone could find in his own conscience if he really searched for it. Ruskin, when asked by a correspondent what honesty should be based on, replied: "Your honesty is *not* to be based either on religion or policy. Both your religion and your policy must be based on *it*. Your honesty must be based, as is the sun, in vacant heaven. . . ." [7]

Gissing thought of moral character as a complex whole whose smallest weakness leads to a general downfall. In his novels little dishonesties are the beginning of a crescendo of immorality that eventually leads to complete ruin, and the more trifling the first misstep, the more impressive is the ultimate disaster likely to be. When the painter, Gresham, intercepts a letter to Helen in *Workers in the Dawn*, Gissing assures us that this small crime is the beginning of his complete demoralization. Richard Mutimer's breach of faith with Emma Vine in *Demos* is precisely the comparatively unimportant personal dishonesty that leads to the wreck of the socialist movement he has founded and to his death. In the story of Mr. Hood, whose error was simply to postpone returning the money until a more convenient time, is contained the warning that an instant of hesitation about moral issues may eventually consume the soul. Obviously, the boy who had been dismissed from Owens College had good reason for feeling that moral character was so susceptible to corruption, especially when it suffered under the pressure of poverty. Though there are no London slums in *A Life's Morning*, poverty and its devastating effects appear in the excellent impressions of daily life in the pinched Hood household. These are presented with a reserve and intimacy that make them far superior to the sensational descriptions of poverty in Gissing's earlier novels.

Except for the insight given into his character, Richard Dagworthy would be a villain of melodrama. A man of strong will and harsh methods, he nevertheless has an unformed poetry of spirit that drives him to seek marriage with a refined woman as a way of satisfying dim but powerful aspirations. Jealousy and desire force him to resort to tactics that are no less futile for being ruthless. Dagworthy achieves a remarkable humanity as Gissing subtly makes the point that he is as much the victim of his passions as Emily is. But this revelation does not dissolve the characterization in sentimentality; Gissing retains his conception of the man, and Dagworthy remains calculating, unimaginative, and unregenerate to the end.

III

Isabel Clarendon was still being considered in its revised form by Chapman and Hall and *A Life's Morning* had not yet been sent to a publisher when Gissing's next novel, *Demos*, was begun. Although his published novels had been failures, and the two still in manuscript were doubtful, Gissing declared in his letters of late 1885 that he found consolation only in unremitting and difficult work. His usual uncertainty had been increased by Meredith's opinion that he had made a mistake in abandoning the slum material of his first two novels, and *Demos* was a return to what he called "my special line of work." The outlook of *Demos*, however, would not be the sympathetic one of *Workers in the Dawn* or *The Unclassed*, for the lessons Gissing had learned about human character and its reactions to poverty and deprivation had now crystallized, and he was ready to write "a savage satire on working-class aims and capacities." He willingly gave it even more time and energy than usual, for he felt that he was expressing his individuality strongly and unequivocally this time. ". . . *Demos*," he wrote to his sister, "will be *something*, I assure you." [8]

The novel tells the story of Richard Mutimer, a Radical working-man who, after unexpectedly inheriting a fortune, becomes the leader of a socialist movement and uses his money to establish a co-operative factory. However, his new wealth and power accentuate the defects of character he brings from his working-class origin. Indifference to the feelings of others, a failing due to the lack of imagination Shelley held responsible for immorality, leads him to abandon the poor London girl to whom he has been engaged, and to deal harshly with some of his workers. He marries an upper-middle-class lady who does not love him, and runs for Parliament. A moral crisis is reached when his wife, Adela, finds a lost will that deprives him of his inheritance. Mutimer wants to destroy this document, but Adela will not permit it. The money goes to the rightful heir, the socialist experiment is shut down, and the Mutimers move to London to live in relative poverty. A new socialist crusade is halted when one of Mutimer's associates dupes him, and he is killed by a stone thrown from a mob of his followers who have turned against him.

Demos is an undisguised *Tendenzroman*. Through Mutimer and his family it exposes the selfishness, narrowness, dishonesty, and weakness of will that Gissing believed to be characteristic of even the respectable poor. Its thesis is that the poverty of the poor debases them beyond remedy and makes them incapable of the self-rule that democratic socialism proposes to grant them.

No idea is expressed more often in Gissing's novels. In explaining why Bob Hewett of *The Nether World* turned to counterfeiting, Gissing says:

Genuine respect for law is the result of possessing something which the law exerts itself to guard. Should it happen that you possess nothing, and that your education in metaphysics has been grievously neglected, the strong probability is, that your mind will reduce the principle of society to its naked formula: Get, by whatever means, so long as with impunity. . . .[9]

Friedrich Engels made the same point in terser language: ". . . for him who has none the sacredness of property dies out of itself." [10] Reardon of *New Grub Street* tells his wife that poverty has the same moral effect in modern times that slavery had in the ancient world, alluding to a line from Homer for authority. "It is not," said Disraeli of Wodgate, the slum region of his novel, *Sybil*, "that the people are immoral, for immorality implies some forethought; or ignorant, for ignorance is relative; but they are animals; unconscious; their minds a blank. . . ." This was the brutality Gissing felt in Bank Holiday crowds and the audiences of working-class meetings. It was, in his view, an inevitable result of poverty, and the only effect of education was to transform it into some form of amorality more socially acceptable but equally vicious.

Gissing was motivated to write *Demos* by important political movements which seemed to him to be based upon ignorance of the facts of working-class life and character. In 1880 socialism in England was hardly more than an ideal proven unworkable by the unsuccessful experiments of the Christian Socialists. In 1881, however, it sprang into vigorous life, and by 1885 three new socialist organizations were in existence, publishing books, pamphlets, and magazines, attracting eminent figures to their membership, organizing frequent public meetings, and even putting up candidates for Parliament. The liberal economic philosophy that had dominated public life and thought during most of the century was showing signs of being exhausted by its own success. It had established laissez-faire principles of trade and employment, widened the franchise by means of the Reform Act of 1867 to include even field laborers and miners, and made education universal and compulsory. The accomplishment of their political aims (whether by Liberals themselves or by their Conservative rivals) put the Liberals in the position of arguing that there was nothing more to be done, but social and economic conditions cried out that there was still a great deal to be done, and it was in answer to this demand that socialist principles were regenerated.

The socialism of the eighties drew its ideas from a long line of thinkers, and counted Robert Owen, Comte, the Christian Socialists, and Ruskin among its forebears. Although the movement was divided by the disagreements and schisms of its leaders, its chief aim, like that of all socialism, was to place the power of government in the hands of the numerical majority of the nation, the working class. According to Sidney Webb, one of the ablest socialist theoreticians of the time, this power would be exercised by means of collective administration of the economic system, government control of the means of production, and the subordination of individual interests to the good of the community as a whole.

The first of the new socialist organizations was the Democratic Federation, a union of Radical clubs of the type described in *Workers in the Dawn*, founded in 1881 by H. M. Hyndman, a wealthy Cambridge graduate who had caught the socialist fire from Marx's *Capital*. The Federation, which soon changed its name to the Social Democratic Federation, gained the support of union leaders and became an active force in English political life, combining some of the vigor of the old Chartists with the sweeping revolutionary vision of the Continental socialist movements. It specialized in propaganda and agitation, making many demands upon the existing government but looking forward at the same time to a dramatic act of deliverance, by violent revolution or other means. In 1884 a number of dissidents, including William Morris, left the Federation to form a new organization called the Socialist League, which had Marx and Engels among its leaders. The third socialist organization of the time was the Fabian Society, founded in 1884 by a group of young intellectuals that included George Bernard Shaw and Sidney Webb. It undertook the task of adapting revolutionary social theory to democratic principles and, by following a more moderate and responsible course than the extreme socialist movements, achieved great success as a propaganda and educational organization.

Socialists could be seen in their most characteristic moods at public meetings, and a number of these are vividly described in *Demos*. While the novel was in progress Gissing went to a meeting of the Socialist League in Hammersmith for the dual purpose of seeing Morris there and gathering material for his crowd scenes. In *Demos* both the behavior of Mutimer on the platform, with his attitudes of self-criticism, devotion, and quasi-religious fervor, and the swift emotional responses of the noisy, uncontrollable audiences have a life of their own. The impassioned Mr. Cullen and the unctuous Mr. Cowles rise like comic twins to subject the meeting to their oratory, disagreeing violently in public, but drinking peacefully together in private. Someone tickles the mob's sense of humor, someone else arouses its passion, and the session ends in an uproar.

In February of 1886, when *Demos* was being written, a huge meeting of the Social Democratic Federation in Trafalgar Square was turned into a disorderly mob as its leaders tried to lead the crowd up Pall Mall to Hyde Park. Stones were thrown, windows broken, shops looted. For a moment it seemed as though the country were on the brink of revolution. Gissing describes a similar scene; Mutimer is attacked at a meeting he is addressing, and he uses the occasion to comment ironically on the character of the common people and their political movement:

The meeting was over, the riot had begun. Picture them, the indignant champions of honesty, the avengers of virtue defamed! Demos was roused, was tired of listening to mere articulate speech; it was time for a good wild-beast roar, for a taste of bloodshed. Scarcely a face in all the mob but distorted itself to express as much savagery as can be got out of the human countenance. . . . On all sides was the thud of blows, the indignant shouting of the few who desired to preserve order mingled with the clamour of those who combated. Demos was having his way; civilisation was blotted out, and club law proclaimed.[11]

Many shades of socialism appear in the novel. The organization of Mutimer's works at New Wanley reflects the spirit of Robert Owen combined with the cooperative ideas of such French theoreticians as St. Simon. His doctrines and speeches seem derived from the fiery and provocative utterances of the Social Democrats. His movement suffers from a schism engineered by an extremist named Roodhouse, and this suggests the defection of some of the Social Democratic Leaders and the formation of the Socialist League. William Morris is represented by Westlake, the cultured and artistic socialist who relies mainly upon public education and whose methods Mutimer grows to dislike. Marxism is brought into the novel by Mr. Keene, a distinctly unsympathetic journalist who is translating *Capital* for a periodical and who helps to destroy Mutimer's socialist movement by the tactic of boring from within.

IV

In essence, *Demos* is an extensive examination of lower-class character as it is exemplified by Mutimer, a superior, though typical, workingman. He joins intelligence, industry, and determination to his revolutionary principles, but Gissing sees evidence of the spiritual sterility of his class in the tasteless furnishings of his home and the shrill radical polemics he studies. A notable exposure of proletarian character occurs when Richard and his family come into an unexpected inheritance. Mutimer's younger brother refuses to work or to accept discipline, and becomes a tramp. His sister immobilizes herself by the fire, reading cheap novels and welcoming the advances of Mr. Keene. Most interesting of all, his mother refuses to have anything to do with the wealth she does not understand and locks herself in her room when she is no longer allowed to perform her usual household tasks. Richard succeeds in learning to dine with his well-do-do neighbors, in courting a girl who is his social superior, and in carrying on elaborate projects of reform, but he fails the ultimate test of character imposed by the somewhat melodramatic device of the lost will. When his wife, Adela, learns that he prefers to destroy the will and keep the money from the rightful heir, she realizes that his deficiency of honor is due to a class difference that Mutimer has never been able to overcome. Once, when he falls asleep on a train, she studies his face carefully.

> It was the face of a man by birth and breeding altogether beneath her. . . . He was not of her class, not of her world; only by violent wrenching of the laws of nature had they come together. She had spent years in trying to convince herself that there were no such distinctions, that only an unworthy prejudice parted class from class. . . . To be her equal this man must be born again, of other parents, in other conditions of life. . . . She had no claims to aristocratic descent, but her parents were gentlefolk; that is to say, they were both born in a position which encouraged personal refinement rather than the contrary, which expected of them a certain education in excess of life's barest need, which authorized them to use the service of ruder men and women in order to secure to themselves a margin of life for life's sake. Perhaps for three generations her ancestors could claim so much gentility; it was more than enough to put a vast gulf between her and the Mutimers. Favourable circumstances of upbringing had endowed her with delicacy of heart and mind not inferior to that of any woman living. . . . And her husband was a man incapable of understanding her idlest thought.[12]

This crucial passage reflects many of Gissing's most characteristic attitudes and betrays the conflict in his mind between the radical doctrine of environment and the conservative one of heredity. Mere environmental changes, Gissing felt, are not enough to reform character; the story of the Mutimer family, which is shattered by a sudden improvement in its standard of living, is enough to show that. The influences must be older, as in the case of the three generations of gentility that have produced Adela. Gissing, whose thinking on these points was still pre-Darwinian, failed to see clearly that the three generations were not enough to establish a difference in heredity, and that the ultimate cause of Adela's superiority—that "margin of life for life's sake" enjoyed by her ancestors—was really environmental.

Throughout his novels Gissing lays great stress upon the effects of both heredity and environment, but, since he never gives a decisive role to either, he never faces the question of whether the poor could be saved by improved living conditions. In spite of the clear answer offered by a long tradition of environmentalism, and by many liberal reformers of the eighties, the issue still remained undecided. Conservatives like W. H. Mallock persisted in regarding "the Poor" as a race apart, and even scientists like Théodule Ribot, whose work on heredity Gissing read a few years later, attributed great cultural importance to heredity. Ribot, following materialist theory, declared that moral characteristics are based on physical ones, and are therefore inherited, just as physical traits are. Thus, the instincts, intellect, national character, and predispositions to vices like gambling and alcoholism are due to heredity. Ribot pointed out that belief in heredity results in a belief in caste, so that Gissing's conviction that class differences were too deep-seated for change is a natural correlate of the importance he attributed to inheritance.

Up to the middle of the century, class status was usually made perfectly clear by outward signs; it would normally have been quite impossible to mistake a workingman for a member of the middle class. Later in the century, however, it became easier for people of low social origin to overcome inferiorities of dress, manners, speech, and education. Nevertheless, Gissing, with characteristic conservatism, continued to look to the small signs of everyday behavior as a guide to the vital distinction between the lower classes and the rest of society. When Mutimer dines with the middle-class Walthams for the first time, Gissing sees in his self-conscious behavior at table a significant betrayal of his plebeian background:

At dinner he found himself behaving circumspectly. He knew already that the cultivated taste objects to the use of a table-knife save for the purposes of cutting; on the whole he saw grounds for the objection. He knew, moreover, that manducation and the absorption of fluids must be performed without audible gusto; the knowledge cost him some self-criticism. But there were numerous minor points of convention on which he was not so clear; it had never occurred to him, for instance . . . that a napkin is a graceful auxiliary in the process of a meal and not rather an embarrassing superfluity of furtive application.[13]

Manners and morality: the two were inseparably linked in Gissing's mind. In 1884, writing to Algernon that he was sorry to see William Morris' work appearing in the radical *Secular Review*, he said, "I confess I get more and more aristocratic in my leanings, and cannot excuse faults of manner in consideration of the end." [14] He felt that middle-class conventions were the counterpart of a moral code which, though it might often be broken, nevertheless did exist. But among the poor, anarchy prevailed, as their noisy, cruel, inconsiderate behavior showed. The rampant disorder of their holidays, which delighted Dickens, was profoundly depressing to Gissing. He was repelled by their food, their table manners, their common eating houses, their low humor and mockery. The furnishings of their homes, even when they were in comfortable circumstances, were dreary, vulgar, and tasteless. He had learned much of this from his association with the working-class relations he had known during his first years in London. He had written of them to Algernon: "Without wishing to be harsh to these people, you must recognise how utterly impossible close relations with them become. . . . I fear they put me down for a prig, an upstart, an abominable aristocrat, but *que voulez-vous?* The matter is entirely intellectual." [15]

This snobbery may not have been "entirely" objective, but it had a rational aspect connected with Gissing's profoundest convictions. The way of life the poor led reflected the materialism and competitiveness of the industrialism that formed it. It favored the survival of the harshest, the cruelest, the most unscrupulous, and these, in accordance with evolutionary doctrine, came to dominate it. In addition, the lives of the poor gave no opportunity for the generous experience of art and beauty which, according to Shelley, enlarged the imagination, the seat of the moral faculties, or for entering the realm of the ideal whose eternal truths, as Pater said, gave men their ethical standards. Gissing declared:

The fatal defect in working people is absence of imagination, the power which may be solely a gift of nature and irrespective of circumstances, but which in most of us owes so much to intellectual training. Half the brutal cruelties perpetrated by uneducated men and women are directly traceable to lack of the imaginative spirit, which comes to mean lack of kindly sympathy.[16]

When Edmund Gosse, in an article on Tennyson's funeral written in 1892, reported that he saw no evidence to support the notion that the general public followed Tennyson's work, Gissing wrote to congratulate him on this insight. He said he suspected that the majority of leisured people paid little attention to poetry, but he could testify that the poor almost never read any; when they did, they read it without feeling, as if it were factual material.

The imaginative and moral capacities lacking in Mutimer and members of his class are, however, found in his wife. It is not the ideals of her middle-class background that make Adela superior to her husband, but her flexibility of mind and the potentialities that leisure and education have conferred upon her. Caught in the conflicting intellectual currents of the time, she responds to various influences, gradually learning a philosophy from her trying experiences. Her development is given intensive analysis in every stage. When Mutimer first meets her she is a refined but immature girl, dominated by her mother and attached to Puritanical religious beliefs. Although she is in love with another man, his character is under a cloud, and she marries Mutimer in obedience to her mother's wishes. At first indifferent to Mutimer's radical ideas, she becomes a socialist out of marital duty, and the studies she undertakes in connection with her new beliefs are her first break with immaturity. Her observations of socialism in action are discouraging, however, and she learns that it is based upon an untenable theory of human nature. Afterward, the death of her child, the recognition of her husband's harshness, and the decay of her faith fill her with a sense of futility.

Gissing exercises considerable subtlety in making Adela retain her integrity in spite of her disillusionment, and in keeping her faithful to the Victorian ideal of the loyal wife in spite of her insight into her husband's faults. Although there are points where he loses the thread of Adela's development, his treatment of her is an able imitation of George Eliot's method of following the interplay of character and experience. Through Stella Westlake, Adela ultimately finds peace of spirit in the contemplation of beauty, which means far more to her now than her husband's social dogmas. Her passionate attachment to this woman has an intensity modern readers will find ambiguous, but Gissing no doubt intended it simply as an expression of her love for the intellect and imagination Stella represents. She reads, enjoys friendship, forsakes socialism for a life of self-fulfillment, and finds in this a lasting satisfaction.

Although he had once attributed importance to the propagandistic power of art, the story of Adela Mutimer shows that Gissing now felt that the value of art, culture, and introspection lay in their capacity for directly strengthening the faculties which poverty and industrialism were doing so much to destroy. Out of the spiritual growth achieved in the passive contemplation of truth and beauty would somehow arise the deliverance the world needed so badly.

This self-culture could be pursued only by withdrawing from the world and its interests.

The distrust of action expressed in Demos led Gissing to disapprove of William Morris, who seemed to him to be sacrificing the better course toward reform for the worse one. Morris, already famous as a writer and designer, had been an active socialist since 1883, when he had joined the Democratic Federation; when the Socialist League was founded in 1884 he became treasurer and editor of its publication. Some of the League's members were arrested at a street-corner meeting in the East End in September of 1885, and when they appeared in court the next morning there was some disturbance in which Morris, who had come to witness the proceedings, was involved. When he read about the incident in the papers, Gissing wrote irritably to his brother:

. . . what the devil is such a man doing in that galley? . . . Why cannot he write poetry in the shade? He will inevitably coarsen himself in the company of ruffians. Keep apart, keep apart, and preserve one's soul alive— that is the teaching for the day. It is ill to have been born in these times, but one can make a world within the world.[17]

Some years later, at a time when he was occupied with a criticism of society as a whole rather than with the lower classes, Gissing found the argument against social reform summed up in an aphorism of Herbert Spencer: "There is no political alchemy by which you can get golden conduct out of leaden instincts." Gissing copied the sentence in his commonplace book, adding, "The whole answer to Socialism is: that if society were ready for a pure socialism, *it would not be such as it now is.*"[18]

V

In offering a life of art and reading as a solution for Adela Mutimer's social perplexities, Gissing was giving practical expression to one of the favorite ideas of his time. The doctrine that esthetic activity and contemplation strengthen the moral capacities is as old as Plato, but some of Gissing's most influential contemporaries considered it particularly relevant to current problems. It is a central idea in the thought of Ruskin and Morris and finds its place in

Pater's philosophy as well. Arnold's *Culture and Anarchy* (1869) is perhaps the most precisely focused statement of the theory that disinterested self-cultivation was the best path to social reform. Arnold said that spiritual growth was a necessary preliminary to any real social advance. He argued that improvement could not be brought about by political fanaticism, or the promotion of the interests of any class, or the mere extension of liberty, but only by a balanced and profound understanding of the welfare of the nation and its historical spirit. Deliverance from the evils of the time must be pursued through "culture," which he defined as the desire "to make reason and the will of God prevail" and "the study of perfection." The "Hellenism" he advocated was the development of intellectual and esthetic qualities that had been obscured by the repressive moral discipline of "Hebraism." He proposed entrusting this task, not to any particular class, for each was corrupted by the prevailing materialism, but to "aliens,"—"persons who are mainly led, not by their class spirit, but by a general *humane* spirit, by the love of human perfection." [19]

Arnold's views were contested by many, including Frederic Harrison, who accused him of ignoring the world's troubles, and characterized him, in Arnold's own words, as "in the midst of the general tribulation, handing out my pouncet-box." [20] To such objections Arnold replied:

. . . we do not at all despair of finding some lasting truth to minister to the diseased spirit of our time; but . . . we have discovered the best way of finding this to be not so much by lending a hand to friends and countrymen in their actual operations for the removal of certain definite evils, but rather in getting our friends and countrymen to seek culture, to let their consciousness play freely round their present operations and the stock notions on which they are founded, show what these are like, and how related to the intelligible law of things, and auxiliary to true human perfection. [21]

Improvement was to be won by a kind of "wise passiveness" consisting of "reading, observing, thinking" exactly like the régime adopted by Adela Mutimer.

Gissing had learned the invigorating power of intellectual pursuits from his own experiences with Greek, music, Dante, Spanish, and other studies he undertook. Unlike social theories, they produce actual improvement in society by improving the human material of which it is formed. So convinced was Gissing of the potential effectiveness of self-cultivation as a social remedy, that in *Demos* he dared to match it against realistic scenes of slum life.

Gissing's high regard for the life of the mind had an important political correlate. Since it was possible to lead such a life, in his experience, only under the sheltering power of money, he came to agree heartily with the characteristic materialism of his time in its regard for wealth. He had learned the immense difference between having and not having in his years of squalor, when a few shillings made all the difference between a day of hunger and a day of peaceful study or writing. He agreed with Mr. Overton, the narrator of Samuel Butler's *The Way of All Flesh*, who will have no nonsense about the improving effects of poverty, but insists, with a fine balance of literal and ironic meaning, that "material prosperity is the safest test of virtue." In describing how the lives of Emily Hood's parents, in *A Life's Morning*, have been poisoned by poverty, Gissing achieves an irony comparable to Butler's:

. . . that love and joy, the delights of eager sense and of hallowed aspiration should be smothered in the foul dust of a brute combat for bread, that the stinted energies of early years should change themselves to the blasted hopes of failing manhood in a world made ill by human perverseness, this is not easily—it may be, not well—borne with patience. Put money in thy purse; and again, put money in thy purse; for, as the world is ordered, to lack current coin is to lack the privileges of humanity, and indigence is the death of the soul.[22]

These views put Gissing on the side of the middle class in the social struggle, for only in a leisured environment could the potentialities of mind and spirit be fulfilled. He knew that the middle class had its faults, and he was to say a great deal about these in his novels. But it was the social level where the things he cared about could be found, and that fact constituted almost the whole of his grievance against the socialists, who threatened to eliminate it. To lose the middle class, in Gissing's view, was to lose everything. Thus, Hubert Eldon of *Demos* speaks for Gissing himself when he says of the workmen who have staged a socialist demonstration: ". . . in the presence of those fellows I feel that I am facing enemies." [23]

Gissing was perfectly aware that the comfortable existence of the middle class was made possible by those injustices and abuses he so vigorously protested. He knew that English industrial civilization was founded upon the poverty of the many. When Eldon is asked whether he is content to have the majority set to labor to support his way of life, he answers that he is. Gissing himself was not quite capable of this patrician indifference. Culture and love of beauty must be served, but Gissing allowed Mutimer to explain clearly enough in one of his platform speeches how the leisure for them was wrung from the twisted bodies of the poor. He was forced to face the fact that his love of art and learning and the demands of his moral nature for social justice were irreconcilable in society as it existed. One could be satisfied only at the expense of the other. Adela Mutimer's pursuit of beauty does nothing to relieve the poverty, overwork, disease, and death that are the lot of Emma Vine and her family, yet these sufferings are too acute to be ignored.

Both sides of the controversy are well presented, with an indecisive resulting effect. The genuinely comprehensive view of the time's social difficulties expressed in the contrasted stories of Mutimer and his wife is blurred by Gissing's conflict of allegiances. This conflict is brought to a focus in the scene between Adela and Eldon in which the latter admits that he is willing to live on the labor of the majority. ". . . I think it very unlikely," he says, "that the majority will ever be fit for anything else. I *know* that at present they desire nothing else." And when Adela replies, "Then they must be taught to desire more," Eldon does not answer, for when radical and conservative stand opposed to each other on the issue of perfectibility, as they do here, Gissing cannot feel that either is wholly right.[24] He has reached the dark center of his dilemma. And when, later in the novel, the conservative Mr. Wyvern is asked what social conditions seem to promise for the future, he can answer only, "Evil." [25]

VI

When James Payn accepted *Demos,* he wrote, according to Gissing, that the style of the writing was better than George Eliot's. For this opinion Gissing termed him a "jackass." But on the eve of publication Gissing himself, in a fit of jubilant optimism, wrote that he felt it to be "distinctly ahead" of any novel since George Eliot's time. When large and encouraging advertisements heralding the publication of *Demos* appeared, Gissing was full of confidence that his day had come at last. Writing to Ellen about an invitation from Mrs. Gaussen, he said: "Thank Heaven I can go without the torture of feeling myself *Nobody*. . . . No, I can't endure to be *nobody*. I knew that would have to come to an end." [26]

Since *Isabel Clarendon* was then being printed, simultaneous publication was avoided by issuing *Demos* anonymously. The combination of anonymity and the controversial issues brought to general attention by the recent socialist disturbances piqued the public's curiosity, so that Harrison could report numerous references to the novel in the press. Several years later Booth alluded to it in his *Life and Labour* as one of the few books that gave a true picture of the lives of the poor. The *Spectator* review was warm, though certainly not extravagant, recommending the descriptions of working-class life and the character of Adela and the accounts of socialist meetings. The Westlakes, however, are "shadows," according to the *Spectator*, and all the scenes of middle-class life are inferior. The characterization of Adela falls just short of excellence, in the opinion of the reviewer, because of her vacillation between a secular and a spiritual standard of morality. The characters of Emma Vine, Mutimer, and Alfred Waltham are heartily praised; the reviewer is so delighted with the latter that he quotes a long conversation to show Gissing's skill in authentic characterization. "Aestheticism," he concludes, is the only alternative to socialism *Demos* has to offer, and the story needs some more spiritual solution to counteract the materialism it criticizes.

Far less cordial was the *Athenaeum* review, which complained that Gissing's ideas about socialism were old-fashioned and belonged to the time of Kingsley and Mrs. Gaskell. In addition, it pointed out (what is very true), that the whole case of socialism was prejudged on the basis of character, for all the socialists are weak and evil, while their opponents are refined and honest. But what the *Athenaeum* called "a blemish in point of art" had been adopted by Gissing as a means of illuminating character through politics and politics through character.

This intention and Gissing's whole purpose in *Demos* were fully understood in at least one contemporary publication. The *Scottish Review* of April, 1886, in an omnibus review of recent novels deal-

ing with ethical questions, pointed to *Demos* as a book of unusual
importance and merit. It said:

It is a book not only to read, but to mark, learn and inwardly digest, a most
thorough exposure of sham, so-called "Socialism," pitiless in its calm com-
pleteness, and total abstinence of any animus or trace of personal feeling.
The author keeps himself entirely out of sight; he deals with a class which it
is abundantly evident he well knows. . . . By the simple means of truthful
portraiture, he shows that the motive force which underlies a fiery crusade
on behalf of the oppressed, wage-earning class is a selfishness as absolute
as any which has helped to produce the evils against which it declaims.[27]

Gissing had always complained about reviews, and the "mixed"
reaction to *Demos* implanted a lifelong aversion to them in his
mind. He asked his publisher not to send him any reviews of his
next book, and read for himself only the *Spectator* reviews, which he
thought sensible. He often found himself misunderstood, for reviewers missed both his irony and his reticence and attributed to him
opinions that he did not hold. Although Gissing occasionally found
examples of carelessness in reviews, the truth is that the fault was
often on his side. His indecision about the complex questions he
dealt with prevented him from expressing his ideas in his stories in a
clear-cut and unambiguous manner. It is not surprising that he
found it painful to read the reviews, for they often told him very
plainly that he had failed to convey his ideas with precision.

The intense labors of 1885 had been punctuated with brief but
pleasant interruptions for recreation and study. During the summer
of the year he had occasionally visited the Harrisons at their house
in Surrey, and was grateful for some glimpses of the countryside. In
December Algernon came to London, staying at 7K with him for a
time. When *Demos* was finished, about the middle of March, 1886,
he had his chance for a real holiday. *Isabel Clarendon* was scheduled for early publication, Smith, Elder had accepted "Emily" the
previous December, and Gissing was temporarily free of his only
pupil, Grahame, who was out of London. Most important of all,
Smith, Elder had just sent him a check for one hundred pounds.
Gissing immediately took advantage of his liberty and his afflu-
ence to make the first of his trips to the Continent, going to Paris
for a stay of three weeks.

As his notes on his later journeys and his fine travel book, *By the*

Ionian Sea, testify, Gissing was an eager, almost a passionate, traveler, and his first reactions to Paris were intense, too intense, it would seem, for communication in his letters. This first escape from London opened unsuspected horizons to him. "It is the beginning of a new life," he wrote. He visited the Morgue, ". . . which was at once very horrible and very simple. . . ." [28] He went to the site of the Bastille, meditated upon the Venus de Milo, saw a performance by Sarah Bernhardt, and admired the new building of the Paris opera. By the middle of April he was back at 7K, concerning himself with the critical reaction to *Demos* and the fate of his two unpublished books.

IV

REVIEWS OF THE PEOPLE

I

HEN Gissing wrote to Margaret, on April 28, 1886, the week after his return from Paris, that he was planning to begin a new novel very soon, he had already established a considerable backlog of unprinted work which slumbered quietly in the hands of publishers. "Emily" was not to be published until the beginning of 1888, about two years after it had been submitted. *Isabel Clarendon,* having been thoroughly revised, was promised by Chapman and Hall first for December, 1885, and then for February of 1886. Gissing was understandably impatient by May, therefore, to see some sign of its appearance. When it was announced at last in May, he was annoyed by the fact that it was made to appear a new book, written after *Demos.*

Demos seemed to be winning him something like the success he was so eager for. About six weeks after publication, Payn told him that five hundred copies had been sold, a satisfactory number for the anonymous and expensive first edition. In June Gissing wrote to Margaret that he detected two signs of his coming "emancipation" from the necessity of teaching in order to make a living. *Demos* had been published in Germany in the Tauchnitz Collection, and George Smith of Smith, Elder, and Company, the publisher of the book, called with a dinner invitation. Even more valuable to Gissing was the praise of John Morley, who wrote to Harrison that he had found "genius throughout."

In spite of all this encouragement, the new book, *Thyrza,* made slow and painful progress. It was to be another novel of working-class life, and in his desire for authenticity Gissing went to Lambeth, the working-class district in the south of London, where he spent many hours gathering material. On the August Bank Holiday he interrupted his work to observe the crowds of pleasure-bound people. Like Zola, he regarded faithful perception of actuality as a necessary preliminary for writing. Zola was, of course, the standard contemporary example of reportorial accuracy in fiction; a cartoon of the time shows him plunging under the hooves of a pair of cab horses, notebook in hand, in search of firsthand experience. English novelists had traditionally been as much concerned as Zola with authenticity, but they tended to make use of experiences they met with instead of undertaking deliberate research. Both Mrs. Gaskell and Kingsley, for example, learned about the poor by doing philanthropic work among them. For them, as for Dickens, the vivid memory of what they saw was enough to incite and control the imagination. Gissing, however, in his eagerness to achieve the most exact and literal realism, embarked on Zola's kind of investigation, kept notes, and introduced his careful observations into his novels.

He seems to have felt that *Demos* was superficial and inaccurate, and he wanted, in *Thyrza*, to write ". . . a book which will contain the very spirit of London working-class life. . . . It will be a stronger and profounder book than *Demos*." [1] He wanted, he said in a revealing remark, to juxtapose Hellas and Lambeth, and he felt that it could be done by studying human nature closely enough. Investigations and meditations of this sort slowed his work. At the end of July an obscure dissatisfaction made him destroy most of what he had done and begin over. He seemed to be pressing his powers to their utmost and searching himself deeply. It would not be useless, he felt, for after *Demos* he could be sure of a hearing.

While he was working on *Thyrza* he wrote to his sister Ellen that he was too occupied to read, but he recommended books and authors. He had extravagant praise for his old favorite, George Sand, and sent Ellen a copy of Heine's *Buch der Lieder* with the suggestive comment: "In all literature he is one of the men most akin to me." [2] He wrote to Margaret that he drew his inspiration from French and Russian authors and disapproved of the English approach to fiction. That was why he feared his works would never be popular. "The mob will go to other people who better suit their taste. Day by day that same mob grows in extent and influence. I fear we are coming to a time when good literature will have a hard struggle to hold its footing at all." [3]

Toward the end of September the pressure became too strong for him, and he escaped from London for a rest. He went to Brighton, but finding it "hideous and vulgar," walked along the coast until he came to Eastbourne, which delighted him. He was soon back in London at work, however. In spite of his feeling that "the mob" was indifferent to his work, a cheap one-volume edition of *Demos*, this one with his name on the title page, was published in November. It was the first of his novels to enter a second edition, and a third, still less expensive, edition of it was to appear in 1888. These reprintings did not bring Gissing any income, for the copyright had been sold outright to Smith, Elder, and all proceeds realized after the first edition belonged to the publisher. Still, the new edition was welcome news, for it meant a kind of popularity which Gissing felt would enable him to ask a higher price for his next book.

But he was disappointed in this expectation. When *Thyrza* was submitted in January, 1887, Smith, Elder gave Gissing the choice of selling it outright for one hundred pounds or taking fifty pounds and 10 per cent of the publisher's sales. He chose the latter arrangement in an experimental mood. He soon realized, however, that this had been a mistake, for he knew that he would worry, regardless of the book's sale, and that his work would suffer.

Although it is Gissing's most sympathetic work about the poor, *Thyrza* is simply a reiteration, in softer terms, of the antidemocratic sentiments of *Demos*. Like *Demos*, it puts on trial a widely supported theory of social reform, and condemns it, this time, however, making some allowances for idealism and good intentions. The plot is complicated and clumsy, an awkward splicing of social interest and love story. A wealthy young idealist named Walter Egremont decides to educate the working people who are the raw material of reform. Recognizing that the lowest poor are for the time being beyond his help, Egremont addresses himself to relatively prosperous and well-educated workmen. He recruits a small band of pupils in Lambeth and, as an antidote for the materialism that their lives and occupations have encouraged, offers a series of talks on English literature. The results are discouraging, except for the response of a bookish workman named Gilbert Grail.

Egremont's educational work is interrupted by a mutual attraction which develops between himself and Thyrza Trent, a beautiful workgirl who is Grail's fiancée. Unable to resist his love for her, Egremont leaves England to wait until Grail and Thyrza have been safely married, but his departure drives Thyrza to leave home in order to avoid marrying Grail. Her whereabouts are discovered by Mrs. Ormonde, a wealthy matron interested in philanthropic work; she takes Thyrza in but refuses to allow Egremont to see her on the ground that she would not be a fit wife for him. She succeeds in making him agree to wait two years before claiming Thyrza. This part of the novel was developed from the outline plot Gissing had sent Algernon in 1883 as material for his first attempt at fiction. Unlike the original outline, however, the novel does not end well for the lovers. Thyrza overhears the bargain between Egremont and Mrs. Ormonde being made, and she confidently awaits Egremont's return, living under Mrs. Ormonde's care and receiving the training and education of a young lady. But when Egremont comes back after two years, Mrs. Ormonde convinces him that Thyrza has become too refined and precious for him, and that the marriage is now as impossible as ever, though for the opposite reason. After this disappointment, Thyrza dies, and at the end of the novel Egremont has turned to a girl of his own class.

The results of Gissing's observant loitering in the streets of Lambeth appear in the accounts of Thyrza's neighborhood and in the numerous working-class scenes and characters of the novel's subplots. Lively and sensitive descriptions of a market, a tiny, crowded shop, and a celebration in a pub are notable for their richness of detail and for the occasional objectionable tone of conscious forbearance. Gissing had apparently set himself to describe the more attractive moments of Lambeth's life, but his disapproval is never suppressed for long.

The many instances of kindness in *Thyrza* make it Gissing's most warmly human novel, although it often threatens to lapse into sentimentality. Its heroine arouses generosity and affection in almost everyone she meets. An infirm old fiddler named Mr. Boddy, who is growing helpless, inspires charitable feelings in the people of the neighborhood. His landlady's daughter secretly brings him food, and when Thyrza and her sister playfully make him a Christmas gift of a badly needed coat, their kindness brings tears to the old man's eyes. Gilbert Grail, however, is sympathetic without being sentimentalized; the reader is given a good insight into the humility, patience, and love of reading that he has managed to preserve through his years of illness and hard manual labor. In spite of his sensitivity and his tender love for Thyrza, he manages to bear her preference for Egremont with fortitude. He is one of a group of characters in the novel whose great virtue is their ability to endure suffering patiently.

More often than any of Gissing's other novels, *Thyrza* reverts to the theme of loss. Unlike Dickens, Morrison, and Maugham, he could not regard his slum material as amusing, or occupy himself solely with the virtues he occasionally found. He could not adopt a tone of hearty acceptance, but maintained a distant point of view that clearly revealed the narrow limits of slum life. The most sordid details point beyond the horizon, evoking sorrow at the waste of life they signify. Gissing feels this waste particularly strongly in the cases of women, and in *Thyrza* the busy scenes of lower class life are dominated by women. Young mothers carry their babies through the crowded market, little girls peddle vegetables shrilly, and in the pub entertainment an ugly workgirl singing a love song becomes an eloquent symbol of deprivation.

Morley Roberts wondered why Gissing, who had a sensitive ear for music, was so fond of common barrel organs. He loved to hear them in the streets when he went to Naples and was upset to learn, on his second visit to Italy, that they had been forbidden. A passage from *Thyrza* reveals the repressed sadness and tenderness that the unlovely music aroused.

Do you know that music of the obscure ways, to which children dance? Not if you have only heard it ground to your ears' affliction beneath yon windows in the square. To hear it aright you must stand in the darkness of such a by-street as this, and for the moment be at one with those who dwell around in the blear-eyed houses, in the dim burrows of poverty, in the unmapped haunts of the semi-human. Then you will know the significance of that vulgar clanging of melody; a pathos of which you did not dream will touch you, and therein the secret of hidden London will be half revealed. The life of the men who toil without hope, yet with the hunger of an unshaped desire; of women in whom the sweetness of their sex is perishing

under labour and misery; the laughs, the song of the girl who strives to enjoy her year or two of youthful vigor, knowing the darkness of the years to
come; the careless defiance of the youth who feels his blood and revolts
against the lot which would tame it; all that is purely human in these
darkened multitudes speaks to you as you listen.[4]

"Vulgar," a favorite word of Gissing's, expressed a great many
aspects of his complicated attitude toward the poor. It meant their
lack of taste in food, music, clothing, and furnishings. It meant their
callow insensitivity to the feelings of others, their narrow and in-
flexible selfishness. But it also meant the rough, childish good nature and kindness they often showed. Vulgarity is the irreverence of
the atheist, Bunce, in *Thyrza*, who expresses his disbelief in God
by sarcasm and gives his child illustrated parodies of the Bible to
read. It is the pompous egotism of Bowers, who harbors a grudge
against Egremont because he has not been offered the librarian's
position given to Grail. A part of vulgarity is the speech of the London workman, made odiously distinctive to Gissing by its cockney
accent and strident tones. But it is also the pert independence and
self-sufficiency of Totty Nancarrow, the workgirl who preserves her
virtue and her Catholicism against the hostile influences of Lambeth.

Thyrza, like *Demos*, has a clear social thesis; it is a vigorous
attack upon mass education. The environmental ideas of Locke and
Owen and the ideal of perfectibility found practical expression in
Gissing's lifetime in the extension of education among the poor.
The School Board system of compulsory education was established
between 1870 and 1880 through a series of Parliamentary acts
which filled in the gaps left by voluntary schools, universalizing
education for boys. By 1880 Victorians of all shades of opinion
could be counted upon to agree that it was necessary to educate
their future masters. "Let us reform our schools," said Ruskin,
"and we shall find little reform needed in our prisons." [5] Graham
Wallas in his contribution to *Fabian Essays* insisted strongly on
the importance of education:

If this generation were wise, it would spend on education not only more
than any other generation has ever spent before, but more than any generation would ever need to spend again. It would fill the school buildings
with the means not only of comfort, but even of the higher luxury. . . . It

would seriously propose to itself the ideal of Ibsen, that every child should be brought up as a nobleman.[6]

In spite of his love of learning, Gissing had no faith in education as a social remedy. In *Workers in the Dawn* Arthur tries desperately to improve his wife's literacy, but the poor girl is unable to muster the necessary self-discipline, and Arthur is forced to recognize that he cannot change her. The government's attempt at mass education, Gissing felt, would be equally futile. Conceived in a commercial spirit, wasted upon hopeless human material, it would only make more efficient helots of the poor and put vulgarity on a higher level, resulting in the lowering of public taste and the general debasement of civilization. Such results are treated in *New Grub Street* and *In the Year of Jubilee*. In *Thyrza* Gissing puts his case against mass education into a speech by a character named Mr. Tyrrell:

The one insuperable difficulty lies in the fact that we have no power greater than commercial enterprise. Nowadays nothing will succeed save on the commercial basis; from church to public-house the principle applies. There is no way of spreading popular literature save on terms of supply and demand. Take the Education Act . . . a more intelligent type of workman is demanded that our manufacturers may keep pace with those of other countries.[7]

Egremont's attempt to lead the poor away from the materialist spirit by helping them to recognize beauty in literature seems to be a critical allusion to F. D. Maurice's pioneer experiment in adult education, the Working Men's College. Egremont's plan is a failure and he himself eventually recognizes that it was a futile idealistic gesture.

Not quite the same problem is that of Gilbert Grail, the intelligent self-educated man, who is a laborer in everything but mind. His gifts and his education are of no use to him in the social struggle. Nobility and inspiration are available to him in books, but in life he finds only monotony and degradation. Even before the educational reforms of the last part of the century, poor men of this type were often to be found. Engels, in his book on the English working class reported in 1844:

I have often heard working-men, whose fustian jackets scarcely held together, speak upon geological, astronomical, and other subjects, with more knowledge than most "cultivated" bourgeois in Germany possess . . . the epoch-making products of modern philosophical, political and poetical literature are read by working-men almost exclusively.[8]

Kingsley's characters Alton Locke and Tregarva, the gamekeeper of *Yeast*, belong to this group, and the hero of Mrs. Humphry Ward's *Robert Elsmere* is surprised to find that the members of the workingmen's clubs where he speaks are often well read. Mr. Wyvern of *Demos* speaks for Gissing in saying that he is less concerned about the ignorant poor than about the educated minority among them.

Thyrza clearly reflects Gissing's painful indecision about the relative importance of heredity and environment in the formation of character. Knowing that the faults of the poor could be attributed to their living conditions, he was nevertheless unable to rid himself of the conviction that heredity was, after all, the more powerful force. He could rationalize Thyrza's transformation into a lady at the hands of Mrs. Ormonde only by providing her with an inheritance superior to that of her ordinary working-class neighbors, a mother who has been a refined schoolteacher. But one of the results of her training is a situation reminiscent of the scene in *Great Expectations* in which Joe Gargery, coming to London to visit his former apprentice, finds him transformed into a fine young gentleman and calls him "sir." When Thyrza's sister, Lydia, comes to see her, she feels ill at ease in the presence of a lady who was once her sister, and who a year before shared her bed and her single small room. No more eloquent evidence for the power of educational influences could be found, yet this development directly contradicts the theme represented by Egremont's failure to achieve social reform through education.

Gissing asked Smith, Elder not to send him any reviews of *Thyrza*, but he saw the *Athenaeum* review, which praised it, incidentally detecting in Gilbert Grail and Egremont a pair of figures resembling Adam Bede and Arthur Donnithorne in George Eliot's novel. Laudatory quotations from reviewers in the advertisements for the book also caught his eye, and he concluded that it would be liked better than *Demos*, though it was not as strong a novel. "It will be a long time before I do anything better than Demos artistically," he wrote.[9] The fact that Mudie's took eighty-five copies was encouraging, but Gissing observed that they had taken two thousand of H. Rider

Haggard's latest novel. "Yes," he added, "but mine will be read when Haggard's is waste paper." [10] "When I write," he said, perhaps defensively, "I think of my *best* readers, not of the mob." [11] He felt that thinking people read and valued his books. An East End clergyman who was enthusiastic about *Thyrza* paid him a visit, and he received a letter from Germany proposing a translation He wrote to his sister Ellen:

I cannot and will not be reckoned among the petty scribblers of the day, and to avoid it, I must for a time issue only one novel a year, and each book must have a distinct character, a book which no one else would be likely to have written. . . . I want money and all it will bring very badly, but I want a respectable position in literature yet more.[12]

In spite of the strong response to *Thyrza*, it was not a marked success. Ultimately, fewer than five hundred copies of the first edition were sold.

II

Gissing went to work industriously after *Thyrza* as usual, and by April, 1887, he had finished the greater part of a new novel, but in spite of constant application everything written for a year after *Thyrza* was either uncompleted or unpublished. It was a year of wasted effort. On April 24 he wrote to his brother that he was planning one of his reorganizations of his working hours. He now planned to work from nine until three so that his evenings would be free. The trouble with this arrangement was that Mrs. King, the charwoman, who came in about noon, disturbed him; but Gissing felt that he could safely give her a quarter of an hour. His novel, *Clement Dorricott*, was almost finished in April, and he planned to write a satire on literati to be called *Sandray the Sophist*. Later in the year he wrote that he was making progress on a novel called *Dust and Dew*, and in December he reported that he was desperately revising *The Insurgents*, which approached completion. Of these four projects, three were certainly finished or nearly finished. Yet none was ever published.

The only one submitted to a publisher, *Clement Dorricott*, was accepted by Bentley, who praised it and offered to publish it in the usual three-volume format, but Gissing felt that it was not sufficiently "characteristic" to be a worthy successor to *Thyrza*, and wanted to restrict it to magazine publication. Bentley returned the manuscript, and Gissing tossed it aside without unwrapping it. It was never mentioned again, and is said to have been destroyed.

He seems to have achieved a satisfying mode of life in 1887 by locking himself away from the world and devoting himself to his writing. He gave some time every day to a single pupil, Walter Grahame, who was a gifted student of Greek, but reserved the rest of the day for his work. He no longer enjoyed visiting and making acquaintances, as he had a year or two earlier. He explained his rejection of an invitation he received in May of 1887 by writing to his sister that his loneliness made him too morose to go into company. "I cannot get the kind of people who would suit me, so I must be content to be alone." [13] He did emerge from his solitude to hear music, however, for in May he saw the new Gilbert and Sullivan opera, *Ruddigore*, attended his first Wagner opera, *Lohengrin*, and heard Adelina Patti sing at the Albert Hall.

In the summer he went to Eastbourne and visited his family at Wakefield, and he was willing enough to accept another invitation from his publisher, George Smith, in July. Smith was a prominent personality in Victorian publishing who, at twenty-two, had taken over the firm of Smith, Elder, founded by his father, and extended it vigorously and imaginatively. He cultivated the personal friendships of the writers he dealt with, and, since Leigh Hunt, G. H. Lewes, George Eliot, Browning, Thackeray, Trollope, and Charlotte Brontë were among them, he had a great deal of knowledge about the leading literary figures of the time. Among Smith's ventures were the *Cornhill*, a periodical whose first editor was Thackeray, the *Pall Mall Gazette*, and the monumental *Dictionary of National Biography*. Gissing had probably first encountered Smith through his work for John Morley and the *Pall Mall Gazette*, and he thought of sending *A Life's Morning* to Smith, Elder, in the fall of 1885; Chapman and Hall, who were still delaying the publication of *Isabel Clarendon*, could not be expected to publish the new novel promptly. Smith, Elder, remained Gissing's regular publisher until *New Grub Street* in 1891 (although *The Emancipated* was brought out by Bentley). While dining with Smith in the summer of 1887, Gissing enjoyed hearing his account of the famous episode early in his publishing career when Charlotte Brontë appeared in his office to reveal that she was Currer Bell, the author of

Jane Eyre. However, he did not always have a good opinion of Smith, whose reader, James Payn, rejected *Born in Exile* in a tactless fashion, and he disapproved of the adulation poured forth by the press on Smith's death in 1901.

In December Gissing broke his self-imposed rule against visits again by attending an "at home" at the Deanery in Westminster in order to meet Dean Bradley's daughter, Mrs. Margareta Louisa Woods; her novel, *A Village Tragedy,* had aroused his enthusiasm. At an art lecture in the same month he saw Oscar Wilde, who had grown fat, shortened his hair, and wore the conventional style of dress. He wrote that he felt fit, in spite of his seven hours' work a day, and was often in good spirits. He was still poor. In a letter to Algernon dated Good Friday, 1887, he asked for five pounds to tide him over for three weeks until the date of publication of *Thyrza.* He said he could make the small sum last that long because he was "desperately economical," even using dripping with his bread instead of butter.

In the middle of 1887 he began to frequent a new working-class neighborhood, Clerkenwell, a venerable slum region, specializing in light metal manufacturing, which was a center of radicalism. The speeches he heard one Sunday evening in August on Clerkenwell Green filled him with outrage at the coarseness and political ambition of the orators. In October and November he reported to Algernon and his sisters that London was constantly disturbed by disorderly meetings of workingmen which were not reported in the papers but which seemed to him to be dangerous.

Early in November, James Payn wrote to him to announce that his novel, "Emily," which had been in his hands for over two years, was to run as a serial in the *Cornhill Magazine,* beginning with the number of January, 1888, but that the title was unsatisfactory. Gissing suggested *Her Will and Her Way,* but that had already been used, and he finally decided on the attractive but inappropriate *A Life's Morning.* He was intensely dissatisfied with the novel on seeing it again after two years, but he later decided that serial publication, which made it impossible to read the book as a whole, was responsible for the poor impression it made.

The beginning of the year found Gissing in "a very shaky state of health" and unable to continue his work. After several weeks of effort he felt that he must escape from London, and he went to spend a week with his brother, who was now married and living at Broadway in Worcestershire. He returned home to work on February 4, but his efforts were so futile that by February 7 he was "almost ready for suicide." The next day he laid aside what he had written and began a new novel, to be called "Marian Dane," which was discontinued in its turn the next day. In desperation, he repeated the experiment of January, 1887, and went to Eastbourne, a strange choice for a winter holiday, which offered the advantages of privacy and cheap accommodations. However, the weather was bad, the wind came through the walls of the old lodginghouse, and loneliness, headaches, and sleeplessness made it impossible for him to work. Roberts came to join him for a week, and the two took long walks in the snow and driving wind, or sat huddled in their overcoats before an inadequate fire, trying to converse. Since he was unable to write, Gissing spent his time reading recent novels and planning the work to be done when he returned to London. On February 29, coming back to his lodgings late in the afternoon after a trip to Lewes, he found a telegram waiting for him which said: "Mrs. Gissing is dead. Come at once."

He telegraphed Roberts, who had gone back to London, took the next train to town, and at eleven o'clock reached 7K, where he found Roberts waiting for him. Exercising characteristic outward control of his emotions, Gissing said little of what he felt, but Roberts interpreted the trembling of his voice and hands as meaning that he hoped intensely, in spite of serious doubts, that the information in the telegram might be true.

After spending the night together at 7K, the two went to Lambeth the next morning. Fearing a trap of some kind, Gissing sent Roberts ahead, to verify Helen's death, and then went to the house himself. He recorded every detail of the following events in his diary, including the names and addresses of the doctor and undertaker, the amount paid to the mourners hired for the funeral, and the pathetic squalor of the room in which Helen had died. There were almost no clothes or bedding, and he found some pawn tickets that showed that she had pawned them during the summer months. In a drawer he found a piece of bread and some butter, the only food in the room. He was moved to see that she had kept certain mementos of him and his influence—his photograph and letters and portraits of Byron and Tennyson. Signs that she had continued to struggle against her alcoholism appeared in three cards pledging to abstain from drink, which she had signed during the last six months. As he examined this room, noting every eloquent detail with a novelist's perception, Gissing experienced a powerful renewal of the indignation that had first drawn him to Helen's cause and to his mission as a social novelist. Her death seemed to draw him into one of those strangely lucid moods of mingled emotion and detachment that animated his creative impulse. Writing about it to Algernon, he said: "Well, now it behooves me to get to work. I have a somewhat clearer task before me than hitherto, and one that will give me enough to do for many years." And, "For me there is yet work to do, and this memory of wretchedness will be an impulse such as few men possess. . . ." [14] Helen would help him more in death, he wrote in his diary, than she had hindered him in life.

He made up a little parcel of a few of her belongings, and took them home with him. He did not intend to go to the funeral, and asked the landlady to make the necessary arrangements. On the next day, however, he did return to Lambeth to see Helen, for the last time, in her coffin. Her face, which had been unrecognizable the day before, now seemed more familiar. Acting upon confused feelings unintelligible to himself, he redeemed her wedding ring, which had been pawned, and cut some of her hair to keep. Then he left her. A few days later, his sister Ellen came to London for a short visit, but he was as spiritless as ever after her departure, and was prevented from writing by a cold. Finally, on March 19, after almost three weeks of unhappy idleness, he began the novel entitled *The Nether World.*

It was now two years since he had sold a book, for every effort to write since the completion of *Thyrza* in January of 1886 had been futile, and there had been signs of disintegration and collapse in his behavior of early 1888. But Helen's death seemed to recall him to himself and give him new energy. *The Nether World,* begun soon after she died, and completed in four months, was his last and most bitter book about the problems of poverty.

III

The Nether World is the only novel by Gissing in which nothing but poverty appears. The reader is immersed in the miserable depths of the slums, and there are no scenes from middle- or upper-class life to relieve their effect or to set them off. Within these limits, however, Gissing is able to discriminate differing degrees of misery. Close to the lowest possible abyss of homeless pauperdom is the Candy family, people of no occupation, whose earnings are always casual. A step above is the family of John Hewett, who works when he can but turns to almost any occupation when he cannot find regular employment, and is one of the first victims of hard times. When Hewett's son marries Penelope Candy, everyone feels that he has married beneath him, so clear are the distinctions between these two ranks of poverty. Considerably above them are the Peckovers, landlords of a lodginghouse in Clerkenwell, and masters of the squalid world they survey. The highest rank of all is reached by the Byasses, who have a modest but commodious house in a different neighborhood, and whose morals and manners have escaped the poisoning effects of deprivation.

Because it has no contrast between rich and poor, *The Nether World* achieves more fully than any of Gissing's other novels the character they all tend to assume—that of a broad, static canvas. The elaborate plot provides constant action and change of situation, but its complexity is easily lost to sight among the many characters and vivid details of daily life. The actions see-saw back and forth, ultimately changing little in the lives of the characters, and they do not alter the general impression of the book—an enormously detailed and accurate panoramic picture, much like one of Frith's crowded and realistic scenes of Victorian life.

The main character, Sidney Kirkwood, is an embittered young workman who cannot resist viewing the suffering about him with irony, although he is essentially kind and good-hearted. Gissing's summary of his development is revealingly autobiographical:

Saved from self-indulgence, he naturally turned into the way of political enthusiasm; thither did his temper point him. With some help . . . he reached the stage of confident and aspiring Radicalism, believing in the perfectibility of man, in human brotherhood, in—anything you like that is the outcome of a noble heart sheltered by ignorance. It had its turn, and passed.[15]

Kirkwood befriends Jane Snowdon, an enslaved child whose sufferings as a household servant are reminiscent of Ida Starr's girlhood, and who leads Gissing to the central thesis of his novel. Jane is discovered and saved from her miserable existence by a grand-father, Michael Snowdon, who returns from Australia laden with wealth which he keeps secret. When Jane grows up, Michael reveals the reason for his secrecy. Having grown repentant of a careless youth, he now wants to use his money for philanthropic works, with Jane as his instrument. He proposes to leave her the bulk of his fortune on condition that she devote herself and the money to improving the lot of the poor.

Jane is not the sort of person, however, who can become a saint of social work. Simple, weak, retiring, she is easily defeated by her first experience in waiting on the poor in a charitable soup kitchen, and wants nothing more than to marry Kirkwood, with whom she has fallen in love, and to live out her life quietly and humbly. However, her grandfather's fanaticism demands that she sacrifice her own happiness for the mission it has thrust upon her. In the end she loses both Kirkwood and the inheritance, and is condemned to a lonely and unhappy life. This plot recalls an observation made by Mr. Wyvern in *Demos* that might serve as the motto of *The Nether World*. To devote oneself to social reform, he said, was not in itself either a good or a bad thing; its value depended upon the relevant facts.

In addition, Jane Snowdon's story expresses Gissing's feeling that philanthropy and social work promised neither real help for the poor nor peace of mind for the rich. Beatrice Webb, who had a great deal of experience with charitable activities and their results in the London of Gissing's day, took a similar view. Discussing the moral dilemmas that plagued the Charity Organization Society, she said, ". . . wherever society is divided into a minority of 'Haves' and a multitude of 'Have Nots,' charity is twice cursed, it curseth him that gives and him that takes." [16] It is not surprising, says Gissing, that the recipients of charity at the soup kitchen in *The Nether World* boldly protest against changes in its administration by pouring their soup on the floor. The poor are too dehumanized to respond with gratitude, and the philanthropist who expects it of them will miss his reward.

The Nether World contains more direct reporting from actuality than earlier books, a result, possibly, of Gissing's new practice of using notes. The fruits of his observations in streets and workshops, at the Crystal Palace, at political meetings on Clerkenwell Green, and in many other places appear in faithful circumstantial accounts. The dialogue is more vivid in its reflection of character, more faithful in phrase and pronunciation to the dialect of working-class speakers. One correspondence between the novel and real life is particularly striking. The cards showing the futility of Helen's repeated efforts to "take the pledge," which Gissing had seen in his dead wife's room, became a detail in his description of the room of Maria Candy, a wretched old woman hopelessly enslaved by alcohol.

In *The Nether World* Gissing demonstrates a more intimate knowledge of the feelings and opinions of ordinary working people, and of the difficulties they encountered in making a living. There is a new reserve and authenticity in his presentation of small physical details. The spectacle of Clem Peckover at tea, the lunch customs of girls working in a paper flower factory, and the arrangement of a sickroom in a crowded lodging are described with meticulous clarity. Numerous instances of the corruption of character by environment occur. The stories of Scawthorne, the unscrupulous clerk, and Bob Hewett, the counterfeiter, are like case histories in their incisive linking of cause and effect.

As always, however, Gissing is less concerned with the causes than with the quality of the facts, and the prevailing impression created by the poor of *The Nether World* is one of animality. Gissing's contempt is apparent as he shows the slum people quarreling, plaguing one another with cruelty, and drinking themselves into violence or insensibility at parties and outings. The chapter describing the wedding excursion of Bob Hewett and his wife to the Crystal Palace is a great panorama of lower-class life, marvelously animated with vivid details of riot and disorder and thoroughly imbued with Gissing's characteristic bitterness. He did not sympathize with the poor in their barbarity, because he knew that they preferred their way of life and would resist change. That men should be rendered so depraved by hardship as to prefer the crude comforts and vicious pleasures of the slums to civilized habits was evidence of a supreme social crime, but that did not make their depravity less real.

Gissing said little directly in his novels about cosmic questions, but his treatment of the slum and its way of life suggests that he felt in it, obscurely enough, a manifestation of the absolute. His most searching explorations suggested further depths of mystery and power. In his novels the slums control the destinies of the rich as well as the poor, sitting astride the paths of their ambitions and sending forth tentacles of guilt and revenge to trouble them in the comfortable fastnesses of their country homes. This spectacle inspired a profound fatalism in him. The social order, with all the evils it produced, seemed to be the expression of a cosmic necessity too powerful for human resources to resist. As Mr. Tollady says in *Workers in the Dawn:* "History pursues its path, using us as its agents for the working out of prescribed ends. To think that we men can modify those ends is the delusion of ignorance or madness." [17]

For all its pretensions to progress, Victorian industrial civilization seemed to be ruled by the same pitiless fates which dominated the world of Homer and Aeschylus, familiar to Gissing since his boyhood. Perhaps that is what he meant when he wrote that he was trying in *Thyrza* to bring Hellas and Lambeth together. The spiritual vacuum of his agnosticism was filled by a combination of the nineteenth century's scientific determinism and his native pessimism. "I see no single piece of strong testimony," he said in the *Ryecroft Papers,* "that justice is the law of the universe; I see suggestions incalculable tending to prove that it is not." [18]

To Hardy, another Victorian fatalist, the hostility of the cosmic power appeared most clearly in the struggle for existence that dominated the world of nature. In Gissing's novels, on the other hand, the malevolence of the universal order manifests itself in the works of man. It is embodied in the operation of the chaotic economy, in the deadening organization of industry, in repressive social and domestic institutions. Its special instrument is the economic system, devised by man but seemingly used against him by other powers. Indifferent to man's well-being, it subjects workers and capitalists alike to the vicissitudes of panics, depressions, and labor disturbances, and it establishes ruthless competition as the law of survival. Throughout Gissing's novels of poverty, the truth of Engels' comment on the insecurity of the workingman is clearly apparent: "Everything that the proletarian can do to improve his position is but a drop in the ocean compared with the floods of varying chances to which he is exposed, over which he has not the slightest control." [19]

Modern industrialism was organized to serve man, yet everywhere, as Carlyle pointed out, man went unserved. Instead the dogma of production became the animating spirit of the slum, in whose filthy tenements untold evils germinated and whose streets and cellars, teeming with corrupting influences, poured forth their army of vulgarians. This is the dark and bristling vision evoked anew by Gissing in each of his novels of poverty, until finally in *The Nether World* it emerges more powerfully than ever before. This book, with its unrelieved amassing of details and its explorations of the mysterious psychological and material depths of poverty, is Gissing's final and most harrowing confrontation of the hostile power that ruled his universe.

The poverty he saw around him seemed to be an integral part of an entrenched social system which was the creation of an omnipotent power. Even the most energetic reforming efforts could not hope to eliminate conditions that were a part of the fundamental order of the universe. These convictions, long operative below the surface of Gissing's novels of poverty, acquire a new and decisive force in *The Nether World*, so that even Gissing's own vague estheticism came under the heel of his satire. In the midst of his description of the disorderly Bank Holiday festivities at the Crystal Palace, he pauses to mock the reformers of his day with the irony of a hollow imitation, which suddenly drops its ironic tone for a terrible directness.

To humanise the multitude two things are necessary—two things of the simplest kind conceivable. In the first place, you must effect an entire change of economic conditions; a preliminary step of which every tyro will recognize the easiness: then you must bring to bear on the new order of things the constant influence of music. Does not the prescription recommend itself? It is jesting in earnest. For, work as you will, there is no chance of a new and better world until the old be utterly destroyed. Destroy, sweep away, prepare the ground; then shall music the holy, music the civiliser, breathe over the renewed earth, and with Orphean magic raise in perfected beauty the towers of the City of Man.[20]

The Nether World was completed, not without many indecisive revisions and failures of inspiration, on July 22, 1888. The last two and one-half pages were written on that day, and the fact entered, with relief, in Gissing's diary. He had worked swiftly, but with little pleasure. He had been prey to even more mental disturbances than usual, including the disturbance of falling in love.

Apart from one or two vague episodes, mentioned by Morley

Roberts, Gissing had little to do with women while Helen was alive. Her death, however, must have suggested that he could now free himself from one of his greatest hardships, that of loneliness. According to his sister Ellen, the family life at Wakefield in his boyhood had been warm and eventful, and he could never accustom himself to the isolation he was forced to endure so often as a man. Two diary entries of May, 1888, suggest a sad little story. Having been pent up for weeks in 7K occupied with his reading and writing, Gissing was driven to despair by loneliness and by thoughts of a Miss Curtis of Eastbourne. The next day he went to see her, and he wrote in his diary simply that his visit and its transparent purpose had failed.

The month after completing *The Nether World* and sending it to Smith, Elder, he went to stay with his mother and sisters at Agbrigg, near Wakefield. While taking the train at King's Cross Station he saw some copies of the third edition of *Demos* with his name on the title page for sale at 3/6. At Agbrigg he passed the time in performing the notable feat of translating the Odyssey aloud to his sister Margaret. He also read Crabbe and Hawthorne, finding in the former an anticipation of his own realism, and re-marking with great interest that he had written some prose tales which did not survive. Finding Wakefield dull, he took his mother and sisters to Seascale for a pleasant two weeks' holiday. Then, in September, he went to stay with Algernon and his wife at their cottage in Worcestershire. From Broadway he made a visit to Stratford, where, in spite of guides and hawkers, he captured the sense of Shakespeare's presence. In the spring of 1888 he had already decided to let 7K and go abroad, but had been vague about his destination. On September 26, however, before hearing whether Payn had accepted *The Nether World*, he left for Paris, accompanied by a German acquaintance named Plitt.

Just before leaving on what was to be an extensive trip that gave him a five-month respite from writing, Gissing had a letter from the Reverend George Bainton of Coventry, who was preparing a lecture for young people on the art of composition and said that he was asking some well-known authors for accounts of their writing methods. With his characteristic sense of duty, Gissing gave considerable time to the composition of a careful answer. In the calm, even sentences of his reply is to be found the disquieting fact that

Gissing, almost thirty and the author of seven novels produced with great effort, felt that he had learned little from his work except despair. He told the young people of Coventry through Mr. Bainton that good English is written intuitively by those who have the gift for it and can succeed without deliberate study. He himself was not that kind of a writer. "My own attempts at authorship," he wrote, ". . . have had the result of making me constantly search, compare, and strive in the matter of style; I would that the issue were more correspondent with the thought I have given such things." [21]

V

TRAVEL AND MARRIAGE

I

ITH the independence typical of the British tourist, Gissing prepared himself for the rigors of Continental travel by buying a frying pan, a spirit lamp, and some other utensils for simple cooking. Both Harrison and Morley Roberts came to see him off from Victoria Station when he left London with Plitt on September 26, 1888. The arrival in Paris the next day was inauspicious. Gissing was suffering from a sore throat, and in addition he and Plitt seemed unable to agree on rooms, for Plitt refused to pay enough rent to secure what Gissing considered to be a minimum of comfort. Plitt's alternate obduracy and indecision, combined with his own illness, made Gissing's first hours in Paris miserable. The two travelers finally agreed on the Hôtel de Londres, Rue Linné, but this was done only by separating, with Plitt's taking a room somewhat cheaper than Gissing's. When Gissing, desperate to close the bargain, offered to pay five francs of Plitt's twenty-five-franc weekly rent, Plitt accepted the offer immediately, without thanks or delicacy. Gissing attributed this boorishness to mere stupidity, reflecting that Plitt was really honest and well intentioned.

He quickly realized, however, that he had chosen an entirely uncongenial companion, who was a serious threat to his pleasure and peace of mind. Plitt had what Gissing considered to be the characteristic faults of the plebeian; he was insensitive and inconsiderate, intolerant of differences of opinion, not interested in art or culture, and unable to understand those who were. He was not of much help in practical matters, for he was vacillating, stupid, and lazy. One of his most trying traits was his stinginess. Gissing, who had good reason to know the value of money, always spent it grudgingly, but he was prodigality itself in comparison with Plitt. His comfort was constantly menaced by the German's drastic economies. Once, for example, Plitt suggested a very cheap restaurant frequented exclusively by workingmen, and, when Gissing refused to dine there, he was taunted with accusations of antidemocratic prejudice.

Plitt's motive in visiting Paris was nominally artistic, for he had some skill as a draughtsman. But his artistic pursuits were very limited. He painted pictures of fruit and flowers, not from life, but from representations which he sought throughout the city. Gissing was revolted by Plitt's taste in art, for, although he found little to admire in the Louvre and spoke disparagingly of the Mona Lisa, he once became enraptured by a gaudy picture of a flower on a soap advertisement in a grocer's shop. Two days later he actually bought this production, paying, to Gissing's horror, two francs for it.

On October 3, five days after his arrival in Paris, Gissing received a letter from Smith, Elder offering £150 for *The Nether World*. It was the highest price he had ever received for a book; yet it was very low, considering the fact that he had now become an established author. The publishers explained that they could not make a better offer because the sale of Gissing's books remained slow. Gissing accepted without hesitation, for the money meant that he could extend his trip to Italy. The next day he made arrangements to go to Naples.

He had hopes that Plitt would not accompany him, for the latter was reluctant to go to Italy, which he had already visited, and could not understand Gissing's eagerness to see Rome. By this time Gissing was wishing he and Plitt could part without rancor. The two were not economizing by sharing rooms and the only effect of their partnership was that Gissing was subjected to constant oppression. But he could not bring himself to do anything that might displease Plitt, "intellectually *borné*" as he might be. When Gissing received a letter from Bertz in Germany, Plitt said that correspondence with Bertz might lead to their being arrested as spies, and Gissing asked Bertz to write to his English address. In fact, Gissing found himself going to extremes to placate his companion, and this led him to write out a painful self-examination in the diary which accompanied him on his travels. He had, he felt, accepted a role of complete submission to Plitt, a person inferior to himself. He guarded his speech, washed the dishes of their common meals, and used the butter sparingly, not out of regard for Plitt, but rather out of "cowardice." It was, he thought, a contemptible weakness, and had always been one of his failings. "Therefore it is that I am never at peace save when alone." [1]

After waiting for a few days until his sore throat improved, Gissing began actively touring, crowding his days with visits to theaters, lectures, museums, galleries, and graves. At the Salle des Conférences he heard a talk on feminism and lectures on Daudet and George Sand, enjoying the speaker's dramatic style of reading from the novels. On October 6 he saw a performance of *Crime and Punishment* adapted for the stage, and objected to the mutilation of a novel he greatly admired. The following week he saw *Athalie*. He was disappointed in this first experience of classical French drama, for he found that the acting did not equal reports he had read of the great French actress Rachel. He spent several hours each day at the Louvre and other galleries, making notes of the pictures he saw there in his diary. He also visited places associated with the gods of his private Pantheon, standing outside Daudet's house for a time, content simply to look at it. At Père Lachaise and the Cimetière de Montmartre he saw the graves of Théophile Gautier, Murger, Heine, Balzac, Rachel, Michelet, and Chopin, entering brief descriptions of each in his diary.

His escape from London and the sight of great cultural achievements in Paris were working curious and subtle changes in him. He felt that he was losing his interest in the poor. While working wearily on *The Nether World* in June of 1888 he had found himself tiring of "this idealism," and vowed that he would soon give it up. At that time he had been reading (in German translation) some plays by a Norwegian named Ibsen, and he found them "extraordinary productions." Perhaps *Pillars of Society, The Wild Duck,* and *Ghosts* suggested to him that it was possible to pursue a criticism of society without espousing the cause of the poor. Toward the end of his stay in Paris he wrote in his diary that he felt little but antipathy toward the common people. "On crossing the Channel," he wrote, "I have become a poet, pure and simple, or perhaps it would be better to say an idealist student of art." [2] In general, this was to be the spirit in which he toured Europe. It was the sign of a permanent change, for when he returned to England and to novel writing, he ignored almost entirely the poverty that had been his usual theme in the first part of his career.

In the spring of 1888, during the weeks of lethargy that had fallen upon him after Helen's death, he had received a letter from a Frenchwoman named Fanny Le Breton, who asked permission to translate *Demos* and also manifested an interest in *A Life's Morning*. Gissing's books had attracted some attention among the French as representatives of a realism resembling that of their own literature. He had granted Mlle. Le Breton permission for her translation, and now he went to visit her at her home in Paris, after learning her address from her publisher, Hachette. He found her to be a plain, elderly woman living with a widowed sister. She told him that her translation of *Demos* was soon to be published and asked Gissing to set a price for the translation rights of *Thyrza*, but he asked nothing.

During his stay in Paris, Gissing prepared himself for the great experience of Italy by refreshing his Italian, communing with the Italian paintings and ancient sculpture in the museums, dreaming of Pompeii and Vesuvius, and reading Goethe's *Italienische Reise*. In Goethe's longing for Italy, so intense that he found references to Roman culture unbearable, Gissing detected feelings exactly like his own.

When the time for the journey to Naples arrived, Plitt at the last moment refused to leave Paris. He said that he had found some new models to copy from, and would now have to pay the price of buying instead of hiring them. Since Gissing would not postpone their departure, Plitt proposed that the extra expense be shared between them. Gissing agreed to this, but soon afterward began to suspect that the whole affair had been a scheme designed to extract a few francs from him. Before they left, Plitt bought some books. He chose difficult works by Pascal and Condorcet, explaining that his reading had to be profound, since he had so little time to give to it. The real difficulty was, Gissing remarked in his diary, that his capacity for attending to a book lasted only ten minutes. The entries about Plitt, which come close to monopolizing Gissing's diary at this time, are a vivid and characteristic mingling of fascination and aversion.

They left for Marseilles from the Gare de Lyons on October 6. From the train windows Gissing saw the autumn foliage of the Rhone Valley, which gleamed with a golden color in the sunlight, and the splendor of the sight moved him deeply. At Marseilles, which had been founded as a Greek colony, he felt that he was crossing the threshold of the ancient world that had called to his imagination since his boyhood. The Mediterranean countries spoke to Gissing with a special power and clarity. The glory of the past seemed to him to form a visible aura over the landscape. "You seem to see the light of the sky *through* the mountains," he said, writing of a sunset on the French coast.[3] What he felt when he looked at the shores the Greeks had colonized, and traveled the seas their ships had sailed, was a nostalgia which lifted him out of himself, offering the release he sought from the world of commerce and industrialism. "Let no one tell me," he wrote from the steamer he had boarded at Marseilles, "I am in the 19th century, nothing of the kind. . . . These are the mountains that the Greek colonists saw. The sea and the shore having nothing altered since the times when Carthage was the great Empire of the Mediterranean." [4] He now felt himself to be entering the realm created in his mind by Gibbon, Horace, Virgil, and Homer, and reliving the great fable of the past.

They went from Marseilles to Naples by a coastwise steamer whose evil smell and crowds of poor emigrants Gissing found oppressive. Freed for a time from Plitt, who took a third class ticket, while Gissing took a second class, he befriended a young American from Missouri who proved to be a rather unstimulating companion. Plitt, finding the third class accommodations unbearable, soon joined them. The American asked whether his companions knew a book named *Don Quixote,* remarking that he had often started it, but could never make much progress with it. Plitt sagely observed that an understanding of *Don Quixote* required a knowledge of Spanish life. To such erudite literary conversation did Gissing listen while the coasts of Italy and her offshore islands slipped by.

They arrived at Naples on October 30, and were established a few days afterward at the Casa di Luca, the house of a German landlady named Frau Häberlin, at Vico Brancaccio 8. Although he had come to Naples primarily for its classical associations, Gissing found his attention attracted by the many small differences of everyday behavior that the observant tourist notices in a part of the world new to him. He noted the high, thick-walled houses, the streets thronged with goats and donkeys in elaborate harness, the bargaining going on in the streets, the cheap and abundant fruit, the sounds of hand organs and peddlers crying their wares about the streets at night. The numerous priests and nuns gave the town a medieval appearance. He enjoyed the food served in the restaurants and quickly adopted the Italian custom of drinking wine with meals. In spite of his thorough Italian studies, he was baffled by the Neapolitan dialect, but his Italian was good enough to allow him to converse with the occasional northerner he met.

He had again arrived at a new place in poor health, but three days afterward felt well enough to go for a long walk through some of the nearby towns. He strolled through Fuorigrotta, Bagnoli, and Pozzuoli, lingering in the squares and along the shore, thinking of the Romans who had once lived there. In Pozzuoli, which had once been the Roman seaport of Puteoli, he sat in the public garden, smoking his pipe and listening to the soft music of a hand organ nearby. Among these placid scenes and their associations he must have felt very far away from Lambeth and Clerkenwell. "I felt happy," he wrote in his diary account of this walk, "more than happy." [5]

Gissing viewed the ruins and landscapes of antiquity with an informed and scholarly eye. He was ready to strip whatever he saw of the centuries that had passed since Virgil and Horace had lived in Naples and its neighborhood. To him Pozzuoli was still Puteoli and Baja was Baiae. Nearby was Cumae, the spot where Aeneas, founder of the Roman nation, was said to have first landed in Italy, and on one of his walks Gissing came upon Lake Avernus, supposed by the ancients to flow into the lower world, and to have been the gateway of Aeneas' visit to the realm of the shades.

In November he visited Pompeii, being careful to go on a Sunday, when admission to the ruins was free, and spent several days touring in the vicinity of Amalfi and Salerno. His only thought of authorship came on November 15, the day *A Life's Morning* was published in book form; he was happy to be far from the scene of the event. Such things were easy to forget among the ruins of Pompeii and the Greek temples of Paestum, with their splendid view of the sea.

On his return from this tour, Gissing stopped at an inn in Pompeii where he encountered a number of German guests. He thought he detected something both familiar and peculiar in the speech of one of them, and after dinner it turned out that this individual was no German at all, but a Yorkshireman named John Wood Shortridge whose strong northern accent had colored his German. Gissing quickly made friends with this man, who had relations in Wakefield, and learned that he had been in Italy seventeen years. Shortridge had a house, an Italian wife, and a large family in Massa Lubrense, near Sorrento, and he promptly invited Gissing to accompany him there.

Before going with Shortridge, however, Gissing devoted a day to climbing Vesuvius. First it was necessary to approach the summit on horseback, and the unaccustomed ride made him sore. After dismounting, he found that volcanoes are more attractive at a distance. The rocks and cinders of the mountainside cut his boots, and he objected to being pulled upward by his guides at the end of a rope. At the top he felt somewhat compensated for the hardships he had endured, for he enjoyed the splendid view and the constant, threatening din of the crater. At lunch two of the guides told him that their names were Raffaelle and Michelangelo, information which Gissing took seriously. When he arrived at the inn near the foot of the mountain on his way back, he had the opportunity of rescuing an American lady who had been temporarily abandoned by her family, and, not knowing enough Italian to order a meal, was in danger of starving. On November 23, the day after his thirty-first birthday, he and Shortridge set out on foot from Pompeii for the latter's home.

Gissing found there a strange and chaotic English-Italian household like the unhappy family described by E. M. Forster in *Where Angels Fear to Tread*. It consisted of Shortridge and his Italian wife, Carmela, their four children, her illiterate parents, and Shortridge's brother. Although Shortridge had some vague intention of giving his children an English education, they were growing up to speak nothing but the local Italian dialect, like his wife. In the vaulted cellar room where he slept, Gissing met his host's brother,

Herbert, who was to be his roommate for the night. He generally
went to bed at seven, as did the rest of the family, but he sat up
late to talk to Gissing. He was, said Gissing, a hopeless drunkard
who had once been a medical student at Edinburgh. The room was
filled with medical books, which he could never bring himself to
open. He ate only at night, for he never had any appetite at other
times, and kept some bread and *salame* by his bedside, which Gissing saw him eat when he woke up at about one in the morning.

After a day with the Shortridges, Gissing spent two days on Capri
and then returned to Naples. The pages of his diary contain some
firmly outlined drawings of local sights: a campanile seen from his
window, a view of Vesuvius, a diagram of a peculiar lock. Rather
abruptly, on November 29, he left by night train for Rome, ridding
himself at last of Plitt. The phrase "a Roma," heard repeatedly on
the train, made him think of the centuries during which the
same word had been used to name the city. Even after a sleepless
night on the train he could not resist going out on his very first
day in Rome to see the Forum and the Colosseum. His first impression of the Roman populace was favorable, for he found them
quieter and more dignified than the Neapolitans.

His first day was given to ancient Rome, but a part of his second
was given to England, for he went to the Protestant Cemetery to
see the graves of Keats, Shelley, and Keats's friend, Joseph Severn,
carefully noting in his diary the situation of the graves, their in-
scriptions, and their condition. The following month was almost
equally divided between Christian and pagan Rome. He wandered
in the Forum and on the Palatine Hill repeatedly, explored the
Campagna, went to see the site of the ancient city of Veii, and
examined the Roman sculpture in the galleries, meditating on the
past which these things evoked, and which had been familiar to him
since his school days in Wakefield. The sight of Mount Soracte,
which recalled the familiar ninth ode of Horace, thrilled him. Of
the long-horned oxen which he saw drawing carts, he said:
". . . they always bring to my mind antique statues and bas-reliefs.
. . . Such oxen Homer had in mind, and Virgil." [6] "The Roman
life and literature," he said, "becomes real in a way hitherto in-
conceivable. I must begin to study it all over again." [7] Looking back
at his experiences in Rome just after he had left it, he wrote to

Ellen: "I am no longer ignorant of the best things the world contains. It only now remains for me to go to Greece. . . ." [8]

The churches and the religious paintings in the Vatican galleries and elsewhere inspired him, not with Christianity, but with the religion of beauty preached by Ruskin and Pater. On December 14, in the midst of his daily explorations of ruins and galleries he wrote in his diary: "Woke early this morning and enjoyed wonderful happiness of mind. It occurs to me, is not this partly due to the fact that I spend my days solely in the consideration of beautiful things, wholly undisturbed by base necessities and considerations?" [9]

He objected violently to the prudery that had draped some of Michelangelo's figures in the Sistine Chapel, where he spent hours at a time. His diary contains a diagram of its walls and ceilings identifying each of the panels, as well as brief comments on many of the works of art in the galleries. It was a good thing, he observed, that only old men became Popes, for a young man in possession of the Vatican's wealth of art would go mad.

After attending Christmas services at St. Peter's, he left, just before the end of the year, to go to Florence, which he found less interesting than Rome. He paid homage to the museums, regretting the lira charged for entrance at each of them, and thought of Florence's association with Walter Savage Landor, but nothing in the city moved him as deeply as had the relics of Roman antiquity he had seen further south. Florence lacked the exuberance and color he had enjoyed in Naples, and it was oppressively cold. In addition, his indigestion returned, and he was forced to consult an English doctor.

About January 15, 1889, he began to think of the novel he would write when he returned to England. It was a comparatively long time since he had had thoughts of this kind. For ten years, beginning in 1878, Gissing had hardly passed a day without working at fiction, either in imagination or by actual writing. Even on his holidays, the project of the moment weighed heavily upon him. This burdensome habit had been broken abruptly in September of 1888. His journey to France and Italy was an escape from all that writing meant, and he scarcely gave a thought even to the events related to his own career that went on in England during his absence. If the experiences he had in Europe suggested material to him—and they did eventually—he said nothing of that in his diary or his letters. However, the news, coming on the fifth of January, that the proofs of *The Nether World* were ready for correction may have recalled future necessities to his mind.

At the end of January he arrived in Venice, where he lived in a house called Palazzo Swift, whose curious name he was unable to account for. The Renaissance atmosphere of the city only served to make him think of how much he preferred the Greek temples at Paestum. About two weeks after arriving in Venice he went to hear a lecture on Zola. He was surprised to find women and schoolboys present, and was amused both by the lecturer's emotional delivery and by his extravagant praise of Zola. Gissing shared the estimate of Zola common among English critics of the time, who found him offensive on both moral and esthetic grounds. Zola was much more appreciated in England after the reopening of the Dreyfus case in 1898, and by that time he had become one of Gissing's literary heroes. It is worth noting, however, that in February of 1889 Gissing agreed with the low estimate of Zola common in England, for it is precisely his novels written before that time, those dealing with poverty, which are supposed by some critics to show a strong influence of Zola.

In Venice Gissing completed the plan of his next book, *The Emancipated*, which was to be set in some of the Italian scenes he had visited. Noting from advertisements in the *Athenaeum* that *The Nether World* was scheduled for publication in March, he sent Smith, Elder a sentence from a lecture by Renan as a motto for the title page of the book: "La peinture d'un fumier peut être justifié pourvu qu'il y pousse une belle fleur; sans cela le fumier n'est que repoussant." [10]

His travels were drawing to a close. On February 26 he left Venice, arriving in Brussels via Milan and Basle on February 28; while waiting for the boat-train, he wandered about Brussels, thinking of Charlotte Brontë, who had once lived there and used it as the setting of her novel *Villette*. His return to London at nine in the morning of March 1 was not an exciting experience to him at all. The only remark entered in his diary on that date observes that his rooms at 7K were badly in need of the cleaning the charwoman was giving them.

II

Gissing had grown tired of his usual theme even before his departure for the Continent, and his traveling experiences made it impossible for him to remain the gloomy poet of the slums. The pleasant, stirring towns of France and Italy reminded him that London was not the world. In observing the poor of other countries he often remarked that they were clean, well-mannered, and considerate, in contrast to their English counterparts. Occasionally, to be sure, he had been pestered by a hawker or cheated by a guide, and he attributed their faults to the influence of generations of slavery. But he found the festivals of the poor lively and colorful, free of the boorishness and disorder that prevailed at the Crystal Palace or Brighton on Bank Holidays. This evidence that people could be poor without becoming brutalized added another complication to the problem of the relationship of character and poverty, deepening his confusion about it.

On the other hand, some of his ideas were strengthened rather than weakened by his experience in Europe. His journey had given him a chance to feel the humanizing power of leisure, art, and culture. He attributed the profound peace of mind he felt on his travels to his frequent communion with art and history, and thought he was drawing a permanent benefit from them. Of the antiquities he saw in Rome he said: "All these things are realities to me, and, as long as I keep my memory, no one can rob me of them. . . . My life is richer a thousand times—aye, a million times—than six months ago." [11] He was still enough of a Comtist to be profoundly moved by the evidences of human achievement visible everywhere. In the beautiful rituals of the Christmas masses at St. Peter's he sensed, not the presence of a supernatural divinity, but the power of inspiring human effort. His feelings toward the priests he saw officiating were divided. "At one moment contempt for them all, at another reverence, seeing that they represent a system which was once so powerful and embodies so much human intellect." [12]

For, in spite of the splendor of the religious art he saw in Italy, his agnosticism was not altered. On the contrary, he strongly preferred pagan art, which reflected the times and spirit of classical literature, and he rated Venice and Florence as second in interest to Rome and Naples. He wrote to Bertz from Venice that he had always been indifferent to Christian art. To Algernon he wrote, "Florence is the city of the Renaissance, but after all the Renaissance was only a shadow of the great times, and like a shadow it has passed away. There is nothing here that impresses me like the poorest of Rome's antiquities." [13] Most Victorian travelers would have taken a contrary view, for interest in the Renaissance had been stimulated by some of the leading figures of the time, including Browning, Pater, Ruskin, and John Addington Symonds.

Gissing's first novel after his return to England, *The Emancipated*, is partially set in Naples and its vicinity. In it he dealt with some of the moral and esthetic issues Italy had suggested to him, as well as some of the streets, pensions, and landscapes he had seen. He found *The Emancipated* a difficult book to write. For one thing, he had broken the habit of regular work. Secondly, it was, as *Isabel Clarendon* had been, a departure from his usual subject. It was, in fact, the beginning of a new phase of his career, and he had to make unusual efforts to arouse and sustain interest in the less sensational material of middle-class life. This phase of Gissing's fiction has often been neglected in favor of his more picturesque early novels of poverty, yet it produced some work of deeper significance, and, on the whole, of more lasting value.

Up to *The Nether World* Gissing's criticism of civilization had been directed at its exploitation of the poor. Now, however, he began to examine the values and achievements by which that civilization justified its shortcomings. His travels on the Continent suggested that the condition of the poor was only one symptom of the malady of money-making that paralyzed the spirit of English society, transforming all potential ideals and aspirations into the values of trade. He now laid aside the theme of poverty, turning in *The Emancipated* to the larger subject of the spiritual condition of modern industrial society.

Many incidental features of his life in London interfered with Gissing's attempt at this new and more complicated task. He had a number of friends and much companionship, but these only served to interrupt him and did not really relieve the loneliness that often discouraged him and prevented him from working. After going north to visit his family, he returned to London to spend a few days writing a piece entitled "Christmas at the Capitol," which had been promised while he was in Italy. On March 18 he was re-united with Roberts, and the next day he went to Acton to pay a promised visit to a sister of Shortridge. On March 23 he went to meet Roberts at the studio of Alfred Hartley, the painter, where he made two new friends, Hartley himself and W. H. Hudson, the novelist. Gissing was eager to meet Hudson, who was then prac-tically unknown as a writer. His first novel, *The Purple Land That England Lost* (1885), had not been well received, and he was to remain an obscure naturalist until 1904, when *Green Mansions* was published. Gissing, who was keenly appreciative of originality, may have liked *The Purple Land* before its qualities were generally un-derstood. Hudson, who had been born in Argentina and migrated to England when he was about forty, was leading a shabby exist-ence on the rents of a boardinghouse kept by his wife. The year be-fore meeting Gissing he had published a curious Utopian novel, *A Crystal Age*, but it had almost no circulation.

After giving much thought to his novel, Gissing began it in March and made gradual progress. On April 1 his former pupil, Bernard Harrison, came to see him, and although Gissing unkindly begrudged the half hour he stayed, the visit did not prevent him from finishing his first chapter. April 3 was the publication date of *The Nether World*; an invitation to dine with the Harrisons on the sixth annoyed him as an interruption, but he was gratified to find, on dining with them again a few nights later, that they had al-ready read his new book.

Visits and conversations with Roberts, Hartley, and Hudson be-came a regular recreation. Once, however, Roberts seriously dis-turbed him. On April 9, when Gissing was expecting his friend, a messenger arrived with the news that Roberts had been arrested for becoming involved in a brawl, and Gissing was asked to come to his rescue. Roberts' account of the incident in *Maitland* de-scribes a cheerful Gissing handing over the three pounds that was Roberts' fine. Actually, he was much annoyed at this incursion on his slim resources. He had not sold a book for a long time. His ac-count at the Wakefield bank was dwindling, and would soon be down to five pounds. In conversations with Roberts he wished for the kind of patron Coleridge had had in Gillman, and, after extemporizing a few whimsical stanzas on the subject, he wrote some more and fashioned them into the comic poem printed in *Maitland*.

On April 18 he had to sustain a visit from Plitt, newly arrived in London from his European travels. Meaning to be entertaining, he told Gissing of a mistress he had kept in Rome, but his story only intensified Gissing's loneliness and prevented him from working for some time afterward. However, Plitt proved to be useful about a month later, on May 14, when he interpreted a German letter whose script Gissing had found impenetrable. It was from a Frau Clara Steinitz, whom Bertz had suggested as a translator of *Demos*, and who wrote, in reply to an encouraging letter from Gissing, to ask permission to publish an abridgment of the novel as part of a periodical. Gissing agreed to her proposal, and the translation was published in 1891.

His work on *The Emancipated* assumed the aspect of a war of attrition. From the middle of March to almost the end of May he alternately attacked and retreated. Often enough he wrote quickly and without hesitation, but he was invariably beaten back by revisions and uncertainty. Twice he was completely routed, for he had to discard long sections of painfully revised manuscript to make new beginnings. On May 25 a final defeat took place. Painters descended on Cornwall Residences (now more splendidly named Cornwall Mansions) and Gissing gave up whatever ground he had gained and fled to his mother's house in Wakefield to begin anew.

He chose his new field of battle without much optimism, for he had always found Wakefield and its neighborhood deadening. His mother and sisters, who had strong religious convictions, disapproved of Gissing's lack of faith, and the atmosphere of the house made him uncomfortable. Though his sisters, who were schoolmistresses, must have had some intellectual interests, Gissing complained of the triviality of mealtime conversations. Nevertheless, by installing himself in the garret and going to work with a will he managed at last, to his own amazement, to make progress. He succeeded in achieving a daily "quantum" of five pages, and at the end of three weeks had already completed the first volume.

Gissing's diary record of the composition of *The Emancipated* explains why his novels were generally written in haste, in spite of the pains they cost him. He wasted a great deal of time in preliminary work that eventually proved useless and, when he found himself in good form, wrote speedily day after day, hardly daring to rest or reconsider anything for fear of losing his facility. In this way, the first volume of *The Emancipated* cost him three months of hard labor, although the story itself was written at top speed in three weeks. By maintaining this rate for the next two months he succeeded in finishing it by the thirteenth of August and sent it off to Bentley, fearing that it might meet with some objection of the kind Bentley had made to *Mrs. Grundy's Enemies* and *The Unclassed*. But Bentley accepted it, and with *The Emancipated* Gissing inaugurated a series of novels concerned with the middle class.

III

Gissing's criticism of the middle class is a logical extension of the social ideas of his novels of poverty. The great horror of poverty was its corruption of human gifts, but Gissing now saw that the competitive spirit of modern civilization produced the same result in all classes, though it might operate in more indirect ways.

The middle class, after gradually coming to power in England during the Industrial Revolution and winning its political rights in the reform of 1832, quickly began to supersede the old landed aristocracy as leaders in most phases of English life. The ideals of a Puritan class engaged in competitive business permeated all of English society from the poorest factory workers to the royal family. It was in effect a new aristocracy, which set fashions and moral standards and based its ideas of social organization upon the exigencies of mass production.

Many of the attitudes typical of the Victorian merchant and manufacturing class can be explained as the result of a need for security; the attachment to custom and tradition, the preference for quiet, the respect for commercial and industrial power, the social pressure in favor of conformity, and the support of imperialist political policies. The solidity and seclusion of prosperous Victorian homes and the comfort of their furnishings seemed to express a wish that nothing would ever happen to unsettle the way of life they represented. The characteristics that such contemporary observers as Mill and Arnold found so detestable in the middle class arose from this desire of its members to put themselves beyond the reach of change. They insisted upon uniformity of manners, dress, and opinions, adhered stubbornly to received religious beliefs, and regarded everything foreign or new with an impregnable sense of their own superiority. Exaggeration was a natural element of this inbred and defensive way of life. Religion was turned into religiosity, and an unquestioning belief in the literal accuracy of the Scripture, a rigid Sabbatarianism, and a despotic prudishness became parts of society's ordinary moral standards. Although spotless respectability was demanded, and the plain terms and common facts of life became unmentionable, human beings remained human beings, and ordinary people seemed no more able to live up to such ideals than the men of other times had been. Prostitution flourished, and respectable gentlemen made suspicious trips to Paris and might be expected to have some such book as a copy of Rabelais locked away out of sight. The need for maintaining an appearance of innocence under any circumstances gave rise to the habit of hypocrisy, institutionalized self-deception which brought with it a general sense of guilt.

The overmastering ambition of Victorian society was money-making. Calvinist religion preached the doctrines of election and economic success as almost equally important to salvation. Engels pointed out how commercial turns of phrase invaded the common speech, betraying the obsession with business. As the schoolroom scenes of *Hard Times* show, mass education was often directed toward the mechanical skills that would produce efficient clerks and good men of business. The novel, like Victorian society in general, spoke the language of money, for it would hardly have been intelligible if it had used any other tongue.

Responsible contemporary observers reported that the Victorian middle class thought, felt, suffered, and rejoiced in terms of money. According to John Stuart Mill, it was incapable of purely esthetic pleasure, and its taste in art and furnishings was based, not on beauty, but on expenditure. "It knows no bliss save that of rapid gain," said Engels, "no pain save that of losing gold." [14] The effects of this thirst for accumulation upon society as a whole were clearly evident to Engels, when he came to England as a young man to work as an executive in the Manchester textile factory partially owned by his father. Although his book, *The Condition of the Working Class in England in 1844*, is mainly concerned with Manchester, he perceived the harm the economic struggle was doing to individuals of every class soon after he arrived in London. His book opens with a vivid, pleasant picture of London's great commercial activity, which is followed by a deeper insight.

But the sacrifices which all this has cost become apparent later. . . . One realizes for the first time that these Londoners have been forced to sacrifice the best qualities of their human nature, to bring to pass all the marvels of civilization which crowd their city; that a hundred powers which slumbered within them have remained inactive, have been suppressed in order that a few might be developed more fully. . . . The very turmoil of the streets has something repulsive, something against which human nature rebels. The hundreds of thousands of all classes and ranks crowding past each other, are they not all human beings with the same qualities and powers, and with the same interest in being happy? . . . They crowd by one another as though they had nothing in common, nothing to do with one another, and their only agreement is the tacit one, that each keep to his own side of the pavement. The brutal indifference, the unfeeling isolation of each in his private interest becomes the more repellent and offensive, the more these individuals are crowded together. . . . Hence comes it, too, that the social war, the war of each against all, is here openly declared.[15]

Toward the end of the century, when *The Emancipated* was written, a reaction to the rigid Puritanism of the mid-century was under way, although there had been no real change in the underlying emotional and economic facts of bourgeois civilization. The mid-Victorian businessman had been proud of his independence and thrift, but his counterpart of the eighties preferred to display his wealth. The children of people who had sought edification in prayers, churchgoing, and moral sentiment turned to art galleries, concerts, the theater, and less respectable indulgences in their search for adventure and enlightenment. Puritanism began to fade. The new middle class began to look to the older aristocratic standard of manners as its model. As a result, Gissing's treatment of the bourgeoisie in *The Emancipated* and later novels was somewhat more complicated than that of Dickens, for he had to deal with the gradual changes that were beginning to mask the rock-ribbed qualities of an older generation personified by such characters as Pecksniff and Dombey.

IV

The hero of *The Emancipated* is a moody and lonely painter named Ross Mallard, Gissing's representative in the novel, a man much like his author in opinions, temperament, and habits. Quietly industrious, suspicious of extremes, sensitive and easily disturbed, he is jealous of art's freedom of expression but refuses to embrace any grandiose theories about its social usefulness. When he is challenged to show how his art serves mankind, he disclaims this purpose altogether, saying: "The one object I have in life is to paint a bit of the world just as I see it. I exhaust myself in vain toil; I shall never succeed; but I am right to persevere, I am right to please myself." [16] These are Gissing's attitudes and Gissing's accents. Jokingly skeptical of innovations, Mallard is at the same time bitterly opposed to the Philistinism of the middle class.

The Emancipated has a curious symmetry of design not found in Gissing's other novels. This characteristic suggests that the intense efforts he expended on the preliminary drafts of the novel were not wasted, but found their way into the final hasty writing in the form of a clear grasp of the contrapuntal plot. The chief characters of the story fall into two groups, and have Mallard, who belongs to neither, between them as a center of balance. On the one hand are "the emancipated," people who have actively taken up arms against convention, and who traffic in pretentious but futile ideas about art and culture. The leader of this group is Cecily Doran, the orphaned daughter of an old friend of Mallard's and his ward. Cecily's education has been entrusted to Mrs. Lessingham, a guardian who has brought her up in a spirit of freedom and enlightenment still shockingly new in a society that felt that girls must be ignorant if they were to be pure. This is how Mallard ironically describes the results of Cecily's education:

Miss Doran is a young woman of her time; she ranks with the emancipated. . . . Miss Doran has no prejudices, and, in the vulgar sense of the word, no principles. She is familiar with the Latin classics and with the Parisian feuilletons; she knows all about the newest religion, and can tell you Sarcey's opinion of the newest play. Miss Doran will discuss with you the merits of Sarah Bernhardt in "La Dame aux Camélias," or the literary theories of the

Brothers Goncourt. I am not sure she knows much about Shakespeare, but her appreciation of Baudelaire is exquisite. I don't think she is naturally very cruel, but she can plead convincingly the cause of vivisection.[17]

But Cecily uses her enlightenment as a shibboleth and a fashionable ornament without having any real convictions about it or understanding of it. She can remark that the artist is free, "a prince among men," but Mallard, a working artist beset by doubts and difficulties, is embarrassed by her ignorance of the truth. Her lover, Reuben Elgar, displaying a similar superficiality, decides upon a career as a writer in preference to business, but is eternally at a loss for anything to write. Cecily's friends, the empty-headed Denyer girls regard themselves as devotees of culture, but when Madeline Denyer's fiancé, who is a painter, seems unable to earn a living, Madeline advises him to work for money until he is able to afford the luxury of painting as he pleases.

Contrasted with these *amateurs* of art is a group of Dissenters, whose religion has made them hostile to the art, freedom of conscience, and breadth of experience that they see about them in Italy. Miriam Baske, the recently widowed sister of Reuben Elgar, a young woman of strict Evangelical education, is the central figure of this group.

To the time of her marriage, her outlook upon the world was incredibly restricted. She had never read a book that would not pass her mother's censorship; she had never seen a work of art; she had never heard any but "sacred" music; she had never perused a journal; she had never been to an entertainment—unless the name could be given to a magic-lantern exhibition of views in Palestine, or the like.[18]

Miriam spends her time in Italy planning a chapel for the people of her north of England manufacturing town and ignores the sights and art works of Italy. She regards Mallard's admission that he paints for his own pleasure as a confession of sinful hedonism, and she is somewhat offended when Cecily plays the piano on Sunday.

Her friends, the Bradshaws, are older and more amusing examples of middle-class parochialism. Prosperous middle-aged business people from the north of England, they can make nothing of the carefree Italians about them or the art of the museums. Stubbornly insular, they do not try to understand the strange customs of the country, but regard it as a kind of madhouse. The nude statues in the museums astonish Mr. Bradshaw and irritate his wife. When he consults Lemprière's *Classical Dictionary*, a book familiar to Gissing from his Wakefield boyhood, Mr. Bradshaw is scandalized and asks indignantly whether boys in England are really given such material to study. This kind of prudery, says Mallard's friend Spence, is an integral element of their hypocritical civilization, where even the most liberal-minded are embarrassed by honesty and innocence. He observes that the same limitations apply to literature, which demands skipping and elisions if it is read in the family. Mallard laments this triumph of Philistinism and declares that his children shall be taught "a natural morality."

Gissing had always objected to conventional ideas of propriety. Once, while visiting Shortridge at Massa Lubrense, he happened to come into a room where Shortridge's wife was bathing her baby girl. The woman laughed and said, "Come è bella nuda!" giving Gissing occasion to think how differently an English mother would have reacted under these circumstances. He had accepted *Punch's* scolding about his views on honesty in literature in silence, but now he began to speak out on the subject, condemning "Grundyism" as one of the blighting forces of middle-class civilization.

The two main groups of characters represent the two ways in which an essentially inartistic age responded to art, and Mallard stands between them as a genuine artist who belongs to neither extreme. The balance into which the characters fall is reflected by the natural opposition of a number of other elements. The art and freedom of Cecily's group is associated with Italy, sunlight, and nature; its opposite, the Puritanism of Miriam and her friends, is related to England (especially the north), smoke, and industrialism. The antithesis is carried further by the contrasting development of the two chief female characters. While the emancipated Cecily follows her modern principles into tragedy and unhappiness, the benighted Miriam learns to escape her provincialism, to open herself to experience, and to fall in love with and marry Mallard.

Mallard's first love is his ward, but since he fails to declare himself, she is won by Miriam's dissolute brother, Reuben Elgar, who woos her by kissing her among the ruins of Pompeii. Cecily is immediately confronted with the formidable defenses of Victorian convention, is refused consent to the marriage, and is forbidden to see Elgar privately. She finds, in short, that she is not allowed to make use of the power of self-determination developed by her advanced education. Against this situation she rebels, eloping with Elgar to England.

Two years of marriage make her position even more difficult, however, for her husband, who is supposed to share her views about the independence of women, reverts to the Puritanism of his upbringing and forbids her to see certain friends. When he tells her that she is incapable of making her own decisions in such matters, she is forced to play the conventional submissive wife. This, and the death of her child, make her see the futility of her old ideals and interests. But Elgar is not strong enough to fill the dominating role that he has assumed. His attempts to write a book are unsuccessful, and, gradually demoralized by his inability to make his life meaningful, he drifts into infidelity and debauchery. When she learns of this, Cecily longs for the old-fashioned wifely resignation with which women of an earlier generation tolerated such disgrace, but the contradictory values of a period of changing social customs have involved her in an insoluble dilemma. She cannot divorce her husband, and according to the general view it is her duty to remain with him in spite of everything. She cannot, however, love a husband whose infidelity she knows; she has already decided that it is right for the woman to leave her husband under such conditions, but only after her own marriage approaches the breaking point does she see how heavy the responsibilities of independence are. Gissing comments:

Life is so simple to people of the old civilization. The rules are laid down so broadly and plainly, and the conscience they have created answers so readily when appealed to. But for these poor instructed persons, what a complex affair has morality become! Hard enough for men, but for women desperate indeed. Each must be her own casuist, and without any criterion save what she can establish by her own experience.[19]

Unable to act upon her principles, Cecily enters into an uneasy reconciliation with Reuben, but his moral disintegration continues until she is forced to leave him. At the end of the book she learns of his death in a sordid street fight over an actress, and the novel closes as she bursts into tears.

Miriam Baske, who is as drearily conventional at the beginning of the novel as Cecily is enlightened, undergoes a contrasting development. Mallard, his talks about art, and a reading of Dante are the first influences that make her begin to see the sterility of her

Evangelical beliefs. After opening her mind to Italy and visiting the Sistine Chapel and the Vatican with Mallard, she can see no point whatever to her former church enthusiasm. When she returns to England to visit her home town, she finds its atmosphere and her fellow church members repulsive. The powerful effect of Italian art upon her recalls the experience recorded by Ruskin in his autobiography, *Praeterita*. He had had the same narrowly pious and repressive Evangelical training as Miriam, and his first step away from it came through discovering the beauty of the illustrations in a Catholic missal he had bought in an Italian town.

Like all of Gissing's novels, *The Emancipated* has a number of minor plots and characters of considerable interest. A bitter comment on the spiritual hollowness of the age is embodied in Mr. Musselwhite, a fellow lodger of Miriam's. Since he has no occupation or interests, his leisure is a fearful burden, and he ultimately finds a calling by marrying the orphaned daughter of a bankrupt commercial traveler. A more harrowing story is that of Madeline Denyer, who is at first engaged to a charming and artistic young man named Clifford Marsh. Madeline's father insists that Clifford become self-sufficient, while Clifford refuses to give up his painting. Under the stress of these differences the young lovers separate, and the tragedy of this becomes clear later in the novel when an accident confines Madeline to her bed and some powerful scenes show her bitterness as a frustrated and resentful invalid.

The Emancipated was written at a time when Gissing had temporarily outstripped his personal resentments. His old fierce, denunciatory tone is gone. Even the note of protest is muted. Instead there is the urbane, perceptive irony suggested in the title, and a mood of sympathy for such innocent victims of social law as Cecily and Madeline Denyer often prevails.

V

Gissing was grieved to learn, while spending the summer at Wakefield, that the bad health of Algernon's wife, Katie, forced them to give up the pleasant cottage in Worcestershire where Gissing had often visited them and move to Harbottle in Northumberland. Algernon remained poor, for he had great difficulty in selling the

novels of country life he had learned to write under Gissing's tute-
lage. His first, *Joy Cometh in the Morning*, had been placed with
the firm of Hurst and Blackett about the beginning of 1888, and
brought him a few pounds. A second novel, *Both of This Parish*,
was accepted in the summer of 1889, but only after it was rejected
by Bentley; Algernon got twenty-five pounds for it only by selling
the copyright as well as the right of publication.

During his quiet stay at Wakefield, Gissing turned for awhile to
religious problems. He received from Bertz a German translation
of *Niels Lyhne*, by the Danish author Jens Peter Jacobsen. This was
to become one of his favorite books, for its profound and sympathetic study of an atheist who is attracted by the consolations of
religion echoed his own spiritual dilemma. Immediately after reading it he reported to Bertz that Jacobsen was having a considerable,
though vague, influence on his own work. While thinking about
the problem treated in *Niels Lyhne*, he turned to Canon Liddon's
Some Elements of Religion; but he found that, like all religious
thought, it was based upon unproven and arbitrary assumptions.

A week after finishing *The Emancipated*, Gissing took his sister
Margaret to the Channel Islands on a holiday that was originally
intended to include Brittany but was ultimately restricted to Guernsey and Sark. The three weeks provided him with a number of little
experiences that later turned up as minor incidents of novels and
stories. The original of one of the unsatisfactory writers' wives in
New Grub Street, for example, was the wife of a painter who made
herself disagreeable in the hotel dining room by complaining about
the food and refusing to eat any of it. Gissing found Margaret a
fearfully uninteresting companion. They were often at a loss for
conversation, and on Sundays her piety reared itself formidably, for
she went to both English and French church services. Gissing
noted that she relaxed her Sabbatarianism to the extent of taking
up a book by Victor Hugo, whom he was himself reading at the
time, having gone through *Toilers of the Sea, 93,* and *Les Misé-
rables* in quick succession. On hearing from Bertz that he was rereading *Workers in the Dawn* and *The Unclassed* as preparation for
an article on Gissing to be written for a German periodical, he wrote
from the placid seclusion of Sark that he would never read them
again himself, for they belonged to a dark period of his life that
Bertz, who had shared it with him, knew well enough, and would

remind him of the imperfection of his early work as well as past suffering.

Bertz also wrote that an article on *The Nether World* by Frederick W. Farrar, the Archdeacon of Westminster, had appeared in the current *Contemporary Review*. Pleased to have his work discussed by so prominent a figure in such an important periodical, Gissing sought the article out when he returned to London, but he was disappointed to find that it was little more than a well-intentioned rhapsody of indignation at social abuses, written in a religious tone. Archdeacon Farrar, having been deeply moved by *The Nether World*, saw in its realism a potent propaganda weapon in the cause of reform, and called the public's attention to it ". . . in order that the rich and the noble may get to know something of the world which lies beneath their feet, and may lay to heart the awful significance of the facts which are here revealed." [20] Noting that Gissing offered no remedies for the evils he depicted, the archdeacon suggested some of his own: sympathy, duty, and a sense of responsibility. Gissing was discouraged to see that his book had been used as the text for a sententious sermon, and that his name had not been mentioned once throughout the article.

Another review of his work, far more competent but hardly more welcome to Gissing than Archdeacon Farrar's, appeared in *Murray's Magazine* in May of 1888, although it did not come to Gissing's attention until the summer of 1889. This was an article called "Two Philanthropic Novelists," by Edith Sichel, a comparative discussion of Gissing's and Walter Besant's social novels. Recognizing the need for useful literature of social reform, Miss Sichel pointed out, with more than a hint of cynicism, that this need had produced the "Philanthropic Romance"; the two leading writers of this genre were Besant the Optimist and Gissing the Pessimist.

The two Besant novels discussed in Edith Sichel's article, *All Sorts and Conditions of Men* (1882) and *Children of Gibeon* (1886), are comedies of social reform that seem to anticipate Shaw's plays. The first and weaker book is about a wealthy girl, a graduate of Newnham College, who sets up a dressmaking establishment in Stepney on the cooperative principles of the Christian Socialist workshops. These workshops had all failed, but that, as Angela Messenger, Besant's heroine, explains, was because they were run by men. Her project is rather unreal, for while there is little work for the needlewomen she employs, there is a great deal of exercise, dancing, tennis, and other activities designed to improve their mental and physical condition.

Angela meets and falls in love with another adventurer in Stepney, a young man who, after being reared as a gentleman, has discovered that he is really the son of a sergeant, and returns to assume his original position in life. Like Gissing's Arthur Golding, he has to choose between the alternatives of social reform and art for its own sake, but Angela shames him out of considering the latter. The novel trudges through a certain number of moderately distressing scenes of poverty and ends with a wedding where the hero marries Angela, not knowing that she is really an heiress. Thus, he has the double happiness of marrying unselfishly and yet gaining a wealthy wife. Angela's reform efforts, which end in a blaze of glory with the establishment of a Palace of Delight containing a library, theater, concert room, and other cultural facilities, are directed toward civilizing the poor by teaching them to enjoy simple pleasures and want better things. Through the lips of his hero Besant derides the aimless fanaticism of radicalism, but he has little to offer himself except a vague estheticism, a denatured derivative from Ruskin and Morris. The thin characterization and comic tone of the novel suggest that it is not intended to be taken seriously as social comment.

More cogent, though still essentially comic, is *Children of Gibeon*. Making use of an artificial plot based on a confusion of identities, the novel follows the attempts of a girl who thinks she is of lower-class stock to establish relations with an oppressed workgirl whom she at first thinks to be her sister. The slum neighborhood of Hoxton, where she takes a room, the ordeal of the long working day suffered by the sweated needlewomen, and the other hardships and hazards of their lives are described with a certain force and a great deal of bitter and satiric comment directed against employers and wealthy people who know nothing of these things. Especially effective is Besant's account of his heroine's transplantation, at her own desire, from her comfortable home with its servants to a single room in a poor lodginghouse where she suddenly discovers what a burden it is to keep herself alive by cleaning, cooking, and marketing. Besant expresses scorn for both socialism and religion. The only remedy that works in *Children of Gibeon* is the heroine's patient kindness to the poor girls she has decided to care for. Thus the novel in effect rejects organized reform in favor of individual philanthropy. In spite of a sensational and unlikely plot and unrealistic characterization, it has some powerful descriptions of hardship and privation and is more successful than *All Sorts and Conditions of Men*, both as a story and as a social document.

As Edith Sichel noted, both of Besant's novels end amid naïve and buoyant optimism with definite schemes for relieving the misery of the people. Gissing, on the other hand, knows too much, she says, and offers no hope. He is ". . . the thorough Conservative, who being powerless to prevent the 'progress' to which he ascribes all the ills of the world, has nothing better left him than to sit and bewail them—the more zealously that he is presumably, at present, a convert from the Radicalism of his youth." [21] As she understood Gissing's position from *Thyrza* and *Demos*, he looked to the upper classes for help and recommended ethical doctrines. In contrast with Besant, he accepts conditions with resignation, and, even though he has the merit of being more factual, the attitudes expressed in his work do little to promote reform.

It must have been the half-sarcastic tone, rather than the content of this article, that stung. In June of 1889 Gissing wrote to its author, denying that his novels were "philanthropic," and declaring that his only motives were esthetic. A correspondence followed, and toward the end of September, after he had returned to London from Wakefield, Gissing paid Miss Sichel a visit at Chiddingford. He found her to be an educated woman of pronounced literary tastes, and a lively conversationalist. Although she was not a member of any organization, she was strongly interested in social reform, and had done social work of her own in Whitechapel and at Holloway Gaol, and the year after Gissing met her she established a nursery at Chiddingford. Later in her career Edith Sichel wrote works on literature and history and became a reviewer for the *Times Literary Supplement*. Gissing attributed her cultivated taste and general refinement to her wealth and her access to books and educated companions. She naturally interested him, and he repeated his visit about six weeks later, this time meeting her in her luxurious London apartment, where, in the course of two hours of literary talk, they discussed his books. She seemed far more interesting—almost beautiful—on this occasion, and thoughts of her remained in his mind for months afterward.

In the fall of 1889, after his return from the Channel Islands, Gissing reverted to the activities of his first years in London, although he was, of course, not so poor or so lonely as he had been then. He often went to the British Museum, no longer to take shelter with the classics, but to read some of the significant scientific works of his time. Though he was not sympathetic with the philosophy of science, the determinist tendency he encountered in these books corresponded with his intuitive fatalism. In Taine's history of English literature, for example, he found the theory that even genius could be attributed to the operation of specific factors. Buckle's *History of Civilization* used the surprisingly regular rates of murder and suicide to argue that history was subject to uniform laws that individual desires could do little to alter, and that a science of history was therefore possible. Théodule Ribot's *L'hérédité psychologique*, which Gissing extracted in his Commonplace Book, advanced what was, in effect, a materialist theory of morals, maintaining that moral and psychological characteristics depended on physical ones and were therefore subject to the laws of heredity. He was less interested in Darwin's *Origin of Species*, which gives environment some power over heredity, for he felt that it was peculiar and confused. Some of his time at the British Museum was spent in research in feminist literature in preparation for a novel about a girls' school; it was to be called *The Headmistress* and was begun in October but never completed. However, he made use of this information in later novels, for "the woman question" soon became one of his leading themes.

VI

Gissing's and Roberts' friendship with Alfred Hartley and W. H. Hudson had now become firmly established. Early in October they all dined together at 7K, with Gissing acting as cook, and after dinner there was lively and intellectual conversation carried on with hearty laughter in clouds of tobacco smoke. It was the kind of relaxed, informal evening that Gissing valued among the best things in life. Roberts dubbed the group "The Quadrilateral" on this occasion (he himself attributed this name to Gissing), but it did not have much stability, for about a month later Gissing reduced it to a triangle by leaving on his second Mediterranean trip.

His travels in Italy had been an enriching experience, but he still wanted to see Greece, which exerted an even stronger attraction on him. When Bentley's firm offered £150 and a royalty for *The Emancipated* on September 27, a visit to Greece became possible. Gissing left behind not only "The Quadrilateral" but also such unfinished business as *The Headmistress* and his new friendship with Edith Sichel. Quickly traversing the route of his earlier trip, he left Victoria Station on the eleventh of November, was in Marseilles the following day, and on the next embarked for Piraeus. By the sixteenth his steamer was in the straits of Messina, and Gissing, seeing the outlines of Stromboli and Mt. Etna and the beautiful colors of seacoast, sea, and sky, felt that he was in the land of Apollo. Two days later the coast of Greece appeared, gleaming, to Gissing's eager eye, with a classical splendor: "It is no use to say that such things are like a vision; no one ever *had* a vision like what this is in reality. . . . The mountains seem translucent; all the coast is incredibly barren and desolate—no sign of habitation—but the light transforms it to indescribable loveliness." [22] As they approached Piraeus, he promised himself that he would never spend another winter in England. "I had rather live in the south on 2d. a day," he wrote to his mother; "here life is worth living. . . ." [23]

By the time he landed at Piraeus on November 19, Gissing had befriended a young Greek fellow passenger named Parigory, whose father met them at the dock and drove them to Athens in a carriage. He was surprised at the oriental atmosphere created by the bazaars and the dress of the common people. Numbers of soldiers appeared on the streets, reminding Gissing that even Greece labored under the militarism he heartily detested. The day after his arrival he went up to the "sacred soil" of the Acropolis, where he made drawings of the views. His diligent touring included a visit to the house where Schliemann, the archaeologist, had lived, examination of the local graveyards and marketing customs, and many walks in the dusty streets. He marveled at the dryness of the soil and the dustiness of the town. The rivers famous since antiquity were mere trickles a foot across. He found, however, that the barren and arid landscape could be beautifully colored by the sun, and that wonderful hues appeared on the hillsides at sunset. He visited the Acropolis repeatedly to see how it looked at different times of the day, once writing in his diary an extremely detailed description of the changes in the sky at twilight. At the site of the battle of Salamis he stood at the spot where Xerxes had watched the fighting, reconstructing it in his mind, and on the banks of the Ilissus he thought of Socrates and the discourse that was to become the *Phaedrus.*

Modern Athens, unlike Naples, seemed featureless to Gissing, and he wrote that it had no attraction for anyone not interested in its classical remains. Parigory reappeared to take Gissing out to dine and to witness a session of Parliament, but the two men were kept out by the police, whose rudeness annoyed Gissing. They did succeed, however, in attending a lecture on Greek literature at the University. Sophocles' *Philoctetes* was the subject, and, although Gissing understood only a little of the modern Greek that was spoken, he enjoyed the experience thoroughly, disapproving, however, of the way the professor treated the meter in his reading.

He left Athens on December 17 by train, having written to Shortridge in Massa Lubrense that he expected to be in Naples soon. Fever and a sore throat had been troubling him, but they seemed to disappear the moment he stepped on the train. The steamer passage from Patras to Brindisi was made in rough weather, so that his arrival in Naples was delayed until the twentieth. With another Greek acquaintance he had met on the steamer he stayed at Frau Häberlin's on the Vico Brancaccio for a few days, observing the lively local Christmas celebrations with their bells and fireworks. However, he was distressed to learn that street organs, whose music he loved, had been forbidden in Naples. On December 31 he went to spend a few days with Shortridge.

He found the strange household at Massa Lubrense in a chaotic state. Herbert Shortridge was now clearly dying of "consumption"; he despised the Italian relations he was living with and swore at Carmela's father, a paralytic who took his meals alone in a corner of the kitchen. The household was as squalid as ever, and the fastidious Gissing found dinner a slovenly and uncomfortable experience. Shortridge opened his heart to Gissing in a long talk. He was greatly disturbed at the loss of his son Jack, who had died not long ago, and resentful of his brother's churlish behavior. He told Gissing that when the boy was ill he had kept a knife under his pillow with which he threatened to kill "zio Herberto" when he grew up. Shortridge said that he hoped to take the whole family to Hartford, Connecticut, to begin a new life, but Gissing thought him too weak to do anything so energetic and felt that he was deceiving himself with idle dreams. Shortridge was practical in small matters, however, had once been a seaman, and was able to demonstrate the operation of the household's macaroni machine. Gissing also thought that some water colors that he brought out and displayed showed signs of talent.

Carmela confided in Gissing just as her husband had done, telling him in the Neapolitan dialect, which he had now learned to understand, that Shortridge often mistreated her. He was moved by her open confession that the poverty and ignorance in which she had grown up prevented her from pleasing her English husband, and he concluded that her complaints against Shortridge were justified.

After a week with this unhappy family, Gissing returned to Naples, where he reluctantly began preparations for leaving Italy. On January 12 Shortridge unexpectedly turned up to spend a week touring the city with him. There were rumors that influenza was on the rise in Naples, and a few days after Shortridge's departure on January 20 Gissing fell ill with a respiratory disorder. After a visit to a doctor he stayed indoors for a few days under the care of Frau Häberlin, but congestion of the right lung developed, and he had to take to his bed for a week, missing the boat he had intended to take back to England. It was the first serious touch of the illness that was eventually to kill him.

The Germans who were filling up the Casa di Luca enabled the convalescent Gissing to practice his German at meals, although after a time he found his new housemates far too noisy. Remembering the discontents of the London life to which he was about to return, he thought of Germany as a possible place of refuge, and wrote to Bertz that he planned to go there to live after completing his next book. On February 20 he was well enough to embark for home.

He was depressed to encounter the atmosphere of England aboard the ship. The wineless English meals and the company of English travelers were equally distressing. Englishmen, he wrote to Bertz, did not know how to travel. They refused to give up any of their usual habits, to cultivate friends in foreign countries, or to speak foreign languages, but spent all their time abroad with their own countrymen. He felt now that he had little in common with them, and that his real home was Naples. An incident that occurred aboard the ship occasioned some bitter reflections on Gissing's part about his place in society. The ship's parson had noticed Gissing's name on some of his belongings and learned from a clergyman traveling first class that he was a well-known author. It was symbolic of his whole life, thought Gissing, that his books were known to first-class passengers while he himself was condemned to associate with those in the second class.

Immediately after arriving in London on February 28, he wrote to Bentley to ask why no notices of *The Emancipated* had appeared. It was time for him to go to work, for he estimated that the seventy-seven pounds he had would last only until September. He saw Roberts the day after his arrival, and they went together to visit Hudson, renewing old times. Writing began on the thirteenth of March; at about the same time Gissing wrote to his brother that his subjects were likely to change, that he felt out of place and lonely in London, and that he planned to move to the Continent soon. "England is a failure with me. . . . I cannot get on with English society, the thing is proved." [24] His reading of the moment included two old favorites that were treatments of spiritual exile, *Niels Lyhne* and *Fathers and Sons*.

When *The Emancipated* appeared at the end of March, 1890, it evoked the usual conflicting opinions. His sister Ellen disapproved of it, suspecting that she had served as the original of Miriam Baske, but Roberts thought it was Gissing's best book. The *Spectator* fully appreciated the criticism of social institutions intended, but declared that it was necessary to distinguish between natural customs and mere conventions.

An April visit to Paris with both of his sisters was planned, and Gissing worked busily in the meantime. He had begun a story about Guernsey and Sark, but after three weeks he abandoned the thirty-one pages he had written to begin something different. The new project, begun on April 8, was called *A Man of Letters*, a title which clearly foreshadows his next novel, *New Grub Street*. However, there were several false starts before *New Grub Street* was actually written. After the trip to Paris between April 18 and April 30 his work went smoothly for a time, but two months later he began to lose confidence in what he was doing, and at the end of June he made a new beginning. A first volume was completed by September 15, but this achievement was followed by a collapse of his creative power. On October 1 he began again, this time having definitely decided that his book would bear the title *New Grub Street*.

While he was threshing about in this desperate way, important emotional changes were taking place in him. He had now lost the pioneering zeal of his youth and yearned for rest, comfort, and companionship. While engaged with the abortive attempts to begin *New Grub Street*, he wrote to Bertz that he wanted to live in the full sense of the word instead of spending all his time in the slavery of writing. On the other hand, his feeling of alienation made it impossible for him to find friends. He had not fulfilled his ambition of becoming so well known that he would be recognized as an author when he went into company. This made him bitter, and he remained aloof, increasing his unhappiness and isolation. He rejected two invitations from Edith Sichel, telling himself that he was finished with the kind of society she represented, and sold his dress suit, convinced that he would never dine "at a civilized table" again. He felt that he ought to follow Roberts' advice to move to Germany or another country on the Continent, where he might do what was impossible for him in England—marry. However, he did not leave England when his lease on 7K expired later in the year, because illness and difficulties delayed his writing.

Having given up hope of gaining the only place in enlightened social circles he would accept—that of a well-known author—Gissing seemed to set about deliberately destroying his social connections in order to follow a course of action that was clear in his mind by the middle of 1890. He entrusted to his diary the observation that he would not be able to do any good work until he was married. On the other hand, although he greatly admired refined and educated women of the type represented by his own heroines and Edith Sichel, he could not hope to marry one. He sent his full thoughts on this subject to Bertz in a letter of September 6, 1890. A poor man like himself, he said, could never marry an educated girl, for women preferred remaining single to marrying men who earned less than £400 a year. In complaining of his loneliness, he said that he must find "some decent work-girl" to live with as a substitute for marriage. He had reason to know that a relationship with a lower-class girl might involve him deeply. But he felt that he had no real chance of marrying a woman of a higher class.

The intention was followed by the deed. On October 25 he wrote to Bertz that he had found just such a "work-girl" as he had hoped for, and he expected her to come to live with him when he moved from 7K. Her name was Edith Underwood, and she was the daughter of a small shopkeeper in Camden Town. Although Roberts says that Gissing made her acquaintance, one day when he found the solitude of his room unendurable, by rushing out into the Marylebone Road and speaking to the first woman he met, a diary notation of September 24 suggests that he met her on that day at a café in Oxford Street. According to Roberts, she was common and unattractive, with no intellectual qualities, "just a female." Wells describes her as "a servant girl." Gissing was not in love with her, and he knew it, but he had reached so desperate a condition that he felt he could consider only his physical needs. Edith seemed to him to be quiet, flexible, and amenable to training. As future events showed, this was one of the greatest errors in the judgment of character ever made.

Gissing did not at first intend to marry her. They went on excursions together, and he came to her home once or twice until her father (who was, according to Roberts, a bootmaker) told him directly that he was an unwelcome visitor. Mr. Underwood seems to have made no objection, however, when Edith spent frequent evenings with Gissing at 7K. They passed their hours there chatting, and on one occasion Gissing read "The Pied Piper" aloud to her. It was apparently as a result of this friendship that *New Grub Street* prospered at last. Begun on the first of October, it was completed, with incredible speed, early in December. This meant that Gissing averaged some four thousand words a day, and the result was one of his best novels.

It is hard to understand why Edith Underwood should have had this effect on Gissing, and above all why, after his first bitter experience with marriage, he married her. There is no reason to doubt that, as he wrote to Bertz, their relations were Platonic, and Roberts explained, in his account of these incidents, that Gissing was not a passionate man. It was Roberts' opinion that Gissing was never really in love, and that his overtures to women, like those of many of his characters, were made in the name of an abstract ideal of "fulfillment." He wanted, as he said, to live. Gissing made use of his relationship with Edith, revealing a great deal about his feelings, in the short story, "A Lodger in Maze Pond," whose protagonist explains how, on the eve of inheriting a fortune, he has happened to commit himself to marry the servant in the lodging-house where he lives.

I am a fool about women. I don't know what it is—certainly not a sensual or passionate nature . . . there's that need in me—the incessant hunger for a woman's sympathy and affection. . . . Day after day we grew more familiar. . . . When she laid a meal for me, we talked. . . . I made a friend of the girl. . . . We were alone in the house one evening. . . . I was lonely and dispirited—wanted to talk—to talk about myself to some one who would give a kind ear. So I went down, and made some excuse for beginning a conversation in the parlor. . . . I didn't persuade myself that I cared for Emma, even then. Her vulgarisms of speech and feeling jarred upon me. But she was feminine; she spoke and looked gently, with sympathy. I enjoyed that evening—and you must bear in mind what I have told you before, that I stand in awe of refined women. . . . Perhaps I have come to regard myself as doomed to live on a lower level. I find it impossible to imagine myself offering marriage—making love—to a girl such as those I meet in the big houses.[25]

All the evidence indicates that Gissing himself was speaking through these words, trying to explain his inexplicable relations with Edith.

Perhaps he contemplated marriage because he was resigned to the fact that the company and approval of a woman were necessary to his creative powers. For a second time, Roberts was shocked to learn of his marriage plans, and for a second time tried to dissuade him. "His mind recognized its truth," said Roberts of the argument he had used, "but his body meant to have its way." [26] In desperation, Roberts tried to save him from the fate he had chosen by a fantastic expedient. He had two unmarried female cousins, who had met and admired Gissing when he was a boy of seventeen, and who knew of his career as a writer. They were gentlewomen of sufficient refinement and education, and Roberts now went to see them, told them of Gissing's misfortunes and hard life, and after a long and tactful introduction, came to the point: he suggested that one of them consider marrying Gissing. After recovering from their surprise, the two ladies agreed to meet him, but when Roberts went to lay his plan before Gissing, he found that Gissing had already asked Edith to marry him, and, much to Roberts' disgust, he refused to retract his proposal.

Roberts thought that Gissing avoided serious attachments to women because he was afraid of having to confess his crime to a woman who loved him, just as he avoided society because he feared that someone he should meet might know of it. A more subtle cause for his conduct is suggested by the fact that *New Grub Street*, which was in progress exactly at this time, contains a number of vignettes about intelligent men victimized by ill-tempered, overbearing, and garrulous wives, so lively and realistic that Roberts wondered, when he read them, how Gissing could have gone ahead with his marriage when he had such a clear knowledge of its probable consequences. It is difficult to escape the obvious conclusion that he married Edith in spite of his foreknowledge because a part of him wanted to suffer those consequences. Apparently, the marriage was another of those acts of self-mortification that Gissing committed from time to time with the subconscious motive of putting himself at a disadvantage.

His plan of life now included leaving London, and he chose Exeter for his new home because of its cathedral, country views, and access to the seacoast. When he learned, on January 7, 1891, after a suspenseful interval, that Smith, Elder were willing to pay £150 for *New Grub Street*, he moved to temporary quarters at 24 Prospect Park in Exeter. The marriage date had been fixed as January 17, but Edith asked for a postponement and continued to hesitate until Gissing wrote to insist that the marriage take place on February 25. On that date he returned to London, went through the ceremony at St. Pancras Registry Office, and brought Edith back to Exeter. In a letter to Mrs. Harrison written two months later, Gissing explained his rejection of an invitation by saying that he had been compelled to marry in order to carry on his work, that he had chosen a woman of "the artisan class" because his income would never be higher than an artisan's, and that he intended to sever all relations with educated people. He thus revealed that his marriage was, at least in part, a foolish gesture of renunciation inspired by his old self-pity and resentment.

VI

THE PROFESSION OF LETTERS

NEW GRUB STREET is an exceptional novel for many reasons. One critic, Q. D. Leavis, has called it Gissing's only great novel; it is certainly one of the most candidly auto-biographical works of fiction ever written; and it has an excellent claim to being the most complete and honest treatment of the writer's life in English fiction. While a natural self-absorption has often led novelists to introduce writers into their work, surprisingly few of the many novels and stories about writers deal directly with the major facts of their occupation: the task of creation, the hazards and profits of publishing, the atmosphere of recommendations and reviews a book breathes, relations among writers and their associates, and the peculiar economic position of the professional writer. *New Grub Street* is probably the only novel wholly dedicated to the theme of authorship. It is a unique exploration of the writer's problem of survival in a commercial age, of the social and professional background that bears upon his work, and of the relations between his activity as an artist and his personal and family life.

The novel was written at a time when the vigorous competition characteristic of the economic system and the methods of the lending libraries, led by Mudie's firm, were creating difficulties for all but the most successful novelists. Lending libraries were already on the scene when Charles Edward Mudie began his bookselling business in 1840, but Mudie bested his rivals by cleverly adapting his stock to middle-class tastes. He had 25,000 subscribers in 1852,

154

and, since he ordered new novels by the hundreds, became an important power in the publishing world. A novel could hardly hope to succeed if it was not suited to the tastes of Mr. Mudie's clientele; in fact, that was exactly what Smith, Elder gave as their reason for rejecting Gissing's *Mrs. Grundy's Enemies* as late as 1882. These tastes were extremely prudish, for Mudie thought of his typical reader as the unmarried daughter of a refined middle-class family. Anything that might be considered "improper" for an adolescent girl was ruled out, and his library was influential enough to enforce this severe limit on the subjects that could be treated in novels for many years.

There were at least two other important effects of the dominance of the lending library system. It kept the three-volume novel alive until the nineties, long after it might otherwise have succumbed to competition; and, in spite of the fact that it promoted the sales of novels in general by making them available to a larger public, it limited the circulation of individual novels and the amount author and publisher could expect to earn from a single work.

An account of the novel-publishing scene in a *Fortnightly Review* article by Alexander Innes Shand in 1886 reported that the lending system had definitely replaced the custom of book buying, and that the old motive of display no longer led people to buy books. Novels were simply too expensive to buy outright. An established author might expect the lending libraries to take 600 copies of his novel, but there would be very little additional demand. Shand compared this with the sales of popular novels and shilling serials earlier in the century, and drew the obvious dismal conclusions about the author's earnings.

The sharp practices of publishers joined with naturally disadvantageous publishing conditions to keep all but the most successful Victorian novelists poor. If an author published on a half-profits or royalty agreement, he had no way of knowing whether the figures of sales and costs presented by the publisher were accurate. When Gissing received an account from Remington showing that his share of the profits of *Workers in the Dawn* was sixteen shillings, he had no way of relieving his grave (and entirely justified) doubts about the publisher's honesty. In agreeing to pay for the cost of his novel, he had fallen into a trap often laid for fledgling authors. His payment eliminated the element of risk to the publisher and was probably based on an inflated estimate of the costs.

He was not alone in falling victim to practices of this kind. Samuel Squire Sprigge, whose *Methods of Publishing* (1891) was designed to warn authors against such dangers, estimated that three-fourths of *all* novels were published under terms requiring a payment from the author; this generally meant that all profits went to the publisher, for the author seldom succeeded in securing a percentage high enough to repay his investment, while the publisher, having ventured nothing, could hardly fail to gain. Arnold Bennet, in his amusing account of the acceptance of his first novel in *The Truth About an Author* tells how the royalty arrangement to which he agreed ultimately gained him a single pound more than he had paid for having his manuscript typed, but he comments that he does not regret this, for many a first novel has cost its author a hundred pounds.

Many such cases were revealed by the Society of Authors, which was founded in 1883 under the leadership of Walter Besant for the purpose of correcting publishing abuses. Besant, after learning what the finances of publishing were by publishing a novel himself, urged authors to insist that the figures of both sides in a royalty agreement be kept open and that no secret profits be allowed. Of the kinds of agreements open to authors, he most strongly condemned outright sale, the method usually adopted by Gissing, for this meant that the author relinquished his copyright to the publisher together with any claim to the profits his novel might make in the future. If the novel went into a second edition, as most of Gissing's did, all the profits belonged to the publisher. However, since the publisher was not compelled to open his books to the author, and since the costs of publication were difficult to learn, a royalty or half-profits agreement enabled the publisher to cheat the author by rendering him a false account. Under these circumstances, it usually seemed advisable to take a modest but sure price for the book in ready cash instead of venturing a double gamble on the book's success and the publisher's honesty.

As a professional writer of only moderate popularity, Gissing learned what conditions like these meant to a novelist who tried to live by his pen. Scott at the height of his fame could expect to make £6,000 from a single novel and was said to earn £15,000 a year.

Even in Gissing's day such a huge success as *David Grieve,* by Mrs. Humphry Ward, was rumored to have earned its author £20,000. Far more usual, however, were the figures given by Anthony Trollope as the earnings of his earlier novels. *Barchester Towers* was published at half-profits with £100 in advance. Trollope estimated that together with *The Warden* it brought him a total of £727 over the years. He sold *The Three Clerks* to Bentley for £250 and was well content to get £400 from Chapman and Hall for each of his next two novels. The sale of *New Grub Street* illustrated one of the problems it described, for it brought Gissing only £150, although he was an established novelist. In explaining this to Algernon, Gissing wrote that he and Roberts were surprised to find, on the basis of calculations they had once made, that publishers earned very modest profits from three-volume novels that had as small a sale as his. Since even Hardy earned little from his books, Gissing wrote that he would have to be content with making just enough to support himself.

On at least two occasions Gissing drew up accounts giving itemized records of the income he earned from literature, and these, together with stray comments in his diary and correspondence, give an indication of the pressures under which he wrote. He could lead his quiet life, taking many of his meals at home and getting his entertainment from books and friends without much expenditure, on a budget of a little over ten pounds a month. Only with *The Nether World* did he begin to earn enough by writing to support himself on this modest scale. *Workers in the Dawn* brought him £2 (though this leaves his own investment of £125 in it out of account); he published nothing after that until 1884, when *The Unclassed* brought £30. In 1886 *Demos* earned £100; according to the "Account Book" kept by Gissing, *Isabel Clarendon* earned nothing, although he once recorded that Chapman and Hall had paid £15 for it. *Thyrza* was sold for £50, and the sale of the copyright brought an additional £10. In 1888 *A Life's Morning* earned £50 as a three-volume novel and an additional £50 as a serial in the *Cornhill.* Beginning in 1889 with *The Nether World* and continuing for three years Gissing published a novel a year, earning £150 for each, or about £30 more than his economical way of life demanded.

Even at best, payment like this meant constant exertion, and for

Gissing, with his difficulties of health and temperament, things were seldom at their best. In his *Fortnightly* article, Alexander Innes Shand observed that although the novelist is privileged in many ways, for he works his own hours and makes no investment of capital, he cannot be sure of writing steadily, must cultivate a public, manifest some versatility, and be able to withstand the pressure of household costs that mount steadily while his pen races frantically over the paper toward the publisher's check. Gissing was peculiarly unable to deal with these hazards; he had almost no versatility; his public was small, and he felt that he could not afford to write more than one novel a year. The fear of poverty and the dwindling of his resources whenever he stopped to plan or revise paralyzed his creative powers. Yet up to the time of *New Grub Street* he never succeeded in escaping from this position. Whenever he sat down to write, he knew that he must finish within a limited time. As chapter after chapter was written and canceled, and one beginning after another was made, he imagined destitution approaching, until the bells of the Marylebone Workhouse across the way from Cornwall Mansions seemed, as he described them in *New Grub Street,* to be calling to him.

New Grub Street is partly a condemnation of the commercialization of literature, partly a moving act of self-revelation. Characters modeled on himself in Gissing's earlier books had been self-justifying idealizations; but he was now ready to reach for a new level of psychological authenticity by using such a figure as a vehicle for divulging the most painful private truths. As a result, the character and career of Edwin Reardon, *New Grub Street*'s protagonist, are copied from Gissing's own with little disguise and with no attempt at extenuation. He is like many of Gissing's weak and morbid heroes, and differs from them only in resembling Gissing more. A provincial boy with a good classical education, he uses his small patrimony to come to London in order to make a career as a writer. After some time divided between the loneliness of squalid lodgings and the reading room of the British Museum, he takes a position as a clerk at a hospital, just as Gissing had once done. On the advice of a successful novelist who tells him that he will be unable to sell the learned essays he writes, he tries fiction, and, mistaking the ease with which he disposes of his first novels for genuine success, leaves his clerkship and turns to novel writing in earnest. After selling a book for a hundred pounds, he visits Europe, and then, as the external events of the novel begin to take a course different from those of Gissing's life, meets and marries Amy Yule, a refined middle-class girl who expects him to become wealthy and famous. He has nightmares about being unable to sell his books and sinking into poverty again, and confesses this lack of confidence to Amy, but they are married nevertheless and go to live in a flat much like 7K.

Reardon eventually finds that he cannot meet his financial needs by writing. He racks his brain for new plots and situations, feels one project after another crumble in his fingers, and struggles against a growing lack of confidence. When we first meet Reardon he has been married for some time, has a child, and is sitting over a blank sheet of paper, trying desperately to continue the novel he has just started. He has been attempting for months to begin a book but has destroyed everything he has written, and he tells his wife that he feels he will never be able to write again. All the difficulties and contradictions of the professional novelist's predicament emerge as Amy and Reardon discuss their problems. He envies the clerk who does work assigned to him and earns his regular wages from day to day regardless of his moods. "What an insane thing it is," he says, "to make literature one's only means of support! When the most trivial accident may at any time prove fatal to one's power of work for weeks or months. No, that is the unpardonable sin! To make a trade of an art!" [1] His wife disagrees with him, urging him to complete his novel in slapdash fashion and sell it quickly. "Art," she tells him, "must be practiced as a trade, at all events in our time. This is the age of trade." [2] Reardon recognizes the truth of this, but is unable to be "practical." He cannot continue with his usual kind of work, he tells a friend, because his trip to the Continent has disrupted his intellectual development, and his growing fear of poverty has kept him from recovering himself.

However, he does manage to go on in a perfectly mechanical way, until he is brought to a stop.

A familiar symptom of the malady which falls upon outwearied imagination. There were floating in his mind five or six possible subjects for a book, all dating back to the time when he first began novel-writing, when ideas came freshly to him. If he grasped desperately at one of these, and did his best to develop it for a day or two he could almost content himself; characters, situations, lines of motive, were laboriously schemed, and he felt ready to begin writing. But scarcely had he done a chapter or two when all the structure fell into flatness. He had made a mistake. Not this story, but that other one, was what he should have taken . . . it invited him, tempted him to throw aside what he had already written. Good; now he was in more hopeful train. But a few days, and the experience repeated itself. No, not this story, but that third one, of which he had not thought for a long time. . . .

For months he had been living in this way; endless circling, perpetual beginning, followed by frustration. A sign of exhaustion, it of course made exhaustion more complete. . . . Little phrases which indicated dolorously the subject of his preoccupation often escaped him in the street. . . . It had happened that he caught the eye of someone passing fixed in surprise upon him; so young a man to be talking to himself in evident distress! [3]

Although his writing day is rigidly organized to allow ten hours of working time, Reardon often makes pathetically slow progress.

Sometimes the three hours' labour of a morning resulted in half a dozen lines, corrected into illegibility. His brain would not work; he could not re-call the simplest synonyms; intolerable faults of composition drove him mad. He would write a sentence beginning thus: "She took a book with a look of ———;" or thus: "A revision of this decision would have made him an object of derision." . . . He had an appreciation of shapely prose which made him scorn himself for the kind of stuff he was now turning out. "I can't help it; it must go; the time is passing." [4]

When he glances at some lines of the *Odyssey*, they only serve to remind him of the baseness of his own work. "Yes, yes; *that* was not written at so many pages a day. . . . How it freshened the soul! How the eyes grew dim with a rare joy in the sounding of these nobly sweet hexameters!" [5]

The mention of reviews is enough to throw Reardon, who despises them, off his stride for days, so that he can neither write nor rest, but sits at his desk absorbed in an exhausting inner struggle. When the book is finished at last he is too worn out to think of a title, and calls it by the name of its chief character. Already in debt by the time the novel is accepted, he now finds that he has reached the end of his powers. Completely demoralized, he continues to write for the sake of appearance, and when his new work is rejected, he gives up authorship, moves to a poor neighborhood and takes an-other humble position as a hospital clerk.

Amy refuses to follow him into poverty, and his failure as a writer is quickly followed by their separation and the dissolution of their home. While she takes their child to her mother's comfortable house, Reardon moves to a garret where he dreams of his trip to Europe, discusses Greek meters with an old crony, and grows withdrawn and eccentric. None of the glamor of art surrounds his poverty. Having lost his ability to write he is no longer a poor artist, but simply a poor man. Still jealous of his independence, he refuses to be reconciled with Amy after she has inherited a fortune and offers to come back to him. His friend Biffen, however, points out that he has ruined his life and his wife's in the name of "an obstinate idealism." "The art of living," says Biffen, "is the art of compromise." Reardon learns this lesson too late, for after Biffen has sent him back to his wife with the words, "Go, and be happy!" and the illness of their child has brought them together, his own illness cheats him of the promised felicity and he sinks into death through delirious nightmares of frustration. The title of the death chapter is "Reardon Becomes Practical."

Around this tragic central figure Gissing ranged a large gallery of smooth opportunists, picturesque pedants, ineffectual bookworms, and fierce quill-drivers, giving a rich panoramic picture of their world. It is a world blighted by the same forces that dehumanize the society of which it is a part: commercialism, competition, and greed. The educational reforms that had increased literacy without cultivating a taste for learning had created a mass market for amusing and superficial reading matter, especially in periodical form. This sort of literature became a valuable commodity, particularly when used in conjunction with illustrations, and numerous magazines like *The Sketch* and *Tit-Bits* depended on it. Thus the customs, standards, and practices of mass production were introduced into literature. Where it is important to command a mass market of "quarter-educated" readers, originality, individuality, or profundity are unwelcome. A flair for notoriety is the best gift for succeeding in this environment. One must apply the principles of trade to writing, try to "hit" the taste of a wide public, make friends among editors and reviewers, and curry favor where it will do the most good. It was a dangerous atmosphere that required astute maneuvering, for irrational animosities filled the air, and the fate of a book or an editorship could be determined by the operation of far-flung alliances.

The conqueror of this literary battlefield is Jasper Milvain, an acquaintance of Reardon's who begins his career as a humble and diligent journalist, confident that a creditable apprenticeship in writing articles (he is not imaginative enough for fiction) will lead him to wealth. The doctrine that literature is a trade is his, and he acts upon it unfailingly. He has no objection to the work of Dante or Shakespeare, but he feels that he is engaged in the entirely different activity of producing material that will attract readers and cause some stir, though it may be of only ephemeral interest. Milvain's success grows as Reardon's ineffectual efforts drag him to disaster, until at the end, after Reardon's death, Milvain achieves wealth by winning an editorship and marrying Reardon's widow.

A contrast to the good-natured optimist, Milvain, is the sour and defeated Alfred Yule, "a battered man of letters," whose lifetime spent in doing odd jobs of writing has taught him nothing so well as envy and hate. Ill-tempered, pedantic, hypercritical, he lives through the arid medium of print. He knows how to punish an enemy through a covert thrust in an article, and how to repay a flattering allusion in a footnote with a pleasant review. Nothing gives him so much pleasure as the misfortune of a rival whose journal has published contradictory reviews of the same book. His friends are writers, his conversation is the gossip of the editorial back stairs, his natural habitat is the reading room of the British Museum. Quaint, bookish mannerisms and turns of speech give this character a convincing individuality. Graspingly ambitious, he tries to induce his daughter to invest some money she has inherited in a journal which he will edit, but he fails in this as in all else, and ends in pathetic blindness.

Another and younger failure is Whelpdale. After suffering through some adventures in America patterned after Gissing's own, he returns to England, and, finding that he cannot sell any of his work, conceives the idea of giving instruction in fiction writing to neophytes. His plans include writing about the middle class and dealing with such topics as boating and riding. Later he writes for a periodical named *Chat*; he plans to improve it by changing its name to *Chit-Chat* and filling it with a potpourri of small items that can be read without effort by the semiliterate products of the democratic educational system. "Everything must be very short," he says, "two inches at the utmost; their attention can't sustain itself beyond two inches. Even chat is too solid for them; they want chit-chat." [6]

Reardon's friend Biffen is a penniless scholar who shares his enthusiasm for Greek poetry and is capable of making fine metrical distinctions, but can do nothing more effective toward earning a living than occasional tutoring. He lives in picturesque squalor, wearing his overcoat indoors to disguise the fact that he has no coat over his shirt sleeves, and eating his bread-and-dripping with a knife and fork to make it seem more filling. He is at work on a new kind of novel, a photographically faithful account of the daily life of a grocer.

What I really aim at is an absolute realism in the sphere of the ignobly decent. The field, as I understand it, is a new one; I don't know any writer who has treated ordinary vulgar life with fidelity and seriousness. . . . I want to deal with the essentially unheroic, with the day-to-day life of that vast majority of people who are at the mercy of paltry circumstance. . . . The result will be something unutterably tedious. Precisely. That is the stamp of the ignobly decent life. If it were anything *but* tedious it would be untrue.[7]

Biffen carries out this project with the devotion of a Flaubert, spending infinite time, patience, and discrimination on the prose style of his drab tale. The masterpiece of tedium is nearly lost when his lodginghouse burns down, but he risks his life to save the manuscript from the flames, thus exhibiting in a dramatic action the courage that enabled him to continue his work through the hardships of his life. *Mr. Bailey, Grocer* actually achieves publication, and Biffen is paid fifteen pounds for it; he does not mind the hostility of the reviewers or the indifference of the public, for he is satisfied with it. But his heroism as an artist and a man turns out to be futile; he cannot escape the habit of isolation developed through years of work, and suffers from being deprived of a woman's love, particularly that of Reardon's widow. Ultimately, he lapses into a state of lonely depression which ends in suicide. His perfectionism asserts itself for the last time as he straightens a book on its shelf and the blotting pad on his desk before going out to poison himself.

The background of the novel swarms with minor literary artisans. There are Milvain's sisters, who find that they can make a living by writing children's books, Quarmby and Hinks, superannuated hacks who haunt the British Museum reading room like shabby ghosts, and Marian Yule, who helps her father as a kind of literary slave, doing research for his articles, copying them when they are completed, and sometimes even writing them herself.

In *New Grub Street* Gissing gives a surprisingly accurate report of the social transition described by Mr. David Riesman in *The Lonely Crowd*. It was natural that he should first sense the emergence of "other-direction" in his own profession. Milvain, Whelpdale, and the crowd of journalists they move with expect to succeed by pleasing the public; they have no abstract convictions about their work, except that it must sell and win approval. They consider it essential that a writer be able to change with the winds of trade and be ready for any sort of an assignment; when Whelpdale says that he has been hired to write a column for a journal, Milvain asks, "Cosmetics? Fashions? Cookery?" and Whelpdale regrets that he is not so versatile. They are less concerned with the instrinsic qualities of their work than with people's opinion of it, and most of their conversations are devoted to gauging the climate of opinion in editorial quarters.

Reardon, on the other hand, is an example of Mr. Riesman's "inner-directed" type, who belongs to an earlier stage of social organization. He is not entirely indifferent to general opinion, but he gives precedence to his own convictions. The easy versatility of men like Milvain seems to him to be simple insincerity. He is attached to one style of writing and one way of conducting himself, and cannot adjust, as Milvain would, to changing conditions. Popularity, Milvain's only motive for writing, means nothing to him, and when he cannot satisfy his own standards he feels no desire to write. In thinking over the actions that have driven Amy from his side, he at first wonders what her relations will say about him, but he then consults moral standards, which he considers absolute, by framing such questions as, "Had he done well? Had he done wisely?" Reardon is caught in a kind of landslide of social standards, for, while he embraces an old moral code in considering it a virtue to be true to his own modest talents, the new concept of success in writing calls for conformity, popularity, and response to public demand.

New Grub Street was a success built with the materials of failure. Gissing's early novels are marred by the tendency toward self-justification apparent in the portrayals of Arthur Golding and Osmond Waymark, and by a resentment that sometimes rendered his depiction of social evils more appropriate to melodrama than to critical realism. Because he had suffered himself, he considered suffering a requirement for merit; according to Roberts, his criticism of any writer who might be mentioned was, "He never starved." He contemplated failure with perverse pleasure because it proved "the native malignity of matter," the injustice of the scheme of things. But after twelve years of writing novels without either gaining popularity or satisfying his own aspirations, he was ready to stake the painful truth of his private deficiencies on an attempt to achieve an ultimate realism. As a result, Reardon is portrayed in *New Grub Street* not as a noble heretic but as a hesitant weakling who is bewildered by the problems of his profession; at the same time the evils of the system that destroys him are incisively analyzed. If *New Grub Street* is more authentic, more cogent, and clearer in construction than Gissing's earlier novels, it is because he had at last learned, through a discipline of self-abnegation, to balance his passionate indignation with the objectivity necessary for genuine realism.

VII

A VICTORIAN DILEMMA IN FICTION

I

WHEN *New Grub Street* was published early in April, 1891, Smith, Elder made the mistake of sending Gissing the reviews, and, although he quickly wrote to stop "this horror," he could not help learning, after about a month, that the book had been well received. The reviews warned readers that it was a depressing novel, but its brave realism was widely recognized and understood. A notice in the *Saturday Review*, which Gissing sent to Bertz, said:

The book is almost terrible in its realism, and gives a picture cruelly precise in every detail, of this commercial age. The degradation of art by the very necessity of its "paying its way" is put forward with merciless plainness. The bitter uselessness of attempting a literary career unless you are prepared to consult the market, and supply only that for which there is a demand, forms a sort of text for the book. Art for art's sake is foredoomed to financial failure.[1]

An especially authoritative accolade, possibly written by Walter Besant, appeared in the June number of *The Author*, the publication of the Society of Authors. "Mr. George Gissing," said the unsigned notice, "ought to be publicly thanked for introducing the world to a form of literary life which has long been known to all who have penetrated into the by-ways and slums of this many-sided calling." Reardon, Milvain, and Yule are said to be true to life, though Gissing has somewhat dramatized the fate of the first two. "I know them all personally," said the reviewer of the novel's characters, ". . . and the fidelity of Mr. Gissing's portraits makes me shudder." [2] Andrew Lang, in the next number of *The Author*, objected to Gissing's pessimism, saying that he knew poor writers who were jolly and hopeful and that there was, after all, a bright side to the picture. Two letters of rejoinder followed Lang's article. One supported Gissing, citing the special case of the free-lance journalist, who led an especially hard life, and the other replied to Lang's remark that the literary feuds in which Yule engaged were harmless. "Slating," or attacking a book in a deliberately critical review was done for pay, said this correspondent, and could be fatal to a book or an author's career.

There were reactions to the novel in all the papers, and the expression "New Grub Street" appeared in the press. Even among his friends and relations Gissing found an unusual unanimity of opinion about the book. His mother, his sister Ellen, Roberts, and his pupil, Walter Grahame, all wrote to say they liked it. Bertz praised it, but objected to the materialism of the characters. Admitting the justice of this criticism, Gissing attributed the fault to his strong conviction that poverty stifled creative powers. The success of *New Grub Street* was capped by a second printing of the three-volume edition after the first month of publication. "The first time," observed Gissing, "I have ever achieved this." [3] Having sold the copyright, he could not hope to profit from the new edition, but he expected that the good sale of *New Grub Street* would be helpful in the future.

A new novel, called "Raymond Peak" or "Godwin Peak" up to the time it was published as *Born in Exile*, had been begun about a week after his marriage and was finished in six months without much difficulty. It was, he wrote to Bertz, "a study of a savagely aristocratic temperament." [4] While working on it he occupied his leisure by botanizing in the countryside, exploring the vicinity of Exeter, and reading Chaucer, Tolstoy, and Hardy's *Far from the Madding Crowd*. He was secure from the emotional disturbances London might have stirred in him, but his new responsibilities as a family man made him feel keenly the limits of his poverty. He remarked in his diary the irony exploited in *New Grub Street*: that it was possible to be a famous author and starve. In spite of the success of *New Grub Street*, he reflected, he still had to work hard to support himself and could not afford to buy books or subscribe to a library; he wrote, "Who of the public would believe that I am still in such poverty?" [5] It was a characteristic exaggeration; actually, he subscribed to the Exeter Literary Society a few days later.

He tried to remedy his poverty by asking Smith, Elder for £250, a substantial increase over his usual price, when he sent them the new novel on July 20, 1891, but "Godwin Peak" proved very difficult to dispose of. This was partly a result of the circumstance that James Payn of Smith, Elder was about to go on a holiday when the manuscript came, and he wrote to Gissing that its consideration would be delayed for a month. He told Gissing in advance that his firm would not give £250 for the novel because *New Grub Street* had been a failure, a reason which must have surprised and grieved Gissing. Instead of rebelling, however, he meekly wrote to say he would take £150 if that were paid immediately. But Payn abruptly sent the manuscript back unread, making use of the opportunity to tell Gissing that his books would not sell until they became more cheerful.

Gissing, who must have been much depressed at this summary treatment of a novel which deeply involved his feelings, met the situation by sending his manuscript to a literary agent, A. P. Watt. Tired of being victimized by "the age of trade," he at last consented to try some of its methods. Toward the end of August, Watt reported that he had received an offer of £120 from Chatto and Windus, but since this fell short of the £200 Gissing had asked him to aim for, the book was sent on to another publisher. In the next few months both Longmans and Bentley rejected it, and Gissing, who now regretted having engaged Watt, wrote to insist that the book had to be placed before the end of the year.

In explaining his difficulties with "Godwin Peak" to Bertz, Gissing said that he thought it was a "rather strong" novel, but that its story of an atheist who tries to create the impression that he is a pious man by studying for orders probably discouraged the publishers. Toward the end of December the novel was at last accepted by the firm of Adam and Charles Black, but on less favorable terms than Gissing had hoped for. The price of £150 after Watt's 10-per-cent commission had been deducted came to hardly more than the original offer of Chatto and Windus. Although the book was not to be published until October, 1892, according to the original understanding, it appeared at the beginning of May. Before that time Gissing spent a month revising it, gave it its final title of *Born in Exile*, and, noting from the proofs that the last volume was too short, wrote in two days a new chapter to be inserted before the last.

Born in Exile, like *New Grub Street*, is a criticism of society in the form of a confession, but the confession goes deeper, and the criticism is more damning. It is the story of a clever young man of lower-class origin and scientific interests who falls in love with a well-to-do young woman, pretends to be a conventional Christian, and even makes a show of preparing himself to become a minister in order to win her family's acceptance. Gissing's knowledge of the thoughts of a philosophic and fundamentally moral man engaged in a deliberate deception must have been drawn from his own experiences at the time of the Owens College episode. Godwin Peak, his hero, is just such a student as Gissing was, industrious, ambitious, and eager for prizes, who is forced to leave college prematurely as Gissing did, though for a different reason. His pride will not let him remain after his Cockney uncle discloses a plan to open a restaurant opposite the college. Sternly honest, Peak suffers feelings of intense guilt when a well-meaning printer shows him an advance copy of an examination. He wants desperately to be a gentleman, like one of his schoolmates whom he sees occupying a box in a theater where he sits in the pit. Because he shares the tastes and interests of the rich, and has nothing in common with his own impoverished family, Peak feels that he is in the wrong social class, and that he has been "born in exile."

He grows up to be a well-dressed, well-mannered intellectual of scientific leanings who believes that "truth is indeterminable" and certainty is impossible. It is his aim "to get through life with as much satisfaction and as little pain as possible," and he believes that moral and intellectual principles are encumbrances to a man who seeks happiness. His motto is *Foris ut moris; intus ut libet.* When a friend suggests that the right thing to do is to act upon conviction, he asks: What if one has no convictions? His own are few, but powerful. He hates religion and the poor, especially the vulgarians of the London slums. And he is certain that he can achieve happiness by marrying a refined and educated woman of the class he admires.

When he meets such a woman in Sidwell Warricombe, however, he finds that her family are faithful churchgoers and that her father, though a devoted geologist, is unintelligent enough to believe that scientific and religious beliefs can be reconciled with each other. In order to win the approval of his new friends, Peak pretends that he is outgrowing his youthful skepticism. He has heard that well-bred women will marry clergymen, no matter how poor, and he returns to his college studies in order to qualify himself for the Church. He impresses the family by commenting brilliantly on a sermon, discusses religious matters with Sidwell's brother, and offers to translate a German theological work for her father. He tells himself that he is no more hypocritical than society, which pays homage to a false religious idealism while pursuing grossly materialistic ends, but he cannot suppress the tormenting self-accusations that rise within him. When Sidwell's brother discovers that he is the author of an atheistic article, Peak's fraud is revealed, and he flees to Germany, where, not long afterward, he dies.

A suggestion that all this takes place within a framework of determinism occurs when Peak acknowledges, before he has carried his deception very far, that forces beyond his control are motivating him. After saying that he intends to enter the Church, he has the feeling that the remark was involuntary, the result of some subconscious influence. Further, he comes to believe that his scheme paradoxically alienates him from the class he is trying to enter, for it is a proof of his lower-class inheritance, an act of dishonesty attributable to the "ancestral vice" of his "base-born predecessors." Sidwell, on the other hand, blames the prevailing hypocrisy of society for Peak's crime, thus explaining it by environment rather than heredity.

" 'Born in Exile,' " Gissing once wrote to Bertz, "was a book I *had* to write." [6] In essence, the novel dramatizes the moral conflict of the Owens College episode, making use of the deeper insight into his motives which Gissing had by now gained. In addition, it is the fruit of a realization, based on his reading of a number of novels about young men inspired by scientific progress to reject traditional beliefs and take morality into their own hands, that his experience was not isolated, but reflected a general crisis of the European spirit.

II

The special attraction of the philosophy of science, as it was presented in such works as Comte's *Philosophie Positive* and Ludwig Büchner's *Kraft und Stoff*, was the hope it offered that the empiric methods that had dealt so successfully with physical facts could be extended to human phenomena, so that they too could be organized under practical and incontrovertible principles. As G. H. Lewes put it: "If the Positive Philosophy be anything, it is a doctrine capable of embracing all that can regulate Humanity. . . ." [7] "Un même déterminisme," asserted Zola, "doit régir le pierre des chemins et le cerveau de l'homme." [8]

A condition of the success of science in government, morals, and ethics was the destruction of theological and metaphysical ideas that still dominated man's regulation of his own life, although they had long surrendered their hold on the physical sciences. Comte held that the human faculties were incapable of solving the problems of essences, first causes, and other mysteries surrounding the conception of God. Man must therefore resign himself to ignorance about these questions and devote his talents to gathering practical knowledge that can be used in promoting his well-being. If there were no divinity, or if He were indifferent to and out of touch with humanity, it followed that man became the arbiter of his own spiritual destiny. If there were no afterlife and no system of rewards and punishments to face after death, man, as the supreme product of evolution and the only possessor of rational intelligence, was free to plan his actions according to his own understanding. Thus, self-realization and service to humanity became the basis of morality. These convictions, the philosophical foundation of English agnosticism and Russian nihilism as well as French Positivism, were shared, for the most part, by Gissing himself. Late in life he wrote to Bertz, with unusual emphasis: "Yes, yes, yes: *Entwicklungsfreiheit!* Whether we like it or not that is the principle of life in this world, and, with you, I cannot help thinking that on the whole it promises for *some day* a true ethical culture." [9]

Gissing could not agree, however, with those of his fellow agnostics who deified humanity. As his novels show, he knew that character is easily corrupted by poverty, jealousy, or power, and even his best men manifest a diffidence and hesitation that are far from godlike. While sharing with other agnostics their respect for human nature, Gissing could not worship it as a substitute for religion.

Among the novels that treated the moral problem taken up in *Born in Exile,* two in particular were pre-eminent in their influence on Gissing: Turgenev's *Fathers and Sons* (1862) and *Niels Lyhne* (1880), by the Danish novelist Jens Peter Jacobsen. Turgenev's novel had an almost hypnotic influence on Gissing, for he reported that he had read it "five or six times." Its hero is a brilliant young scientist who has adopted rationalist ideas and finds any sort of faith impossible. He is scornful of the feelings that bind his parents to each other and to their land, of the "animal passion" of love, and of all the institutions of his country supported by authority or religious belief. He is interested only in the kind of certainty he finds in the dissection of frogs and beetles. "There are no general principles . . ." declares Bazarov. "There are feelings. Everything depends on them." [10] But as he undergoes emotional conflicts for which he cannot account on rational grounds, and which make him hate himself, he grows to envy the happy innocence of his parents. He cannot hold convictions or organize his experience, and, when he contemplates the universe, feels himself to be naked in the withering presence of the infinite and inexplicable.

The tiny space I occupy is so infinitely small in comparison with the rest of space, in which I am not, and which has nothing to do with me; and the period of time in which it is my lot to live is so petty besides the eternity in which I have not been, and shall not be. . . . And in this atom, this mathematical point, the blood is circulating, the brain is working and wanting something. . . . Isn't it loathsome? Isn't it petty? [11]

Ultimately, Bazarov escapes his despised identity to find peace in death, which, like every other event in his chaotic world, occurs by chance.

The hero of Jacobsen's novel is a dreamy and imaginative man whose religious faith has been shattered by a childhood experience. The vague poetic narrative describes a number of emotional trials that make Niels realize that he is deeply at odds with life. Although he idealizes valiantly, believing that his doctrine of atheism will ennoble humanity by giving it freedom and inner strength, his wife calls for the parson when she dies, and Niels himself, worn out with suffering at the death of his son, prays desperately, confessing the power of God. Afterward he regrets this lapse.

. . . he ought to have resisted it, for he knew with the innermost fibres of his brain that gods were dreams. . . . He had not been able to bear life as it was . . . in the stress of the fight he had deserted the banner to which he had sworn allegiance; for after all, the new ideal, atheism, the sacred cause of truth—what did it all mean, what was it all but tinsel names for one simple thing; to bear life as it was and allow life to shape itself according to its own laws.[12]

At the close of the novel Niels is wounded in battle, but refuses to see the minister, preferring to face death alone, thus winning the hardest battle of all.

In another of Gissing's favorite novels, *Crime and Punishment*, the hero feels himself to be free of the usual claims of morality, family affection, and friendship, for modern thought has taught him that superior individuals like himself are justified in adopting any means of fulfilling their destinies. Raskolnikov's murder of the old moneylender and her sister is committed to demonstrate his freedom from conventional moral laws. But he is surprised and frightened to see how weak his feelings of sympathy and fear have grown, and how detached he can become in emergencies. Only the quasi-divine intervention of Sonia and the purgative suffering of his Siberian exile can save him from the moral disintegration represented by Svidrigaïlov.

Similar characters appear in two novels, both known to Gissing, by the French author Paul Bourget. The hero of *Le Disciple* (1881), Robert Greslou, is a fanatical admirer of a scholar, a "French Spencer," who has put the science of psychology on a positivist basis, showing that the human passions and will are subject to determinist laws. The brilliant young student decides to put the speculations of the unworldly scholar into practice, and as an experiment, makes a girl of noble family fall in love with him. When she discovers the motive of his courtship she commits suicide, and Greslou himself is shot by her brother. The old scholar whose theories have inspired Greslou's actions wonders bitterly whether the responsibility for all this destruction does not really belong to the "truths" he has discovered.

In *Un Crime d'Amour* (1886), a wealthy young idler who

suffers from an "inward nihilism" which makes him incapable of enjoying life, seduces the wife of his closest friend without loving her. When their relationship is discovered, and the hero's mistress offers to sacrifice everything to go away with him, he is compelled to admit his lack of feeling for her. The terrible effects of this confession upon a sincere and virtuous woman make him realize that his course of action constitutes "a crime of love." Profoundly disturbed by her suffering and his own coldness of feeling, he reviews his past and his education, concluding that his capacity for belief has been destroyed by science, misanthropy, and debauchery.

Whether or not any of these novels influenced *Born in Exile* directly, they show that in Godwin Peak Gissing was dealing with a characteristic figure and a characteristic problem of nineteenth-century civilization. All over Europe young men were making an ideal of science, and the fictional record of this development shows how their contempt for feelings resulted in a stifling of their own emotional capacities; what began as an exile from environment ended as an exile from the self. The individual became an amoral desperado, committing some affront to society that aroused in him feelings of guilt and remorse he had hitherto suppressed, and these feelings forced him to recognize the inadequacy of the scientific ideal.

The passionate and gloomy *Sturm und Drang* heroes of the romantic period were forerunners of the Peaks, Bazarovs, and Raskolnikovs who appear in later European literature. The actual psychic experience must have been the same both at the beginning and after the middle of the century: a feeling of estrangement from the world, an inability to share the common attitudes, an awareness that spiritual certainty is impossible. There are striking differences, however, in its external manifestations. In the romantic works the crisis of the disturbance was generally brought on by an intense self-consciousness accompanied by dandyism, sensationalism, and megalomania. In the Victorian novels, on the other hand, its source is the social and intellectual environment. New scientific truths or political ideals make it impossible for young men to accept traditional beliefs. They are, in contrast to the romantic rebels, cold, intellectual, indifferent to such externals as sunsets, landscape, or impressive costumes. Where the romantics erred in enthroning passion, they committed the parallel and contrary error of enthroning intellect.

Born in Exile dramatizes the limitations of the scientific materialist philosophy as a spiritual guide; Godwin Peak's tragedy shows that it can destroy traditional beliefs but is unable to rebuild. The novel's lesson recalls the conclusion reached by Helen Norman in *Workers in the Dawn*: that even though Christianity was a false belief, its sudden extinction might be a worse evil than its continued existence. Peak's rebellion is motivated by a moral ideal, but it is a remote one and has no means of dealing with immediate spiritual problems. Contemptuous of faith and feeling, he would like to believe that his freedom from emotion brings with it freedom of action and conscience. But the vacuum of the perfect objectivity he thinks he has achieved is invaded by fears and passions. His pride corrupts the abstract doctrine of self-fulfillment into mere anarchic selfishness. Ethical morality dissolves into no morality at all. Ultimately, however, the strict honesty that has forbidden him to accept the moral dictates of supernatural religion forbid him to accept those of his own egotism, and he is forced to recognize the true nature of his motivation. He finds that he has wandered into a strange amoral realm, where certainty, on either scientific or religious grounds is impossible, and every question of right and wrong is an intolerable nightmare.

In giving Peak's hypocrisy the form of a belief that religious doctrines can be reconciled with scientific knowledge, Gissing was directing criticism at one of the most characteristic products of the Victorian compromise. Both agnostics and orthodox Christians turned to it as a way of ending the conflict of beliefs. Even the most aggressive of the agnostics tended to drift toward the view that the order of the universe supported Christian morality. Samuel Butler's *God the Known and God the Unknown*, after offering some highly unorthodox speculations about the nature of God, arrived at conclusions that were mere religious truisms. Herbert Spencer in *First Principles* (1860) suggested that religion and science could come to terms on the basis of a recognition that knowledge of the universal Power was inaccessible to either. When Huxley's little son, Noel, died in 1860, Kingsley wrote to the bereaved father, urging him to take consolation in the doctrine of immortality. Huxley's reply was a courageous reaffirmation of his belief in scientific method, and a refusal to abandon it in his grief, but he also said that he felt an order in the physical universe that inspired something akin to a sense of religion. "The absolute justice of the system of things," wrote Huxley, "is as clear to me as any scientific fact. The gravitation of sin to sorrow is as certain as that of the earth to the sun, and more so. . . ." [13]

Religious thinkers, on the other hand, undertook the task of absorbing scientific discoveries into the body of religious dogma; such a policy is the touchstone of Peak's hypocrisy. He borrows this line of thought from Chilvers, a young clergyman who acts as a sort of counterbalance to him in the novel, and seriously defends it.

There is distinct need of an infusion of the scientific spirit into the work of the Church. . . . It behooves us to go in for science—physical, economic—science of every kind. . . . What we have to do is to construct a spiritual basis on the basis of scientific revelation. I use the word revelation advisedly. The results of science are the divine message of our age. . . . [14]

Gissing made this compromise the master fallacy of *Born in Exile* because it seemed to him a typical example of the Victorian spiritual failure. Both science and theology claimed to shed light on the nature of the cosmos and the moral duty of man, yet Gissing could accept the claims of neither. And he could not accept a sophistical combination of both as a formula for exempting man from the need for wrestling with the paradoxical realities of his universe.

In writing to Edward Clodd of metaphysical questions, Gissing said:

Well, well, let us agree that it is very good to acknowledge a great mystery. . . . How to go further than this recognition I know not. That there is *some order, some purpose*, seems a certainty; my mind, at all events, refuses to grasp an idea of a Universe which means nothing at all. But just as unable am I to accept any of the solutions ever proposed. . . . These things have a meaning—but I doubt, I doubt—whether the mind of man will ever be permitted to know it. [15]

Gissing was one of a minority of Victorians who felt with equal force the attraction and the impossibility of faith. The agnostic position meant spiritual peace and intellectual freedom to most of his contemporaries who adopted it. To the artistic mind, however, agnosticism must seem, not an answer to the problem of man's place in the universe, but only a way of posing that problem in its most unequivocal terms. The feeling that there is a divine order, but that it is inaccessible to man, a view accepted without any strong emotions by John Stuart Mill and Herbert Spencer, meant to Gissing that life was a tragedy of the spirit. To many, agnosticism offered relief from the impossible task of solving the riddle of the universe, but to Gissing it meant only that man was doomed to pitiful ignorance and loneliness in a harsh universe he could never understand.

Although he rarely dealt directly with the problem of universal order in his novels, it seems clear that Gissing's indecision about metaphysical questions is the ultimate source of his indecision about social and economic themes. Moral values depend on man's relation to the universe, yet agnosticism held that it is impossible to understand fully the nature of that relation. Gissing could neither understand nor ignore it. His conflict about his artistic intentions, and his ambiguous attitudes toward the poor and the middle class were counterparts of his metaphysical doubts. Behind the pessimism and contradictions of his novels there lurks the anguish of the unknowable, the feeling that filled him when he contemplated the ultimate problems of existence as they were embodied in the immediate problems of his age.

Born in Exile is an important spiritual document, and the only novel by Gissing that can be called European in character. Although it is a profound and honest book, its workmanship is undistinguished. The plot progresses by minute stages through many scenes of little dramatic value, so that its effect is extremely diffuse. Peak himself is very thoroughly explored as a character, and the most living parts of the book are his meditations and his reactions to the world about him. His youthful intolerance of his family, the tortuous rationalizations of his actions, and his response to the comfort and refined society he has always admired are marked by Gissing's authoritative skill in describing states of mind. There are no other interesting characters, however, and the large portion of the book devoted to subplots and minor characters is exceptionally flat.

Because it is slow-moving and esthetically uninteresting, *Born in Exile* has never won its due recognition as a novel of ideas. Contemporary reviewers missed its ideological implications entirely.

The *Spectator* wondered at the perversity of people who refused to enjoy life, termed Peak's crime a "specially despicable hypocrisy," and found the novel "devoid of charm," a quality it made no pretension of offering. The *Athenaeum* warned its readers that following Peak's psychological development would demand attention, but would be ultimately rewarding. Gissing was particularly outraged by the review in the *Pall Mall Gazette*, which said, "The material is of the slightest, but it is cleverly worked up." Gissing copied this obtuse comment into his diary, following it with an inarticulately wrathful "Ye gods!" [16]

III

His trouble in placing *Born in Exile* caused Gissing some anxious moments in the middle of 1891, for, as he noted in October, he was down to only twenty-seven pounds. In addition, Edith was expecting a baby, and disagreements with his landlady forced him to undertake the task, always particularly painful for him, of looking for a new house and moving his household. Toward the end of August he moved from the rooms he had been occupying to a pleasant eight-room house at 1 St. Leonard's Terrace in Exeter. The removal was a considerable improvement, for he now had a quiet study of his own, with views of flowers and greenery in all directions, where he spent his first month in almost uninterrupted reading.

On September 26, not long after moving to St. Leonard's Terrace, Gissing had the unprecedented experience of being approached by a publisher. The new firm of Lawrence and Bullen, having heard from Roberts that Gissing was working on a one-volume novel, offered to publish it in a six-shilling format, giving Gissing a royalty of one shilling on every copy sold, with one hundred pounds in advance. This news, coming while *Born in Exile* was drifting from one publisher to another, must have cheered Gissing considerably, for it gave new impetus to his current project, which he now titled "The Radical Candidate." Early in November one of the new firm's partners, A. H. Bullen, who was making the rounds of booksellers to introduce himself, appeared in Exeter and invited Gissing to dine with him.

Bullen was a man of exactly Gissing's age, who had studied classics at Oxford, been a schoolmaster, and earned a reputation as an expert on the sixteenth and seventeenth centuries in English literature. After applying for, and failing to win, the Chair of English at University College, London, he had gone into publishing in partnership with H. W. Lawrence. On his initiative the firm published valuable editions of Elizabethan playwrights and poets, later extending its publications to a ten-volume edition of Shakespeare and some of the most important scholarly material of the period, including Henslowe's diaries. Gissing found Bullen to be younger and less intellectual than he had expected, but he seemed optimistic about Gissing's future as a novelist.

When Gissing sent the completed short novel to them toward the end of November, Lawrence and Bullen promptly paid him £105 on account, although they wrote that the novel did not seem "very strong," and that its title would have to be changed to *Denzil Quarrier*, for the original political title might alarm women readers. The publication of *Denzil Quarrier* was the beginning for Gissing of a long, pleasant, and profitable association with Lawrence and Bullen. Unlike other publishers Gissing had dealt with, Bullen was candid, friendly, and encouraging. He set out to capture Gissing for his firm by asking first refusal of his next book, proposing inexpensive reprints of his early novels, and offering royalties, which enabled him to share in the profits of his books, instead of a flat price.

There were two reasons for Gissing's change to shorter forms in *Denzil Quarrier* and the numerous short stories he was to write after 1892. It was a way of making money quickly. In addition, the three-volume novel was being overtaken by history at last. Writing to Algernon in 1885, Gissing said he approved of the new practice which allowed the novelist to present a series of episodes rather than a biography, and to use the "dramatic" method of suggesting thoughts instead of analyzing them at length. Although he continued to use the three-volume style and form, his preference for the new method continued to grow, and one of the lessons on writing he sent to Algernon in 1891 reads, "I am convinced that the less you think about analysis, the better and more acceptable work you will do. Let the reader analyse character and motive . . . do you simply present facts, events, dialogue, scenery." [17]

He admitted the need for "condensation" in his work, and made practical acknowledgment of it by sharply cutting *Thyrza*, *The Unclassed*, and *Workers in the Dawn* when he revised them for new editions. (The revision of *Workers in the Dawn* was never completed.) His method of revision was to eliminate or condense passages of dialogue, psychological analysis, and authorial exposition, as well as to make minor changes of diction. Although he said that it would be pleasant to be free of the three-volume novel, he came to the new methods slowly. When he did adopt them, his work benefited from the newly fashionable economies of technique, but the confining forms of short stories and short novels did not suit him; before long he applied his more dramatic narrative style to full-length stories, as before.

Although *Denzil Quarrier* was written primarily to take advantage of Bullen's offer, it represents a step in Gissing's development and is on the whole a pleasing book, mingling with a melodramatic plot some of Gissing's most characteristic touches. Its hero, a strong-minded and vigorous man of action, enters politics as the Liberal candidate for Parliament in a provincial town named Polterham. To a supposedly friendly rival named Eustace Glazzard, whom he has bested for the nomination, he confides the unusual story of his marriage, which is not really a marriage at all. He met his wife, Lilian, while she was a governess in Sweden, and discovered only after proposing to her twice that she was already married, though only in a technical sense, for her husband was arrested for forgery while leaving the church after the wedding, and has never lived with her. Quarrier tells Glazzard how, after hearing this account, he induced Lilian to live with him in London, and now proposes to take her to Paris for the sake of appearing to be married there, and to brave the social law, that would keep them apart by settling down with her in Polterham as man and wife. After this mock marriage, Lilian, who is a frail creature, takes up her social duties in Polterham with reluctance.

When Parliament is dissolved and an election approaches, Quarrier begins active campaigning. In the meantime, Eustace Glazzard, vaguely resentful at Quarrier's new importance, has succeeded in tracing Lilian's missing husband. He goes to see him without any clear motive at first, but soon plans to embarrass Quarrier's campaign by having him appear in Polterham to claim his wife just before the election. The husband accordingly wanders through the town until he meets Lilian, demands that she return to him, and renews his demand on the eve of the election. This drives the unstable Lilian to kill herself by drowning herself in a pond. The grief-stricken Quarrier, who is elected the next day, finds himself at once a member of Parliament and a widower. The final chapter, which takes place a year after Lilian's death, unmasks Glazzard as the betrayer of Quarrier's secret. The novel ends as Glazzard quietly confesses his guilt and Quarrier sadly admits that he now sees the need for the social law he violated.

The book was, as Gissing wrote to Algernon, "a strong defence of conventionality"; yet it would be a mistake to conclude that his feelings were genuinely involved, for he repudiated "conventionality" a few years later when, by what must be one of the oddest coincidences in literature, he found himself in precisely the same situation he had contrived for his characters. When he was prevented from marrying Gabrielle Fleury by his own former marriage, he followed the course his novel warned against, made a pretence of marriage, and lived with her as man and wife, though he cautiously set up his home outside of England. It is impossible, therefore, to attribute much sincerity to the lesson of *Denzil Quarrier*, or to take it seriously as an acceptance of convention on Gissing's part. It can be explained as the beginning of a policy of following two simultaneous writing careers; in one Gissing courted popularity and tried to increase his income by short stories and light novels that offered no challenge to convention, and in the other he pursued the social criticism that was his real vocation, in such longer novels as *The Odd Women, In the Year of Jubilee,* and *The Whirlpool.*

As Gissing's first attempt at a shorter novel, *Denzil Quarrier* is comparatively lively and fast-moving, but its structural difficulties betray his inexpertness with the new genre. The weak motivation and thin characterization might have been improved if he had had more space to work in. The accumulation of detail, dialogue, and minor action, which he had recommended to Algernon as a means of maintaining interest, may have given the novels of Dickens and George Eliot their solidity, but they interfered with the unity and pace of a short novel. Some of the minor elements, however, seem to spring from Gissing's deeper feelings and to be connected with his general opinions. For example, Lilian's sympathy with the poor is presented as weakness of character, and Quarrier's lecture on the rights of women and his relations with a feminist named Mrs. Wade foreshadow Gissing's interest in the woman question. His treatment of the Polterham townsfolk is Gissing's first moderately successful attempt at social comedy, a genre he had occasionally tried before, and was to take up again in the future.

VIII

HEN his first son was born early in the stormy morning of December 10, 1891, Gissing felt no excitement at this beginning of a new life but only a savage resentment at the pain Edith had to undergo. At 4:15 in the morning he wrote that the "blackguard business" was almost finished. An hour later he recorded, "So, the poor girl's misery is over, and she has what she earnestly desired." [1] It was some time before Gissing expressed any enthusiasm for his son, who began life by disrupting his sensitive father's routine. The child's crying depressed Gissing; when the birth was registered he chose the names Walter Leonard for no better reason than that they were inoffensive. Edith was ailing and had begun, in addition, to show the first signs of the bad temper that poisoned the atmosphere of the house and eventually led to their separation. When, early in 1892, the servant (whose name happened to be Thyrza) became ill, domestic responsibilities fell heavily on Gissing and made him frantic. He had to interrupt his work on the revision of *Born in Exile* to engage a woman to take the child, nicknamed "Gubsey," out to board at her farmhouse.

A period of peace followed. After the revision of *Born in Exile* was completed, Gissing took Edith to Penzance for a week's holiday, returning to Exeter and work on February 15. He was in an aggressive mood. Forgetting his earlier struggle to subdue the didactic element in his work, he now wanted to write something that would reveal the vulgarity of modern civilization. In the past, he wrote to Bertz, he had dealt with gifted people who occupied a lower social position than the one they really deserved; now he wanted to write about stupid people who were placed higher than they should be. At first he thought of a novel about fools in positions of authority to be called "Jacks in Office." Democracy, he explained to Bertz, was leveling society down, partly through the influence of America, and partly through the education provided by the Board Schools. A class higher than the lowest was emerging, but it was still very far from being truly educated.

While Gissing was occupied with ideas like these, and with a series of useless attempts to begin his novel, Gubsey was brought home in the middle of April, and disorder erupted. Edith, who was incapable of getting along with servants, had continual disagreements with the baby's nurse, and Gissing was constantly being interrupted to hear complaints or settle disputes. It was not long, of course, before the nurse left, and then Gissing himself had to nurse the child, care for it, prepare its meals, and perform other duties that even in modest households like his were invariably left to servants.

Gissing must now have begun to gain some disquieting insights into his wife's character. The depths of ignorance he discovered in her did not disturb him; he simply noted them as examples of the plebeian mind at work. He observed with clinical interest that she had never heard of *Pilgrim's Progress*, said "amusing" when she meant "interesting," and did not realize that "Henry" and "Harry" were forms of the same name. But he suffered at what he called "uproar in the house," quarrelsome scenes with servants or neighbors that left him unable to work for days. He must already have begun to fear that he had sacrificed too much to his physical needs by marrying. In January of 1893, after less than two years of marriage with Edith, he was compelled to acknowledge to himself that he had needs that she could not possibly satisfy. He wrote in his diary:

On way home at night, an anguish of suffering in the thought that I can never hope to have an intellectual companion at home. Condemned for ever to associate with inferiors—and so crassly unintelligent. Never a word exchanged on anything but the paltry everyday life of the household. Never a word to me, from anyone, of understanding sympathy—or of encouragement.[2]

The summer of 1892 passed as Gissing, between crises created by Edith's neuralgia, the baby's illness, and an incredible succession of dissatisfied nurses who came and went every week, tried ineffectually to start another novel. By July 10 he had recorded eight unsuccessful attempts, and on August 2 he stopped making entries in his diary because, as he later wrote, he was "sick of chronicling endless beginnings." By September 2, however, he had finished the first volume of a novel, after making *twelve* starts. By October 4 he completed the book, gave it the title *The Odd Women*, and sent it to Lawrence and Bullen.

Gissing had been concerned all his life with the subject of *The Odd Women*, the problem of the social status of women. When his sisters were girls he urged them to take their studies more seriously than girls generally did, and he wrote to them that he preferred the kind of knowledgeable and self-reliant woman who could travel alone. Four of his novels, *The Emancipated, The Odd Women, In the Year of Jubilee,* and *The Whirlpool,* form a searching examination of such aspects of the problem as courtship, marriage, sexual mores, and the fate of single women. The theme is important in *Workers in the Dawn,* where it is represented by Carrie Mitchell, and it forms a more or less significant interest in nearly every subsequent novel.

On this subject at least, Gissing's opinions were clear, consistent, and uncompromising. An enemy of the Victorian myth of the inferiority of women, he believed firmly that women were the intellectual and spiritual equals of men. His favorite novelists, George Eliot, Charlotte Brontë, and George Sand, were women; he admired such clever women as Edith Sichel and Mrs. Woods without the usual reservations. Like John Stuart Mill, he felt that the emancipation of women was an important phase of the general struggle for liberty. In addition, he was convinced that the one false idea of the inferiority of women subtly poisoned the most intimate social relationships and undermined the happiness of marriage and the home. He might legitimately have attributed his own marital difficulties to the Victorian conception of the role of women. He wrote to Bertz that he was in favor of equality for women because "social peace" would be impossible until women had the same education as men. "More than half the misery of life," he wrote, "is due to the ignorance and childishness of women." [3] He admitted that the readjustment would bring "sexual anarchy" for a time, but he claimed that it would not destroy anything of value.

According to such spokesmen for the Victorian ideal as Ruskin and Coventry Patmore, a woman was no more than the pillar of the home and the helpmeet of man. By assuming that every woman would find a place as the protected and inferior partner in marriage, the law, custom, moral standards, and women's education rendered women incapable of independence. As Mrs. Annie Besant put it, a woman counted only as somebody's wife, somebody's daughter, or somebody's mother. Under the law, as it stood through most of the century, married women simply did not exist; a married woman could not hold property or be party to a lawsuit. Because they were legally accountable for the actions of their wives, husbands had the right to impose severe physical discipline upon them. The thread-bare legal fiction that husbands could control their wives is demolished by the henpecked Mr. Bumble of *Oliver Twist*, who, when he is told that he is guilty of his wife's crime in destroying evidence pertaining to Oliver's birth because "the law supposes that your wife acts under your direction," bitterly replies: "If the law supposes that . . . the law is a ass—a idiot. If that's the eye of the law, the law is a bachelor; and the worst I wish the law is, that his eye may be opened by experience—by experience." [4]

Marriage, which was supposed to sanctify the relation between the sexes, often proved to be its ultimate corruption, for the ignorant and dependent woman produced by the Victorian education could be expected to share neither her husband's emotional nor his practical life. Her training as a kind of superior servant with limited responsibility thrust upon husbands powers that no husband who respected his wife as a human being would wish to possess. "The relative position," said Mrs. Besant, "is as dishonouring to the man as it is insulting to the woman. . . ." [5] In effect, a woman surrendered her identity to the man she married. She had, for example, no redress whatever for infidelity on the part of her husband. The English divorce laws were almost as rigid and cumbersome as they had been in Milton's time; divorces could be obtained only at great expense and at the cost of dishonoring one of the partners. A wife separated from her husband was, in law, a nonentity. She had no claim over her children or her property; her husband retained the right to discipline, coerce, or confine her, and he could even have her legally imprisoned.

Although the process of women's emancipation was well under way in 1892, when *The Odd Women* was written, many of the serious social disabilities still existed. A first recognition of the legal rights of married women had been won earlier in the century by Mrs. Caroline Norton, who, after being separated from her husband and learning that she had no power under the law to see her children, keep what she might earn, or defend her reputation in court, led a propaganda campaign that resulted in the Infants' Custody Act of 1839. This was followed by a series of enactments on divorce and the economic rights of married women, including the introduction by John Stuart Mill of a motion on woman suffrage in connection with the Reform Bill of 1867, and the Married Woman's Property Act of 1882. The woman suffrage movement grew steadily until it met a paralyzing Parliamentary defeat in 1884.

At the beginning of the century no trades were open to women except, oddly enough, a few rough ones, like coal mining. A middle-class spinster could work as a governess, and this ill-paid profession was crowded by thousands of impoverished gentlewomen, in spite of the hardships and inferiority of station it involved. By 1850 working women had won a recognized place in the factories, and by 1880 various agencies had been set up to train women as clerks, commercial artists, and even engineers and architects. On the assumption that the "female brain" was incapable of any but the most superficial learning, the usual girls' school limited itself to teaching elementary subjects and accomplishments like dancing, music, and needlework. The first step beyond these educational standards was the founding of Queens College for women in London in 1848. Other girls' colleges began to appear, and a group of girls challenged masculine academic superiority by sitting successfully for the Cambridge University Local Examinations in 1863. The founding of Newnham College in 1871 and Girton College in 1873, both boarding colleges with standards based on those of Cambridge, put women's education on the same level as men's. When London University opened all its degrees (including the crucial medical degree) to women in 1878, the fight for equal educational opportunities was won.

The Odd Women surveys the emancipation process through the experiences of four women in their encounters with the shifting customs of the time. Alice and Virginia Madden, helpless and genteel spinsters in their middle thirties, are typical victims of the Victorian ideal of womanhood. Unemployable, unmarriageable, unwanted by society, they live together on a pitifully small income in a single room, clinging desperately to some shreds of refinement and to the illusion that they may someday be employed again as governesses or companions. While their poverty is in itself a nearly unbearable hardship, Gissing perceives that the most desperate element of their plight is the loneliness and barrenness of lives in which an invitation to tea or a slice of roast beef are events of supreme importance.

Their hopes are based on their younger sister, Monica, who is sure to marry because she is pretty. But Monica's marriage becomes a sad instance of the inadequacy of traditional marriage customs in a period of social transition. Seeking to rise from her position as a kind of slave in a draper's establishment, she tries to learn the new skill of using the typewriter but, unable to muster the necessary self-discipline, drifts into marriage with a wealthy, dull, middle-aged bachelor whom she has met on a public boat on the Thames. Her husband, Widdowson, a partisan of the most old-fashioned ideas about marriage, imposes a life of strict seclusion upon her. When Monica, who is fatally bored by her dull husband, ventures the opinion that women are not so different from men as Widdowson believes, and asks to be allowed to pay visits and seek entertainment, Widdowson feels that she is in rebellion against him. Before long, his tyranny drives her into unfaithfulness. Brooding over his shattered marriage, Widdowson is forced to recognize that he has no real understanding of his wife as a personality, that their union is mainly physical, and that the marriage bond holds Monica against her will. But when Monica's adultery and attempt to run away are revealed, Widdowson grows stern, and he remains unforgiving even after she dies in childbirth, leaving a written confession. Like the unhappy Elgars of *The Emancipated*, the Widdowsons learn that the Victorian ideal of marriage does not fit the facts of life.

Monica Widdowson is not an emancipated woman, but merely a girl who has responded to some of the new ideas about equality and has grown accustomed to a freer life than old-fashioned marriage allowed. The cause of emancipation is represented by Mary Barfoot, who runs an agency devoted to training middle-class women in occupations that will enable them to live independently, and Rhoda Nunn, one of her followers, who is the heroine of the novel. Miss Barfoot's enterprise must have been suggested to Gissing by the Society for Promoting the Employment of Women, an organization founded in 1859 by Jessie Boucherett, which had developed a number of subsidiary branches by the nineties.

In contrast to Miss Barfoot, whose moderate ideal is that of enabling girls who do not marry to find positions in offices, where they are still far from welcome, Rhoda feels that women can be saved only by a sweeping reorganization of society. A fanatic of feminism, she believes, like Herminia Barton of Grant Allen's *The Woman Who Did* (1895), that the marriage custom itself is responsible for the subjection of women, and when she falls in love with Everard Barfoot, Mary's active and adventurous cousin, she contemplates a free union of the kind Herminia enters into, a marriage in all but legal fact. While Monica's story exemplifies the danger of marriage on the old plan, Rhoda's shows how impossible the new plan is in a society governed by the old suppositions. The engagement between Everard and Rhoda is a kind of treaty based on principle, and it is promptly destroyed by a matter of principle. Each partner proposes to allow the other freedom, yet Rhoda cannot ignore certain doubts about Everard's fidelity. Demanding that she have faith in him, Everard refuses to enter into an explanation of suspicious circumstances, but Rhoda cannot overcome the distrust of men at the root of her militant feminism. After they have parted, and she has learned that Everard is innocent of any wrongdoing, she realizes that her independent attitude makes it impossible for her to marry. Everard calmly turns to another woman, entering into a conventional and advantageous marriage, while Rhoda is left to pity the little girl born to Monica Widdowson at the close of the novel. She has failed, not because feminism is an impossible ideal, but because her real motive as a feminist, pride, prevents her from making the compromises necessary to apply it to practical affairs.

Bullen asked Gissing to rewrite the first chapter of *The Odd Women* when he accepted it, and there were some other revisions while the book was in proof. However, in spite of its excellence as a varied and scrupulously realistic examination of a single problem (the *Athenaeum* called it Gissing's best book), many of Gissing's typical structural weaknesses remain. The twist in the plot that leads Widdowson to believe that Barfoot is Monica's lover is brought about by the most flagrant of coincidences. Everard can end his disagreement with Rhoda by the very simple means of denying something that is, in fact, untrue, and his refusal stems from an implausible insistence upon a fine point of principle that hardly seems worth the loss of his fiancée. There are, as usual, too many characters, although some of the minor ones are excellent, and the major feminine characters are notable examples of Gissing's ability to dramatize the interplay of social forces and individual psychology. There are also too many pointless incidents and too many conversations, and the value of the illustrative anecdotes in and out of the dialogue seems to diminish as they multiply.

Lawrence and Bullen were pleased with *The Odd Women*, and they offered to pay nine shillings per copy for the first edition in three volumes and sixpence per copy for the 3/6 edition to follow, with a hundred guineas in advance. They also proposed to republish *The Emancipated* in a cheap edition, an offer which put Gissing into an embarrassing position. Only 492 copies of Bentley's edition of *The Emancipated* had been sold. When Gissing asked to buy the copyright back, Bentley wrote that he could have it if he made up the fifty-two pounds that the book had lost. With characteristic candor, Gissing forwarded this letter to Bullen, who was shocked to learn how slowly the books of his new author had sold. However, when Bentley reduced his demand to twenty guineas, Bullen met it, and the new edition of *The Emancipated* was published in October, 1893; Gissing was to receive half profits.

Lawrence and Bullen's eagerness to have Gissing's work, and their generosity in sharing profits with him, did much to relieve his mind at this time. They distributed his books widely by selling the copyrights of *Denzil Quarrier* and *The Odd Women* to firms on the Continent, and in the United States, Australia, and the colonies. The profits of these foreign sales were small, but, such as they were, Gissing shared in them. Bullen did not succeed in increasing the sale of Gissing's books, but he strengthened his self-respect by telling him that it was a "privilege" to publish his books at a loss, and that in any case he hoped they would bring future profits. Gissing's dealings with the agent, Watt, and with Lawrence and Bullen seem to have taught him to take a more professional approach to the marketing of his work; he made more businesslike financial arrangements and saw the merit of using agents, social connections, and other means to make the most of his abilities.

II

After completing *The Odd Women*, Gissing took a long holiday alone while Edith went to stay with a sister in London. He spent a week at the seashore, visited his family at Broadway, and early in November took rooms in Birmingham for three weeks in order to gather material for a novel about the industrial north. He explained his intentions to Bertz, writing: "It is not my purpose to deal with the working-class of that district. I shall use it as a picturesque background to a story of middle-class life, insisting on the degree to which people have become *machines*, in harmony with the machinery amid which they spend their lives." [6]

Because the study of the house in St. Leonard's Terrace no longer afforded enough protection from domestic disturbances, Gissing hired a sitting room to work in when he returned. The Birmingham novel went well. He told Bertz that it was better than his recent work, was concerned with characters who did "social work of the higher—the intellectual kind," and was generally cheerful in tone. He even hit upon an excellent title for it, *The Iron Gods*. But by March, 1893, when he was within twenty pages of completing it, he doubted that it would ever be finished. It never was. He gave it up for unexplained reasons, turning to other projects.

At the end of March Gissing spent a week alone in London. He wandered through the streets, feeling as if he had never left the city, and visited the office of Lawrence and Bullen, who were very friendly; but his real purpose was finding a new home in London. The feeling he had once expressed to Bertz that "my London life is in the past" had now changed, perhaps because of the comparative success of his recent books. On May 15 he rented a house at 76 Burton Road in Brixton, and toward the end of June, 1893, the move was made. Edith remained in Exeter while Gissing underwent more than a week of misery at the hated work of unpacking in hot weather. When they were settled, he hired a separate place to work in as before, this time a bare attic in Kennington.

Not long after his return to London, Gissing made the acquaintance of a woman who was to become one of his closest and most valuable friends, Clara E. Collet. He had first heard of her in March, 1892, when his sister Ellen had called his attention to a brief and rather confused report of a lecture on his novels by Miss Collet appearing in *The Queen*, a ladies' magazine. In May, 1893, Miss Collet wrote asking to meet Gissing, and after he had characteristically declined, sent him some of her articles from the *Charity Organization Review*. These included a report on the proceedings of a Royal Commission on the Depression of Trade which pointed out that the inhuman exploitation of labor was one of the reasons for the success of Britain's competitors in the world market, and an article on Gissing himself which he liked.

After declining a number of other invitations, he at last paid her a visit at her home in Richmond on July 18. Although he did not record his reaction, he must have found her to be an intelligent, strong-minded woman whose attitude toward social problems was a blend of sympathy and practical method resembling that of the Fabian Society and the Charity Organization Society. She had worked as a Labour Correspondent for the Board of Trade, submitting detailed statistical reports on economic matters, and she wrote a number of articles on her special interest, the social and economic position of women. A paper on "The Economic Position of Educated Working Women," which she had read before the London Ethical Society in February of 1890, might almost have served as a text for *The Odd Women*, for it showed by statistical analysis that unmarried middle-class women outnumbered middle-class bachelors, sometimes by as much as two to one, and that many of them must therefore be accepted on the labor market. Gissing was hesitant about Miss Collet's suggestion that she come to his home to meet Edith, but he ultimately gave way, for in August she came to tea in Brixton, and a week later Edith and Miss Collet spent a day boating on the Thames. Miss Collet was quick to gain insight into Gissing's special problems. About two months after first meeting him, she took Edith out of the way one evening by inviting her to the theater, and sent Gissing a note saying that she was ready to pay for Walter's expenses if Gissing should ever find himself unable to continue working. He felt this offer to be "a wonderful piece of kindness."

Toward the end of 1892 occurred an incident which led Gissing to believe that he could bolster his income by writing short stories. He had always had misgivings about them. When Algernon had sent one for criticism in 1889, he observed that they required a striking central incident or character. He said that he could not do them himself, and could not possibly invent the fifteen or twenty a year that he would have to write to earn a living by them. The fact remains, however, that he had begun his career as a short-story writer in America, and had published "The Four Silverpennys" and "Phoebe" in *Temple Bar* in 1883. Two years after writing so pessimistically to Algernon about short stories, he tried his hand at one again but gave it up, saying he needed a larger canvas. After finishing *Denzil Quarrier* in November, 1891, however, he made another attempt, and sent the result, "A Victim of Circumstances," to *Blackwood's Magazine*. When nothing was heard from *Blackwood's* for a year, he wrote to inquire and was pleasantly surprised to be answered, late in 1892, with a payment of twenty pounds and a request for more contributions.

"A Victim of Circumstances," an ironic and artificial contrivance, concerns a poor, untalented painter who occupies himself with a grandiose picture while his wife supports him by selling little water colors of her own, which dealers accept on the understanding that they are her husband's work. The painter, blaming his failure on "circumstances," gives up his great project. In the second scene, twenty years later, we see him boasting to some companions of the talent displayed in the water colors, which have gained some recognition since his wife's death, and which he has continued to claim as his own. It becomes clear, as he complains of the hardships that prevented him from fulfilling the promise shown in them, that he is a pathetic victim of his delusions.

Blackwood's rejected Gissing's next story, submitted in January, 1893. Soon after, however, Clement Shorter, editor of no fewer than three periodicals, the *English Illustrated Magazine*, the *Illustrated London News*, and the *Sketch*, asked Gissing for a story of lower-class life. Gissing sent the tale "Lou and Liz." After giving up *The Iron Gods* Gissing devoted himself exclusively to short stories for a time. Ultimately he wrote scores of them. His first and most important market was Shorter, who distributed them between the *Illustrated London News* and the *English Illustrated,* paying eleven or twelve guineas for each. Trying for a higher price, Gissing in September of 1893 took some of the stories he had written during the summer to William Morris Colles, the agent of the Society of Authors, who proposed to market them at the rate of three guineas per thousand words, and succeeded in selling "The Day of Silence" to the *National Review* and "Under an Umbrella" to *To-Day.* Although Gissing's demand of eighteen guineas per story instead of twelve had silenced Shorter in September, he was very affable when Gissing went to see him a few months later, asking him to write a serial for the *Illustrated London News* and then inviting him to submit six more stories at the old price of twelve guineas. After receiving the letter containing this proposal on December 4, Gissing set vigorously to work, completing all six of the stories by December 26. Conscious that his dealings with Shorter and Colles were leading him into the "commercial path," Gissing wrote to Bertz that he would nevertheless try not to write "rubbish."

On September 12 he had begun a new novel, "Miss Lord," moving his workshop to Camberwell, which he had chosen as its setting. After a number of fruitless starts (he had recorded six by October 16), he put the work aside to devote most of December to the six stories promised to Shorter; he began again on January 1. The novel moved ahead rapidly this time, being completed by April, 1894. During these months his career as a short-story writer prospered, while his success as a novelist seemed to decline. When he took his stories to Shorter on January 15, he agreed to do the serial the latter had requested for a price of £130. The six stories— three weeks' work—brought him more than £88. Two stories placed by Colles with the *National Review* brought £25. On the other hand, Bullen's account of the sales of *The Odd Women* and *Denzil Quarrier* reported a loss of exactly £53–12–11. Bullen added, however, that he expected to recover this loss eventually, and he sent Gissing a check for twenty-five guineas, which the sensitive author felt he had no right to accept. In the meantime, Bullen bought the copyright of *Born in Exile* and issued a cheap edition.

On January 15, 1894, Gissing took a step that was to bring him both professional and social advantages; he formally joined the

Society of Authors. The society, now over ten years old, had about a thousand members and was doing much to teach authors their rights and to expose the dishonest practices of publishers. Its founder, Walter Besant, campaigned vigorously to bring literature under the control of generally accepted business principles. By brandishing the term "literary property" in the society's periodical, *The Author,* he succeeded in promoting the view that authors, while they were primarily artists and worked for other than financial motives, were entitled to a fair share of whatever money their work might earn. Gissing joined the society because he felt that the service of its secretary, Colles, in marketing his stories, had put him under an obligation, but it was a natural thing for him to do. He had to see Colles often, he had dined at the Authors' Club more than once with Roberts, and he knew some of the members, including Shorter and John Davidson. In addition, he had now accepted, though with considerable distaste, the need for the kind of help in selling his work that the society could give.

Gissing's work proceeded under difficulties, for Walter, who had a bad cold, had to be taken south for the winter, and this involved a number of moves. From February until April of 1894 the family lived in lodgings in Hastings, St. Leonard's, and Eastbourne. (Miss Collet lived near them in Hastings for a week, and Gissing saw her every day.) Under these inconvenient conditions Gissing completed "Miss Lord," which was soon retitled *In the Year of Jubilee.*

A sprawling story about marriage problems and the corruption of values in industrial society, it covers a great deal of ground by shifting its attention frequently over a large group of loosely linked characters. Its central plot is concerned with Nancy Lord and Lionel Tarrant, two young people who find that the marriage they are compelled to enter into interferes with their independence. Because a provision of her father's will makes it necessary for her to conceal her marriage, Nancy has her child in secret, supports herself, and endures Tarrant's neglect without losing courage. Tarrant, who likes the freedom of a bachelor's life, believes that the best married life is a separate one, yet at the same time he is jealous of Nancy's affection and her reputation. Ultimately these two strong-willed people settle down to a more or less conventional married life, after overcoming the barriers of temperament that stand in their way.

Because *In the Year of Jubilee* suffers from a lack of tone and from the sketchy development of its major characters, its minor elements are unusually prominent. Possessing little plot value, they are important as illustrations that repeat and augment the book's central ideas. Nancy Lord, for example, is surrounded with characters who are beset, in different ways, with difficulties arising from the changing status of women. The dire results of reforms in women's education are illustrated by the French sisters, *parvenues* whose superficial studies and fashionable frocks hardly disguise the quarrelsome selfishness characteristic of Gissing's slum women, and by Jessica Morgan, whose frantic preparation for university examinations, undertaken without any real incentive or love of knowledge, results in a pathetic emotional breakdown.

A second major concern of *In the Year of Jubilee* is the influence upon society of the lower classes to which mass education and mass production had given new power. This new social force is symbolized by the idle holidaying crowds that pour through the streets during the celebration of Victoria's Jubilee. The characters of the book drift through this menacing tide of humanity, meeting and parting at the random mercy of the crowd. The gross materialistic aspirations of the vulgar are expressed by Luckworth Crewe, a suitor of Nancy's who is in the process of raising himself by unscrupulous means from low social origins. Clever, greedy, and obsessed by thoughts of fortune, he exploits the new force used to direct the power of mass production and mass thought—advertising. Crewe represents the phenomenon that Gissing feared, the low risen to places of authority; extremely knowing and energetic, he is blind to any but material values and unhampered by moral or spiritual convictions, a man capable, in Gissing's view, of infinite destruction.

The most abject worshipper of the materialist superstition of progress, however, is Samuel Barmby, one of Gissing's most savagely satirical character creations. His maiden sisters maintain their old-fashioned middle-class ways; they leave home rarely, read Evangelical periodicals, and lead a kind of life whose greatest events are Chapel functions and headaches. Samuel, on the other hand, leads a vigorous, though pointless, social life. His memberships in a debating society and an excursion club enable him to glory in the achievements of progress and industry, which he usually describes in overwhelming statistics. The Barmby family is a microcosm of the change taking place in middle-class customs. The narrow-minded, stubborn, independent bourgeoisie described by Matthew Arnold in "My Countrymen" was being superseded by a generation born to comfort which combined attitudes of the old aristocracy and the new democracy. They were capable of amusement, and even of culture, but they still believed, as their fathers did, that money was the only reality, and that civilization was primarily a matter of production. The rapaciousness and unscrupulousness that Gissing associated with commerce is found in the dress-shop scheme of Beatrice French, an enterprise calculated to succeed by bilking ignorant women. With the aid of Luckworth Crewe, Beatrice plays upon the parsimony and snobbery of bourgeois women, and achieves a dazzling financial success that Gissing felt to be perfectly typical of the ideals of a materialistic society indifferent to moral values.

Whatever is vivid or vigorous in In the Year of Jubilee is the product of Gissing's animosities. His experience in writing short stories seems to have led him to think in terms of the vignette, for while there are excellent patches of characterization or description, the novel's larger qualities are unusually weak. The plot, unnecessarily intricate and artificial, contains a number of anomalies. Nancy writes a novel in order to support herself, but she does not publish it and, of course, makes no money from it. A peculiar matron named Mrs. Damerel sits behind the scenes, wielding an unaccountable influence over the characters; her own motives and personality are rather confused, and they are hardly clarified by the revelation that she is Nancy's mother.

III

For two years after completing In the Year of Jubilee, Gissing occupied himself with shorter tales and stories which enabled him to capitalize on his growing reputation. His short stories have neither the social idealism nor the earnestness of his earlier work, but they are usually interesting nevertheless. Some of them deal with the manners of lower-class people like those in The Nether

World. Others exploit the quaintness of character exhibited by helpless bibliophiles, underdogs, and social outcasts, often displaying sympathy but ending with a cruelly ironic twist.

He wasted all of May, 1894, in unsuccessful beginnings of the serial requested by Shorter. Once during this interval he made a trip to Halesworth, where his father was born, and found the record of his birth in the church register. He greatly enjoyed seeing the place and talking to the sexton, whose father had been a schoolmate of Thomas Gissing. After buying, at the railway station, a copy of the *Illustrated London News* that carried one of his stories, Gissing thought that his father would have been proud to know that his son would one day buy his own "literary work" at Halesworth.

Only after giving up the house in Brixton and moving his family to lodgings in Clevedon for the summer did Gissing succeed in making progress with the serial. *Eve's Ransom,* which was finished on June 29 after twenty-five days of actual writing, is primarily a story of love and character, with both ingredients present in the thinnest amounts. It concerns a young man of humble origin, Maurice Hilliard, who, coming unexpectedly into some money, is enabled to cultivate his obsession with Eve Madeley, a girl from his own town and social class. Although Eve is mysteriously and unhappily involved with a married man, Hilliard forces himself upon her, buys her company with money, which she seems to need badly, and suffers patiently through her indifference. He tells himself that her sense of obligation prevents her from loving him, but he later finds that she has been interested in another man, whom she marries. When the two meet later, Eve thanks him for the double ransom: the money he gave her, which enabled her to save her old lover, and his forbearance in not forcing her to accept himself. Hilliard feels that both sacrifices have been justified by the fact that Eve has turned out to be a genuine English lady and has overcome her proletarian background, but the real point of the story, Gissing told Bertz, was that she was not really worth his trouble. The book displays an unaccustomed deftness. However, in deliberately avoiding character exposition, Gissing exposed more clearly than ever the coincidences and weak motivations that always marred his plots.

Shorter was eager to have the manuscript of *Eve's Ransom* early in order to give the illustrator time to work, but the art work itself became the cause for the delay of the serial's appearance. The artist chosen by Shorter was Frederick Barnard, the brilliant illustrator of Dickens' works, who was a heavy drinker. Gissing found some of the drawings Barnard submitted in August unsatisfactory. When he went to see him about the matter in September, a month before *Eve's Ransom* was scheduled for publication, he found Barnard drunk, living in poverty, and hopelessly out of control. Eventually the illustrations were done by another artist, and *Eve's Ransom* ran in the *Illustrated London News* from January to March, 1895. It was published as a six-shilling volume by Lawrence and Bullen in April, sold well, and went into a second edition before the end of the month.

His disturbing home life and his interest in stories and short projects that would bring in money prevented Gissing from undertaking another novel for some time after *Eve's Ransom* was completed. He spent the end of the summer in desperate house hunting, and only after moving Edith and Walter into lodgings for a time did he succeed in finding a house in Epsom early in September.

The diary entry of October 10, 1894, marks the point at which Gissing began to realize that his marriage might become too great a hardship for him to bear. He had given up hope of winning affectionate companionship from Edith within two years after their marriage. Her bad temper and vulgarity made his home life a daily ordeal. Now, in addition, after the birth of the child, her incompetence as a mother and housekeeper overwhelmed him with difficulties. Not long after moving to the new house in Epsom he recorded in detail one of her quarrels with the servant and her abuse of Walter, saying that he could not continue to live with her if it were not necessary for the child's sake. In later years when he became intimate with H. G. Wells and his wife, he told them flatly that he could not invite them to his home. "Impossible," he is quoted as saying, "—quite impossible. I have to dismiss any such ideas. I have no home." [7]

Perhaps because of the uncomfortable atmosphere at home, Gissing now changed his habits of seclusion, and began to dine out often, to make visits, and, somewhat reluctantly, to befriend other writers. When he attended his first Society of Authors dinner on October 19, 1894, he found it to be "a mere gathering of tradesmen." He had become known, through *New Grub Street,* as a spokesman for the society's aim of improving the economic conditions under which writers worked, but he disapproved of it nevertheless, and for a characteristic reason; in the manners and conversation of its members he found damning evidence in support of his book's contention that literature was becoming nothing more than a business. Although he was extremely critical of Walter Besant, Marion Crawford, and Anthony Hope, whom he met at the society's dinner, he accepted an invitation to a second dinner, held in November in honor of Hope, whose *Prisoner of Zenda* had been a great success that year; Gissing even bought a dress suit for the occasion. This time he sat next to Besant, the leading spirit of the society, whom he considered largely responsible for the commercialization of literature. His diary comment about Besant is unsparing: "Commonplace to the last degree; a respectable draper." He was somewhat more charitable, even cordial in fact, toward writers he met at private luncheons and gatherings; these included John Davidson, who presented him with a copy of his *Ballads and Poems,* W. Robertson Nicoll, Sir Edmund Gosse, Grant Allen, Edward Clodd, and C. F. Keary.

His letters to Bertz, which had once spoken piercingly of his loneliness, now complained that he was deluged with invitations. Nevertheless, he accepted a number of them willingly as a refuge from his life at home, which had become so troublesome that one day in May, 1895, Edith's "blackguardism" drove him from the house. He was no longer the shy youth of his early twenties, or the soured and withdrawn man of his early thirties, but an urbane gentleman whose unhappy private life gave him a certain reserve. W. Robertson Nicoll, who knew him at this time, said: "He looked like the very last man to have cultivated an intimacy with the slums. He was well dressed, bland, debonair and communicative. . . ." [8] The civilized company into which he often went did little to meet his need for warm understanding; his deep loneliness persisted, so that he created a grave, dignified, and aloof impression.

In June of 1895 Gissing was one of a party of literary men who spent a weekend at the home of Edward Clodd in Aldeburgh, exchanging the news and gossip of the profession and even doing some business. He was pleased with Grant Allen, whom he found genial and open, and who must have aroused his envy. Not only had Allen made a thousand pounds from his book *The Woman Who Did*, in royalties that continued to come in at the rate of twenty-five pounds a week, but he told Gissing that he was genuinely fond of his wife. "Says his wife suits him admirably," wrote Gissing in his diary in a mood, one imagines, of quiet wonder, "and shares his views of several matters." [9] The ubiquitous Shorter was also at Aldeburgh, and Gissing came away from the weekend with an agreement to write six short stories and twenty "sketches" for him.

Many of the writers he knew belonged to the Omar Khayyám Club, a dinner club of men active or interested in literature, whose dinners he began to attend in 1895, being elected a member in December of that year. Gissing's first Omar Khayyám dinner in July, 1895, seems to have been the most important social occasion of his career. Held in honor of Meredith, it took place at the Burford Bridge Hotel near Box Hill, and Gissing attended as a guest of Clement Shorter. When Meredith, now a deaf, garrulous, and lionized old man of sixty-seven, came in after dinner, the company rose and applauded. Meredith went around the table to greet the guests, who included Hardy, Henry Norman, W. Robertson Nicoll, Max Pemberton, L. F. Austin, George Whale, William Sharp, and Theodore Watts. When someone presented Gissing, he said, no doubt remembering *The Unclassed*, "Mr. Gissing! Ah, where is Mr. Gissing?" before shaking hands with him.

Meredith gave a short speech, and Hardy spoke afterward, referring to the time, twenty-six years earlier, when he had first met Meredith. Actually, the occasion had not been a very pleasant one, for it had fallen to Meredith's lot to advise Hardy that his first novel, *The Poor Man and the Lady*, which had been accepted by Chapman and Hall, was too radical and had better be withheld from publication after all. After Hardy had concluded his talk, Gissing was surprised to find himself spontaneously called upon to speak, as another novelist who had dealt with Meredith as a young man. He rose and told the story of the publication of *The Unclassed*, no doubt omitting his grievance over the delayed check. After dinner he spoke briefly with both Hardy and Meredith, promising each that he would soon come to visit. The report of this dinner in *The Chronicle* grouped Meredith, Hardy, and Gissing as the three most important novelists of the day, but Gissing, who remembered his speech with embarrassment, feared that this exaggeration would harm his career.

His feeling was that he had a firmly established reputation, but only with a small, choice reading public. Actually, his public, both in England and abroad, had been growing slowly but steadily. Each of his novels since *Demos* had been reprinted for mass distribution in inexpensive single-volume form; some had appeared in the editions published expressly for the foreign market by Tauchnitz and by Heinemann and Balestier; and his more recent novels had been published or distributed in America, Australia, and the colonies. Translations into French and German had appeared, and in 1892 Gissing learned that a German translation of *New Grub Street* was running as a serial in a Budapest newspaper.

In watching over the growth of his reputation, Gissing attributed importance to references to himself and his books in popular periodicals, particularly valuing casual allusions which suggested that he was already known to the public. A little entanglement of September, 1893, had produced some publicity of the sort that he considered useful. In reading a review in the *Times* of a book called *The Social Problem,* by the Reverend Osborne Jay, he noticed that a passage quoted from the book contained several complete sentences from *The Nether World.* Gissing's letter of protest to the *Times,* printed under the heading, "Borrowed Feathers," elicited a pleasant scattering of comments in other publications. The Reverend Mr. Jay wrote to say that he had meant to quote the passage, and a letter from the proofreader confessed that he had been responsible for omitting quotation marks. The difficulty was settled so amicably that Mr. Jay continued to correspond with Gissing, and at Christmas, 1894, invited him to pay a visit, an invitation which Gissing accepted in March, 1895. Early in January, 1895, he began to find references to himself in the press multiplying. On January 2 he observed that a recent issue of the *Times* had carried a notice about a lecture on him given in Paris by a French critic. Within two weeks after *Eve's Ransom* began its run in the *Illustrated London News* on January 5, he noticed that he had been mentioned in four periodicals. At about the same time, he was astonished to receive a request for a novel from Smith, Elder, who had rejected *Born in Exile* unread. "I never considered it possible," he wrote, "that they would come to me. Times are altered." [10] Even his bank balance was prospering; by the end of 1895 it had reached the very satisfactory total of £560.

The demand for a second edition of *The Unclassed* in 1895 indicated a clearly perceptible growth of interest in Gissing's work and career, particularly among literary people. Gissing had heard of some inquiries about it in 1893. W. Robertson Nicoll reported that Hardy, when asked if there were any young novelist he liked, had named Gissing and described *The Unclassed*. When Lawrence and Bullen proposed that it be republished, Gissing revised it, eliminating whole scenes, descriptions, and episodes, as well as altering details of style. The changes seem to have been dictated by two motives: making the narrative more swift and direct, in accordance with the newer fictional style, and toning down the note of social protest.

Gissing's next story after *Eve's Ransom* was a thirty-thousand word novelette, *Sleeping Fires*, written between January and March, 1895, for the firm of Fisher, Unwin, who paid £150 for it. A weak effort that made use of Gissing's Greek voyage for its setting, it tells of a middle-aged Englishman named Edmund Langley, who, while staying in Athens, meets attractive young Louis Reed and offers to help overcome his guardian's objection to his marriage with an older woman. The guardian, Lady Revill, is a sweetheart of Langley's youth, and when he returns to England to plead Louis' cause, he learns that the boy is his illegitimate son by another woman. Louis dies in Greece, and his death has the effect of drawing the two former lovers together again.

During the early part of 1895 Gissing considered editing for the Muses' Library series, published by Lawrence and Bullen, a volume of the works of Crabbe, a poet in whom he found a congenial realism. The editor of *To-Day*, Jerome K. Jerome, had approached Gissing through Colles, asking him for a series of five hundred-word character sketches. Gissing devoted some time to this task in March, and the series, entitled "Nobodies at Home," was published in the six numbers of *To-Day* which appeared between May 4 and June 8, 1895. A short statement on realism for the *Humanitarian Review*, a novelette called *The Paying Guest*, a large number of stories for Shorter, and the revision of *The Unclassed* occupied him for the rest of the year. While in the midst of this work he wrote to Bertz that he intended to refuse future requests for short stories, for he needed more space if he were to do good work.

The Paying Guest was written, after a number of false starts, in the first two weeks of July, 1895, on commission for Cassell's Pocket Library; it is the best of Gissing's heavy attempts at comedy, a little intrigue about a girl from the lower section of the middle class who seeks to rise into the middle part of it by taking lodgings with a suburban family. But the manners of her own social level are too firmly established to be reformed. Instead of profiting from her new environment, she gives way to restlessness and temper, disrupting the household with unwelcome visitors and, as a climax, a fire in the drawing room. She finally returns to her proper sphere, to the relief of her hosts, by marrying the sturdy young man who has been pursuing her.

In September, accepting the invitations he had received at the Omar Khayyám dinner, Gissing visited Meredith twice and Hardy once. During his talk with Gissing, Meredith made a plea for imagination in fiction; also, he annoyed his visitor by his deferential behavior toward a titled lady who called while Gissing was there. Gissing's visit to Hardy took the form of a weekend spent at Max Gate. Hardy talked about his current writing, *Jude the Obscure*, and reported that he was finding it difficult to avoid impropriety in narrating the scene where Arabella attracts Jude's attention by flinging a pig's pizzle at him. Gissing thought Hardy inferior to Meredith in intellect, culture, and even in knowledge of country things. He sensed a "coarseness" in him attributable to his poor parentage, and found fault with him for cultivating his social superiors. Gissing's account of his conversation with Mrs. Hardy suggests some of the reasons for the unhappiness of Hardy's first marriage. She told Gissing, who was practically a stranger to her, that she found it hard to live with a man "of humble origin," and that their frequent visits in London were a nuisance. "Oh, a painful woman!" exclaimed Gissing in his diary account of the visit.

Having been elected a member of the Omar Khayyám Club, Gissing attended the December 6 dinner at Frascati's, thoroughly enjoying the conviviality of the occasion and the experience of receiving many invitations. In January of 1896 he joined a dinner group of writers which included C. F. Keary, John Collier, and

Shorter; together they abused the new poet laureate, Alfred Austin. At this gathering Shorter told the story of the acquisition of the Charlotte Brontë manuscripts, which were to form the basis of his work on her. He said he had paid Charlotte Brontë's widower, Arthur B. Nicolls, five hundred pounds for them, but Gissing suspected that the amount was exaggerated.

Toward the end of December, 1895, Gissing resolved to give up short stories, and on the first day of the new year he began to make notes for a full-length novel. The work was interrupted, however, by difficulties at home. The birth of a second son, Alfred Charles, on January 20, disrupted the household; Gissing had to take charge of Walter and sleep on the sofa for a few nights. Things had hardly settled down when, at the beginning of March, some gasfitters who were "laying on" the gas caused an explosion that created a considerable amount of damage and made it necessary for the family to take shelter elsewhere while the repairs were in progress. Another crisis occurred in April, this one caused by Gissing himself. He had been watching Walter's development with proud interest, noting such things as his ability to memorize the copy of *Struuwelpeter* given him by Miss Collet, and he now came to the conclusion that the boy must be raised away from the quarrelsome atmosphere of his home. Taking him on what was supposed to be a visit to his two aunts and his grandmother in Wakefield, Gissing left the boy in their care. He returned home after a delightful tour in Chester and Wales at the end of April, resigned to the necessity of facing the inevitable scene with Edith.

IV

Work on his new long novel was slowed by a variety of causes. He went out so often that, he wrote to Bertz, he feared he was getting to know too many people; he wrote some short stories, one of them, "A Yorkshire Lass," for the short-lived periodical, *Cosmopolis*; and during the winter he suffered from a serious cough. In June he attended a dinner at the Savoy in honor of *Cosmopolis*, at which Frederic Harrison spoke. Gissing had not seen Harrison for years, although he had written to him in November, 1895. About a month after the *Cosmopolis* dinner, he went to visit the Harrisons in the country, where he met his two former students. Austin was preparing to enter the Foreign Office, and Bernard had spent five years studying art in Paris, had just sold his first picture, and had become a Catholic, a step which Gissing attributed to his nervousness of temperament.

Gissing made some interesting new acquaintances in 1896. At a National Club luncheon Edmund Gosse introduced him to Austin Dobson, Andrew Lang, and Israel Zangwill. At an Omar Khayyám dinner in November, he met a young writer named H. G. Wells, who told him that *New Grub Street* was an exact picture of his own life at one time, for he had lived in a flat near Regents Park as a struggling author with a wife named Amy. Wells had written agreeable reviews of *Eve's Ransom* and *The Paying Guest*, while Gissing had been following Wells's work. Gissing accepted an invitation to visit Wells and his wife in December, writing in his diary the comment, "He seems the right kind of man." [11] This was the beginning of a warm friendship, which lasted until Gissing's death. Though there were certain reservations on both sides, Gissing's relationship with Wells stimulated and comforted him and did much to break down his solitary habits.

Wells's origins were somewhat similar to Gissing's (his father had been a shopkeeper in Bromley), but he was very different in intellect and temperament. He was cheerful, aggressive, resilient and insensitive to adversity. After an embattled adolescence as an apprentice in drapers' shops and an assistant at a grammar school, he won a scholarship in 1884 to the Normal School of Science in London, where he studied under Huxley. Here he acquired a scientific education, but his boredom with the work eventually led to academic failure. There followed a period of miscellaneous educational work and poverty in London lodginghouses while he absorbed socialism and enlightenment and composed literary efforts of all sorts, which were (with a single chance exception) rejected by editors. His resemblance to Gissing and Gissing's early heroes was only superficial, however, for he was made of durable stuff, and took adversity in stride. Poor health and an uncomfortable marriage and divorce hardly interfered with his development. Through a combination of persistence and ingenuity he sold an article to the *Fortnightly Review*, caught the attention of some editors, and eventually placed a revision of a youthful fantasy, *The Time Ma-*

chine, as a serial in 1894. It was the beginning of a swift success. By the time he met Gissing in 1896, Wells was fairly begun on a lucrative career as a writer of science-fiction novels and stories. His income had already gone up to over a thousand pounds, he was vigorously courting gentility and literary friends, and was soon to branch out into other kinds of writing.

It is surprising that the friendship prospered as well as it did. To Gissing, Wells's speech and manner must have seemed unbearably proletarian. His education was a vast assemblage of scientific lore assimilated by a retentive mind in preparation for endless examinations; he was ignorant of languages, living or dead, and had never been out of England. Wells, on his side, considered Gissing confused, ineffectual, and repressed, and blamed his old-fashioned education for the preoccupation with classical learning that had made him a misfit in the dynamic society Wells himself fell in with so successfully. Nevertheless, the two felt a strong affection for each other and enjoyed each other's company. Gissing admired Wells for his success in educating himself, and thought him a talented man. Even more important, he felt able to confide his marital difficulties to him, and to turn to him for advice and sympathy.

The novel Gissing was working on in 1896, *Benedict's Household*, apparently incorporated some of his unhappy family experiences, but it was laid aside before the end of summer when he turned to a new novel, completed on the eighteenth of December, 1896, which was ultimately titled *The Whirlpool*. It was difficult work, requiring much rewriting. "I often marvel," he wrote to Bertz, "at my own stubborn patience." [12] *The Whirlpool* is both a subtle psychological study of marriage and a criticism of the commercialism and libertinism of the nineties. Its protagonist, Harvey Rolfe, a bookish middle-aged bachelor, sees modern life as a whirlpool of uncontrollable and irrational forces that sweep individuals to their doom. When the Britannia Loan Company fails through irresponsible speculation, spreading hardship far and wide among innocent families and causing two suicides, Rolfe is divided between acceptance of the inevitable and sympathy for the victims of the crash. He is grateful "that no theological or scientific dogma constrained him to a justification of the laws of life." [13] All the activity and energy of modern life seem to Rolfe to be aimed at "artificial necessities" and to contradict natural human feelings and desires; he congratulates himself on having avoided "the whirlpool" by remaining single.

But it is not long before he involves himself in it by marrying the talented and ambitious Alma Frothingham. Eager to succeed as a concert violinist, and to be recognized socially, Alma cultivates the company of poseurs, dilettantes, and opportunists, allowing herself to be flattered and cheated by them and engaging in illogical rivalries and irresponsible flirtations. All this leads Rolfe to realize that he has lost the quiet, peaceful life he loved. As Alma, deeply troubled by neurotic fears and cravings, grows away from him, Rolfe comes to feel that his life is bleak and empty, and that his only happiness comes from his little son. Eventually, Alma is trapped in one of her own intrigues. She is discovered in the house of a predatory bachelor by a jealous husband who mistakes her for his own wife and kills the man he takes to be her seducer. Feeling that she is responsible for this crime, Alma hysterically protests her innocence to Rolfe, but his assurances that he believes her are not enough, and she kills herself with an overdose of sedative. Afterward Rolfe lives in the country with his little boy, feeling himself to be freer than he was while his wife was living.

The Whirlpool is Gissing's most perceptive study of the psychology of marriage. The Rolfes agree, in marrying, that marriage is a state of freedom, and at first Alma freely chooses to give up her musical and social activities and to move to the country in order to lead the kind of quiet life her husband prefers. But Rolfe senses her subconscious resentment at this sacrifice, and insists that she follow her real desires. Alma cannot do this, however, without experiencing feelings of guilt which she tries to ease by telling herself that her husband is unfaithful to her. When Rolfe clears himself she finds no comfort in the truth, for she is left to bear the burden of remorse for her own selfishness; she grows preoccupied and ill, and finally collapses altogether.

Like Hardy's novels, The Whirlpool gives the impression that life is ruled by a malevolent determinism. In social affairs, as in business, trivial causes produce grotesquely disproportionate effects. Alma goes to her fatal rendezvous only to frustrate a friend of whom she is jealous, not because she cares for the man; yet this frivolous and innocent action sets off a train of events that includes murder, imprisonment, and her own suicide. That Gissing patterned Rolfe upon himself is obvious; he too withdrew from a hostile wife to find comfort in his child. But Rolfe learns a lesson in middle life that Gissing had known since his youth. At first he considers the merchant virtues of competitiveness and self-seeking to be necessary evils in a world governed by the cruel laws of evolution, but he sees, in reading Kipling's *Barrack Room Ballads,* that they may lead to war. His only way of meeting this threat is to go for a quiet walk with his son, so that the moral of the book becomes something like Ryecroft's observation that ". . . most of the wrong and folly which darken earth is due to those who cannot possess their souls in quiet." [14]

Miss Collet, writing to Roberts after Gissing's death, said that *The Whirlpool* reflected his anxieties about Walter, and that the weak Rolfe was a remorseful self-portrait. In its revelation of Rolfe's thoughts and its depiction of the brittle society surrounding Alma, she thought it might be called his truest book. It was a greater success, both with the public and the critics, than any of his earlier books. The first edition of two thousand copies was sold out in a month. The puzzled critics now sought to account for the fact that a novelist of Gissing's talent had failed to win much attention in his years of work. The *Spectator* reviewer thought it might be due to his "uncompromising" study of character and his interest in ordinary people. The *Athenaeum* attributed it to his pessimism. An enthusiastic article by G. White in the *Sewanee Review* called the novel "startlingly modern" in its objectivity and freedom from obvious pathos. It praised the book's realism and the clarity with which the psychology of the characters was revealed in their speeches.

"Modern" was a word that had long been used by Gissing's reviewers to refer to his realism, pessimism, and preoccupation with problems peculiar to industrial society. However, his new friend, H. G. Wells, gave the word a somewhat different application in an article on Gissing published in the *Contemporary Review,* which carefully examined the whole sequence of his novels as a background to a consideration of *The Whirlpool.* Gissing, he said, wrote a new kind of novel primarily concerned, not with individual character, but with general social forces studied through their effects on individuals. While the operation of such forces could be discerned in Dickens and in some of Turgenev's works, said Wells, they dominated Gissing's novels, with the result that the latter could be called "deliberate attempts to present in typical groupings distinct phases of our social order." [15] This gave them a "contemporary" quality. As might be expected, Wells objected to the "hopeless ideal of scholarly refinement" that appeared in some of the novels. He tactfully referred to such weaknesses of Gissing's work as "the exponent character" and the tone of personal bias as faults that showed signs of disappearing as the novelist developed, but Gissing, giving his reaction to Wells's article, wrote that he was afraid he lacked the energy for the improvements Wells expected to see.

V

On February 10, 1897, about two months after *The Whirlpool* had been completed, Gissing's situation at home, which he had borne with a patience that Roberts considered superhuman, exploded in a scene that drove him from the house. Roberts was not present, of course, but he said, on the basis of "Maitland's" information: "The wife behaved like a maniac; she shrieked, and struck him. She abused him in the vilest terms, such as he could not or would not repeat to me. It was with the greatest difficulty that I at last got him calm enough to meet anyone else." [16]

He went to New Romney, to stay with Harry Hick, an old friend he had known at school. Hick, who was a doctor, examined him, and recommended that he consult a specialist. Gissing had already been warned that the respiratory disorders that had first attacked him seriously at Naples in 1890 were now developing into a definite disease, and that he had a weak spot in his right lung which might prove to be serious. Accordingly, after seeing a physician named Philip Pye-Smith, who recommended the air of South Devon, Gissing spent the next few months at the little seaside town of Budleigh Salterton, which he had discovered in February, 1891, when he was living in Exeter.

There followed a pleasant and fruitful interlude of about three months and two weeks. Margaret came to stay with him, and Wells and his wife joined them for a fortnight; the visit, in Gissing's words, "did me a great deal of good." [17] Toward the end of March the unsettled Algernon proposed that he solve his occupational problem by becoming a clergyman. Interestingly, the author of *Born in Exile* raised no doctrinal objections but approved of the plan if the practical obstacles could be overcome, saying that Algernon would be a great improvement over the usual clergyman, and could do useful work in the church. Reverting to a general consideration of his brother's situation from the detached point of view that his retreat at Budleigh Salterton gave him, he wrote, with characteristic pessimism, that he was glad most of his life was over. "It is nothing less than a miracle that we, with our total lack of practical strength, have escaped sheer beggary. I wonder, often and often, whether this family curse will show itself in the next generation. I shall do my best to bring up my boys in a spirit of savage egotism." [18]

He seems to have recovered his spirits, however, for it was at Budleigh Salterton, while reading a book by Ferdinand Gregorovius (no doubt his *Geschichte der Stadt Rom im Mittelalter*), that Gissing conceived the idea of writing the historical novel about sixth-century Rome that was to become *Veranilda*. His preparations for this project were long and thorough; he began by reading Cassiodorus' *Variae*, sought out information about St. Benedict and the daily life of the period, and laid plans for returning to Italy to gather material. He discussed his novel with Wells when he came to Budleigh Salterton in April, and it was agreed that Wells and his wife should join him in Rome the following year. The novel, he wrote to Bertz, was to be the fulfillment of an old ambition.

Peace with Edith was established through the intervention of Eliza Orme, a friend Gissing had met at dinner with Lawrence and Bullen in 1894, and a person who was to play a significant part in his family affairs. On May 31, somewhat pacified, no doubt, by the recent success of *The Whirlpool*, he returned home, where Edith soon joined him.

His main occupation now was serious research into Roman history of the sixth century in connection with his historical novel, and he persuaded the London Library to purchase some of the books he needed. At the same time he was working casually at another congenial undertaking, a book-length study of Dickens. On December 27, 1896, he had received a note from an old Owens College friend, John Holland Rose, asking him to write a book on Dickens to be published as part of a Victorian Era Series, and he welcomed the assignment as a change from fiction. He gathered notes for this book throughout the summer and began to reread John Forster's *Life of Dickens* in the early part of August. As a third project he began, on June 8, the humorous novelette, *The Town Traveller*, which was written, as he told Bertz, expressly to make money. Gissing committed little of his talent to this story. A comic intrigue having to do with the search for the rich uncle of a spirited London girl named Polly Sparkes, it is notable only for its good-humored, though still faintly patronizing, treatment of lodginghouse life, and it is hardly recognizable as Gissing's work. The first half was sent to Colles before the end of June with the request that he make as much as he could from it.

On July 24 Gissing took Edith and the baby to Castle Bolton in Yorkshire where Walter later joined them for what proved to be a turbulent month's holiday. The chaotic journey was made more troublesome by Edith's grumbling and scolding, but Gissing had learned that "stern silence" was the best policy for him to follow. Her constant ill humor now seemed to be strengthening a half-formed resolution in his mind to make the earlier separation permanent. In the past he had generally kept the misery Edith caused him to himself, but on August 17, a day when her behavior was worse than usual, he sent Margaret a letter containing a detailed account of her actions, telling her the letter was to be kept for possible use as evidence. In the next few days Edith's ill temper spoiled an excursion to a picturesque mountain torrent and caused a disagreement with the landlady's daughter. Determined to escape from her, Gissing wrote to Miss Orme that he had decided to spend the winter in Italy.

On August 25 Edith's behavior reached a climax, which Gissing recorded in his diary as a "crucial instance." Angry at being unable to find a small object which had rolled out of the hands of one of the children into the room where Gissing was sitting, she imagined that Gissing was hiding it to annoy her, and accused him at tea, in Walter's presence, of lying to her about it. During the ensuing argument she threatened to throw a plate at him. Gissing, grown suddenly calm, asked Walter to repeat the words and recorded them in his pocketbook to confront her with when she denied having said them, as he knew she would. The scene ended as she told Walter she pitied him for having such an ill-tempered father. "There it is," wrote Gissing. "Decisive, I should think, forever." [19]

While his family was on its way home from this holiday toward the end of August, Gissing stayed behind at King's Cross Station to meet Algernon and turn Walter over to him. As a result, he was alone when he met James B. Pinker, the literary agent, in Waterloo Station. Gissing rode with Pinker as far as Epsom, and then wrote to ask him to handle the American rights of his forthcoming book, *Human Odds and Ends,* a collection of his short stories to be published by Lawrence and Bullen. Eventually, Gissing was to put all his business into Pinker's hands.

At home, Gissing prepared secretly for his Italian trip by reading the work of the archeologist François Lenormant and making a start on the Dickens book, which was to be completed abroad. The purpose of his trip, he wrote to Bertz, was to examine the scenes of his Roman novel; he thought he might also make use of his experiences for a book of "travel-sketches." On September 6 he revealed his intention to Edith, who reacted with anger, as he expected her to. The household was to be broken up, the furniture put into storage, and lodgings were to be found for Edith and the child; at the last moment, however, Miss Orme earned Gissing's profound gratitude by offering to take Edith in to live with her at a reasonable rent. A resentful parting took place on September 17; it was the end of a miserable marriage that had lasted nearly seven years, for Gissing and Edith were never to live together again.

Gissing suffered one serious disappointment before he left England. Early in September his friend Henry Norman had suggested that it was time for a collected edition of his novels. Aroused to enthusiasm by the idea, Gissing wrote to Bullen about it, saying he did not want his work to pass out of circulation. However, when he dined with Bullen in London on the evening before his departure, the publisher, who had been so helpful about his work a few years earlier, met his proposal of a collected edition with pessimism.

IX

DICKENS AND ITALY

I

LEAVING London on September 22, 1897, Gissing traveled by way of Basle and Florence to Siena, where he soon found a room that pleased him at Via delle Belle Arti 18, with a family named Gabrielli. At first the intoxication of being in Italy again allowed him to take pleasure in small things; a *festa* was in progress, his room commanded a view of the Duomo, the landlady and her sister promised to give him good practice in Italian, for they did not speak English, and he made the acquaintance of a congenial young American lodger named Dunne, who played the zither. He was able to work long hours on the Dickens book, in spite of ominous indications about his health; a cough that had started in Florence left stains of blood on his handkerchief, and he noticed that he was losing weight but told himself that he would get more fresh air after finishing his book.

Two weeks later, in the middle of October, he was feeling, as he wandered about Siena and read an English newspaper, that he had been away from home for months. But new developments began to trouble him. A gloomy atmosphere prevailed in the boarding-house, for Signor Gabrielli, a bedridden paralytic, was now approaching his end. Gissing and Dunne tried to dissipate the sadness with a little party held to celebrate another lodger's completion of his military service, but weeping could be heard from other parts of the house. On October 17 Signor Gabrielli died in strikingly dramatic circumstances; a thunderstorm was raging, and Gissing could hear, between the loud peals of thunder, Gabrielli's wife crying

214

"*Addio*" as she was led from his bedside. Not long afterward the entire household, together with its boarders, moved, and Gissing was assigned to a pleasant room in the new house.

Here he brought his work on Dickens to a close on November 5, not without some weariness and impatience. Although few of its ideas are original, *Charles Dickens: A Critical Study* is a workmanlike and engaging book. In spite of his great popularity, Dickens did not fare well at the hands of the most discriminating critics of his time, partly because his novels lacked realism, partly because the philosophy they expressed seemed superficial and naïve. Toward the end of the century, however, realism was coming to seem less inevitable as a canon of excellence in fiction, and this made it possible for Gissing to admit Dickens' limitations and express admiration for him without seeming inconsistent. Adopting a tone of broad tolerance, he examined Dickens' talent on its own terms, without applying any external critical standards to it. Essentially, his book is an act of homage whose sincerity is deepened by its conscientious recognition of Dickens' shortcomings and deficiencies.

The most striking contribution to Dickens criticism Gissing made was that of putting the novelist and his work into their appropriate sociological setting. He began by attributing two social motivations to Dickens: avenging himself on the middle class in retaliation for his suffering as a child, and winning the status of a middle-class gentleman himself. Then, in a brief review of labor conditions and reform legislation between 1812 and 1834, Gissing mentioned the historical facts most relevant to the early social novels, adding that Dickens' interest in the poor arose from his sympathy with the neglected and exploited children described in Parliamentary reports on factories and mines.

Most responsible critics had said that Dickens could not properly be called a realist, and Gissing agreed with this view, but while others had been content to cite flagrant examples of Dickens' distortions and exaggerations, Gissing offered some reasons for them. He felt that a good deal about Dickens could be explained by his wholehearted acceptance of middle-class tastes and feelings. His primary aims were not to imitate reality but to please his readers, softening and suppressing the facts of life when necessary, and to express a simple and familiar moral code. Gissing's discussion of this point seems to be indebted to the astute analysis of the morality of Dickens' novels in an article by George Stott appearing in the *Contemporary Review* in 1869. Observing that Dickens' novels originated in his moral convictions and were embodiments of his doctrines, Stott termed him an "Idealist" rather than a "Realist." He explained that he was using the term "Idealism" to mean the process of locating the types or essences of things, not that of en-nobling them. Their abundance of details lends Dickens' novels a superficially realistic air, but a closer examination, says Stott, reveals that the details are usually improbable, and have been chosen for their expressive qualities rather than their reflection of reality.

Adopting some of the distinctions and terms used by Stott, Gis-sing described Dickens' usual method of character portrayal as a process of careful selection intended to achieve an "essence" rather than an authentic impression of a personage. Mrs. Gamp, one of its finest products, is constructed of perfectly recognizable materials drawn from actuality, but she is not realistic, for she does not make the impression that her real-life counterpart would make; she does not disgust, but amuses. She is no more than "the Platonic *idea* of London's hired nurse early in Victoria's reign." [1] The difference be-tween this method and true realism is the difference between Dick-ens and Hogarth. Dickens idealizes, but Hogarth, says Gissing, ". . . gives us life—and we cannot bear it." [2] Gissing thought that Dickens was willing to depict life with faithful realism, but that the desire to entertain and to support a moral view were far stronger motives with him, even if they often led him to falsify actuality. To some, Gissing added, this practice would make Dickens un-acceptable as a serious artist. Indeed, Andrew Lang rejected Gis-sing's term "idealist" as an unjustifiable condemnation of Dickens (though it was not intended to condemn) and irritably waved aside such critical distinctions as valueless.

In generally approving of Dickens' powers of characterization, Gissing dissented from most respectable critics. He said that most of Dickens' characters were true to life, but their human nature was distorted by the implausible motivations required by Dickens' sensational plots. It was no more than a critical commonplace to ad-mit, as Gissing did, that Dickens was weakest in depicting normal or virtuous characters. An anonymous critic writing in the *West-minster Review* of October, 1864, had pointed out that Dickens could not create people who were genuinely admirable or fearful; and the author of an article in the June, 1871, number of *Blackwood's Magazine* had said that his inability to portray noble individuals debarred him from ranking with the greatest writers. Like the *Westminster* critic, Gissing found the sudden conversions Dickens' people sometimes experienced unconvincing. In the evaluation of Dickens' grotesque and lower-class characters, however, critical opinion was divided. It was common to dismiss them as "caricatures," and Taine, G. H. Lewes, and Stott all agreed in using this word. Stott, in fact, defined Dickens' failure as the use of the methods of caricature in fields where they were not appropriate. In defending Dickens, Gissing pointed out that he must have found much oddity about him in real life, and that exaggeration of this quality was a natural result of his "idealism." But he denied that Dickens' method was caricature, for he was not "broad and simple," but complex and richly detailed; indeed, he considered the portrayal of such eccentrics as Micawber to be Dickens' great and distinctive power.

Dickens' humor was universally recognized, of course, but Gissing was almost alone in feeling that it contained thought as well as wit. "The humorist . . . implies more than he can possibly have thought out; and therefore it is that we find the best humour inexhaustible, ever fresh when we return to it, ever, as our knowledge of life increases, more suggestive of wisdom." [3]

The values of Dickens' humor, Gissing said, were that it depicted manners vividly, mocked stupidity, and led people to take an interest in the serious social questions he treated. Taine had remarked on the punitive element in Dickens' satire; but Gissing insisted that his satire was never strong enough to alienate readers, even when it was directed against "national character." Of all the critics, only Taine and Gissing pointed out the English quality of Dickens' work, and they disagreed about its significance. Taine held up Dickens' narrow-minded, grasping businessmen as embodiments of a national fault of character; Gissing, however, felt that Dickens' "*Englishness*" and his love of "the homely English race" formed the ultimate source of his strength.

Gissing's study of Dickens reflects many of his most characteristic attitudes. Unwilling to face the fact that Dickens had unmercifully satirized the classical learning he loved, Gissing explained his gibes at scholarship as a result of his feeling that his education had been inadequate, and he observed that Dickens was willing enough to have his sons given the conventional classical education. Stott, who shows that Dickens was unable to appreciate the value of any of the learned professions, including politics and the law, is more convincing. Gissing's prejudice against the theater led him to pronounce Dickens' love of the drama "assuredly a misfortune to him as author and as man," [4] and to ascribe the melodramatic effects and improbable plots of his novels to it. He betrayed envy and admiration in describing Dickens' gift for fluent composition and in telling of his irresponsibility in beginning a serial story without a fixed plan. Thinking, no doubt, of his own very different treatment of the subject in New Grub Street, he insisted that Dickens had not intended David Copperfield to be an honest portrayal of the profession of authorship. "The attempt," said Gissing, "would have cost him half his public." [5]

In Dickens' treatment of women, especially vulgar and ignorant women, Gissing, guided by his own generous knowledge of irate landladies, recalcitrant servants, and difficult wives, found "incontestable fidelity." Unable to resist a digression on one of his favorite grievances, he predicted that, when women won social and educational equality, they would see in Dickens' vast gallery of scolds, coquettes, and giddy girls a force moving toward the reform of "the ancient deformity of their sex."

As might be expected, Gissing did not admire Dickens' sympathetic treatment of the poor as a class. He felt that Dickens was not entirely successful in dealing with the poor because he was reluctant to criticize them. He was skeptical of such lower-class "gentlemen" as Tom Pinch and Joe Gargery, though he was forced to admit the charm of these characterizations. In evaluating Dickens' political position, he passed over the sympathy for the poor and the hostility toward the aristocracy, so obvious in his novels, to one of his public speeches in which he found a dubious justification for arguing that Dickens was no democrat and was unwilling to allow the majority to exercise political power. He preferred, says Gissing, to put his hope in the sort of private philanthropy personified by the Cheeryble brothers and the converted Scrooge; this is the attitude that Stott contemptuously called "an expansion of the idea of Christmas," and that appeared in Gissing's own novels as a weak-minded substitute for genuine reform. Nevertheless, said Gissing, Dickens' feeling that the poor deserved succor, though it may have seemed old-fashioned and tame in the days of the Marxists and Fabians, was sufficiently extreme to make him a Radical in his own time.

Charles Dickens was successful enough to be reissued in an elaborate Imperial Edition, with topographical illustrations and notes by George Kitton, after Gissing's death. It also resulted in Gissing's becoming involved in a number of other Dickens projects. At the request of the publisher Methuen, he wrote prefaces to some of the novels for publication in the Rochester Edition of Dickens' works. Only nine of the novels were published in this set, and Gissing's prefaces to these were later collected in a separate volume entitled *The Immortal Dickens*. He also wrote some articles on Dickens for magazines and in 1901 was approached by Chapman and Hall to do a new biography of Dickens based on Forster's *Life*. This was one of the most familiar and beloved of all books to Gissing; he had first read it when he was a schoolboy of sixteen at Lindow Grove, and he referred to it from time to time in his letters and other writings throughout his life. He was too ill to write a new biography, but agreed instead to do an abridgment of Forster's work.

II

Soon after finishing the Dickens book in the early part of November, 1897, Gissing left Siena for Rome and Naples to begin the Calabrian journey described in *By the Ionian Sea*. The poor and backward province at the toe of the Italian boot has attracted few sightseers. Gissing's book is one of a short line of modest descriptive accounts by intrepid English travelers. The others are Henry Swinburne's *Travels in Two Sicilies* (1783), Edward Lear's *Journal of a Landscape Painter in Southern Calabria* (1852), and Norman Douglas' *Old Calabria* (1915). The Neapolitans warned Gissing before he left that the country was unpleasant, and at one town he visited he was told that they had a traveler only once in a hundred years. But Gissing persisted in his aim of seeing the country that had once been "*Magna Graecia*," because, as he explained in *By the Ionian Sea*, it combined the two cultures that he loved most, those of Greece and Rome. Before entering it, however, he took the precaution of executing his will at the British Consulate in Naples.

Actually, only an imagination saturated with the past could feel in the poverty and squalor of nineteenth-century Calabria any of its former historical interest. The only facilities available for Gissing's landing at the coastal town of Paola were the arms of two strong men who carried him through the surf. After a scenic carriage ride inland he found that the inn he had planned to stay at in Cosenza, the *Due Lionetti*, was "really alarming." Dilapidated, dirty, and smelly, it seemed to have as its only staff a man, either a waiter or the proprietor, who wore the shabbiest clothes Gissing had ever seen. Cosenza interested him because as the ancient town of Cosentia it had marked the furthest point of the Gothic invasion of Italy, and it contained the grave of Alaric, the Gothic conqueror. While exploring the town's geography in detail, Gissing came to the conclusion that the story about the prisoners who had been killed after digging Alaric's grave to prevent their divulging the secret of its situation was illogical, for the river Busento, which had been diverted to cover the grave, was in full view of the town.

After a few days at Cosenza, Gissing traveled by rail to Taranto. There he made the acquaintance of the museum director and, in spite of his warnings that he was wasting his time, sought out the river Galesus, a place mentioned lovingly by Horace. He was disappointed, after all, to find that it was less than half a mile long and entirely uninteresting. In the same way, his eagerness to see Fontanella, a spot near Taranto whose murex shells had been famous in antiquity for their purple dye, was turned to disgust when he discovered that the spot was occupied by a modern arsenal. On November 25 he began to retrace his journey along the coast that faced Greece, stopping first at the town of Metaponto, which had been a thriving place in antiquity but now seemed to consist solely of a railway station. Nevertheless, Gissing, enlisting a boy as a guide, made his way to some ancient temples and, remembering that Pythagoras had died there in 497 B.C., tried to imagine the barren countryside as a fertile and flourishing Greek colony.

On the evening of the same day he arrived at Cotrone, the ancient city of Croton, from whose shore he could see the single surviving column of a temple of Hera that had once stood on the coast nearby. He had planned to visit these remains, but since a fresh gale prevented the boat trip, he spent a few days wandering about the ugly and depressing town, sketching what he saw. On November 28 a sudden feebleness and loss of appetite sent him to bed. The doctor who came to the Albergo Concordia to see him diagnosed "rheumatism" caught from exposure to the wind and recommended strong doses of quinine. Confined to bed for several days, Gissing was forced to give up his visit to the temple and to find some interest instead in observing the people of the inn who attended him. The average Englishman, he wrote, would have taken them for ragged ruffians, but, through the closer acquaintance forced by his illness, Gissing found in his landlady, the kitchen maid, a newspaper seller, and the boy who cleaned his room a good deal of kindness, pathos, and cheerfulness.

Gissing had often had curiously vivid dreams, which he took some care to record, and he found that the quinine he took improved them. It seemed to liberate remote subconscious imaginings, so that he saw splendid visions of ancient life, street scenes, and armies, which astonished him by their unfamiliarity and wealth of color and detail. Dr. Sculco, sympathizing with his patient's frustrated yearning to see the temple of Hera, did his best to satisfy his curiosity by describing the spot and relating some of the customs of Cotrone. Norman Douglas, who wrote his book about Calabria some eighteen years later, retraced Gissing's steps through Cotrone, using *By the Ionian Sea* as a guide. He sought out some of the local people mentioned by Gissing and even talked about Gissing with Dr. Sculco, who, however, was rather uncommunicative. As soon as he was well enough to leave his bed, Gissing moved on to Catanzaro, the next stop on his itinerary, where letters were awaiting him.

He arrived on December 6 and found the air of the mountain town invigorating. The English vice-consul there, to whom he had a letter of introduction, turned out to be an Italian who spoke no English but was overwhelmingly kind and attentive. While sitting in a café in Catanzaro Gissing was struck by the superiority of the conversation he heard around him to the sort of talk that would have been its counterpart in England. The casual talk of poor

Italians, he noted, was not profound or closely reasoned, but it accorded respect to reason and often dealt, however superficially, with abstract subjects.

Gissing's enthusiasm for antiquity plunged him into a last disaster before he left Calabria. He was determined to visit Squillace, the town where Cassiodorus, the founder of the medieval scribal tradition, had set up his two monasteries with their scriptoria. He made a carriage trip there through the rain only to find modern Squillace "a filthy ruin." The inn was too squalid even for him, who had braved the *Due Lionetti* at Cosenza; it served the only wine he had ever found undrinkable. Unable to stay over, he visited some of the places mentioned by Cassiodorus and learned from some laborers he befriended that the historian's name was still associated with local landmarks. Then he left for his last stopping place, Reggio di Calabria. While musing on his trip at Reggio, in view of Mount Etna, he felt anger at the modern Italians, who were destroying the old associations. "These countries," he wrote with unreasonable fervor, "ought to be desolate." [6] Just before going back to Naples, he was pleased and touched to note, on the first page of the museum's registry book, the signature of François Lenormant, whose book *La Grande grèce* had guided him through "*Magna Graecia.*"

On his way from Naples to Rome, Gissing spent a night at the Abbey of Cassino, which he planned to use for some scenes in *Veranilda*. Going up to the monastery in the afternoon on the back of a donkey, he was received by the prior, to whom he explained the plan for his novel. As he took a frugal supper with the monks and three other visitors, he absorbed the medieval atmosphere of the place. After sleeping in a comfortable room with an excellent view he explored the monastery's grounds in the morning, then took the train to Rome.

In Rome his main employments were gathering material for *Veranilda*, by reading historical works at the Biblioteca Vittorio Emanuele, and exploring the city minutely. He spent a great deal of time with English friends and was curious enough to attend some Church ceremonies, including a Requiem Mass for Pius IX held in the Sistine Chapel, where he had to wear a dress suit and stand throughout the proceedings. When Wells wrote in January to say that he meant to come to Rome in accordance with the plans they had made the year before at Budleigh Salterton, Gissing busied himself to make arrangements, ultimately reserving a room for the Wellses at the Hotel Alibert. He himself was still in ill health after an attack of influenza and, deciding that life in lodgings was now too hard for him, moved into the hotel on February 14, in spite of the expense. When Wells and his wife arrived on March 9, the three toured Rome vigorously together. A lively group was formed and gradually extended as they were joined by Dunne, Gissing's American acquaintance from Siena, E. W. Hornung, the future author of *The Amateur Cracksman* and creator of Raffles, and Conan Doyle, who was Hornung's brother-in-law. Touring, visits, dinners, and conversations brought them together often in the next couple of weeks; a kind of climax was reached on April 8 when several of these friends dined together at a *trattoria* and spent the rest of the evening at the Hornungs' quarters.

Gissing did little writing in Rome. Soon after arriving he corrected the proofs of *Charles Dickens*, which had caught up with him at Catanzaro, and in March met a commitment for a short story by writing "The Ring Finger." On March 7 he learned from Colles that an agreement reached with Methuen about *The Town Traveller* would bring him an advance of £350 for British and American rights, more than any of his other books had earned! Disquieting news about Edith made it hard for him to concentrate on his work at the library. Miss Orme wrote to him regularly, and, while her reports had been satisfactory at first, he now began to hear that Edith was quarreling with the neighbors and disrupting the household. Gissing now began to write to Algernon about various places where they might share a house together; it would have to be away from London, possibly in the Midlands, with Edith settled elsewhere. "What I want," he wrote, "is a *home* in England, where I can know that my books and papers are safe." [7] Toward the end of February, Miss Orme wrote that she had found separate lodgings for Edith. In a frantic series of notes to Algernon, Gissing asked him to spend two days in London at the end of March, moving the furniture from the warehouse to the four-room house Edith was to occupy, and sent him a list of the furniture together with detailed instructions. The complicated arrangements, all directed by letters from Rome, were completed by April 1, and on April 4 Gissing heard that Edith was settled.

In the meantime, a legal separation was being planned with the help of Miss Orme. In the middle of March Gissing had received from an attorney named Brewster a document fixing the separation agreement. Miss Orme had suggested that Edith be allowed a pound a week for expenses, but Gissing changed this to twenty-five shillings, and Brewster continued to negotiate with Edith.

On April 12 the Wellses left Rome for Naples and Gissing entrained for Berlin, where he was to see Bertz for the first time since they had parted in London fifteen years before. He had taken the precaution of writing that he wanted to see no one but Bertz himself, for he felt himself "a wretched invalid, weak in body and mind." [8] When Bertz met him at the station in Berlin, Gissing found that his old friend had aged but was apparently in good health. Although he had once planned to come to Germany to live, Gissing found much to complain of during the two days he spent living in Bertz's house in Potsdam and touring Berlin. He was disstressed by the "rampant militarism" he saw about him, and complained of "the sheer *commonness* of it all, after Italy." [9] There were many signs of wealth and ambition, but there was little beauty. On the whole, he must have been glad to leave Berlin on April 18, going, via Cologne, Ostend, and Dover, to Harry Hick's house in New Romney, where he arrived at eleven in the evening.

III

Re-establishing himself in England occupied Gissing for a month. After taking a room in London at the Hotel Previtali, he began a busy round of business and social visits. First he learned that his bank balance was two hundred pounds; then he saw two publishers, an old one, Bullen, and a new one, Grant Richards. Then, after visits with Roberts, Miss Collet, and Henry Norman, he went up to spend a week at Wakefield, where Walter was still living with his mother and sisters. On May 6 he rented a house at 7 Clifton Terrace, Dorking, and, on a day spent in London to buy furnishings, dined with a party that included Clodd, Shorter, Barrie, and G. W. Cable. The last two joined him the following evening when they dined at Meredith's. On May 20 Gissing moved into his new house, which was by now equipped with furnishings and a housekeeper.

It is significant that he asked the Wellses to come to dinner there two days later, for he had never felt able to invite them to his home when he was living with Edith. Finding that he had spent seventy pounds in setting up his household, he thought it was time to go to work, and by June 3 he had written three short stories, which he sent to Colles.

Having insured some income in this way, Gissing now for the second time in his life tried to write a play. For more than a month he worked on a dramatic project called "The Golden Trust." Then, after an interlude of a few days spent on a three-act comedy to be called "Clare's Engagement," he went back to a new plan for "The Golden Trust." After some indecision and such complaints in his diary as "Desperate struggle, this," he finished the first act, but got no further.

Not long after his arrival in England, Gissing received a novel and interesting proposal from the publisher Grant Richards, who offered to buy the rights to all of his work for the next five years at a price higher than the sum it would ordinarily bring. After considering the offer for a month, Gissing accepted it, but on terms that he must have known would be refused. Although he had never earned more than five hundred pounds a year through his writing (and that only in the very best years), he asked Richards for a thousand pounds a year, assuring him that he would receive "a fair return in work." He described his plans in this way:

I want to write (I think you know that I write to please myself) two kinds of novel: one running to about 150,000 words, the other to some 80,000. I want also to write short pieces of between 3,000 and 10,000 words. As to character of work, that must be entirely my own affair. For twenty years I have written what I thought good in spite of every difficulty, and I cannot imagine myself being induced by any circumstances to do otherwise.[10]

Richards kept the question open by replying that he was considering Gissing's proposal.

Edith was actively seeking Gissing, who was terrified that she might find him; he maintained his only contact with her through Miss Orme. He asked Roberts to spread the rumor that he was planning to live in Worcestershire, near Algernon. "It is not strictly true," he wrote, "—but a very great deal depends on my real abode being protected from invasion."[11] Early in June he learned from Miss Orme that Edith's landlord, grown impatient at her troublesome behavior, had given her notice, and that she had disappeared from her lodgings. Later he heard that, acting upon the rumor he had planted, she had appeared at Algernon's house in Worcestershire. Faced with the necessity of moving her again, Gissing urged Miss Orme to prod Brewster into working out a separation agreement. His only condition was that Edith was to give up Alfred, the younger child. Early in August he learned that she had attacked her landlady with a stick and had almost been arrested. Half blaming himself for not facing his responsibilities with respect to Edith, he wrote to Roberts: "My behaviour is bestial, but I am so hard driven that it is perhaps excusable. All work impossible, owing to ceaseless reports of mad behaviour in London." [12] Before the end of August, Edith, in the first of a long series of moves caused by her inability to get along with her neighbors, was installed in a new house. Consulting with Brewster, Gissing learned that her terms for agreeing to a separation included possession of both children. Negotiations were stalemated. One dreadful day in September, 1898, the scene Gissing had feared actually took place. Learning his address from an employee at a warehouse where he had stored some furniture, Edith came to see him, bringing little Alfred with her. Gissing told her firmly that they could never live together again, and she went away quietly, without arguing. Gissing remembered afterward that he had been too agitated to speak to Alfred, and that the boy had not paid any attention to him. This was the last time he saw Edith or his younger son.

Now that a divorce seemed finally to have become impossible, Gissing had a stronger reason than ever for wanting one. In the summer of 1898 he had met the woman who was to give him some years of happiness, although he was never able to marry her. On June 23, the day after he had completed the first and only act of "The Golden Trust," Gissing received a letter from "a Frenchwoman," who asked permission to translate *New Grub Street*.

At first he replied that another translator, Georges Art, was interested in the book. However, he agreed to see the French lady and asked Wells, who was giving him bicycle lessons at this time, to invite both of them to lunch at Worcester Park, so that they could meet without violating the proprieties. There Gissing and Gabrielle Fleury saw each other for the first time, and walked in the garden together after lunch. He gave her permission to do the translation, though Georges Art later protested at his displacement, and Mlle. Fleury soon reached an agreement with the novel's copyright holders, Smith, Elder. She came to Dorking on July 26 to report to Gissing that her translation would appear serially in either the *Journal des Débats* or *Le Temps*. "As explanation of this rather extraordinary state of things," he wrote to Bertz, "you must remember that I am at present almost as well known in Paris as in London— that French papers have abounded in flattering paragraphs about me. . . ." [13] Gissing noted in his diary that Gabrielle had arrived on the 11:28 and left on the 8:35. The day he spent with her convinced him that she was "a sweet and intelligent creature." [14] After receiving a letter from her, written in a style he greatly admired, he wrote to Wells that "Mlle. Fleury has a mind of rare delicacy, emotional without emotionalism, sensitive to every appeal of art, and rich in womanly perceptiveness." [15] He added that he was looking forward to her probable return to England in October.

During August and September he wrote introductions for Methuen's Rochester Edition of *Pickwick Papers, David Copperfield,* and *Nicholas Nickleby*. Richards did not accept his offer to sell the rights in his production for a five-year period, but he did write early in September to inquire about Gissing's next book. Although a new novel had not yet been begun, and was hardly thought of at this time, Richards promptly accepted Gissing's offer to sell him an option on it for twenty-five pounds. At about the same time Methuen reported that *The Town Traveller* had sold 1,400 copies in England and 1,000 in the colonies and asked Gissing to send his next book when it was ready. This demand for his work was, of course, a new experience for Gissing, and he was determined to take full advantage of it. Recording the letter from Methuen's representative in his diary, he wrote, "I shall make him and Richards bid against each other." [16]

Gabrielle Fleury and Gissing continued to write to each other after she had returned to Paris to work on her translation. Through these letters their relationship changed and deepened; they had met only twice, but after a summer of correspondence they were in love. Gabrielle returned to England early in October, and after meeting her at East Croydon, Gissing took her to Dorking, where they spent a week together. Their coming union was by now a settled thing. They had many long talks and walks in the neighborhood, and read favorite poems to each other, Gissing choosing Browning and Tennyson and Gabrielle, Victor Hugo. When they parted, Gissing accompanied her for part of the trip home; the lovers were so engrossed in each other that they took the wrong train at Dorking, and found themselves at the London Bridge station instead of East Croydon. Eventually however, Gabrielle took a channel steamer at Newhaven. "We have decided," wrote Gissing in his diary, "that our life together will begin in the spring." [17]

In reporting these developments to Bertz, Gissing wrote, "The thing is a miracle, nothing less." [18] Eight years earlier, in telling the same friend that he could not bear his loneliness, he had said that he must find some "work-girl" to live with. "Marriage, in the best sense, is impossible," he wrote at that time, "owing to my insufficient income; educated English girls *will* not face poverty in marriage. . . ." He said that he knew the danger of befriending a lower-class girl. "But then, reflect: there is no *real* hope of my ever marrying any one of a better kind—no *real* hope whatever! I say it with the gravest conviction." [19] His marriage with Edith had been the outcome of these feelings.

Gabrielle Fleury was precisely the sort of woman Gissing had always admired from afar but felt he could never hope to marry. Twenty-nine years old at the time she met Gissing, she was described by Roberts as a refined, intelligent, charming woman of good family. She had an especially melodious voice: "It was perhaps the most beautiful human voice for speaking that I ever heard." [20] The daughter of a chief of customs at the port of Marseilles, where she grew up, Gabrielle had, like Gissing, been an ardent student, and had advanced as far as the Brevet Supérieur, an accomplishment unusual in those days for a girl who was not preparing herself as a teacher. She spoke English fluently, knew German and Italian, had had a thorough musical education, and was an accomplished pianist. She betrayed a certain independence of mind, after her family moved to Paris, by going unescorted to call on well-known writers and asking for their autographs, a practice her family naturally disapproved, but one that led to a number of friendships and acquaintances among literary people. At one time she had been engaged to the Parnassian poet Sully Prudhomme, who was thirty years her senior. Prudhomme wrote some verses to her and gave her a valuable collection of holographs, but the intended marriage was prevented by a member of Gabrielle's family. In spite of her general cultivation and the gift for expression revealed in her letters, she apparently never thought of doing any literary work until her enthusiasm was aroused by *New Grub Street*.

The fact that Gabrielle was his superior socially and had been born to a standard of manners he had had to acquire was not lost on Gissing. Her parents, "people in comfortable circumstances," lived in Passy; she had some "semi-aristocratic" relatives; and she was acquainted with intellectual people of several nationalities, including a sister of Alfred de Musset, the widow of the German poet George Herwegh, and the first wife of the Austrian author Leopold von Sacher-Masoch.

Edith's refusal to agree to a divorce presented no obstacle to the lovers, for neither Gissing nor Gabrielle had any moral reservations about the step they were about to take. Gabrielle was sure of her feelings toward Gissing, and her parents made no objections; her father was an invalid who was to die before their union took place, and her mother approved wholeheartedly of their plans, writing to Gissing to tell him so soon after the decision had been made. But Gissing, who seems to have been troubled both by his timidity in social matters and by his usual reserve in dealing with women, had some doubts. The death of Gabrielle's father in January, 1899, created a new difficulty, for her new status would have to be reflected in the signatures she used on legal documents connected with the transfer of his property. Gissing continued to entertain futile thoughts about a divorce. He made some inquiries about obtaining an American divorce, which could be granted without Edith's agreement, and, hearing from Gabrielle that Von Sacher-Masoch had remarried in Heligoland without divorcing his first wife, he urged Bertz to learn the details; but it turned out that he had simply concealed his first marriage. After these frustrations, Gissing wrote to Roberts, "We have discussed the possibility of braving the world with the simple truth. But it is a tremendous step for G., whose mother would suffer terribly from the results, I fear. She has all sorts of semi-aristocratic relatives; it would be a terrific scandal. And, upon my word, I feel that I should be taking a very grave responsibility." [21]

Gabrielle, less timorous than Gissing, reassured him by writing:

"Nous nous marions parce que nous nous aimons, parce que nous sommes surs l'un de l'autre, non par convenance mondaine." [22] Nevertheless, Gissing told Roberts, they would have to present the appearance of being formally married for the sake of Gabrielle's relatives. He would have to give up the idea of ever obtaining a divorce and would have to live abroad and conceal his whereabouts. "You will be the only man in England who knows this story. Absolute silence!—it goes without saying," he told Roberts. [23]

After his week with Gabrielle, Gissing's creative powers asserted themselves, just as they had after he had been accepted by Edith. Three days after Gabrielle returned to Paris, he began working on *The Crown of Life*, noting that he could now keep at his writing for hours at a time, and had returned to his old schedule of writing from nine to one and five to eight. In spite of his concern about the ambiguities of his relationship to Gabrielle and a harassing attack of eczema which sent him to see a doctor, he worked quickly, finishing the novel by the middle of January, 1899.

IV

The Crown of Life is a love story without a genuine love affair. Its hero, Piers Otway, experiences a number of feelings toward women, but they are attenuated so far beyond the requirements even of Victorian gentility that they arouse suspicions about Gissing's own emotions. Piers begins by worshiping some pictures of ideal women, displayed in a shop window, which arouse vague and troubling aspirations in him. He experiences a stronger form of the same emotion when he falls in love with a girl named Irene Derwent. He idealizes her as "a pearl of women, the prize of wealth, distinction and high manliness." He is, in fact, less in love with Irene than dazzled by the manners, refinement, and position he associates with her. This thoroughly social passion is brought to a temporary end by a social *gaffe*. After being reproached by Irene for coming to a soireé slightly drunk and in inelegant company, Piers gives up his hopes of becoming a civil servant, and goes to Russia to work for an English importing firm. Having in this way spent a few years growing up, he returns to win Irene after all.

Gissing's inability to tell a love story was probably due to the fact that his relations with women had always been substitutes for love. He could admire refined and educated women intensely from a distance, and he could make use of women he did not respect to satisfy his sexual needs, but until his meeting with Gabrielle he seems to have been unable to commit himself to any other relationship. The lovers of *The Crown of Life* are brought together for the happy ending by a common interest in Russian language and culture; apparently, Gissing did not think of a more fundamental motivation. Worst of all, he took Otway's "passion" quite seriously, failing to see that, as H. G. Wells unkindly said, it amounted to little more than "love—in a frock coat."

In spite of its insipid love story, *The Crown of Life* has some interest as an expression of Gissing's pacifism. Imperial interests had kept Britain on the brink of war almost continuously between 1895 and 1899, the year of the Boer War. A protracted disagreement with France, first over possessions in West Africa and then over territories adjacent to the Sudan, had filled the newspapers with Empire propaganda and threats of war. Gissing, who blamed Imperialism on "the syndicates," hated and feared it as a mingling of greed and violence. He had often written to Bertz, while the nations of Europe were energetically building up their colonies, that it was the mission of men like themselves to keep apart from the new barbarism. His letters of the time frequently criticize Kipling and the historical tendency he represented; to Roberts, who thought that Gissing's pacifism was unrealistic and cowardly, he wrote that he detested Imperialism and felt India and Africa to be "an abomination."

In *The Crown of Life* Gissing made some attempt to characterize Imperialism and to suggest a remedy for it. Its best representative in the novel is Arnold Jacks, a handsome young businessman who displays in his personal life, as well as in his attitude toward international problems, what Gissing considered typical English arrogance. He is an admirer of Lee Hannaford, an ingenious and cold-blooded chemist whose specialty is inventing explosives to be used in warfare. Otway's brother Alexander, one of the more vivid people in the novel, represents the common people who support Imperialism. An improvident journalist, he entertains Piers in the single shabby room he shares with his wife and child, praising the Empire while he grows drunk on ale and chauvinism. In contrast with these characters, Jerome Otway, Piers's old father, a vigorous mid-century socialist of the school of Herzen and Bakunin, appears as a gentle libertarian.

The sympathetic characters in the novel who are opposed to Imperialism, draw their inspiration from Russia. The knowledge Gissing had about Russia, based, no doubt, on his reading of Turgenev, Dostoevsky, and Tolstoy, had made him feel that Russian spirituality could serve as an antidote to British Imperialism. He thought he saw his own opposition to militarism crystallized in its purest form in the beliefs of the Dukhobors, who embraced a militant pacifism and resisted army service in the name of a mystic ideal. Otway is much impressed by the sacrifice of a Russian friend who gives up his ambitions to join the Dukhobors. Such actions, he says, are the hope of the future, "peace made a religion." Probably because he felt they might be interested in his criticism of the warlike spirit of the times, Gissing sent copies of *The Crown of Life* to Ibsen and Tolstoy. By coincidence, Tsar Nicholas' "Peace Crusade" was reported in the London newspapers in the same week that Gissing finished his novel and turned it over to Pinker. It was not the first time, he wrote to Bertz, that his writings had anticipated such developments.

During his last few months in England Gissing seems to have made an effort to see nearly all of his acquaintances. Clodd came to spend the night with him on November 12, and on the next day the two paid a visit to Meredith at Box Hill and went to meet Roberts, who had just returned from South Africa. Gissing went to his last Omar Khayyám dinner on December 16. At this dinner, or shortly afterward, he learned of the situation that had come to light following the recent death of Harold Frederic, the London correspondent for the New York *Times*, who had been living in Europe since 1884. Frederic had done a great deal of distinguished reporting in France, Italy, and Russia, and was the author of a number of novels about American and English life. He had been a hard drinker who turned to Christian Science, and, when he died at Henley-on-Thames on October 19 after refusing medical aid, he left, in addition to his wife and children, an illegitimate family consisting of a mistress and four children. This woman and her children, who had, of course, no legal claim upon Frederic's estate, must have seemed to Gissing to be innocent victims of the marriage convention he himself was wrestling with so bitterly. He contributed two guineas to a fund for them and was interested to learn from the fund's executor that Frederic's mistress, herself a Christian Scientist, had saved him from alcoholism, and that the children were being cared for temporarily by the American novelist Stephen Crane, who was then living in England.

Another demand on Gissing's resources came toward the end of January when, as part of his farewell tour, he visited his family in Wakefield. Algernon paid him a visit there, and Gissing, alarmed to find his brother in poor health, committed himself to giving him £150 in the next few months in order to enable him to rest. At the beginning of February Gissing himself fell seriously ill. It was, he wrote to Bertz, "an attack of influenza, followed by lung-congestion, pleurisy, and all sorts of things." [24] The illness lasted for six weeks, leaving him in a weakened condition. By March 22, however, he was strong enough to pay a last visit to Algernon in Worcestershire, where Margaret and Walter were staying on a holiday. He said nothing of Gabrielle. Probably because he knew they would disapprove, he kept his family ignorant of his real reason for moving to France, so that they did not learn of his relationship with Gabrielle until after his death. By May 1 he was staying at Lewes, where he awaited Gabrielle's message summoning him to Rouen.

X

FRANCE AND ENGLAND

I

ON THE evening of May 7, at the Hôtel de Paris in Rouen, Gabrielle and Gissing solemnized their relationship in a private ceremony. Mme. Fleury was present at this scene, and in all probability she was the only witness. She notified her circle of Gabrielle's new status by sending out Gabrielle's visiting card with her maiden name canceled and "Gissing" substituted for it in her own writing. The day after this ceremony, Mme. Fleury returned to Paris while Gissing and Gabrielle stayed at a hotel near Fécamp. They remained on the Normandy coast for nearly a month and went to their permanent residence in Paris at the begining of June.

They lived with Mme. Fleury in her flat at 13 Rue de Siam, a large modern apartment house in Passy not far from the Bois de Boulogne. Although he was now living under the most pleasant physical conditions he had ever known, Gissing had no relief from financial pressures. In addition to the sum he had guaranteed Algernon, he had to put Walter through school and send Edith two pounds a week. Accordingly, he set seriously to work soon after arriving in Paris and, after writing three more Dickens prefaces, turned to the notes of his Calabrian trip and began *By the Ionian Sea*. The work went wonderfully well. On July 11, after less than two weeks of writing, he sent the first nine chapters of the placid little travel book to Pinker. The book was completed about a month later in the course of a long Swiss holiday, while he, Gabrielle, and Mme. Fleury were at Trient. Proofs of *The Crown of Life* which

234

reached him there convinced him that it was "my best book yet for style." He had not written short stories for a long time, but in the middle of this holiday the striking little tale "Humplebee" suggested itself to him. In the first weeks of September they traveled through a number of Swiss cities, and at Airolo Gissing enjoyed the chance of speaking Italian to the local people.

Soon after returning to the Rue de Siam late in September, 1899, he began another novel, "The Coming Man." Although *The Crown of Life* was to meet with a poor reception from reviewers when it was published, it brought him £254 at this time for English and American rights. The new novel went badly; in addition to his old uncertainties, Gissing was depressed by the Boer War, which had broken out in June, and the servant's illness disrupted the household for a few days. After working at "The Coming Man" for about six weeks, Gissing turned to a new project, a novel about people who sought inward peace through Spiritualism, Theosophy, and "things still more foolish." This book, first called "Oracles," then "Among the Prophets," was begun optimistically, for Gissing wrote to Bertz that he thought he could make something "exciting" of it. But his enthusiasm faded by the time it was completed in February of 1900; he complained that financial pressures and the war had distracted him. After reading it, Pinker advised him to lay it aside for a time before sending it out. "Among the Prophets" was never published and never submitted to a publisher. In March, 1901, Gissing asked Pinker to burn both of the typewritten copies in his possession. In the meantime, in the spring of 1900, he wrote more of the Dickens prefaces, spent a few weeks on short stories, and ultimately returned to "The Coming Man."

Gissing spent most of April, 1900, in England, where he stayed with his family in Wakefield, with Clodd in London, and with Wells at Sandgate. The secret behind his residence in Paris was divulged to Wells and very probably to Clodd as well. Gissing was now able to use Wells as an intermediary with English correspondents, so that when Stephen Crane died that summer Gissing sent his note of condolence through Wells.

After Gissing's return to France, he, Gabrielle, and Mme. Fleury moved to a villa with a large garden in St. Honoré les Bains where, in spite of periods of hot weather that reduced him to writing in his underclothes, he worked steadily at "The Coming Man," completing it on August 29. He wrote to Pinker that he considered it the best book he had written for some time. It was vital, he thought, that "The Coming Man" be published as quickly as possible for all sorts of reasons. He needed the money, his public had not had a novel from him for years, and in addition: "I am in good working trim, and have a novel on hand greatly more important than 'The Coming Man,' and decks must be clear for autumn. . . ." [1] The new novel could only have been his historical project, first called "The Vanquished Roman" and finally, *Veranilda*. In spite of Gissing's eagerness for speed, however, the publication of his novel was delayed as Pinker negotiated with a number of American firms, hoping to secure simultaneous publication in England and America. By January, 1901, Gissing was writing with desperate and almost pathetic insistence that it must be published no later than the spring of that year. Soon afterward there were two favorable bids. Chapman and Hall offered £350, and the American firm of Henry Holt offered £150. This was excellent news to Gissing, whose original price had been £150, but the arrangement caused more delay, for the English and American companies could not agree on a date of publication. While these transactions were going on, Gissing's old difficulty with titles reasserted itself. Holt disapproved of "The Coming Man." Desperately, Gissing bombarded Pinker with a succession of infelicitous suggestions until, at almost the last minute, while he was correcting the proofs in March, he hit upon the final title, *Our Friend the Charlatan*.

This book, which was finally published in May, 1901, is a reworking of the problem of *Born in Exile* on a far lower level. Its protagonist, Dyce Lashmar, is a poor young man who uses his eloquence and personal magnetism to court the favor of an eccentric old invalid, Lady Ogram. She is sufficiently impressed by Lashmar and the pseudoscientific social theory he has cribbed from a French treatise to arrange for him to run as a candidate for Parliament against an old enemy of hers. Lashmar, bent on making the most of his good luck, falls out of Lady Ogram's favor by courting her niece, who is her heiress, instead of following the old lady's dictates by marrying her secretary. When Lady Ogram dies, Lashmar is caught in the web of his intrigues, for it turns out that the secretary is the real heiress. After losing the election, Lashmar resigns himself to marrying the unattractive mother of a boy he has been tutoring. The book ends as he finds, just after the marriage, that his bride's modest fortune has been stolen by its dishonest trustee, and that, in spite of his strenuous pursuit of the main chance, he has been left penniless.

Unlike Godwin Peak, Lashmar is a wholehearted opportunist, incapable of moral conflict or remorse. *Our Friend the Charlatan* does not address itself to a moral problem, as *Born in Exile* did, but is concerned with the simpler satisfaction of showing a villain defeated by his own schemes. The ironies of the plot often verge on comedy; however, the fact that their victim, the frustrated and often ridiculous Lashmar, resembles Gissing in surface particulars lends the novel a touch of pathos. Lashmar is bookish and fastidious in speech and manner; he believes in aristocracy, supports a matter-of-fact feminism, and cannot tolerate the vulgarity of the London poor. Accordingly, it seems that this dexterous and farcical novel is also an exercise in self-criticism of a particularly masochistic kind.

The most interesting aspect of *Our Friend the Charlatan* is its criticism of the application of evolutionary theory to government. Capitalists held up evolution as a justification for economic competition, which was defended as an inevitable and ultimately beneficent variant of the Darwinian struggle. Socialists made a somewhat different use of biological theory. Sidney Webb praised the collective state as an advanced development in the evolution of government, which is precisely the point of view attacked by Gissing in *Our Friend the Charlatan*. He clearly saw the pernicious implications of this idea, for he had previously put into Denzil Quarrier's mouth the words: "Nature gives no rights; she will produce an infinite number of creatures only to torture and eventually destroy them. But civilization is at war with nature, and as civilized beings we *have* rights." [2]

Two contemporary works stand behind the issue of social evolution as it is presented in *Our Friend the Charlatan*. The book to which Lashmar owes his "bio-sociological" theory of the state is identified in a prefatory note as Jean Izoulet's *La Cité moderne*. This work, after observing that evolution results in the association of cells, and examining the principle of association with its corollary of specialization in chemistry and biology, applies it to human affairs. "Comme l'animal est une association de cellules, ainsi la cité sera une association d'animaux. . . ." Izoulet then pursues the familiar "body politic" analogy to quaint extremes, comparing the different sensory organs of a dog to administrative departments in a government, and arguing that the corpus of a state must have as its brain an aristocracy. In *Our Friend the Charlatan* Lashmar parades as his own the principle of association. He argues:

Just as cells combine to form the physiological unit, so do human beings combine to form the social-political unit—the State. . . . A cell in itself is blind motion; an aggregate of cells is a living creature. A man by himself is only an animal with superior possibilities; men associated produce reason, civilization, the body politic.[3]

Gissing opposed to this acceptance of the laws of evolution in human affairs the doctrines of Huxley's "Evolution and Ethics," a work he had read in 1895. Huxley had warned that ". . . cosmic nature is no school of virtue, but the headquarters of the enemy of ethical nature." [4] Evolutionary principles cannot be applied to government, he argued, for the standards of the breeder and gardener are completely opposed to those of an ethical, civilized society. Organized society is like a garden in which the plants live in a "state of Art" created by man as protection against the "state of Nature." Both society and the garden exist as defenses against the competitive and selective forces of the evolutionary process. "Let us understand, once for all, that the ethical progress of society depends, not on imitating the cosmic process, still less on running away from it, but on combating it." [5]

In the novel Huxley's view is represented by Lord Dymchurch, an impoverished young nobleman in search of a vocation. One day he meets a pathetic old man of the kind Wordsworth liked to use in his poems, who has grown unable to care for his garden. Dymchurch lends him a hand, and while digging, experiences the revelation that man's livelihood depends on the conflict with nature. Thus, in the very garden of Huxley's analogy he sees that his friend Lashmar's acceptance of the system of nature as a principle in human affairs is wrong. While Lashmar goes on to tumble disastrously from the height of his pretentious theory, Dymchurch sees that it is his duty to return quietly to his small farm and learn to cultivate it. Thus, the organization of society on scientific principles is made the dominant fallacy of *Our Friend the Charlatan*, just as the reconciliation of science and religion was the dominant fallacy of *Born in Exile.*

II

While working on *Our Friend the Charlatan,* Gissing had returned to the problem of bringing out a collected edition of his novels. He wrote to Pinker in August, 1900, that Lawrence and Bullen had failed to reply to a letter of his, and that he understood they were no longer publishing. Lamenting that the books of his to which they owned the rights were "lost property," he tried to arrange for these rights to be sold to some other firm which would be willing to publish a collected edition. His motivation was not his need for money, but a fear that his life's work would be forgotten. "Naturally enough," he wrote, "I have a certain faith in the vitality of what I have written. . . ." [6] Both Methuen and Heinemann displayed some interest in the proposal, but Gissing hoped that a "better" publisher would eventually make an offer.

In spite of his anxiety over matters of business, which sometimes prompted him to write to Pinker twice a day, Gissing continued to work steadily. Just two days after finishing *Our Friend the Charlatan,* he began what was to be his most successful book, *The Private Papers of Henry Ryecroft.* Although most of it was actually written in less than two months, between September 1 and October 24, 1900, while he was living at the Villa des Roses in St. Honoré, the book had had a long genesis in Gissing's mind. His own commonplace book contains some of the ideas which were later developed into passages in the Ryecroft papers, and the thought of writing a book of essays with the title "Thoughts and Reveries" is recorded in an entry made some time before July, 1887. In September of 1900 he wrote to Pinker that he was working on "a queer little book—not a novel—which will amuse you some day," and in the following month he assured him that he felt it was his best work stylistically. Gissing continued to revise and add to the manuscript for nearly a year until it appeared as a serial in the *Fortnightly Review,* under the title "An Author at Grass." It was published as a volume in 1903, and Gissing had the satisfaction of seeing it go through three editions before he died. The clearest and most direct expression of his temperament, it has been frequently reprinted after his death and has achieved the status of a minor classic.

The Private Papers of Henry Ryecroft is a more or less disconnected series of meditations supposedly drawn by Gissing from the private journal of a middle-aged writer who has inherited an unexpected competence and has retired to a cottage near Exeter. Ryecroft, as he is described in Gissing's "Preface," is and is not an autobiographical device. The personality and opinions of these "private papers" are close to Gissing's own; the placid, mellow contentment that pervades the book, on the other hand, is a mood Gissing aspired to but did not achieve. Like Gissing, Ryecroft experienced poverty in London as a young writer, and he shares his author's love of Italy and England, his need for quiet and his bookishness. Ryecroft's "solitary friend," as Gissing wrote to Roberts, was Roberts himself, and Bertz, Henry Norman, and Grant Allen are referred to by their initials. Unlike Gissing, he is a widower, but he lives with a housekeeper under conditions like those at Gissing's house in Dorking. He seems to have been a writer of magazine articles, translations, and reviews rather than a novelist. The most important difference of all is that Ryecroft wrote for money and not as an artist, so that when he became financially independent he stopped writing altogether. He is less like Reardon (who resembles Gissing) than like one of the minor *New Grub Street* writers who haunt the British Museum.

According to the "Preface," Gissing purports to feel, while reading his friend's diary, that Ryecroft might have intended to publish parts of it as a book written for its own sake rather than for money, and ultimately decides to publish it for its "human interest." It consists of fragments of prose on all sorts of subjects suggested to Ryecroft by the weather, the newspapers, his walks, his memories, and the atmosphere of his quiet and comfortable cottage. For lack of a better organization, says Gissing, he has grouped the fragments according to the season of the year in which they were written, without regard to their actual chronology.

In some respects the character of Ryecroft is a sort of confession. The old writer describes himself as a man who does not inspire affection; yet he regrets that his insistence on independence has led him to reject help and friendship throughout his life, so that he is still lonely and cannot regard himself as "part of the social order." He lives alone, enjoying the utter silence of his house; even his housekeeper is praised because she makes no noise and performs her tasks unobtrusively. He is a constant reader but cannot be a genuine scholar because care has made him forgetful. Sensitive and fastidious, he is easily upset by small incidents and deeply thrilled by the small, intense experiences of beautiful flowers or sunsets. He takes his pleasure sparingly. There is no music in his house, but the music he sometimes overhears in the street provides him with an overwhelming esthetic experience. His life consists of thinking, reading, walking, and observing nature in solitude and quiet. Convinced that most of the world's ills are caused by noisy and combative people "who cannot possess their souls in quiet," he feels that the quiet life he leads for his own satisfaction is a positive social good. ". . . Most of the good which saves mankind from destruction comes of life that is led in thoughtful stillness. . . . How well would the revenues of a country be expended, if, by mere pensioning, one-fifth of its population could be induced to live as I do!" [7]

One of the old man's most appealing qualities is his willingness to face bitter personal truths with candor.

. . . never a page of my writing deserved to live. I can say that now without bitterness. . . . The world has done me no injustice; thank Heaven I have grown wise enough not to rail at it for this! [8]

For me Nature has comforts, raptures but no more invigoration.[9]

I read much less than I used to do; I think much more. Yet what is the use of thought which can no longer serve to direct life? [10]

. . . for me there is no more activity, no ambition. I have had my chance—and see what I made of it.[11]

Thoughts like these do not torment him, for he realizes that his life is not supremely important, but "a little thing." ". . . That is best, to smile, not in scorn, but in all forbearance, without too much self-compassion. . . . Better to see the truth now, and accept it, than to fall into dread surprise on some day of weakness, and foolishly to cry against fate." [12] Gissing did not, like Ryecroft, feel that his life had been wasted on useless work; but he did understand the wisdom of calm resignation.

Ryecroft bitterly acknowledges the power of money, both for good and evil. The terrible thing about his youthful poverty, he says, was not that it forced him to live under squalid conditions, for he was happy enough in the slums, but that it drove him to waste his energy in desperate labor. On the other hand, he feels that his past struggles enable him to appreciate his present security and to be grateful to the unknown working people whose labor makes his quiet life possible. The reverse truism, "Money is time," expresses the real value of money for Ryecroft; it enables him to spend his time reading and meditating instead of drudging.

Ryecroft confesses that he is innately undemocratic. He does not love everyone and is glad to be free of the obligation of pretending that he does. Although he made the youthful error of allying himself with the poor, he now understands that their aims are very different from his. Once a socialist, he understands himself now to be a man who loves privacy and his possessions passionately. On the other hand, he is more capable than before of real sympathy with the common people, for, while he valued only intellect when he was young, he has now learned to respect "the intelligence of the heart" often manifested by the rude and ignorant. He recognizes that learning does not necessarily civilize, and that it is possible for a man to remain a lettered barbarian. Wondering how many households are as peaceful as his own, he is led to the reflection that men are naturally selfish and aggressive rather than sociable and cooperative. Peace is less natural to man than war.

Ryecroft's pacifism is based in part at least on his hatred of military discipline. While he was drilled at school, he recalls, his individualism rebelled violently at the mechanical conformity of the parade ground. He feels that a combination of democratic brutality and greed for profit make war inevitable, and he turns his thoughts from it. There is, of course, no doubt, that in his hatred of war Ryecroft speaks for Gissing, who had once written to Walter:

. . . War is a horrible thing which ought to be left to savages—a thing to be ashamed of and not to glory in. It is wicked and dreadful for the people of one country to go and kill those of another. . . . What we ought to be proud of is peace and kindness—not fighting and hatred.[13]

With his pacifism and hatred of chauvinism, Gissing was far from patriotic in the commonest sense of the term. Yet the Ryecroft papers, written from the distance of St. Honoré, comprise a genuine and candid tribute to England. Ryecroft says that in spite of his pleasure in travel, he will never leave England again. He muses lovingly on the peculiarities of English manners, English cookery, and English government. It is a characteristic English trait, he feels, to admire and preserve the concept of nobility; in England democracy is unnatural and destructive. The future poses the problem of whether nobility in manners and mores can be retained while the social class itself disappears. The English, he feels, are fundamentally generous and free; what is mistaken for prudery is a form of Puritan spirituality whose motives are excellent. Giving more praise than blame, the expatriate Gissing describes his countrymen with a calm objectivity very different from the feelings of a time when, returning from Italy on an English steamer, he *suffered* from the presence of English people.

Although his inability to tolerate the pain of a headache with detachment leads Ryecroft to repudiate Marcus Aurelius, the essential quality of the *Ryecroft Papers* is Stoicism with, perhaps, an infusion of detached Oriental mysticism. Ryecroft cannot master the self-discipline recommended by the Stoics, and he does not share Marcus Aurelius' pious belief that evils must be borne because the world is ultimately just, but his conviction that the good life consists of study and meditation pursued in spite of the turmoil of the outside world is a Stoic ideal. Ryecroft's self-improvement does not have the strenuous earnestness recommended by Arnold and Carlyle. It is enough, he feels, to be fully oneself and to have one's own thoughts, even if they are not particularly wise or constructive. Wisdom comes, not from striving for it, but from revery.

For not, surely, by deliberate effort of thought does a man grow wise. The truths of life are not discovered by us. At moments unforeseen, some gracious influence descends upon the soul, touching it to an emotion which, we know not how, the mind transmutes into thought. This can happen only in a calm of the senses, a surrender of the whole being to passionless contemplation.[14]

Ryecroft includes Gissing's only direct discussion of the problem of belief, and it is significant as an expression of the despairing agnosticism that gives his novels their pessimistic temper. In his meditations about God, immortality, and other ultimate problems he is impressed with the pathetic fact of human ignorance. Although it is a mistake to take this ignorance for knowledge, Gissing does feel that beyond the physical world is some "Reason of the All" which he will never begin to understand. The sense that man is doomed to loneliness in a harsh and inexplicable universe leads Gissing to the lamentation:

The most tragic aspect of such a tragedy is that it is not unthinkable. The soul revolts, but dare not see in this revolt the assurance of its higher destiny. Viewing our life thus, is it not easier to believe that the tragedy is played with no spectator? And of a truth, of a truth, what spectator can there be? [15]

When he was young, Gissing felt that agnosticism implied that man was the self-sufficient master of his destiny; in the pages of *Ryecroft* the "insoluble problem" of man's existence gives rise to a despair which can only be alleviated by the necessary "self-deception" of turning away from it. Still, adds Ryecroft, reasserting, but in infinitely tentative language, the hopes of the youthful Gissing, an era of positivism based on scientific methods may come when "everything will be as lucid and serene as a geometric demonstration."

While many of Ryecroft's opinions and experiences are Gissing's own, it would be a mistake to regard the *Ryecroft Papers* as an occasion taken by Gissing to lay aside his fictional mask. Ryecroft's affection for England and his pacifism come directly from Gissing's heart. Whether his balanced, if not precisely warm attitude toward the common people is one Gissing himself had finally achieved is questionable. It is certain that Gissing was not indifferent to recognition, as Ryecroft is, for he continued to lament his poor sales, and when *Ryecroft* itself proved successful his triumph was embittered by the fact that he did not profit proportionately.

"I hope too much will not be made of the few autobiographical pages in this book," Gissing wrote to Harrison. "The thing is much more an aspiration than a memory." [16] Yet this mistake was made even by Roberts, who was irritated by Gissing's apparent profession of attitudes he did not hold. Gissing himself, according to a letter written after his death by Gabrielle, was angry with the *Athenaeum* review that took Ryecroft's preference for scholarship as a bit of autobiography. He felt that it implied that he ought not to have written his novels at all. His letters make it obvious that Ryecroft's gentle resignation did not represent a change in his own character, for in his last years he continued to fume and fret as impatiently as ever. Though it is often difficult to tell where the character, Ryecroft, ends, and the real Gissing begins in these pages, the important fact remains that Ryecroft is a fiction distinct from his author.

Gissing was undoubtedly right in considering the *Ryecroft Papers* his best book stylistically. Its sentences, generally short and uncomplicated, have a certain quiet steadiness that appears only occasionally in his novels, in descriptive passages. Except when he uses it to secure an effect of gentle irony, the language is free of the verbosity that is one of Gissing's worst stylistic faults. It is a gray, reserved prose with a touch of bookish stiffness. It can summon vigor for such subjects as militarism and English cooking, but when it ponders cosmic dilemmas, it melts into a preoccupied indecision which recalls the inconclusiveness of Gissing's social novels. Ryecroft's thought seems to slip into and through issues without resolving them, leaving behind, instead of a verdict, some hint of his mood or personality.

III

Gissing and his family left St. Honoré on November 1 to stay with cousins of Gabrielle at the Châteaux de Chasnay and Tazières at Fourchambault in Nièvre. After visits lasting about six weeks, they returned to Paris, where, on Christmas Day of 1900, in the "dreary flat," as he called it, on the Rue de Siam, Gissing began the historical novel he had been planning since his stay at Budleigh Salterton in the spring of 1897. His recent Italian trip, his research at the Biblioteca Vittorio Emanuele in Rome in 1898, and much of his occasional reading had been preparations for this novel. He had gathered a thick sheaf of notes under such headings as "Topography," "Religion," "Daily Customs," and "Senate," and a sketch of the history of the years 532 to 553.

His interests went well while he worked on "A Vanquished Roman" through the early months of 1901. Gabrielle's translation of *New Grub Street* was serialized in the *Journal des Débats* beginning in February, under the title *La Rue des Meurt-de-faim*, and the *de luxe* edition of *By the Ionian Sea* with illustrations based on Gissing's sketches was going through the press. He enjoyed a visit from Wells and his wife, who passed through Paris on their way from Italy in March, and felt himself in good health but later had a serious attack of influenza which left him weakened; he also had a troublesome skin condition on his face and forehead. A French doctor whom he consulted diagnosed his ailments as "emphysema, chronic bronchitis, and moist spot on right lung." [17] He was ordered to stop working and had to put "A Vanquished Roman" aside. However, instead of seeking mountain air, as the doctor had suggested, he gave way to his longing for the English countryside and English food, and made a trip across the Channel. His pretext was that he had been asked to pose for a photograph to be published in the periodical *Literature*, and did not feel that he could decline this chance for publicity. Wells agreed to put him up, and at the last minute Gabrielle was included in his travel plans. Accordingly, the two went to England the last week in May, staying first with the Wellses at Sandgate, and then with the Pinkers in London, where Gissing had business to transact. Wells arranged for Gissing to pay a visit to Henry James, who lived at Rye, and who had once written an article praising Gissing's feeling for "the general gray grim comedy" of vulgar life.

Instead of returning to Paris after a week, Gissing stayed behind, while Gabrielle went home alone, angered at the decision, reached without her consent, to keep Gissing in England for his health. It seems that the meagre meals customary in his French household had lowered Gissing's resistance and led him to lose weight, so that the moment he began to live at the homes of his English friends, he began to grow heavier, and his health improved. The passages about food in the *Ryecroft Papers* and the letters written from France certainly suggest that Gissing lived in a state of continual yearning for hearty English meals. Apparently the Wellses, probably with the advice of Harry Hick, decided that Gissing must stay in England to consult Pye-Smith, who seconded the French doctor's pessimistic diagnosis and told Gissing that he needed a rest in a sanatorium.

Unfortunately, Gabrielle took the view that these steps implied a criticism of her ability to care for Gissing and also reflected on the effect the French climate had on his health. Unstrung by the illness of her mother and by the fear that Edith might discover Gissing's presence in England, she wrote to Mrs. Wells to protest the separation. It was a step a French doctor would not have approved, she said. Feeling that she had an insufficient hold upon Gissing's affection, she reviewed their relationship, revealing that it had been marked by painful disagreements. She declared that the Wakefield family had always been her rivals for Gissing's love, that the desire to see them had drawn him to England the year before and might well be keeping him there now, and that he kept his relationship with her from them because he was afraid of offending them. Mrs. Wells expressed a justifiable skepticism about this attachment, for Gissing invariably found the company of his mother and sisters tiresome, even unbearable; but Gabrielle insisted that it was unconscious, and stronger than his conscious will —"the voice of the blood." Unless all other indications are wrong, Gabrielle seriously misinterpreted Gissing's attitude toward his family. Walter, who was still living with them, seems to have caused some difficulties, and Gissing's preoccupation with Wakefield was probably due, not to his emotional dependence upon the people there, but to his feeling of guilt at imposing his responsibility for the boy upon others. His unwillingness to tell them about Gabrielle was an aspect of his exaggerated regard for gentility, not the result of his respect for them.

These misunderstandings are a study in national differences; they show that Gabrielle, in spite of her sensitivity, failed to read some of Gissing's characteristic English qualities correctly. But she could hardly fail to grasp the essential element of his nature, which was suspected by everyone who knew him. She said she never felt secure about him, because he was the victim of "an extraordinary, terrible, perhaps morbid *unstability* in mind, views, decisions, feelings," which made him dissatisfied, sooner or later, with any one way of life. He suffered from the "delusion" that the practical problems with which he was so unable to deal were not natural and inevitable but were due to his particular situation, and could be eliminated if only everything were changed. In addition, she wrote, he demonstrated a querulous dissatisfaction with the management of the household, and objected when Gabrielle refused to give up her friends in order to share his solitary habits. "He *can't* be unreservedly happy," she wrote; "it is not in his nature. . . ." [18]

Toward the end of June, after spending a month with Wells, Gissing went to Dr. Jane Walker's East Anglian Sanatorium at Nayland in Suffolk, where for a month he took an "open air and over-feeding cure." He was unhappy at being separated from Gabrielle, aware of her dissatisfaction, and conscious that "as always in things practical, I bungled this affair from the first." [19] But he gained weight and improved in health at the sanatorium. The windows were never closed and food was served in quantities so huge that even Gissing found it somewhat sickening. When he proposed making a visit to Wakefield late in August before returning to France, Gabrielle objected strenuously, saying that the climate of the town would be harmful; and he seems to have gone directly to France, where they stayed in Autun until October 12, and then paid a long visit to Gabrielle's cousin at the Château de Tazières. A warning by a French doctor who examined Gissing sent them further south early in December to spend the winter in the supposedly beneficial warm air at Arcachon. Here, at a *pension* occupied mainly by invalids, Gissing passed most of his day in the open air on a *chaise longue* in the garden, as did many of the guests.

In December Gissing wrote to Ellen that he had at last learned the truth of his condition. His lungs, he wrote, were undergoing a "gradual hardening of all the surface." [20] This seems to be a layman's description of cirrhosis of the lungs, a condition in which the lungs are gradually overgrown with fibrous tissue. Gissing certainly had one of the symptoms, labored breathing, for he reported his "snoring" or "wheezing" as an old peculiarity. The doctor who told him of his disease said that improvement was possible. It is still considered incurable, although the patient may live for ten or twenty years, appearing to enjoy good health.

Naturally, Gissing was hardly able to work during most of this time. Apart from some additions to "An Author at Grass" and an essay called "Dickens in Memory" he wrote nothing. Even his diary, left behind in Paris, was neglected for a whole year. He had begun his abridgment of Forster's *Life of Dickens* after returning from England in the spring, and he continued this project, working an hour or two a day while sitting in his *chaise longue* in Arcachon, but attempting no writing of his own. "Who could write on a *chaise longue?*" he wrote irritably to Roberts. [21]

Early in February, 1902, a serious piece of news came from England. Miss Orme informed him that Edith had been taken in charge, found to be insane, and committed to an asylum. Little Alfred was to live with a farmer's family under the supervision of a sister of Miss Orme. On the whole, said Gissing, he was relieved at this development, for it meant that Edith would no longer cause trouble for everyone around her, and that the child would be well cared for. Only one more allusion to Edith occurs in Gissing's letters after this time. When *The Private Papers of Henry Ryecroft* was published, her name appeared on Gissing's list of those who were to receive author's copies.

When he felt that his health had improved, Gissing returned to his preparations for "A Vanquished Roman" by reading Gregorovius again. However, he did not work on it at this time, but turned instead to the last novel he was to complete before his death, *Will Warburton*. He also had to find a new home, for he had grown to hate Paris, and its climate was bad for him. He and Gabrielle decided on St. Jean de Luz, which had moderate temperatures, an excellent view, and, unlike Arcachon, some claim to beauty. Accordingly, Gissing left Arcachon on April 24 and after some searching rented an apartment on the Place de la Mairie in St. Jean de Luz. A week after the move from the Rue de Siam was made, on July 10, he began *Will Warburton*.

In the autumn, Gabrielle's translation of *New Grub Street* was published in book form in a series put out by the *Revue Blanche*, and the first part of "An Author at Grass" appeared in a May number of the *Fortnightly Review*, after Gissing had waited long and impatiently for it to begin. In June, Constable accepted it for book publication, changing the original title, which was felt to be a little facetious, to *The Private Papers of Henry Ryecroft*.

The remainder of 1902 passed as Gissing, in ill health, studied Spanish, read *Don Quixote* in the original with enjoyment, and worked at his novel at the rate of a page a day, ". . . a poor account," he wrote to Bertz, "for a man who used to write his 8 or 10 hours daily. . . ." [22] After three months' work the novel had to be begun over, amid many complaints of poverty. Since he lived only a few miles from Roncesvalles, he crossed over to Spain early in November for a sight-seeing tour. Thus, toward the end of his life, he visited the scene of the historic battle he had described in a poem of his boyhood. The entry of November 8, 1902, mentioning this excursion is the last in the three-volume diary that Gissing had kept, with few interruptions, for fifteen years.

Early in 1903 he suffered from a new and uncomfortable disorder, sciatica, but was cheered by the success of the *Ryecroft Papers*, which appeared as a volume in January. It was the only one of his books that could be called a decided success. The reviews were enthusiastic, a third edition was published in March, the book became a frequent topic of conversation in London, and in the English colony of St. Jean de Luz it was being read by everyone. Gissing received many letters about it, including one from a clergyman who asked whether Ryecroft's exemplary housekeeper was now free and enclosed a stamped envelope for Gissing's reply. These admirers of his would find it hard to believe, grumbled Gissing, that in spite of the recognition it had won, the book brought him very little money. He wrote to Edward Clodd that it had earned him less than two hundred pounds.

Roberts paid a visit to Gissing while he was at St. Jean de Luz, meeting Gabrielle for the first time, and for the first time approving of a woman his friend loved. During his week-long stay he found that Gissing was unhappy with the food and bare furnishings of his home and thought longingly of returning to England with Gabrielle, but the poor health of Mme. Fleury made any such move impossible. He mused over his historical novel but wrote little, and Roberts was impatient to see that he had grown so timorous about his health that he was reluctant to go out of the house, even in good weather.

When he finished *Will Warburton* in March, Gissing sent it to Pinker, asking that it be placed as a serial, even if that delayed its appearance. In April, 1903, he was approached for the first time by an American publisher, McClure's, who wanted to publish a new edition of *New Grub Street*. Gissing agreed to shorten the novel and write an introduction for it, plans he never carried out. He returned to his work on "A Vanquished Roman" after he had moved, at the end of June, to the neighboring town of St. Jean Pied de Port in order to be away from the seaside, which his doctor felt was injurious to his health. The name of the novel had been changed to *Veranilda* by October, and by November he wrote to Ellen that it was "two-thirds" finished.

But *Veranilda* was never actually completed. A few days before Christmas, 1903, Gissing, who was recovering from a case of pneumonia, made an excursion in bad weather with some friends who were staying with him, and the next day fell seriously ill. A consultation was held, and his condition was diagnosed as myocarditis.

He was not expected to live through the night of December 21, but he lingered, suffering severely, and lapsing into periods of delirium and unconsciousness. On the twenty-fourth, at Gissing's request, Gabrielle sent a telegram to Wells, asking him to come to the dying man's bedside; thinking it would encourage Gissing to speak to an Englishman, she sent for the Reverend Theodore Cooper, the English chaplain at St. Jean de Luz, who had been friendly with Gissing and had given him copies of English periodicals.

Mr. Cooper arrived at three in the afternoon and found Gissing well enough to chat for a couple of hours. Almost as soon as they began to talk, Gissing told Mr. Cooper that he knew he was dying. He asked him to persuade Wells, whose arrival was expected, to take him back to England so that he could see an English doctor. When Mr. Cooper offered to send for an English doctor who lived in nearby Biarritz, the patient was satisfied. Mr. Cooper returned after dinner to relieve Gabrielle at the bedside and continued a relaxed conversation with Gissing. He stayed at St. Jean Pied de Port overnight, going up to see the sick man again on the morning of Christmas Day.

Meanwhile, Wells had received Gabrielle's summons but, because he was busy with his own affairs and was suffering from a cold, sent a telegram to Roberts, telling him of Gissing's condition and saying he could not go. Roberts was convalescent himself, and telegraphed both Wells and Gabrielle to say that he could come only if it was necessary. But Wells had already taken a steamer at Folkestone, and, after traveling all night, he reached St. Jean Pied de Port at three o'clock on Christmas Day. He and the English doctor for whom Mr. Cooper had sent arrived on the same train. The doctor left, after reporting that Gissing was in grave condition and might die that night. Wells was not permitted to go into the sickroom at first, but Mr. Cooper returned to see Gissing in the evening. He reported, in a letter to Gissing's sisters, "After a few minutes he opened his eyes suddenly, thrust out his hand and grasped mine firmly, murmuring 'Patience, patience' (with the French accent). I leaned over him and said 'My friend, you are going home.' Distinct and clear came the words 'God's will be done.' " [23]

Wells found Gissing delirious when he came up to see him the next day. In a moment of clarity, the sick man begged Wells to take him back to England. At other times he sat up in bed, thinking himself in the Rome of his imaginings, raved disconnectedly of his visions, and spoke and chanted in Latin. The antagonism between Wells and Gabrielle was renewed at the bedside. Wells disapproved of what he saw in the sickroom, including Gabrielle's ineffectiveness, the light diet that had been prescribed for the patient, and even the handkerchief Gabrielle was using to wipe his mouth. According to Gabrielle, Wells took advantage of the night of the twenty-sixth, when he was alone with the sick man, to feed him beef-tea, wine, coffee, and milk in quantity, in order to build up his strength. The result was a rise in temperature, and when the doctor heard of this treatment, Gabrielle reported, he exclaimed that it would kill the patient. Wells obtained the services of a nun, who nursed Gissing until an English nurse arrived to take charge. On the twenty-seventh, he and Mr. Cooper left together, the former going to the nearby town of Cambo and Wells returning to England.

By this time Roberts, who had received an urgent telegram from Wells, was on his way south, so that he and Wells passed each other *en route*. At Bayonne, Roberts found that he had missed the last train for St. Jean Pied de Port and had to spend the night in a hotel. Because of this delay, he failed to see Gissing again before his death. He describes his arrival at Gissing's house in this way: "On entering the hall I found a servant washing down the stone flooring. I said to her, 'Comment Monsieur se porte-t-il?' and she replied, 'Monsieur est mort.' " [24] Gissing had died at 1:15 p.m. on December 28; the immediate cause of death was myocarditis.

Roberts comforted the distraught Gabrielle and her mother as well as he could and, because Gabrielle did not want to have Gissing buried at St. Jean Pied de Port, conferred with Mr. Cooper, who made arrangements for the burial to take place in the English cemetery at St. Jean de Luz. The next day Roberts and the nurse who had cared for Gissing went with the body to St. Jean de Luz, where they were met by Mr. Cooper. Gabrielle and her mother had requested that Gissing be buried according to the Anglican ritual. The body rested in the English chapel before the altar for the night and was interred with the usual ceremony in the morning in the presence of a number of English people who had gathered for the service.

XI

SEQUELS

I

THE helpful and well-intentioned Mr. Cooper was the cause of an unfortunate sequel to Gissing's death. He gathered the impression during his hours at the dying man's bedside that Gissing had returned to religious faith, and he sent a letter containing this information to the *Church Times.* When a paragraph appeared in the *Church Times* announcing that Gissing had died in "the Catholic faith," both Roberts and Edward Clodd were outraged. Roberts wrote a strong note to the *Church Times* in January of 1904, declaring that Gissing had been steadfastly hostile to theological dogmas throughout his life, and that no importance should be attributed to what he might have said in his dying delirium. With characteristic vigor, he pursued information about the point by writing to Gabrielle and to the nurse who had attended Gissing during his last twenty-four hours. Gabrielle explained the mutterings of prayers and visions of hell in Gissing's last hours as the effects of the ecclesiastical works he had been reading in connection with *Veranilda.* The nurse, Miss E. Robertson Bayman, repeated this explanation, given to her by Gabrielle, for the chanting of the *Te Deum* and references to "the Holy Father" she had heard from her patient, and agreed that he was not in a responsible condition.

The information from Miss Bayman and Gabrielle raises some serious doubts about the accuracy of Mr. Cooper's reports of Gissing's death. It was perhaps natural that, in replying to an inquiry from Margaret Gissing as to whether her brother had emerged from

253

"his darkness" before death, he should have tried to offer her comfort. But there is little doubt that he strained the facts. According to Mr. Cooper, Gissing was capable of taking part in long conversations, yet he said nothing more about spiritual matters than "God's will be done." Gissing, who was discriminating in speech, would not have used the conventional religious phrase attributed to him as a matter of habit, and he certainly cannot be imagined as resorting to such language to express a spiritual illumination. Mr. Cooper wrote to Margaret that he felt that he and Gissing were "in sympathy," but a startling ellipsis follows the published version of this very general comment. He had taken it upon himself to pronounce a blessing while holding the dying man's hand, and he had then felt Gissing's grip relax as he grew unconscious. In telling Miss Bayman that he intended to telegraph a short report of Gissing's death to England, he said (with, apparently, some disingenuousness) that it was intended for "the *Times*," and it had not occurred to her, until Roberts wrote his letter of inquiry, that he meant the *Church Times*.

The *Church Times* took Roberts' denial seriously enough to write to Mr. Cooper upbraiding him for the misinformation he had supplied, but it did not follow Roberts' request to publish his letter, printing instead, a short acknowledgment of it. Mr. Cooper hurriedly telegraphed to deny that he had written the report of Gissing's conversion. When Roberts wrote to Miss Bayman to ask about this, she replied that it was true only in the most literal sense, for Mr. Cooper, who was weak and ill, had asked a friend to take care of his correspondence for him. She added that he seemed to regret the whole affair, and Roberts, after sending the facts about Gissing's religious belief to a London newspaper, dropped the matter until he reviewed it in detail in *The Private Life of Henry Maitland*.

II

Gissing left two novels of considerable interest which were published posthumously. *Will Warburton* is a study of a man who moves down the social ladder into a lower class. Its hero is a hearty, generous young businessman, a gentleman but no artist, whose modest funds are lost through the business ventures of an unreliable friend. Faced with the need of providing for his mother and sister, Warburton secretly becomes a grocer, subjecting himself to the ignominy of wearing the professional apron and serving customers behind the counter. He experiences firsthand the truth of Gissing's axiom that poverty deadens the soul, for he is forced to compete ruthlessly, both with his poor customers and with a hapless rival grocer, and he finds that his feelings of sympathy and kindness are melting away. His adoption of the grocer's trade, at first intended to be temporary, becomes permanent. Warburton's resignation to his lot is capped by the outcome of his love affairs. He loses the woman who objects to marrying a grocer, but gains the one who feels the claims of love more strongly than those of class. Warburton's humble resignation contrasts with the meretricious success of a friend who exploits his superficial gifts as a painter to make his way. The implication is that it is better to surrender honestly and fully to "an age of trade" than to seek a corrupting compromise. At the end of the novel Warburton is moving away from his upper-class friends, and there is the clear suggestion (somewhat surprising in Gissing) that he is well rid of them.

In spite of the sense of novelty with which Gissing approached Veranilda, it resembles his other novels in essential elements. Its central interest is in following the perplexed thoughts of the hero, Basil, as he pursues his beloved through a net of subtle intrigue. As usual, there is little action, though the novel is set in the time of the Gothic wars, a period of great turmoil and many battles. The plot is carried forward steadily but slowly through conversations and journeys; many of its important developments take place off stage. A certain interest is supplied by minor characters and the atmosphere and mood of decadent Rome, cunningly but unobtrusively woven of the details gleaned in Gissing's patient researches. Veranilda has no lesson or ideological point; its place is taken by another interest extraneous to the esthetic requirements of fiction, the historical one.

Basil is a young nobleman of only moderate intelligence, the scion of a decadent aristocracy and a member of a disintegrating culture. Though capable of fiery anger at times, he is generally melancholy and introspective. The lassitude and impotence that have overtaken the old Roman nobility give him a marked resemblance, in fact, to Gissing's moody English heroes. Basil is not learned; he hardly reads, the ideas of literature he has derived from his education are petty and artificial, and he is easily tempted and terrorized by the Huns, Byzantines, and other foreigners who have come to govern Italy.

The story of *Veranilda* opens in the year 544, a time when the Ostrogothic king, Totila, was gradually moving upon Rome from the south, undoing the conquests of the Greek general, Belisarius. At the home of his uncle near Naples Basil woos and wins Veranilda, a Gothic princess related by marriage to a member of his family. When Veranilda is mysteriously kidnapped, Basil goes with his friend Marcian to Rome to seek her, but it is a whole year before Marcian, who is practiced in intrigue, succeeds in finding and freeing her. However, he falls in love with her himself, and betrays Basil by telling Veranilda that her lover has been unfaithful. Basil, hearing of Veranilda's liberation, travels across a countryside made restive by war and kills Marcian in a fit of jealousy. He takes refuge at the Abbey of Cassino, where his inner turmoil is somewhat soothed by the spiritual guidance of St. Benedict, and where he meets Totila and agrees to serve him in fighting the Greeks. After leaving Cassino and accomplishing some missions in the Gothic cause, he is briefly reunited with Veranilda. The unfinished narrative stops in the middle of a minor plot development, five chapters short of the ending Gissing had planned, as the Goths besiege Rome and the city grows restless with hunger. If, as Wells said, Gissing meant to end the story at the moment after the Greek garrison had fled and before the Gothic army entered the city, when Rome, for a dramatic moment in its history, stood deserted, he might have had a happy ending in mind. It is easy to imagine Basil and Veranilda together again and rejoicing in Totila's victory and the delivery of Rome from the tyranny of the Byzantines. It was only a temporary victory, of course, for the city was retaken within a year by Belisarius.

Veranilda resembles Scott's historical novels in having actual historical figures as minor characters and protagonists who are fictional. However, Gissing made no attempt to rival the color and excitement of Scott or Bulwer-Lytton. His intention seems to have been closer to the effect achieved by George Eliot in *Romola* and Jacobsen in *Marie Grubbe*, that of a mature study of character, foregoing nearly entirely the more obvious and attractive trappings of historical fiction, while ensuring the thorough authenticity of physical details. In place of color and action there is an impression of smoothly-modeled narrative and a play of incident that hardly ripples the placid atmosphere. Apart from its success in presenting the feelings and moods of sixth-century Romans, *Veranilda* is not very notable as a study of character, partly because its plot is more suited to melodrama, partly because Basil is a fundamentally uninteresting personality.

As usual, Gissing's friends disagreed about the merits of his novel. H. G. Wells, at the request of Gissing's family, wrote a preface for it that combined honesty and generosity in moderate amounts, admiring its "comprehensive design" and skillful integration of details. In this preface Wells included a biographical sketch, describing Gissing as impractical and self-defeating and addicted to joyless drudgery, and giving some excellent characterizing facts about him. However, the family, obtaining proofs of this preface in advance of printing, refused to allow it to appear. They had always disapproved of Gissing's moral and religious views, and they must have been alarmed, on learning for the first time of his life with Gabrielle, to find that his posthumous reputation was likely to be that of a libertine as well as an atheist. They seem to have rejected Wells's preface because it made some references, tactful and obscure enough, to the episode at Owens College and to his early marriage, and they turned to Frederic Harrison for an introduction to *Veranilda*.

Harrison wrote a preface, accurately described by Roberts as a "frigid performance," praising *Veranilda* at the expense of Gissing's other work, and saying that it represented Gissing's real ability, in contrast to his novels of social realism. Roberts, however, thought that *Veranilda* was a tragic failure, and that it did not justify the enthusiasm and faith Gissing brought to it. It lacked the strong feeling of his social novels; on the other hand, since it was not a direct treatment of the classical antiquity he loved, it did not, in Roberts' opinion, have the quality of *By the Ionian Sea*.

Wells's rejected preface was published as an article in the *Monthly Review* of August, 1904. Although Wells seems to have made some changes in his essay before publishing it in an effort to satisfy Gissing's family, he satisfied no one. The muted references to Gissing's private life aroused general indignation, though nothing whatever was said about Edith or Gabrielle. Gabrielle heard of the reaction to the article, but asked Roberts not to send her a copy, for it would upset her. Miss Collet, while admitting that Wells had been "badly treated," opposed the publication of the article, and wrote to Roberts that it would shock Gabrielle deeply, for Gissing had never been able to bring himself to tell her about the Owens College incident or his first marriage. Wells was mistaken, she wrote, in describing Gissing's aim as the creation of an English *"Comédie Humaine,"* for she knew that after 1893 he had no such plan. Both Gabrielle and Miss Collet urged Roberts to write on Gissing in order to offset the effect of Wells's article. Gabrielle added that Gissing had distrusted Wells as a critic and felt that Wells had not understood his work.

III

It is generally acknowledged that Gissing was handicapped by his loyalty to the traditions of the Victorian novel. The intricate plotting typical of Victorian novels was due to the requirements of the serial or the three-volume form, but it was a necessity of which important virtues could be made. Dickens, who has often been wrongly regarded as the most important influence on Gissing, filled his novels with a multiplicity of plots and characters, achieving interesting effects of balance and counterpoint, and ranged widely over the scale of social classes, tracing the small, firm tendrils that linked them. Gissing followed the form used by Dickens, throwing together many plots to produce a richness of episode, but not all of his events carry the action forward; many are merely illustrative or irrelevant altogether. Furthermore, Gissing lacked Dickens' ability to make an incident unnecessary to the plot vivid and entertaining enough to justify itself. As the coincidences, trite situations and unintegrated subplots of Gissing's novels suggest, the necessity for devising a number of interlocking actions and keeping them in motion put considerable strain upon his powers of invention. He lacked the talents necessary for a follower of Dickens, but, even more important, he did not wish to be anything of the kind. The admiration for Dickens expressed in *Charles Dickens* is qualified by an awareness of his limitations, which Gissing would have considered fatal to any other author, including himself.

The fact is that, as Frank Swinnerton shrewdly observed, he began by modeling himself upon another novelist. In 1892 Gissing wrote to Bertz of Mrs. Humphry Ward, whose *David Grieve* had just been published, that she was a follower of George Eliot, adding parenthetically that he had been one himself many years earlier. This clue, revealing as it does the source of Gissing's conception of the novel, is illuminating. There are many points of resemblance between Gissing's and George Eliot's novels. His books were essentially the expressions of an enlightened didacticism directed to an ideological end. Like George Eliot, he devoted great attention to the intellectual and emotional development of mature characters. He felt the need for clearly realizing and explaining subtle shifts of feeling or attitude, and for providing sound motivations for the actions of his characters. Every incident of the plot justified its occurrence, ideally, by some important effect, often a psychological one. The cause-effect relationships in the minds of the characters are often analyzed at length and evaluated by instructive references to general experience. The fullness of description and detail, the elaborate compound plots, the passages of authorial commentary, and the slow and sometimes ponderous thoroughness of the narration in Gissing's novels are all imitations of George Eliot. As he strove for greater directness and economy of style, Gissing eliminated some of these characteristics from his work, but he continued to think of the novel as a form suited to the serious treatment of ideas through the narration of psychological experiences.

In following the example of George Eliot, Gissing had adopted a fictional method inappropriate to his own views and temperament. The closely woven fabric of a George Eliot novel is calculated to exhibit the subtle progression of moral and social forces to a just and inevitable conclusion. In seeing life as "the stealthy convergence of human lots . . . a slow preparation of effects from one life on another," as she puts it in *Middlemarch*, she pursued a mission comparable to the one nineteenth century scientists had set for themselves: that of formulating reality as a system of relationships governed by intelligible principles. This was not Gissing's view of reality, and his adaptation of George Eliot's techniques to his own use fails to achieve the satisfying sense of logical process that is felt in her best work. His was a divided mind, for while he had discarded the Comtism of his youth, he did not doubt that the scientific method was, as Huxley explained, the natural mode of all practical thought. However, he discounted entirely the optimistic implication that the natural processes revealed by science were forces for improvement. The real meaning of Gissing's attitude toward science has been pointed out by Mme. Cazamian: "Presque partout G. Gissing dénonce les effets nuisibles de la science; mais cela ne signifie pas qu'il n'en ait point senti la force, au contraire. Ces idées, ces doctrines qu'il a montrées néfastes, il les croyait justifiés ou inévitables. Et c'est là un des aspects les plus profonds de son pessimisme." [1] Thus, the underlying orderliness of events, which represents ultimate justice in George Eliot's universe, becomes, in Gissing's, the embodiment of a sinister determinism.

Like all novelists influenced by the example of George Eliot, Gissing brought to fiction a new conception of its responsibilities. The development of the English novel can be expressed in terms of two gradual tendencies: a turning from motives of entertainment and propaganda to the illumination of genuinely controversial moral issues, and an expansion of the social and psychological areas in which it could feel at home. Both of these developments arrived at new thresholds with George Eliot. After her, the novel could act, in the phrase borrowed by Mrs. Humphry Ward from Arnold, as "a criticism of life." Established tastes, which preferred the entertaining and edifying novels of Dickens and Thackeray, were repelled by the new novelists for two reasons. It was felt that some subjects necessary to a "serious" treatment of life, such as sex, violence, and the honest portrayal of certain emotions, were out of place in fiction. Secondly, many of those who had been brought up to think of Dickens as the representative novelist could not believe that the novel was a form suited to the treatment of profound intellectual or spiritual issues.

Against these views the new novelists prevailed only with difficulty. Hardy, who had had his share of troubles after *Tess of the D'Urbervilles*, expressed the ambition of the modern novelist in this way:

. . . conscientious fiction alone it is which can excite a reflecting and abiding interest in the minds of thoughtful readers of mature age, who are weary of puerile inventions and famishing for accuracy; who consider that in representations of the world, the passions ought to be proportioned as in the world itself. This is the interest which was excited in the minds of the Athenians by their immortal tragedies, and in the minds of Londoners at the first performances of the finer plays of three hundred years ago. They reflected life, revealed life, criticized life.[2]

Because he shared this view of the novel's mission, Gissing extended his concern with authenticity beyond the presentation of social problems themselves to the thoughts of the characters who faced them. His people are not mere bundles of traits floating in a social and economic vacuum but persons belonging to particular classes and occupations who have clear parts to play in the historical developments of their time. They are well realized both as spiritual and sociological beings. Exemplifying the effects of social changes, they in turn illuminate these social changes by their actions and their destinies. Even their private meditations take place in a loneliness where history seems always present, for each personal situation is a microcosm of some general one.

If Gissing's novels can be said to have a dominant theme, it is the destruction of human character in the crushing mill of social evils. He found that the social institutions men worked so hard to create and to maintain were, after all, hostile to dignity, honor, intellect, and sensibility. His opinions were varied and even inconsistent, but he felt clearly that the remedy for the evils he described lay in a change of the spirit of society rather than its form, and that the most advanced reform theories of his time missed that fact. His novels are indecisive because he was denied a vision of life as a well-ordered whole. He had convictions and perceptions, but they were isolated, disjointed, baffling even to himself. Instead of enabling him to arrive at coherent conclusions about the problems that troubled him, they delivered him into a nightmare of conflicting aims. His sympathy with the poor and oppressed was contradicted by his hatred of the barbarism their living conditions produced in them. He was jealous of the purity and independence of his art, but was also eager to accomplish a moral mission through his novels. He could not advocate the radical remedy of sweeping away the classes that lived on the labor of the poor because everything he felt to be of importance in man's intellectual life seemed possible only in the kind of environment produced by wealth and leisure.

Paradoxically, Gissing's inability to make up his mind about social issues was an advantage to him as a novelist. He used this failing as one of his literary talents. His active dislike of the poor sharpened his eye for details of their lives and manners; his doubts about cosmic problems gave him insight into crises of the soul; and his indecision about the civilization of his day led him to present it as a complex entity rich in minor characteristics. A wordy passage from *Workers in the Dawn* explains how skepticism can be an asset to the artist:

The man who convinces himself that he has ever at his elbow the key to the mystery of the universe . . . who conceives that the great laws of duty have long ago been written down in black and white for the use of man, and are not capable of discovery otherwise; such a man *cannot* but regard the world in a more or less prosaic light, compared with the point of view of one who recognises no patent key as in existence, for whom the mystery of life and death begins and ends with a vast doubt, whose very thought is the fruit of, and leads to, boundless conjecture. . . .[3]

Frank Swinnerton, arguing that Gissing's attempts at objectivity were foreign to his talent, says that he did his best work when he was confident of his point of view and was writing on some theme which aroused his partisanship. But Gissing's fictional powers were disabled by certainty, while doubt and curiosity seemed to liberate them. He firmly believed that great art and literature enriched character, yet his attempts to show this happening in his novels are unsuccessful. On the other hand, his attitude toward such men as Peak and Reardon was unsettled and ambiguous, yet his depiction of this type is one of his strong points. "Boundless conjecture" is perhaps not enough in itself to serve as an artistic principle, but it seemed to disarm Gissing's preconceptions and prejudices and give him access to a more authentic realism.

IV

Gissing's death was the occasion for some critical estimates which carried to extremes the growing recognition of his work. In an obituary notice in the *Athenaeum*, C. F. Keary described his work as the "almost unique" English expression of a spirit represented on the Continent by Zola and Hauptmann. Arthur Waugh mistakenly insisted in the *Fortnightly Review* that Gissing had never given in to the temptation to write for money. Both of these critics agreed in calling him "sincere" or "conscientious" and in attributing his relative unpopularity to the unpalatable truths he revealed.

It was not long, however, before the "sincerity" of Gissing's work was given another evaluation. Critics like Frank Swinnerton and Edmund Gosse pointed out that there was in Gissing's criticism of society an element of self-justification and revenge. "His books were ground out of him by the contemplation of his own misery," said Gosse, "and nothing but his fine artistic conscientiousness kept them from being openly egocentric." [4] Gissing would have argued that this relation of his novels to his own experiences insured their authenticity. He saw nothing wrong in the fact that his poor young intellectual heroes were obviously autobiographical; he regarded his treatment of this type as his most important achievement. In 1895, while complaining to Roberts of the obtuseness of reviewers, he wrote, ". . . the most characteristic, the most important, part of my work is that which deals with a class of young men distinctive of our time—well-educated, fairly bred, *but without money*. . . . This side of my work, to me the most important, I have never yet seen recognised." [5]

He wrote about rootless young intellectuals, not merely to plead his own cause, but to present instances of the problem they represented. He saw that new developments in Victorian civilization had conspired to isolate such men as Waymark, Peak, and Reardon between an old system that was going out and a new one not yet brought into being. He had knowledge of the spiritual ordeals such men suffered from his own experiences, and he was willing to expose his own conflicts for the sake of illuminating a general moral crisis.

The subjective quality that sometimes makes Gissing's readers uneasy can be accounted for by the conservative principles he brought forward in *Charles Dickens* to defend Dickens' veracity against critics who found him to be unrealistic. Like most Victorians, Gissing felt that "truth to life" was the most important single standard for fiction; the common terms of critical approbation among the Victorians, such as "genuine," "convincing," and "authentic," show that they considered it essential for a novel to prove itself a close representation of actuality. When an unlettered neighbor who was reading *Robinson Crusoe* observed, "Some of it seems like fiction," Gissing noted the remark as a tribute to Defoe's power. Having written, in his school essay on Milton that "truth" was one of the attributes of great poetry, he never had any reason to alter an opinion which agreed so well with the taste and theory of his time.

His difference with the critics of Dickens arose, however, from the fact that he adhered to the mid-Victorian concept of "truth" as the honest expression of the writer's reactions, and not to the naturalist view, then gaining currency, that nothing short of objective reporting could qualify as realism. Gissing's views are well represented in G. H. Lewes' *Principles of Success in Literature* (1865), which put "truth" under the general heading of "The Principle of Sincerity," and discussed accuracy in literature as if it were analogous to honesty in everyday behavior. The Victorians did not feel that the novels of Dickens and Thackeray were less realistic or less accurate because they reflected personal attitudes; on the contrary, it was precisely the presence of a strong and responsible individuality that guaranteed their authenticity. "Whatever is sincerely felt or believed," said Lewes, ". . . may fitly be given to the world. . . ." [6] Only with Flaubert, Zola, and Moore did "realism" come to mean the impersonal photographic accuracy which Baudelaire (who did not approve of it) formulated as "*L'univers sans l'homme*," and whose purpose he phrased as follows: "Je veux représenter les choses telles qu'elles sont ou bien qu'elles seraient, en supposant que je n'existe pas." [7]

Distrusting science, Gissing also distrusted such adaptations of its aims to fiction as Zola had attempted in *Le Roman expérimental*, and he declared flatly in two short critical essays written a few years before his book on Dickens that objectivity is impossible: "There is no science of fiction." [8] In *Charles Dickens* he concludes that "that very idle word 'realism' " is useless as a critical standard, and contends that even the realist, if he is wise, acknowledges the essentially subjective quality of fiction and is satisfied with the view ". . . that truth, for the artist, is the impression produced on *him*, and that to convey this impression with entire sincerity is his sole reason for existing." [9] Writing to Bertz in 1892 he said that he would never try to suppress his own spirit for the sake of achieving an "impersonal" effect. In fact, he considered the personal tone to be the element that distinguished the novelist from the playwright, and observed in a later letter that a successful book must be strongly marked by its author's personality.

Thus, the writer is to be judged, not by his accuracy as an imitator of actuality, but by his fidelity to his own perceptions. Dickens, Gissing found, generally followed this principle, and the many instances where the truthfulness of his work fails to convince can be traced to a conscious refusal, usually on moral grounds, to give a faithful representation of his own impressions. Comparing the two charity boys, Oliver Twist and Rob the Grinder, Gissing points out that the latter showed how accurately Dickens could observe, while the former showed how far he was willing to go in distorting his observations. Dickens might heighten his effects or omit unpleasant facts of life or character in the name of morality, but to Gissing the novelist's supreme morality was the principle of truth to his own knowledge of life, however limited it might be. If he feared the barbarism of the poor, disapproved of progress and democracy, experienced a profound pessimism when he considered civilization as a whole, and failed to see in the human drama the intention of a benevolent divine power, he was bound to convey these feelings without regard to public taste or the advice of publishers' readers. "After all," he once wrote to Algernon,[10] in defending the poor judgment he had shown in one of his early novels, "one must write what is in one to write. . . ."

NOTES

Sources of factual information are given in informal statements easily associated with the material they account for. Quotations are footnoted in the conventional manner. In referring to manuscripts I have consulted that have subsequently been published, I have generally cited the original document. The only significant instances of this kind are the letters to Bertz, published as *The Letters of George Gissing to Eduard Bertz, 1887–1903*, edited by Arthur C. Young (New Brunswick, N.J.: Rutgers University Press, 1961) and the Commonplace Book, published as *George Gissing's Commonplace Book*, edited by Jacob Korg (New York: New York Public Library, 1962). The latter has also been published in parts in the *Bulletin of the New York Public Library*, LXV, Nos. 7–9 (September, October, November, 1961).

CHAPTER I

SECTION I

For impressions about Gissing's appearance and his relations with the Harrison family, see *Frederic Harrison: Thoughts and Memories*, by Austin Harrison (London: W. Heinemann, Ltd., 1926), pp. 80–84; and "George Gissing," by Austin Harrison, *Nineteenth Century and After*, LX (September, 1906), 453–63. For Frederic Harrison's career and opinions, see his *Autobiographic Memoirs* (London: Macmillan & Co.; Ltd., 1911) and *Early Victorian Literature* (London: E. Arnold, 1894–95), as well as Austin Harrison's *Thoughts and Memories*. The informative schoolfellow is mentioned in a letter from Harrison to H. G. Wells, January 27, 1904, found in *George Gissing and H. G. Wells*, edited by Royal A. Gettmann (Urbana, Ill.: University of Illinois Press, 1961), p. 230.

1. *Letters of George Gissing to Members of His Family*, Collected and Arranged by Algernon and Ellen Gissing (London: Constable, 1927), pp. 77–78. This book is hereafter referred to as *Letters*.
2. A. Harrison, *Thoughts and Memories*, p. 83.
3. F. Harrison, *Autobiographic Memoirs*, I, 238.

SECTION II

Thomas Gissing is described in the unpublished manuscript, "Reminscences [*sic*] of My Father," which is in the Yale University Library (hereafter abbreviated as YUL). Gissing's "List of Books" and "John Milton" are in the Henry W. and Albert A. Berg Collection of the New York Public Library. His reading of *The Old Curiosity Shop* is from Gissing's *The Immortal Dickens* (London: Cecil Palmer, 1925), p. 1. Harrison's Back Lane School is mentioned in *Letters*, p. 259. Gissing's caricatures and the Roncesvalles and Fingal manuscripts are in YUL. "The English Novel of the Eighteenth Century" is a manuscript in the Carl H. Pforzheimer Library. The school and college prizes are listed in "The Adams-Gissing Collection," *Yale University Library Gazette*, XVIII, No. 3 (1944), 49. The letters to Bowes are in YUL.

For details of Gissing's career at Owens College, see *The Private Life of Henry Maitland*, by Morley Roberts (New and Revised Edition; London: Eveleigh, Nash and Grayson, 1923), pp. 21–22; Austin Harrison's "George Gissing"; and Robert Shafer's introduction to the Doubleday, Doran edition of *Workers in the Dawn* (Garden City, 1935). Gissing's first wife is identified in *George Gissing: Grave Comedian*, by Mabel Collins Donnelly (Cambridge, Mass.: Harvard University Press, 1954), p. 22.

4. Ellen Gissing, "Some Personal Recollections of George Gissing," *Blackwood's Magazine*, CCXXV (May, 1929), 658.
5. The sentence from Lecky is transcribed on p. 35 of the Commonplace Book kept by Gissing between 1887 and 1903 (Berg Collection).
6. Winwood Reade, *The Martyrdom of Man* (24th ed.; New York: E. P. Dutton & Co., Inc., 1926), pp. 479–80.
7. Chapter 31. Though not published until 1903, *The Way of All Flesh* was written between 1872 and 1885 and so belongs to the period of Gissing's youth.
8. Henry Maudsley, "Materialism and Its Lessons," *Fortnightly Review*, XXXII (1879), 260.
9. Letter to Eduard Bertz, May 20, 1892. (All correspondence with Bertz referred to is in YUL.)

SECTION III

For Gissing's reactions to America, see *Letters*, pp. 12–21. His "sketches" are mentioned in a letter to Algernon dated November 13, 1876 (Berg Collection). Gissing's characteristic comment on matter is from Roberts' *Maitland*, p. 51. For the Chicago stories and information about them, see *Sins of the Fathers and Other Tales* (Chicago: Covici, 1924), *Brownie* (New York: Columbia University Press, 1931), and the appendix to *Maitland*. Details about Gissing's New England travels are from the American notebook (YUL); Roberts, *Maitland*, pp. 36–37; Shafer's introduction to *Workers in the Dawn*, pp. xiv–xv, and Donnelly, *Gissing*, p. 29. The mistake about the trip to Germany was made by Thomas Seccombe in his article on Gissing for the *Dictionary of National Biography*, Second Supplement, and by Frank Swinnerton. Bertz's help with the chapter about Germany is mentioned in "George Gissing's Friendship with Eduard Bertz," by Arthur C. Young, *Nineteenth Century Fiction*, XIII, No. 3 (December, 1958), 227–37.

10. *Letters*, p. 17.
11. *New Grub Street* (New York: Modern Library, 1926) p. 419.
12. *Sins of the Fathers and Other Tales*, p. 13.

SECTION IV

Among the sources of information about poor London lodgings in the last quarter of the nineteenth century, see Gissing's novels, especially *The Nether World* (London: Murray, 1903); Charles Booth's *Life and Labour of the People in London* (London: Macmillan & Co., Ltd., 1889); Reverend Andrew Mearns's *The Bitter Cry of Outcast London* (London: James Clarke & Co., 1883); Beatrice Webb's *My Apprenticeship* (New York and London: Longmans, Green & Co., Inc., 1926), pp. 228–29; and H. G. Wells's *Experiment in Autobiography* (New York: The Macmillan Co., 1934), pp. 217–27. For details of Gissing's first year in London, see *Letters*, pp. 22–50. The Colville Place address appears in a letter to Algernon dated January 12, 1878 (Berg Collection). Other facts about this period are from the following letters to Algernon (Berg Collection): February 28, 1878; March 14, 1878; September 9, 1878; September 26, 1878; December 17, 1878; March 2, 1879; March 23, 1879; and June 16, 1879.

Information about Bertz is from Young's introduction to *The Letters of George Gissing to Eduard Bertz*, and Young's "George Gissing's Friendship with Eduard Bertz." The unpublished letter of November 9, 1878, dealing with Comte, is in the Berg Collection. The letter to Harrison dated July 9, 1880, which accompanied a copy of *Workers in the Dawn*, is No. 20 in the Gissing collection of the Pforzheimer Library. Readings for the lecture are listed in letters to Algernon of March 9 and March 15, 1879 (Berg Collection).

Letters guiding Algernon in his studies are all omitted from the published letters. They are dated February 28, 1878; March 14, 1878; April 15, 1878; May 22, 1878; September 9, 1878 (Berg Collection). Helen is first mentioned by name in a letter to Algernon, March 2, 1879 (Berg Collection). The date of the marriage is given in Donnelly, *Gissing*, p. 35. Information about their married life is found in Roberts, *Maitland*, pp. 38–42, and in the following letters to Algernon: March 23, 1879, June 16, 1879 (Berg Collection); April 23, 1880, October 13, 1880, November 3, 1880, and February 25, 1881 (YUL).

13. Commonplace Book, p. 16 (Berg Collection).
14. *Letters*, p. 28.
15. *Ibid.*, p. 32.
16. Letter to Algernon, September 26, 1878 (YUL).
17. Roberts, *Maitland*, p. 39.
18. *Letters*, p. 69.
19. Poem dated August 10, 1872, in MS notebook, "Verses" (YUL).
20. *Letters*, p. 53.
21. *Ibid.*, pp. 73–74.

SECTION V

Most of the facts in the survey of social conditions are from *England in the Eighteen-Eighties*, by Helen Merrell Lynd (New York: Oxford University Press, 1945), and *A Short History of the British Working-Class Movement*, by G. D. H. Cole (New York: The Macmillan Co., 1930–37), Vol. II. The social novels of the midcentury are treated in Louis Cazamian's *Le Roman social en Angleterre* (Paris: Société nouvelle de librairie et d'édition, 1904). Bertz's help with *Workers in the Dawn* is mentioned in a letter by him published in Young's "George Gissing's Friendship with Eduard Bertz," p. 30. Rejections of the novel are mentioned in *Letters*, pp. 50–57. The contract for the publication of the novel is in YUL. James's remarks on Gissing are in "London Notes, July, 1897," *Notes On Novelists with Some Other Notes* (New York: Scribner's, 1914), pp. 437–43. Mrs. Harrison's comment, transmitted in her husband's letter, appears in *Letters*, p. 79.

22. Webb, *My Apprenticeship*, p. 126.
23. *Letters*, p. 57.
24. *Ibid.*, p. 73.

25. *Workers in the Dawn*, I, 158.
26. *Ibid.*, I, 131.

SECTION VI

27. Robert Owen, *A New View of Society* (London: Cadell and Davies, 1813), p. 37.
28. Cazamian, *Le Roman social en Angleterre*, p. 555.
29. John Ruskin, *Fors Clavigera*, in *Works*, ed. Cook and Wedderburn (London: Longmans, Roberts and Green, 1903–12), XXVII, 13.
30. Percy Bysshe Shelley, "A Defence of Poetry," *Prose Works* (London: Chatto and Windus, 1888), I, 11–12.
31. *Workers in the Dawn*, II, 269.
32. Letter to Algernon, May 9, 1880 (YUL).
33. Letter to Bertz, November 4, 1889.

CHAPTER II

SECTION I

Gissing's comments about the sale, advertising, and proceeds of *Workers in the Dawn* are from *Letters of George Gissing to Members of His Family*, ed. Algernon and Ellen Gissing (London: Constable, 1927), p. 94, and a letter of June 30, 1880, to Algernon (YUL). The letter of July 9, 1880, to Harrison is No. 20 in the Pforzheimer Library's Gissing collection. Harrison's recommendations are mentioned in a letter of July 29, 1880, to Algernon (Pforzheimer Library No. 43). Gissing's work for John Morley is mentioned in letters to Algernon of September 10, 1880 (Pforzheimer Library No. 44) and September 15, 1880 (YUL). For the contents of the *Pall Mall Gazette* articles on socialism, see Mabel C. Donnelly, *George Gissing: Grave Comedian* (Cambridge, Mass.: Harvard University Press, 1954), pp. 40–41. Gissing's relations with the Positivist Society are described in *Letters*, pp. 84 and 96, and in letters to Algernon of November 3 and November 15, 1880 (YUL).

The Wornington Road flat and the novel written there are first mentioned in a letter to Algernon of February 25, 1881 (YUL). Bertz's trip to America is from Arthur C. Young's "George Gissing's Friendship with Eduard Bertz," *Nineteenth Century Fiction*, XIII, No. 3, (December, 1958) 227–37. Gissing's work for the *Messager de l'Europe* is mentioned in *Letters*, p. 85, and in letters to Algernon of November 15, 1880, April 20, 1881, and October 6, 1882 (YUL). Gissing wrote eight of these articles, which appeared in *Vestnik Evropy* at quarterly intervals between May, 1881, and November, 1882, under the heading "Correspondence from London." Morchard Bishop's new edition of Roberts' *Maitland* (London: Richards Press, 1958) has informative footnotes and an introduction defending Roberts' biographical methods. It also contains an index of characters that agrees, in most respects, with the less complete key written into a copy in the Berg Collection, probably by Clement Shorter.

Gissing's money troubles are mentioned in a letter to Algernon of February 25, 1881 (YUL). The information about Helen's illness and behavior is from letters to Algernon dated April 9, 1881; June 19, 1881; June 24, 1881; January 16, 1882; January 19, 1882; October 6, 1882; and October 31, 1882 (YUL). Gissing describes his cat in *Letters*, pp. 105–6, and in a letter to Margaret, June 18, 1881 (Berg Collection). For Jumbo, see *Letters*, pp. 108–9; for Sarah Bernhardt, *Letters*, p. 117; and for Gissing's meals with Roberts, see Morley Roberts, *The Private Life of Henry Maitland* (New and Revised Edition; London: Eveleigh, Nash and Grayson, 1923), p. 47. Helen's June disturbance is described in a letter to Algernon, June 17, 1882 (YUL). The facts about *Mrs. Grundy's Enemies* are from *Letters*, pp. 119, 121–23; *George Gissing: 1857–1903*, by John D. Gordan (Catalogue for an exhibition of materials from the Berg Collection of the New York Public Library [New York: New York Public Library, 1954]), p. 10; Donnelly, *Gissing*, p. 80; and *A Victorian Publisher*, by Royal A. Gettmann (Cambridge, Engl.: Cambridge University Press, 1960), pp. 215–20. Helen's eye operation and its sequel are described in a letter to Algernon, October 6, 1882 (YUL).

The manuscript of "Hope of Pessimism" is No. 15 in the Gissing collection of the Pforzheimer Library. Gissing's feelings about crowds and the theater are expressed, among other places, in *Letters*, p. 116, a letter to Bertz, March 5, 1891, and *Charles Dickens: A Critical Study* (London: Gresham Publishing Company, 1904).

1. *Athenaeum*, June 12, 1880.
2. Letter to Harrison, July 23, 1880 (Pforzheimer Library No. 21).
3. *Ibid.*
4. *Letters*, p. 97.
5. Letter to Algernon, October 6, 1882 (YUL).
6. *Letters*, p. 103.
7. *Ibid.*, p. 87.
8. The poem, in "Verses" (YUL), dated 1869, reads, in part:

> Attend all ye who love the play, and to the theatre go,
> I sing a theatre's history that stands in Bunkum row,
> How on one famous boxing night, to suffocation cramm'd
> The people paying for the pit were in the boxes ramm'd

'Tis getting near to eight a'clock, a thick crowd outside roar
And with increased impatience waits the opening of the door.
At last, the doors are open flung and through the people rush
And some are almost squeezed to death, tremendous is the
  crush. . . .
At last the curtain rises up and "Hats off" is the cry
And at the sight the actors turn and whisper "Oh my eye"
But still they stamp and shout hurrah as loud as they can bawl
And half the people didn't know the play'd begun at all.
In vain the actors raise their voice in hope of being heard
In vain the orchestra struck up "I would I were a bird"
But still they stamp and shout behind, the blackguards of the
  town
And the thunder of the audience nearly brought the gallery
  down. . . .

9. *Letters*, p. 116.
10. *Ibid.*

SECTION II

Gissing's comments on newspaper stories are from *Letters*, pp. 86 and 91, and a letter to Algernon, June 19, 1881 (YUL). For his reaction to the death of Carlyle, see *Letters*, pp. 92–93. For the Rossetti pictures and Gilbert and Sullivan operas, see *Letters*, pp. 121, 123–24. For his opinion of Ruskin, see *Letters*, p. 126. For John Ruskin's economic theories see his *Unto This Last*, in *Works*, ed. Cook and Wedderburn (London: Longmans, Roberts and Green, 1903–12), XVII, 25–114. Bertz's conversion is mentioned in a letter to Algernon, September 2, 1883 (YUL). Helen's new difficulties and Gissing's attempt to find evidence for a divorce are narrated in the following letters to Algernon (YUL): September 24, 1883; September 29, 1883; October 1, 1883; October 10, 1883; October 30, 1883; November 24, 1883.

11. *Letters*, p. 86.
12. *Ibid.*, p. 126.
13. *Ibid.*, p. 132.

SECTION III

"The Four Silverpennys" appeared anonymously in *Temple Bar*, January, 1884, pp. 120–28. "Phoebe" appeared in the number of March, 1884, pp. 391–406. It was originally set up to be published anonymously, but Gissing added his name to the proofs, as he told Algernon in a letter of January 11, 1884 (YUL). "Song" led Gissing into a foolish situation, for when the "Literary Gossip" column of the *Athenaeum* reported, on November 10, 1883, that "a very pretty song" had been contributed to a recent number of *Temple Bar* under a pseudonym by Leonard Huxley, the son of Thomas Henry Huxley, Gissing took this for a reference to his own poem and wrote to the editor demanding an explanation. There was no reply, but a letter to Bentley brought forth the explanation that the remark referred to a previous number of *Temple Bar*. Although Gissing wrote to Algernon that he was dissatisfied with this, there was really no cause for confusion. The previous edition of the magazine had carried a "Birthday Ballade of September 21st," signed with the initials N.O.E.L.; it was a poem addressed to his sister, Jessie, which Leonard Huxley had signed with the name of the brother who had died before he was born.

The outline of "Pastures New" is in a letter to Algernon dated October 21, 1883 (YUL). Remarks about Scott and George Eliot as models are in a letter of November 11, 1883 (YUL). The phrases about literature as a profession are from a letter of January 9, 1895 (YUL). Gissing mentions his writing difficulties in *Letters*, p. 137, a letter to Bertz of October 21, 1889, and entries in his Holograph Diary of December 27, 1887, January 6, 1888, and February 7, 1888. This diary, which is in the Berg Collection, is an important source of information about Gissing's daily activities, personal feelings, and private thoughts; it also supplies the biographer with much factual material. A number of pages in the first of the three notebooks appear to have been cut out; the first surviving entry is that of December 27, 1887.

The negotiations over the publication and revision of *The Unclassed* are mentioned in *Letters*, p. 135, in letters to Algernon dated February 28, 1884, March 13, 1884, and April 10, 1884 (YUL), and in Gordan, *George Gissing*, pp. 10–11. A letter from George Bentley rejecting the novel, dated January 4, 1884, is to be found in Gettmann's *A Victorian Publisher*, p. 220. For the discovery of Meredith's identity, see *Letters*, p. 138. Repeated references to Bentley's silence about *Mrs. Grundy's Enemies* are in letters to Algernon dated October 10, 1883, October 30, 1883, and February 28, 1884 (YUL). Details about Bertz's book and departure from England are from Young's "George Gissing's Friendship with Eduard Bertz" and a letter to Algernon of March 21, 1884 (YUL). The recommendation that Algernon write essays is in a letter of May 15, 1884 (YUL).

14. Letter to Algernon, July 25, 1891 (YUL).

15. Holograph Diary, entry of July 8, 1888 (Berg Collection).

16. *The Bookman*, IV (September, 1896), 18. This note was probably based on information Gissing gave in a speech made at a dinner in honor of Meredith in November, 1895.

Gissing had once commented on the problem of landlordism, which is treated in *The Unclassed*, in a letter of June 19, 1881 to Algernon (YUL): "Someone owns all these slums and alleys," he wrote, "and draws endless rents from them." Gissing's reference to his typical young man is in a letter to Roberts, February 10, 1895 (Berg Collection). The letter to Harrison following the discussion of *The Unclassed* is No. 57 in the Gissing collection of the Pforzheimer Library. The remarks about irony and indirectness relative to "Sewage Farm" are in a letter to Algernon dated September 7, 1884 (Berg Collection).

17. *The Unclassed* (London: Sidgwick and Jackson, 1911), pp. 116–17.
18. *Ibid.*, p. 212
19. *Letters*, p. 135.
20. *Ibid.*, p. 141.
21. *Athenaeum*, July 27, 1889, p. 126.

The summer holiday of 1884 is described in *Letters*, pp. 143–47. Gissing's relations with Mrs. Gaussen and her family are mentioned in *Letters*, pp. 147–48, and a letter to Algernon, September 1, 1884 (YUL). His wider social activities are mentioned in *Letters*, pp. 149–50.

His letters to Ellen about her visit to Mrs. Gaussen are published in Jacqueline Steiner, "George Gissing to His Sister: Letters of George Gissing," *More Books* (Bulletin of the Boston Public Library), XXII (November, December, 1947), 323–36, 376–86. They were written in May, 1885.

22. *Letters*, p. 167.
23. Dated August 10, 1872, in "Verses" (YUL).
24. *Letters*, pp. 128–29.
25. *Ibid.*, pp. 138–39.

CHAPTER III

Various observations about 7K are found in *Letters of George Gissing to Members of His Family*, ed. Algernon and Ellen Gissing (London: Constable, 1927), pp. 150–51; a letter to Algernon, December 20, 1884 (YUL); Austin Harrison, "George Gissing," *Nineteenth Century and After*, LX (September, 1906), 453–63; Morley Roberts, *The Private Life of Henry Maitland* (New and Revised Edition; London: Eveleigh,

Nash and Grayson, 1923), p. 43; and a letter to Ellen of March 14, 1888, *Letters*, p. 210. For "The Graven Image" and "Madcaps," see John D. Gordan, *George Gissing: 1857–1903* (Catalogue for an exhibition of materials from the Berg Collection of the New York Public Library [New York: New York Public Library, 1954]), p. 11. For his change of writing habits in 1885, see *Letters*, p. 157. His manuscript copies are exemplified by holographs of his novels in the Berg Collection and the Huntington Library.

For Roberts on Gissing's learning, see Roberts, *Maitland*, pp. 49–50, 79–80, 81–82, and 97. "He knew by heart a hundred choruses of the Greek tragedies. . . ." For H. G. Wells on this subject, see his *Experiment in Autobiography* (New York: The Macmillan Co., 1934), pp. 483–84. For Gissing on Gibbon see *The Private Papers of Henry Ryecroft* (New York: Modern Library, n.d.), pp. 33–35. For his interest in the early Christian sects, see *Letters*, pp. 165–66. For his interest in the dissolution of the Roman Empire, see *Letters*, p. 351. His diary *passim* gives evidence of his grasp of French and German. For his purchase of Turgenev's novels, see *Letters*, p. 136; for his interest in Turgenev, *Letters*, p. 138. The suggestion that Turgenev influenced *A Life's Morning* is Roberts'; see Roberts, *Maitland*, p. 162. For Gissing's difficulty with titles, see *Letters*, pp. 49–50, 53, 65. For the change of *Isabel Clarendon's* title, see *Letters*, pp. 150, 160.

1. Quoted in *Punch*, January 3, 1885, p. 1.
2. *Ibid.*
3. *Letters*, p. 157.
4. Holograph Diary (Berg Collection).
5. *Letters*, pp. 160–61.
6. *Ibid.*, pp. 163–64.

SECTION II

For the revision of *Isabel Clarendon*, see *Letters*, p. 157. On the question of payment for it, see Gordan, *George Gissing*, pp. 12–13. For Gissing's opinion of "Emily," see *Letters*, p. 173. For Payn's reaction, see *Letters*, p. 174. For the enforced revision, see Roberts, *Maitland*, p. 88.

7. John Ruskin, *Time and Tide*, in *Works*, ed. Cook and Wedderburn (London: Longmans, Roberts and Green, 1903–12), XVII, 348.

SECTION III

Gissing describes his work as a "consolation" in a letter to Algernon, September, 1885 (YUL). For his confidence in *Demos*, see *Letters*, pp.

174–75. For information about socialism, see Max Beer, A *History of British Socialism* (2 vols.; London: G. Bell and Sons, Ltd., 1919); Sidney Webb, "Socialism in England," *Publications of the American Economic Association*, Vol. II, No. 2 (April, 1889); and John Stuart Mill, "Chapters on Socialism," *Fortnightly Review*, Vols. CXLVI–CXLVIII, New Series (February–April, 1879). For Gissing's visit to Hammersmith, see *Letters*, p. 174.

8. *Letters*, p. 174.

9. *The Nether World* (London: Murray, 1903) chap. xxiv, p. 217.

10. Friedrich Engels, *Condition of the Working Class in England in 1844*, trans. Florence Kelley Wischnewetzky (London: G. Allen & Unwin, Ltd., 1926), p. 115.

11. *Demos: A Story of English Socialism* (New York: E. P. Dutton & Co., Inc., n.d.), chap. xxxv, pp. 453–54.

SECTION IV

For W. H. Mallock on the poor, see "Social Equality," *Saturday Review*, LIV, 380 ff. For Théodule Ribot on the inheritance of moral characteristics, see *L'Hérédité psychologique* (Paris: F. Alean, 1914), particularly pp. 320 ff.

For the class war, see Benjamin Disraeli's *Sybil* (Bradenham edition; London: Peter Davies, 1927), IX, 190; and Engels, *Condition of the Working Class*, p. 298: ". . . the war of the poor against the rich now carried on in detail and indirectly will become direct and universal. It is too late now for a peaceful solution."

12. *Demos*, chap. xxvi, pp. 350–51. (There are two chapters numbered xxvi; this reference is to the second one.)

13. *Ibid.*, chap. viii, p. 89.

14. Letter to Algernon, June 21, 1884 (YUL).

15. Letter to Algernon, December 21, 1880 (YUL).

16. *Demos*, chap. x, p. 136.

17. *Letters*, p. 169.

18. Commonplace Book, p. 40 (Berg Collection).

SECTION V

For Arnold on "aliens" and "the saving remnant," see chapter iii of *Culture and Anarchy*, *Culture and Anarchy and Friendship's Garland* (New York: The Macmillan Co., 1913), pp. 1–206; and the essay, "Numbers," *Discourses in America* (New York: The Macmillan Co., 1912), pp. 158–64. For ethical implications in Pater, see Ruth C. Child's *The Aesthetic of Walter Pater* (New York: The Macmillan

Co., 1940), particularly p. 41, where a parallel with Shelley is pointed out, and pp. 102–3.

19. Arnold, *Culture and Anarchy*, p. 85.
20. *Ibid.*, p. 41.
21. *Ibid.*, pp. 150–51.
22. *A Life's Morning* (London: Home and Van Thal, 1947), chap. v, p. 93.
23. *Demos*, chap. xxix, p. 376.
24. *Ibid.*, chap. xxvi, p. 339.
25. *Ibid.*, chap. xxix, p. 385.

SECTION VI

Gissing's comment about Payn and his own comparison with George Eliot are in letters to Ellen of November 26, 1885, and March 6, 1886 (Berg Collection). Details about his position in March of 1886 are from *Letters*, pp. 175–76.

26. Letter to Ellen, March 14, 1886 (Berg Collection).
27. "Ethics and Art in Recent Novels," *Scottish Review*, April, 1886, pp. 328–29.
28. *Letters*, p. 177.

CHAPTER IV

SECTION I

For Chapman and Hall's promise to publish *Isabel Clarendon*, see *Letters of George Gissing to Members of His Family*, ed. Algernon and Ellen Gissing (London: Constable, 1927), pp. 174, 175. Gissing's annoyance at the way it was advertised is expressed in a letter to Ellen, May 8, 1886 (Berg Collection). For the sale of *Demos*, see *Letters*, p. 180, and for signs of Gissing's "emancipation," *Letters*, p. 182. Morley's comment is on p. 185 of *Letters*. For his frequenting of Lambeth, see *Letters*, pp. 182, 183. For the remark about Hellas and Lambeth, see *Letters*, p. 184. For the new beginning in July, *Letters*, p. 183. For Gissing's debt to French and Russian rather than English writers, see *Letters*, p. 183. The final agreement on *Thyrza* is described in a letter to Algernon, January, 1887 (YUL). For the copies of *Thyrza* taken by Mudie's, see *Letters*, p. 196. The fact that it sold fewer than 500 is in an undated letter to Algernon (1887?) (YUL).

1. *Letters*, p. 184.
2. *Ibid.*, p. 188.
3. *Ibid.*, p. 183.

4. *Thyrza* (London: Eveleigh, Nash and Grayson, 1928), p. 111.

5. John Ruskin, *Unto This Last*, in *Works*, ed. Cook and Wedderburn (London: Longmans, Roberts and Green, 1903–12), XVII, 48, note.

6. Graham Wallas, "Property Under Socialism," *Fabian Essays* (London: G. Allen & Unwin, Ltd., 1948), pp. 137–38.

7. *Thyrza*, pp. 12–13.

8. Friedrich Engels, *Condition of the Working Class in England in 1844*, trans. Florence Kelley Wischnewetzky (London: G. Allen & Unwin, Ltd., 1926), p. 115.

9. *Letters*, p. 193.

10. This sentence, omitted from the published version, appears in a letter to Ellen, July 8, 1887 (YUL).

11. *Letters*, p. 196.

12. *Ibid.*

SECTION II

Gissing's planned reorganization, *Clement Dorricott*, and *Sandray the Sophist* are mentioned in a letter to Algernon dated April 24, 1887 (YUL). For *Dust and Dew*, see *Letters*, pp. 196, 201; for *The Insurgents*, *Letters*, p. 204. *Clement Dorricott* is also mentioned in a letter without salutation dated 1887 (Berg Collection); its final fate is described in the diary entry of June 7, 1888. For Gissing's visit to Smith, see *Letters*, p. 197; for his visit to the Deanery and his glimpse of Oscar Wilde, see *Letters*, p. 205. The five pounds are requested from Algernon in a letter dated Good Friday, 1887 (YUL). His good health is insisted upon in *Letters*, p. 201, and a letter to Ellen, October 16, 1887 (Berg Collection). For speeches at Clerkenwell, see *Letters*, p. 199; diary entries of March, 1888, mention repeated visits to the district. London disturbances are mentioned in *Letters*, p. 203, and a letter to Algernon, October 19, 1887 (YUL). For the difficulty with the title of *A Life's Morning*, see *Letters*, p. 202; his distaste for the novel is from *Letters*, p. 205, and his change of mind from the same, p. 212. Visits to Worcestershire and Eastbourne are in *Letters*, pp. 207–8. Details of the death of Helen and the wording of the telegram are from the diary. Gissing's reaction and other particulars are given by Morley Roberts in *The Private Life of Henry Maitland* (New and Revised Edition; London: Eveleigh, Nash and Grayson, 1923), pp. 54–59. Roberts' account is not entirely clear or complete, but he was with Gissing at this time.

Gissing's visit to Helen's room is in the diary entry of March 1, 1888. See John D. Gordan, *George Gissing: 1857–1903* (Catalogue for an exhibition of materials from the Berg Collection of the New York Public Library [New York: New York Public Library, 1954]), p. 16, for some details of it. The creative impulse this experience stimulated is mentioned in the diary, and in letters to Algernon of March 1 and March 3 (Berg Collection).

13. *Letters,* p. 192.
14. Letters to Algernon, March 1 and 3, 1888 (Berg Collection).

SECTION III

Some information about Gissing's family life in boyhood is given in Ellen Gissing's "George Gissing: A Character-Sketch," *Nineteenth Century and After,* CII (September, 1927), 419–20. The story of Miss Curtis is suggested in brief diary entries of May 8 and 9, 1888. For his visit to Wakefield, see *Letters,* p. 221; the copies of the new edition of *Demos* are mentioned in a letter to Algernon, August 4, 1888 (YUL); for Gissing's reading of Crabbe, Hawthorne, and the *Odyssey,* see *Letters,* p. 222. The departure for Paris is mentioned in a diary entry of September 26, 1888. For Gissing's contribution to the Reverend Mr. Bainton's book, see *Letters,* p. 224.

15. *The Nether World* (London: Murray, 1903), chap. vi, p. 57.
16. Beatrice Webb, *My Apprenticeship* (New York and London: Longmans, Green and Co., 1926), pp. 196–97.
17. *Workers in the Dawn,* ed. Robert Shafer (2 vols.; New York: Doubleday, Doran, 1935), p. 161.
18. *The Private Papers of Henry Ryecroft* (New York: Modern Library, n.d.), p. 157.
19. Engels, *Condition of the Working Class,* p. 116.
20. *The Nether World,* chap. xii, p. 109.
21. George Bainton, *The Art of Authorship* (London: J. Clarke & Co., 1890), p. 82.

CHAPTER V

SECTION I

Information about Gissing's Paris trip and details about Plitt are in diary entries from September 26 to October 26, 1888. Terms for *The Nether World* and Smith, Elder's explanation are from *Letters of George Gissing to Members of His Family,* ed. Algernon and Ellen Gissing (London: Constable, 1927), p. 225, and the diary entry of October 3, 1888. For Gissing's self-analysis, see *Letters,* p. 227. His impatience with "idealism" is from the diary, June 13, 1888; readings of Ibsen are recorded in the diary, June 10 to 13, 1888. See also *Letters,*

p. 217. For his change of feeling on crossing the Channel, see *Letters*, p. 228; the explanation of the change is somewhat fuller in the diary entry of October 19, 1888.

Mlle. Le Breton is mentioned in diary entries of March 14, October 10, and October 13, 1888. Her translation, not published until the spring of 1890, was a source of intense dissatisfaction to Gissing, as he says in a letter to Bertz of May 25, 1890; it was a summary rather than a translation. His sympathy with Goethe's feelings is from *Letters*, p. 228. The conversation with the young American is described in the diary entry of October 29, 1888. Gissing's impressions of Naples are from *Letters*, pp. 232–39, and the diary, November 2, 1888. Publication of *A Life's Morning* is noted, November 15, 1888, in the diary.

For his meetings with Shortridge, see *Letters*, p. 245; the full name is given in the diary, November 20, 1888. For the ascent of Vesuvius, see *Letters*, pp. 245–46. The Shortridge household is described in the diary entry of November 23, 1888. For Gissing's trip to Rome, see *Letters*, p. 248; his parting from Plitt is in the diary, November 29, 1888. For Gissing's experiences in Rome, see *Letters*, pp. 249–67. The Sistine Chapel diagram is in the diary, December 12, 1888. For Florence see *Letters*, pp. 267–74.

Proofs of *The Nether World* are mentioned in the diary, January 5, 1889. His thoughts of a new novel are recorded in diary entries of January 15 and February 9, 1889. For Gissing's journey to Venice see *Letters*, pp. 276–78. The lecture on Zola and Gissing's reaction are described in the diary, February 11, 1889, and in a letter to Bertz dated February 13, 1889. For English opinion of Zola, see *The Victorian Conscience*, by Clarence R. Decker (New York: Twayne Publishers, Inc., 1952), chap. v. Gissing followed Zola's work closely, as the references in the dialogue of chap. x of *New Grub Street* (New York: Modern Library, 1926) suggest. In a letter to Bertz dated September 29, 1893, he wrote that Zola was universally respected in England, in spite of the arrest of Vizetelly a year or so earlier. In a letter to Bertz of February 23, 1896, he praised *La Débacle*; in letters to the same correspondent dated January 13, 1898, and March 8, 1898, Gissing expressed admiration for Zola and the part he was playing in the Dreyfus case. The return to England is from diary entries of February 26 to March 1, 1889. For the thoughts of Charlotte Brontë, see *Letters*, p. 281.

1. *Letters*, p. 227.
2. *Ibid.*, p. 228.
3. *Ibid.*, p. 229.
4. *Ibid.*, pp. 229–30.

5. *Ibid.*, p. 233.
6. *Ibid.*, p. 258.
7. *Ibid.*, p. 262.
8. *Ibid.*, p. 269.
9. *Ibid.*, p. 264.
10. Diary, February 24, 1888.

SECTION II

Favorable reactions to the poor of Europe are recorded in diary entries of December 9, 1888, in Rome; January 20, 1889, in Florence; and February 2, 1889, in Venice. Indifference to Christian art is expressed in a letter to Bertz, February 14, 1889. Information about Gissing's activities in London after his return is from the diary, March 1 to 19, 1889. The planning and actual start of *The Emancipated* are from the diary, March 20 to 28, 1889. Intercourse with the Harrison family is mentioned in the diary, April 1, 6, and 9, 1889. Roberts' arrest and Gissing's part in it are described in a letter to Algernon, April 14, 1889 (YUL); a diary entry of April 9, 1889; and Morley Roberts' *The Private Life of Henry Maitland* (New and Revised Edition; London: Eveleigh, Nash and Grayson, 1923), pp. 90–92. The verses, "The Humble Aspirations of H. M., Novelist," as Roberts called them, are in his *Maitland*, pp. 158–60. Gissing's meetings with Hartley and Hudson are mentioned in diary entries of March 23, April 13, April 27, and May 11, 1889. Plitt's reappearance and the letter from Frau Steinitz are mentioned in the diary, April 18 and May 14, 1889. Gissing's removal to Wakefield is from the diary, May 25, 1889. The complaint about family conversation is from the diary, May 30, 1889. The completion of Volume I of *The Emancipated* is from the diary, June 25, 1889.

11. *Letters*, p. 269.
12. *Ibid.*, p. 266.
13. *Ibid.*, p. 273.

SECTION III

For observations about the middle class, see Friedrich Engels, *Condition of the Working Class in England in 1844*, trans. Florence Kelley Wischnewetzky (London: G. Allen & Unwin, Ltd., 1926), particularly pp. 276–98; Matthew Arnold, "My Countrymen," *Culture and Anarchy and Friendship's Garland* (New York: The Macmillan Co., 1913), pp. 317–57; Charles Booth, *Life and Labour of the People in London* (London: Macmillan and Co., Ltd., 1889), Vol. VIII, Part II; Helen Merrell Lynd, *England in the Eighteen-Eighties* (New York: Oxford

University Press, 1945), Part II, chap. viii; and John Stuart Mill, *Principles of Political Economy* (London: Longmans, Roberts and Green, 1940), Vol. I.

14. Engels, *Condition of the Working Class*, p. 276.
15. *Ibid*, pp. 23–24.

SECTION IV

The incident involving the baby is from the diary entry of January 2, 1890.

16. *The Emancipated* (London: Bentley and Son, 1890), I, 190–92.
17. *Ibid.*, I, 25–26.
18. *Ibid.*, II, 94–95.
19. *Ibid.*, III, 243–44.

SECTION V

Algernon's removal to Harbottle is mentioned in a letter to Algernon, May 21, 1889 (YUL). Among the references to Algernon's novels and dealings with publishers are the following letters to Algernon (YUL): January 20, 1888; July 15, 1888; November 13, 1888; January 22, 1889; April (no date), 1889; April 14, 1889; April 21, 1889; July 27, 1889; June 6, 1890. See also *Letters*, p. 215. Gissing described his reaction to *Niels Lyhne* in a letter to Bertz, October 21, 1889 (YUL). His opinion of *Some Elements of Religion* is in the diary, July 21, 1889.

The painter's wife is described in the diary entry of August 26, 1889. His observations about Margaret's piety are from the diary entry of September 1, 1889. His reading of Hugo is recorded in the diary, July 21, August 31, and September 12, 1889. Gissing's remarks about his early novels are in a letter to Bertz of September 11, 1889. Receipt of Bertz's letter about Farrar's article is recorded in the diary on September 11, 1889. His reading of and reaction to it are from the diary, September 16, 1889, and a letter to Bertz, October 21, 1889. Gissing recorded the receipt of a letter from Edith Sichel in the diary on June 8, 1889. His visits to her are in diary entries of September 28, 1889, and November 9, 1889, and in a letter to Ellen, September 29, 1889 (Berg Collection). For biographical information about Edith Sichel, see F. W. Cornish, "Edith Sichel, A Study in Friendship," *Cornhill Magazine*, August, 1915, pp. 217–30. Gissing's reading is recorded in the diary, September 22 to November 9, 1889. *The Headmistress* is mentioned in the diary, October 17, 1889.

20. F. W. Farrar, "The Nether World," *Contemporary Review*, LVI (September, 1889), 371.

21. From Edith Sichel, "Two Philanthropic Novelists: Mr. Walter Besant and Mr. George Gissing," *Murray's Magazine*, III (April, 1888), 506–18.

SECTION VI

The dinner of "The Quadrilateral" is described in the diary entry of October 5, 1889. See also Roberts' biography, *W. H. Hudson, a Portrait* (New York: E. P. Dutton & Co., 1924). The terms for *The Emancipated* are given in the diary entry of September 27, 1889. Gissing's Mediterranean voyage is described in the diary, November 11 to 19, 1889. His reaction to Athens and his Greek friend are mentioned in the diary from November 19 to 24, 1889. See also *Letters*, pp. 294–301. His visit to the university is from the diary, December 14, 1889. The trip to Naples is recorded in the diary, December 17 to 22, 1889, and in a letter to Bertz, January 8, 1890. The visit to the Shortridge household is from the diary, December 31, 1889, to January 5, 1890. Gissing's illness is mentioned in diary entries of January 23 and January 31. He expressed his reaction to English people and customs in the diary entry of February 22, 1890, and a letter to Bertz, February 22, 1890.

For reactions to *The Emancipated*, see letters to Ellen of April 1, 3, and 15, 1890, in Jacqueline Steiner, "George Gissing to His Sister: Letters of George Gissing," *More Books* (Bulletin of the Boston Public Library), XXII (November, December, 1947), 323–36; also, diary, April 3, 1890. "A Man of Letters" is first mentioned in the diary, April 8, 1890. The title *New Grub Street* first appears in the diary, October 1, 1890. The trip to Paris is recorded in the diary, April 16, 1890, to May 1, 1890. Gissing's loneliness at this time and his thoughts about marrying in Germany are expressed in letters to Bertz of June 22 and August 15, 1890. Edith Sichel's invitations are mentioned in the diary, June 20 and 22, 1890. The remark about the connection between good work and marriage is from the diary, September 16, 1890. The explanation of the impossibility of his marrying is in a letter to Bertz of September 6, 1890.

For his meeting with Edith Underwood, see Roberts, *Maitland*, pp. 139–46; Mabel Collins Donnelly, *George Gissing: Grave Comedian* (Cambridge, Mass.: Harvard University Press, 1954), p. 136; and John D. Gordan, *George Gissing: 1857–1903* (Catalogue for an exhibition of materials from the Berg Collection of the New York Public Library [New York: New York Public Library, 1954]), pp. 20–21. For Roberts' opinion of her, see his *Maitland*, pp. 151–52; for H. G. Wells's opinion, his *Experiment in Autobiography* (New York: The Macmillan Co., 1934), pp. 487–88. Visits and excursions with Edith are mentioned in the diary, September 28, 1890, October 15, 1890, November 2, 5, 16, etc., 1890. His opinion of Edith and the nature of his relationship with her are from letters to Bertz of October 25, 1890, and January 23–24, 1891. Roberts gives an account of his visit to his cousins in *Maitland*, pp. 148–50. The acceptance of *New Grub Street* is from the diary, January 7, 1891. The removal to Exeter is mentioned in the diary, January 10, 1891. The uncomfortable marriage negotiations can be traced through diary entries of January 13, February 3, 5, 9, and 13, 1891. The marriage is recorded in the diary on February 25, 1891. The letter to Mrs. Harrison dated April 21, 1891, is No. 55 in the Pforzheimer Library's Gissing collection.

22. *Letters*, p. 293.
23. *Ibid.*, p. 294.
24. *Ibid.*, pp. 308–9.
25. *The House of Cobwebs* (London: Constable, 1926), pp. 257–60.
26. Roberts, *Maitland*, p. 140.

CHAPTER VI

For Q. D. Leavis' opinion of *New Grub Street*, see "Gissing and the English Novel," *Scrutiny*, VII (June, 1938), 73–81. For Smith, Elder's rejection of *Mrs. Grundy's Enemies*, see *Letters of George Gissing to Members of His Family*, ed. Algernon and Ellen Gissing (London: Constable, 1927), p. 119. For the dishonesty of publishers, see Samuel Squire Sprigge, *Methods of Publishing* (London: H. Glaisher, 1891). Information about the relations of authors and publishers may be found in *Publishing and Bookselling* by Frank Arthur Mumby (New and Revised Edition; London: Jonathan Cape, 1949) and Royal A. Gettmann's *A Victorian Publisher* (Cambridge, Engl.: Cambridge University Press, 1960), chap. iv and v. Gissing's small profit from *Workers in the Dawn* is mentioned in *Letters*, p. 94. For the Society of Authors, see Walter Besant's *Autobiography* (New York: Dodd, Mead & Co., 1902). In spite of his disapproval of outright sale, Besant seems to have disposed of his own books on these terms; see Mumby, p. 188. Gissing's reference to the supposed income from *David Grieve* is in a letter to Bertz of August 7, 1892. The earnings of Trollope's novels are from his *Autobiography* (Berkeley, Calif.: University of California Press, 1948). Gissing's calculations of profits are mentioned in a letter to Algernon of January 19, 1891 (YUL). His "Account Book" covering 1880–98 appears in facsimile in "How and Why I Collect George Gissing," by George Matthew Adams, *The Colophon*, Part XVIII

(1934). Another document of this kind, "Account of Literary Work," covering the years 1899–1902, is No. 89 in the Pforzheimer Gissing collection.

1. *New Grub Street* (New York: Modern Library, 1926), pp. 50–51.
2. *Ibid.*, p. 51.
3. *Ibid.*, pp. 128–29.
4. *Ibid.*, pp. 129–30.
5. *Ibid.*, p. 131.
6. *Ibid.*, p. 492.
7. *Ibid.*, pp. 150–51.

CHAPTER VII

SECTION I

For reactions of Gissing's friends and relations to *New Grub Street,* as well as press references to it, see *Letters of George Gissing to Members of His Family,* ed. Algernon and Ellen Gissing (London: Constable, 1927), pp. 317–19. The reaction of Roberts is recorded in the diary, April 30, 1891; of Grahame, in the diary, May 6, 1891. Gissing replied to Bertz's criticism in a letter dated April 26, 1891. Gissing's complaint about the ironic relationship between fame and starvation is from the diary, May 27, 1891; his membership in the library is recorded in the diary, June 2, 1891. His price for "Godwin Peak" is from the diary, July 20, 1891. Payn's holiday and Gissing's retreat to £150 are from the diary, August 7, 1891. In this entry, Gissing recorded an objection to Payn's penmanship: "His handwriting alone is an insult." The return of the manuscript of "Godwin Peak" and Gissing's approach to Watt are from the diary, August 9, 1891. Watt's reports on the publishers' offers for "Godwin Peak" are from the diary, August 29 and December 29, 1891. Gissing's explanation of his difficulty in placing it is in a letter to Bertz, December 16, 1891. The revision of the book is described in the diary, January 12 to February 5, 1892.

1. The quotation, in a letter to Bertz dated May 15, 1891, is from the *Saturday Review,* LXXI, No. 1854 (May 9, 1891), 572.
2. *The Author,* Vol. II, No. 1 (June 1, 1891). The next number, dated July 1, 1891, contains Lang's reply, and the rejoinders to it are in the August number.
3. Diary, May 23, 1891.
4. Postcard to Bertz, April 9, 1891.
5. Diary, May 27, 1891.
6. Letter to Bertz, May 20, 1892.

SECTION II

Gissing refers to his frequent rereading of *Väter und Söhne* in the diary, March 16, 1890. He once wrote to Ellen of "Bazaroff": "It is the purely *negative* mind, common enough now-a-days in men of thought" —Letter of June 17, 1888 (Berg Collection). References to *Niels Lyhne* are from the diary, March 18, 1890, and a letter to Bertz, March 26, 1890. Bourget is praised in a letter to Bertz, September 6, 1890. For Samuel Butler's views, see *God the Known and God the Unknown* (London: A. C. Fifield, 1909), pp. 82 ff. For Herbert Spencer on the reconciliation of science and religion, see *First Principles* (New York: D. Appleton, 1894), p. 46. For his reaction to the agnostic dilemma, see *First Principles*, pp. 29 ff; for John Stuart Mill's views on the question, see *Three Essays on Religion* (3rd ed.; London: Longmans, Roberts and Green, 1923). Reviews of *Born in Exile* are from the *Spectator*, June 25, 1892, p. 883, and *Athenaeum*, May 28, 1892, p. 693. The *Pall Mall Gazette* observation and Gissing's reaction are from the diary, July 2, 1892.

7. G. H. Lewes, *Comte's Philosophy of the Sciences* (London: Bell and Daldy, 1871), p. 9.

8. Émile Zola, *Le Roman expérimental* (Paris: Charpentier, 1893), p. 15.

9. Letter to Bertz, May 7, 1900.

10. Ivan Turgenev, *Fathers and Children*, trans. Constance Garnett (London: Heinemann, 1915), p. 226.

11. *Ibid.*, p. 222.

12. Jens Peter Jacobsen, *Niels Lyhne*, trans. Hanna Astrup Larsen (New York: The American-Scandinavian Foundation, 1919), pp. 278–79.

13. *Life and Letters of Thomas Henry Huxley* (New York: D. Appleton & Co., 1900), I, 236.

14. *Born in Exile* (London: T. Nelson and Sons, 1913), p. 377.

15. Edward Clodd, *Memories* (London: Chapman and Hall, 1916), pp. 180–81.

16. Diary, July 2, 1892.

SECTION III

The removal to St. Leonard's Terrace is from the diary, August 19, 1891. The letter from Lawrence and Bullen is from the diary, September 26, 1891. The title "The Radical Candidate" is from the diary, September 29, 1891. Bullen's visit is from the diary, November 6, 1891. Lawrence and Bullen's acceptance of *Denzil Quarrier* is from the diary,

November 25, 1891. Gissing's comments on the shorter and more dramatic mode in fiction are from the *Letters*, p. 166, and letters to Bertz of May 25, 1890, and October 18, 1891. He revised *Thyrza* in March, 1891, and *The Unclassed* in September, 1895. Joseph J. Wolff's "Gissing's Revision of *The Unclassed*," *Nineteenth Century Fiction*, VIII (June, 1953), 42–52, and Robert Shafer's edition of *Workers in the Dawn* (New York: Doubleday, Doran, 1935), give information about the new forms of these novels. See also the discussion of Gissing and the three-volume novel in Royal A. Gettmann's *A Victorian Publisher* (Cambridge, Engl.: Cambridge University Press, 1960), pp. 252–56. In this passage, he is quoted as saying, in a letter written to a French critic in 1901: "If ever I get the opportunity, I shall give all my books a vigorous revision, and cut them down." Gissing's description of *Denzil Quarrier* as a "defence of conventionality" is in *Letters*, p. 326.

17. Letter to Algernon, July 25, 1891 (Berg Collection).

CHAPTER VIII

SECTION I

Gissing's choice of his son's names is from a letter to Algernon, December 10, 1891 (YUL), and the diary entry of December 29, 1891. Domestic difficulties are described in diary entries of December 16, 1891, and January 4, 12, and 14, 1892. The Penzance trip is from the diary, February 8–15, 1892. Gissing's plan of dealing with people placed too high is expressed in letters to Bertz, February 16 and May 1, 1892. The same idea and the title "Jacks in Office" are found in a letter to Algernon, December 17, 1891. The baby's return home and the difficult period that followed are from the diary, April 13–23, 1892. Gissing's difficulties in making progress in 1892 are recorded in the diary, June 9, July 1, July 31, and September 2, 1892, and in a letter to Bertz, December 2, 1892. Observations about Edith's ignorance are recorded in the Commonplace Book, pp. 28, 33, and 37. The completion of *The Odd Women* is from the diary, October 4, 1892.

Gissing expressed his views on "female equality" in a letter to Bertz, June 2, 1893. For the usual Victorian view of woman's role, see Coventry Patmore, *Angel in the House* in *The Poems of Coventry Patmore* (London: Oxford University Press, 1949), pp. 61–210; and John Ruskin, *Sesame and Lilies* in *Works*, ed. Cook and Wedderburn (London: Longmans, Roberts and Green, 1903–12), XVIII, 21–127. For criticism of it, see Annie Besant, *Marriage As It Is, As It Was, As It Should Be* (London: Freethought Publishing Co., [1879]); Bernard

Shaw, *Quintessence of Ibsenism* (New York: Brentano's, 1928); John Stuart Mill, *Subjection of Women* (Philadelphia: J. B. Lippincott Co., 1869); and the volume entitled *Ideas and Beliefs of the Victorians* (London: British Broadcasting Corp., 1949), by various contributors. For the history of women's emancipation, see *The Woman Question in Europe*, by Theodore Stanton (New York: G. P. Putnam's Sons, 1884), and *The Cause*, by Ray Strachey (London: G. Bell and Sons, Ltd., 1928). For a vivid description of the kind of shop Monica Widdowson was employed in, see H. G. Wells, *Experiment in Autobiography* (New York: The Macmillan Co., 1934), pp. 88–95, 115–21. Gissing's revision of *The Odd Women* is recorded in the diary, October 22 and December 1, 1892. Lawrence and Bullen's terms are from the diary, October 22, 1892. Their offer to republish *The Emancipated* and the ensuing complications are from the diary, October 22, November 17, and November 29, 1892. The publisher's account, giving somewhat different figures, appears in "Bentley and Gissing" by Royal A. Gettmann, *Nineteenth Century Fiction*, XI, No. 4 (March, 1957), 306–14.

1. Diary, December 10, 1891.
2. Diary, January 24, 1893.
3. Letter to Bertz, June 2, 1893.
4. Dickens, *Oliver Twist*, chap. li.
5. Annie Besant, *Marriage*, p. 29.

SECTION II

Gissing's visit to Birmingham and its neighborhood is from the diary, November 3–24, 1892. The projected Birmingham novel is described in letters to Bertz of December 2, 1892, January 15, 1893, and March 11, 1893, and in a letter to Algernon of February 28, 1893 (YUL). His abandonment of it is noted in the diary, April 22, 1893. For his move to Brixton, see *Letters of George Gissing to Members of His Family*, ed. Algernon and Ellen Gissing (London: Constable, 1927), p. 334. Miss Collet's first letter to him is noted in the diary, May 10, 1893. Her lecture was reported in *The Queen*, March 5, 1892, p. 395. Gissing recorded the receipt of her articles in the diary, May 13 and 14, 1893. In 1902, Miss Collet published some of her articles in a volume entitled *Educated Working Women* (London: D. S. King and Son, 1902). Gissing's first meeting with her is recorded in the diary, July 18, 1893. Her offer to support Walter is recorded in the entry of September 16, 1893. Information about her and her relations with Gissing are found in "George Gissing and Clara Collet," by Ruth M. Adams, *Nineteenth Century Fiction*, XI (June, 1956), 72–77.

Gissing's original opinion about short stories is in a letter to Algernon, April 9, 1889 (YUL). The composition of "A Victim of Circumstances" is recorded in the diary, November 19–20, 1891. Its acceptance is noted in the diary, November 19, 1892. Blackwood's request for more contributions is from the diary, December 29, 1892. Another early short story, "Letty Coe," was published in *Temple Bar* in August, 1891, though it had been accepted years before. For Gissing's first relations with Shorter, see John D. Gordan, *George Gissing: 1857–1903* (Catalogue for an exhibition of materials from the Berg Collection of the New York Public Library [New York: New York Public Library, 1954]), p. 25.

"Lou and Liz" is recorded in the diary April 17, 1893. His attempt to get a higher price from Shorter is noted in the diary, September 15, 1893. His approach to Colles is from the diary, September 19 and 22, 1893. The re-establishment of his relations with Shorter is from the diary, December 4, 1893; the completion of the six stories is noted December 26, 1893. His letter to Bertz about the "commercial path" is dated September 29, 1893. "Miss Lord" can be traced through diary entries of September 12, October 16, 1893, and January 1 and April 13, 1894. The serial agreement with Shorter that resulted in *Eve's Ransom* is recorded in the diary, January 15, 1894. Payment for the six stories is noted February 24, 1894. Bullen's account of sales is recorded in the diary, January 25, 1894. Gissing's membership in the Society of Authors is recorded January 15, 1894.

6. Letter to Bertz, December 2, 1892.

SECTION III

His difficulty with the beginning of *Eve's Ransom* is from the diary, May 10–18 and May 26, 1894. The visit to Halesworth is described in the diary, May 26, 1894. The move to Clevedon is from the diary, June 2, 1894. The completion of *Eve's Ransom* is from the diary, June 29, 1894. Gissing's dealings with Barnard are mentioned in the diary, August 4, 1894, September 17, 1894, and November 22, 1894, and in a letter to Bertz, November 24, 1894. The sale of *Eve's Ransom* is recorded in the diary, April 3 and 29, 1895. Gissing's first Society of Authors dinner is recorded in the diary, October 19, 1894. The second, with his comment on Besant, is from the diary, November 19, 1894. His letter of complaint to Bertz is dated June 23, 1895. Other complaints about writers—especially Besant—are in a letter to Bertz, August 27, 1895.

The weekend at Clodd's is from the diary, June 6, 1895. The Omar

Khayyám dinner is from the diary, July 13, 1895. The meeting between Meredith and Gissing is also described in A *Bookman's Letters*, by Sir W. Robertson Nicoll (London: Hodder and Stoughton, 1913), pp. 5–6. This meeting between Hardy and Gissing was not the first. A letter to Margaret in March, 1887, speaks of an earlier acquaintance (*Letters*, p. 190), and the copy of *Isabel Clarendon* in the Berg Collection was inscribed to Hardy on June 30, 1886 (Gordan, *George Gissing*, p. 13). The appearance of *New Grub Street* in the Budapest paper *Pester Lloyd*, is mentioned in a letter to Bertz, February 16, 1892. The matter of the Reverend Osborne Jay is in diary entries of September 8, 9, 11, and 13, 1893, and a letter to Bertz, September 29, 1893. The Reverend Mr. Jay's invitation and Gissing's visit are from the diary, December 21, 1894, and March 31, 1895. The French critic was Blaze de Bury, who had asked Gissing for permission to translate *The Odd Women* in a letter mentioned in the diary, November 30, 1894. He had allowed translations of his earlier books for nothing, but now, on the advice of Lawrence and Bullen, he asked twenty guineas. The periodical references are noted in a diary entry of January 16, 1895. The figures of his bank balance are in a diary entry of January 4, 1896. Hardy's remark to Nicoll is from W. Robertson Nicoll, *People and Books* (London: Hodder & Stoughton, Ltd., 1926), pp. 190–91. His recommendation was so strong that Nicoll read all of Gissing's work.

The beginning of the revision of *The Unclassed* is mentioned in the diary, September 8, 1895, and in a letter to Bertz, September 22, 1895. For a study of this revision, see "Gissing's Revision of *The Unclassed*," by Joseph J. Wolff, *Nineteenth Century Fiction*, VIII (June, 1953), 42–52. The sale of *Sleeping Fires* is recorded in the diary, March 27, 1895. The possibility of editing Crabbe is mentioned in the diary, February 4, 1895, and Crabbe is discussed in *Letters*, p. 222. Jerome's approach to Gissing is from the diary, March 14, 1895. The visits to Meredith are recorded September 3 and 12, 1895. The visit to Hardy is from the diary, September 15–16, 1895, and from a letter to Algernon, September 22, 1895, published in "George Gissing at Max Gate, 1895," by Richard L. Purdy, *Yale University Library Gazette*, XVII, No. 3 (January, 1943), 51–52. The winter Omar Khayyám dinner is from the diary, December 6, 1895. The lunch with Shorter and others is from the diary, January 11, 1896. The beginning of notes for a new novel is from the diary, January 1, 1896. The birth of Alfred and attendant complications are from the diary, January 20–25, 1896. Gissing's decision to leave Walter in Wakefield is recorded, April 10 and 22, 1896, in the diary. His motives and the situation at home are described in a letter to Algernon of April 22, 1896 (YUL).

7. Wells, *Experiment in Autobiography*, p. 483.
8. Nicoll, *A Bookman's Letters*, p. 291.
9. Diary, June 6, 1895.
10. Diary, January 12, 1895.

SECTION IV

Gissing's visit to the Harrisons in 1896 is in the diary, August 24, 1896. His meeting with Wells is from the diary, November 20, 1896. Biographical information about Wells is from his *Experiment in Autobiography*. His comments on Gissing are on pp. 481–94. "Benedict's Household" is mentioned in a letter to Bertz, May 9, 1896. The completion of *The Whirlpool* is recorded in the diary, December 18, 1896. Miss Collet contended that Gissing identified himself with Harvey Rolfe as a form of self-reproach; she explains this in a letter to Roberts dated November 23, 1904 (Berg Collection). Though its ironic tone is not unmistakable, Rolfe's dialogue about Kipling is intended to be hostile. By this time Gissing detested Kipling as a spokesman for imperialism ("That fellow has done terrible harm"—Letter to Bertz, January 17, 1899); but he thought very highly of him before jingoism became an important issue in his mind. In letters to Bertz of May 20, 1892, and October 2, 1894, he praised *Barrack-Room Ballads* and Kipling's short stories. For the success of *The Whirlpool*, see a letter to Bertz, May 9, 1897.

11. Diary, November 26, 1896.
12. Letter to Bertz, September 27, 1896.
13. *The Whirlpool* (London: Lawrence and Bullen, 1897), p. 45.
14. *The Private Papers of Henry Ryecroft* (New York: Modern Library, n.d.), p. 10.
15. H. G. Wells, "The Novels of Mr. George Gissing," *Contemporary Review*, LXII (August, 1897), p. 193. Gissing's reaction appears in a letter to Wells of August 7, 1897; see *George Gissing and H. G. Wells*, ed. Royal A. Gettmann (Urbana, Ill.: University of Illinois Press, 1961), p. 47.

SECTION V

References to Gissing's flight from home and the events between February and June, when he was separated from his diary, are recorded in the entry of June 2, 1897. His earlier visit to Budleigh Salterton is mentioned in a letter to Algernon of February 9, 1891 (in the Huntington Library). His plan to write a historical novel is in a letter to Bertz, June 15, 1897. Miss Orme is mentioned in the diary entry of June 4,

1897. A conference with the librarian of the London Library is from the diary entry of July 10, 1897. The letter from Rose proposing the Dickens book is noted in the diary entry of December 27, 1896. *The Town Traveller* is mentioned in diary entries of June 8 and 28, 1897, and a letter to Bertz of June 15, 1897.

The unhappy summer holiday of 1897 is from the diary entries of July and August. His letter to Margaret is recorded in the diary, August 17, 1897. His meeting with Pinker is described in the diary, August 27, 1897. His decision to go to Italy is from the diary, August 28, 1897, and a letter to Bertz, September 13, 1897. Miss Orme's helpful intervention is described in the diary, September 10 and 14, 1897, and in letters to Roberts of March 12 and July 19, 1897 (Berg Collection). Norman's suggestion is recorded in the diary, September 9, 1897; Bullen's reaction is from the diary, September 21, 1897.

16. Morley Roberts, *The Private Life of Henry Maitland* (New and Revised Edition; London: Eveleigh, Nash and Grayson, 1923), p. 193.

17. Diary, June 2, 1897.

18. Letter to Algernon, March 26 (?), 1897 (YUL).

19. Diary, August 25, 1897.

CHAPTER IX

SECTION I

Gissing's trip to Siena and his activities there are from the diary, September 22 to October 20, 1897. The completion of *Charles Dickens: A Critical Study* is recorded in the diary, November 5, 1897. The fellow lodger whom Gissing called "O'Donne" was actually Brian Ború Dunne. See *George Gissing and H. G. Wells*, ed. Royal A. Gettmann (Urbana, Ill.: University of Illinois Press, 1951), p. 108. The article by George Stott referred to here is "Charles Dickens," *Contemporary Review*, X (1869), 203–25. Andrew Lang's observations are from the *Fortnightly Review*, December, 1898. The references to Taine are from Hippolyte A. Taine, *History of English Literature*, trans. H. van Laun (New York: Henry Holt & Co., 1886), pp. 339–66.

Information about the prefaces to the Rochester Edition and magazine articles on Dickens is from John D. Gordan, *George Gissing: 1857–1903* (Catalogue for an exhibition of materials from the Berg Collection of the New York Public Library [New York: New York Public Library, 1954]), pp. 34–35. A series of letters to George Kitton about his work on the Imperial Edition of *Charles Dickens* and related matters is Nos. 27–38 in the Gissing collection of the Pforzheimer Library. Information about the abridgment of Forster's *Life of Dickens* is in a letter to J. B. Pinker, October 13, 1901 (Berg Collection). Gissing's first reading of Forster is described in a letter to Bowes, February 21 [1873] (YUL).

1. *Charles Dickens: A Critical Study* (London: Gresham Publishing Co., 1904), p. 106.
2. *Ibid.,* p. 103.
3. *Ibid.,* p. 202.
4. *Ibid.,* p. 48.
5. *Ibid.,* p. 117.

SECTION II

The beginning of the Calabrian trip is from the diary, November 10–17, 1897. His conclusions about Alaric's grave are from the diary, November 18, 1897. The events at Taranto are from the diary, November 21, 1897, and *By the Ionian Sea* (London: Chapman and Hall, 1921). The visits to Metaponto and Cotrone are from the diary, November 25, 1897. Gissing's illness at Cotrone is described in *By the Ionian Sea*. The quinine dreams are described in the diary, November 29, 1897. Norman Douglas in *Old Calabria* (Boston: Houghton Mifflin Company, 1915) described again the Cotrone scenes associated with Gissing, discussing them in the chapter "Memories of Gissing," pp. 296–302. The visit to Catanzaro is from the diary, December 6–7, 1897. The visit to Squillace and the arrival at Reggio are from the diary, December 10, 1897. The visit to Cassino is from the diary, December 14–15, 1897. Gissing's visit to Rome and his activities there are from the diary, December 19, 1897, to April 11, 1898. His somewhat hysterical preparations for the arrival of the Wellses may be followed in the letters in Gettmann's *Gissing and Wells*, pp. 76–95. The agreement for *The Town Traveller* is from the diary, February 12, 1898. Miss Orme's reports about Edith are recorded in the diary, January 6, February 24, and March 25, 1898, and in a letter to Algernon, December 28, 1897 (YUL). The letters about Edith's removal are all to Algernon, February 22, March 13, and March 17, 1898 (YUL). The negotiations through Brewster are mentioned in the diary, March 14, 1898. Gissing's visit to Germany and his return to England are from the diary, April 14–18, 1898.

6. Diary, December 11, 1897.
7. Letter to Algernon, January 27, 1898 (YUL).
8. Letter to Bertz, February 10, 1898.
9. Diary, April 15, 1898.

Gissing's activities on his return to England in the spring are from the diary, April 18 to June 3, 1898. His invitation to the Wellses is in Gettmann's *Gissing and Wells*, p. 101. His attempt at drama is chronicled in the diary, June 3–17, 1898. His reply to Richards' proposal is recorded in the diary, June 24, 1898; the letter itself, dated from Wakefield, is in the Berg Collection. Richards had recently entered publishing, and was engaged in aggressive "author-hunting." Details about Edith's behavior are from a letter to Roberts, August 14, 1898 (Berg Collection); diary entries of June 6, 11, and 17, August 4 and 23, 1898; and from a letter to Bertz, September 4, 1898. Edith's terms are noted in the diary, August 27, 1898. Her visit is from the diary, September 7, 1898. "In mild intervals," Gissing wrote to Roberts in a letter dated February 6, 1899 (Berg Collection), "she spread the rumour that she refused to live with me because *I was a disciple of Oscar Wilde!*"

His first letter from Gabrielle Fleury is noted in the diary, June 23, 1898. Their first meeting at Wells's house is described in *Experiment in Autobiography*, by H. G. Wells (New York: The Macmillan Co.; 1934), p. 489, and the diary, July 6, 1898. Gabrielle's visit to Dorking is from the diary, July 26, 1898. The composition of the first Dickens preface is from the diary, August 10–13, 1898. Richards' inquiry about his next book is from the diary, September 6, 1898; his acceptance of the option offered by Gissing is from the diary, September 10, 1898. The same entry records Methuen's report on *The Town Traveller*.

Gabrielle's return to England is from the diary, October 5 and 8, 1898. The visit is recorded in the diary, October 9–15, 1898. Details about Gabrielle are from Morley Roberts, *The Private Life of Henry Maitland* (New and Revised Edition; London: Eveleigh, Nash and Grayson, 1923), pp. 222–25; Wells, *Experiment in Autobiography*, p. 489; and a letter to Bertz of November 1, 1898. I am indebted for further information about Gabrielle to Mme. Denise Le Mallier. A letter received by Gissing from Mme. Fleury is recorded in the diary, October 17, 1898. Gissing's attempts to obtain a divorce are mentioned in letters to Bertz of February 1 and 11, 1899, and July 23, 1899. The beginning of *The Crown of Life* is from the diary, October 18, 1898; its completion is recorded January 16, 1899.

10. Letter to Grant Richards, June 24, 1898 (Berg Collection).
11. Letter to Roberts, May 7, 1898 (Berg Collection).
12. Letter to Roberts, August 14, 1898 (Berg Collection).
13. Letter to Bertz, November 1, 1898.
14. Diary, July 26, 1898.

15. July 30, 1898 (Gettmann, *Gissing and Wells*, p. 110).
16. Diary, September 10, 1898.
17. Diary, October 15, 1898.
18. Letter to Bertz, November 1, 1898.
19. Letter to Bertz, September 6, 1890.
20. Roberts, *Maitland*, p. 222.
21. Letter to Roberts, February 3, 1899 (Berg Collection).
22. Quoted in a letter to Roberts, February 6, 1899 (Berg Collection).
23. *Ibid.*

SECTION IV

For Roberts' opinion of Gissing as a lover, see his *Maitland*, pp. 141–45. Gissing's ideas on war and imperialism are found in a letter to Roberts, April 5, 1899 (Berg Collection), and letters to Bertz of January 17, and December 11 and 31, 1899. Gissing observed that his novel coincided with the "peace crusade" in a letter to Bertz of January 17, 1899. Visits with Clodd, Meredith, and Roberts are from the diary, November 12 and 13, 1898. Entries relating to Harold Frederic are dated December 29, 1898, and January 1, 2, and 7, 1899. Gissing's anger about the ostracism of Frederic's mistress and her children is plain from his letter to Wells of January 2, 1899 (Gettmann's *Gissing and Wells*, p. 132). His commitment to Algernon is from the diary, January 20 and 26, 1899. His last visit to Worcestershire is recorded in the diary, March 22, 1899; his stay at Lewes is from the diary, May 1, 1899.

24. Letter to Bertz, March 31, 1899.

CHAPTER X

SECTION I

The ceremony at Rouen is recorded in the diary, May 7, 1899. See also H. G. Wells, *Experiment in Autobiography* (New York: The Macmillan Co., 1934), p. 489. The beginning of *By the Ionian Sea* is from the diary, June 29, 1899. The trip to Switzerland is mentioned in the diary, July 28 to September 25, 1899. The beginning of "The Coming Man" is from the diary, October 1, 1899. Payment for *The Crown of Life* is from the diary, September 27, 1899. His intentions in "Among the Prophets" are from a letter to Bertz, December 11, 1899. The ultimate fate of this novel is from a letter to Pinker, March 13, 1901 (Berg Collection). His return to work on "The Coming Man" is from the diary, May 28, 1900. He was not as skeptical of Izoulet's ideas as his use of them in his book would suggest. He recommended Izoulet's work enthusiastically to Bertz in a letter of January 22, 1900. Gabrielle met Izoulet in the summer of 1901; the latter had heard of Gissing's use of his book, and was both puzzled and mildly resentful about it. See Gabrielle's letter to Mrs. Wells, July 12 [1901], *George Gissing and H. G. Wells*, ed. Royal A. Gettmann (Urbana, Ill.: University of Illinois Press, 1951), p. 189.

Gissing's visit to England is from the diary, April 21, 1900, and May 1, 1900. The letter to Crane's widow is mentioned in the diary, June 9, 1900. The removal to St. Honoré les Bains is from the diary, May 25, 1900. Gissing's opinion of "The Coming Man" is from a letter to Pinker, August 29, 1900. His anxiety over Pinker's efforts to place it is evident from letters to Pinker of November 6, 11, and 29, 1900, which also contain suggestions for titles. These letters are in the Berg Collection.

1. Letter to Pinker, January 3, 1901 (Berg Collection).
2. *Denzil Quarrier* (London: Lawrence and Bullen, 1892), pp. 32–33.
3. *Our Friend the Charlatan* (London: Chapman and Hall, 1901), p. 38.
4. Thomas Henry Huxley, "Evolution and Ethics," *Selected Works* (Westminster Edition; New York and London: D. Appleton, 1896–1902), IX, 75. See also John Stuart Mill, "On Nature," *Three Essays on Religion* (3rd ed.; London: Longmans, Roberts and Green, 1923).
5. Huxley, "Evolution and Ethics," p. 83.

SECTION II

Gissing's letters to Pinker about the proposed collected edition are dated August 12, September 14, and October 6, 1900 (there are two letters on this date), in the Berg Collection. The composition of *The Private Papers of Henry Ryecroft* is recorded in the diary, September 1 to October 28, 1900. An early intention to write a book of essays is suggested on page two of the Commonplace Book, where Gissing makes a note of the title "Thought & Reverie" for such a book. The note cannot be dated exactly, but it was probably made not long before July, 1887. The identification of the "solitary friend" as Roberts is in a letter to Roberts, May 7, 1902 (Berg Collection). His complaint about the "circumfluence" of English people was written, after a visit to Italy, in a letter to Bertz, February 22, 1890. Gissing's lack of resignation to poverty and obscurity is obvious from letters to Roberts, December 15, 1901 (Berg Collection), and to Bertz, October 25, 1902. The letter from Gabrielle describing Gissing's indignation at the *Athenaeum* review is dated September 21–22, 1904 (Berg Collection).

6. Letter to Pinker, October 6, 1900 (Berg Collection). (One of two letters with this date.)

7. *The Private Papers of Henry Ryecroft* (New York: Modern Library, n.d.), pp. 10–11.

8. *Ibid.*, p. 2.

9. *Ibid.*, p. 82.

10. *Ibid.*, p. 83.

11. *Ibid.*, p. 183.

12. *Ibid.*, pp. 184–85.

13. *Letters of George Gissing to Members of His Family*, ed. Algernon and Ellen Gissing (London: Constable, 1927), p. 367. Ironically, Walter Gissing was killed in combat in World War I while fighting in France.

14. *Ryecroft Papers*, p. 138.

15. *Ibid.*, p. 151.

16. Letter to Harrison, February 11, 1903 (Pforzheimer Gissing collection, No. 60).

SECTION III

The beginning of "A Vanquished Roman" is from the diary, December 25, 1900. The visit of Wells and his wife is recorded March 8, 1901. The influenza is mentioned in the diary, March 22 to April 3, 1901. Gissing's trip to England is from the diary, April 7, 1902, and from letters to the Wellses of May 21 and 24, 1901 (Gettmann, *Gissing and Wells*, pp. 157–62). Information about the sanatorium is from the diary, April 7, 1902, and from letters to the Wellses, both June 25, 1901 (Gettmann, *Gissing and Wells*, pp. 178–81). The visit with James is from *Letters*, p. 377. For opinions about food in Gissing's French household, see Morley Roberts, *The Private Life of Henry Maitland* (New and Revised Edition; London: Eveleigh, Nash and Grayson, 1923), pp. 247–48; and Wells, *Experiment in Autobiography*, p. 490. Gabrielle's views of her difficulties with Gissing are expressed in letters to the Wellses of June 10 and 24, and July 12, 1901 (Gettmann, *Gissing and Wells*, pp. 162–77, 182–90). Villa Souvenir, the pension at Arcachon, is mentioned in a letter to Roberts, December 15, 1901 (Berg Collection). Gissing described his labored breathing in a letter to Roberts quoted in Roberts, *Maitland*, pp. 241–42.

The work done toward the end of 1901 is from the diary, April 7, 1902. Discussion of the Forster abridgment is from letters to Pinker, October 13 and 20, 1901 (Berg Collection). Edith's insanity and Gissing's reaction to it are from a letter to Bertz, February 24, 1902. The list of presentation copies containing her name is in a letter to Pinker,

January 26, 1903 (Berg Collection). The decision to leave Paris is re-
corded in the diary, April 14, 1902. His house-seeking in St. Jean de
Luz is in the diary, April 28 to May 12, 1902. The beginning of *Will
Warburton* is from the diary, July 10, 1902. The change of title for the
Ryecroft Papers is mentioned in a letter to Pinker, July 27, 1902 (Berg
Collection). The new beginning of *Will Warburton* is from the diary,
November 1, 1902. For Gissing's sciatica, see *Letters*, p. 392; it is also
mentioned in a letter to Roberts, February 22, 1903 (Berg Collection).
For the popularity of the *Ryecroft Papers*, see *Letters*, p. 393. The
clergyman's letter is mentioned in a letter to Bertz, April 5, 1903.

For Roberts' account of his last visit to Gissing, see his *Maitland*,
pp. 252–55. The interest shown by McClure's in *New Grub Street* is
from a letter to Pinker, April 14, 1903 (Berg Collection). The move
to St. Jean Pied de Port is from *Letters*, p. 393. Progress on *Veranilda*
can be traced through a letter to Pinker, July 10, 1903 (Berg Collection), and *Letters*, pp. 393 and 395. Details of Gissing's last illness and
the circumstances surrounding it are from the following sources: Roberts, *Maitland*, p. 271 ff., Mr. Cooper's account in *Letters*, pp. 397–99,
Wells, *Experiment in Autobiography*, pp. 491–93, and "The Death of
Gissing: A Fourth Report" by Arthur C. Young, *Essays in Literary
History* edited by Rudolf Kirk and C. F. Main (New Brunswick:
Rutgers University Press, 1960), pp. 217–28. Mr. Young's essay gives
Gabrielle's views as they are expressed in five letters to Bertz. There are
a number of factual discrepancies among these accounts. Roberts does
not say that he received a telegram from Gabrielle, though Wells
thought he did. He also says he arrived on the morning of the twenty-
eighth to find that Gissing had already died, but the time of death was
the afternoon of the twenty-eighth. The consultation is mentioned in
a letter from the English nurse, Miss E. Robertson Bayman, written to
Roberts on January 14, 1904 (Berg Collection). For a description of
the sickroom, see Wells, *ibid.*, pp. 491–92. For the time and date of
Gissing's death, I am indebted to M. Pierre Coustillas, who has consulted the official death certificate. A postcard from Gabrielle to Bertz
postmarked St. Jean Pied de Port, December 28 (YUL), was written
to say that Gissing was dying, but it ends with the added words "Mon-
day. Died today 1 h. afternoon." The fact that the immediate cause of
death was a "miocardite" resulting from bronchial pneumonia is given
in a letter from Gabrielle to Roberts, January 17, 1904 (Berg Collection).

17. Diary, April 18, 1901. The French doctor, Chauffard, was called
"Piffard" by Roberts.

18. Letter from Gabrielle to Mrs. Wells, July 12, 1901 (Gettmann, *Gissing and Wells*, p. 185).
19. Letter to Wells, June 25, 1901 (Gettmann, *Gissing and Wells*, p. 181).
20. *Letters*, p. 378.
21. Letter to Roberts, December 15, 1901 (Berg Collection).
22. Letter to Bertz, July 27, 1902.
23. *Letters*, pp. 398–99.
24. Roberts, *Maitland*, p. 270

CHAPTER XI

SECTION I

The matter of the *Church Times* announcement and Roberts' reply to it is from Morley Roberts, *The Private Life of Henry Maitland* (New and Revised Edition; London: Eveleigh, Nash and Grayson, 1923), pp. 276–81. Letters on this subject to Roberts from Gabrielle, January 17, 1904, and from the nurse, Miss Bayman, January 14, 1904, are in the Berg Collection. A portion of Mr. Cooper's letter to Margaret is in *Letters of George Gissing to Members of His Family*, ed. Algernon and Ellen Gissing (London: Constable, 1927), pp. 397–99.

SECTION II

The Wells preface is mentioned by Miss Collet in letters to Roberts of September 30, 1904, and October 1, 1904 (Berg Collection). For Roberts' opinion, see his *Maitland*, pp. 292–93. Gabrielle's letter referring to the Wells article is dated September 21–22, 1904 (Berg Collection). The H. G. Wells article, "George Gissing: An Impression," appeared in the *Monthly Review*, XVI (August, 1904), 159–72, and has been republished in Gettmann's *Gissing and Wells*, pp. 260–77.

SECTION III

For two observations about Gissing and the Victorian novel, see Q. D. Leavis, "Gissing and the English Novel," *Scrutiny*, VII (June, 1938), 73–81; and Frank Swinnerton, *George Gissing: A Critical Study* (London: M. Secker, 1912), pp. 165–68. Swinnerton's remark about Gissing's debt to George Eliot is on p. 51. Gissing's letter to Bertz identifying himself as a disciple of George Eliot "some ten years ago" is dated February 16, 1892 (Berg Collection).

1. Madeleine L. Cazamian, *Le Roman et les idées en Angleterre* (Strasbourg and Paris: Librairie Istra, 1923), p. 309.

2. Thomas Hardy, "Candour in English Fiction," *Life and Art* (New York: Greenberg, 1925), pp. 77–78.

3. *Workers in the Dawn*, ed. Robert Shafer (New York: Doubleday, Doran, 1935), I, 282.

SECTION IV

Keary's article is from the *Athenaeum*, January 16, 1904, p. 82. Waugh's article is from the *Fortnightly Review*, February, 1904, pp. 244 ff. Gissing's reaction to the man who read *Robinson Crusoe* is from the Commonplace Book, p. 29 (Berg Collection). For G. H. Lewes on "truth" and "The Principle of Sincerity," see *The Principles of Success in Literature* (Boston: Allyn and Bacon, 1891), pp. 86–91. Gissing's two critical essays were: "Why I Don't Write Plays," *Pall Mall Gazette*, September 10, 1892, and "Realism in Fiction," *The Humanitarian*, July, 1895. The comment on "impersonal" writing is from a letter to Bertz, March 17, 1892, and the letter stressing personality is also to Bertz, December 6, 1896.

4. Edmund Gosse, *Leaves and Fruit* (London: W. Heinemann, Ltd., 1927), p. 277.

5. Letter to Roberts, February 10, 1895 (Berg Collection); printed in part in Roberts, *Maitland*, p. 301, and in Morley Roberts, "The Letters of George Gissing," *Virginia Quarterly Review*, VII (July, 1931) 409–26.

6. Lewes, *Principles of Success in Literature*, p. 102.

7. Charles Baudelaire, "Le gouvernement de l'imagination," in Oeuvres Complètes (Brussels: Editions "La Boetie," 1948), II, 170.

8. "Realism in Fiction," *Selections Autobiographical and Imaginative from the Works of George Gissing*, ed. A. C. Gissing (London: Jonathan Cape, 1929), p. 220.

9. *Charles Dickens: A Critical Study* (London: Gresham Publishing Co., 1904), p. 85.

10. *Letters*, p. 141.

SELECTED BIBLIOGRAPHY

WORKS BY GISSING

Listed in order of original publication. The dates in parentheses are those of the first editions.

(1880) *Workers in the Dawn*, ed. Robert Shafer. 2 vols. New York: Doubleday, Doran, 1935.
(1884) *The Unclassed*. London: Sidgwick and Jackson, 1911.
(1886) *Isabel Clarendon*. 2 vols. London: Chapman and Hall, 1886.
(1886) *Demos: A Story of English Socialism*. New York: E. P. Dutton & Co., Inc., n.d.
(1887) *Thyrza*. London: Eveleigh, Nash and Grayson, 1928.
(1888) *A Life's Morning*. London: Home and Van Thal, 1947.
(1889) *The Nether World*. London: Murray, 1903.
(1890) *The Emancipated*. London: Bentley and Son, 1890.
(1891) *New Grub Street*. New York: Modern Library, 1926.
(1892) *Denzil Quarrier*. London: Lawrence and Bullen, 1892.
(1892) *Born in Exile*. London: T. Nelson and Sons, 1913.
(1893) *The Odd Women*. New York and London: Macmillan, 1893.
(1894) *In the Year of Jubilee*. New York: D. Appleton and Company, 1895.
(1895) *Eve's Ransom*. New York: D. Appleton and Company, 1895.
(1895) *The Paying Guest*. New York: Dodd, Mead and Company, 1895.
(1895) *Sleeping Fires*. London: Fisher, Unwin, 1895.
(1897) *The Whirlpool*. London: Lawrence and Bullen, 1897.
(1898) *Human Odds and Ends*. London: Sidgwick and Jackson, 1915.
(1898) *Charles Dickens: A Critical Study*. London: Gresham Publishing Company, 1904.

(1898)   *The Town Traveller.* New York: F. A. Stokes, 1898.
(1899)   *The Crown of Life.* London: Methuen, 1899.
(1901)   *Our Friend the Charlatan.* London: Chapman and Hall, 1901.
(1901)   *By the Ionian Sea.* London: Chapman and Hall, 1921.
(1903)   *The Private Papers of Henry Ryecroft.* New York: Modern Library, n.d.
(1904)   *Veranilda.* New York: Dutton, 1905.
(1905)   *Will Warburton.* London: Constable, 1915.
(1906)   *The House of Cobwebs.* London: Constable, 1926.
(1924)   *Sins of the Fathers and Other Tales.* Chicago: Covici, 1924.
(1924)   *Critical Studies of the Works of Charles Dickens.* New York: Greenberg, 1924.
(1925)   *The Immortal Dickens.* London: Cecil Palmer, 1925.
(1927)   *A Victim of Circumstances.* London: Constable, 1927.
(1929)   *Selections, Autobiographical and Imaginative from the Works of George Gissing,* ed. A. C. Gissing. Introduction by Virginia Woolf. London: Jonathan Cape, 1929.
(1931)   *Brownie.* New York: Columbia University Press, 1931.
(1938)   *Stories and Sketches.* London: Michael Joseph, 1938.
(1962)   *George Gissing's Commonplace Book,* ed. Jacob Korg. New York: New York Public Library, 1962.

LETTERS

Letters of George Gissing to Members of His Family, ed. Algernon and Ellen Gissing. London: Constable, 1927.
George Gissing and H. G. Wells, Their Friendship and Correspondence, ed. Royal A. Gettmann. Urbana: University of Illinois Press, 1961.
The Letters of George Gissing to Eduard Bertz, 1887–1903, ed. Arthur C. Young. New Brunswick, N.J.: Rutgers University Press, 1961.

CHIEF MANUSCRIPT SOURCES

Berg Collection, New York Public Library
Holograph Diary, 1887–1902, 3 volumes.
Commonplace Book, 1887–1903.
Miscellaneous Notes of Childhood, 12 leaves.
"John Milton," dated Lindow Grove, 1871.
Letters to Algernon Gissing, January 12, 1878—March 14, 1902.
Letters to Ellen Gissing, February 27, 1883—November 5, 1889.
Letters to Margaret Gissing, October 26, 1879—June 16, 1902.
Letters to Morley Roberts, December 6, 1894—November 6, 1903.

Letters to James B. Pinker, August 12, 1900—December 20, 1903.
Letters of Gabrielle Gissing to Mr. and Mrs. Morley Roberts, November 4, 1904—June 1, 1912 (?).

Yale University Library

"Verses," 1869 to 1882 (?), a notebook of 93 pages.
17 letters to Bowes, 1870 (?)–December, 1873.
Notebook kept by Gissing in America, 1877.
189 letters to Eduard Bertz, 1887–1903.
86 letters and postcards to Algernon Gissing, 1878–1891.
20 letters to Ellen Gissing.
8 letters to Harry Hick.

Carl H. Pforzheimer Library (Gissing Collection)

No. 15 "Hope of Pessimism," 28 leaves.
No. 20 Letter to Frederic Harrison, July 9, 1880.
No. 57 Letter to Frederic Harrison, June 24, 1884.
No. 58 Letter to Frederic Harrison, August 17, 1884.
No. 59 Letter to Frederic Harrison, November 7, 1895.
No. 83 "The English Novel of the Eighteenth Century," 18 folio sheets.
No. 89 "Account of Literary Work, 1902."
Miscellaneous letters to Algernon and Ellen Gissing, Mr. and Mrs. Frederic Harrison, F. G. Kitton, Edward Clodd and C. K. Shorter.

CRITICAL AND BIOGRAPHICAL

Adams, George Matthew. "How and Why I Collect George Gissing," *The Colophon*, Part XVIII (1934), no pagination.
Adams, Ruth M. "George Gissing and Clara Collet," *Nineteenth Century Fiction*, XI (June, 1956), 72–77.
Bergonzi, Bernard. "The Novelist as Hero," *Twentieth Century*, CLXIV (November, 1958), 444–55.
Brewster, Dorothy, and Angus Burrell. *Adventure or Experience*. New York: Columbia University Press, 1930.
Cazamian, Madeleine L. *Le Roman et les idées en Angleterre*. Strasbourg and Paris: Librairie Istra, 1923.
Clodd, Edward. *Memories*. London: Chapman and Hall, 1916.
Donnelly, Mabel Collins. *George Gissing: Grave Comedian*. Cambridge, Mass.: Harvard University Press, 1954.
Farrar, F. W. "The Nether World," *Contemporary Review*, LVI (September, 1889), 370–80.
Gapp, Samuel Vogt. *George Gissing, Classicist*. Philadelphia: University of Pennsylvania Press, 1936.

Gettmann, Royal A. "Bentley and Gissing," *Nineteenth Century Fiction*, XI (March, 1957), 306–14.

Gissing, Alfred C. "George Gissing—Some Aspects of His Life and Work," *National Review*, XCIII (August, 1929), 932–41.

——. "Gissing's Unfinished Romance," *National Review*, CVII (January, 1937), 82–91.

Gissing, Ellen. "George Gissing: A Character Sketch," *Nineteenth Century and After*, CII (September, 1927), 417–24.

——. "Some Personal Recollections of George Gissing," *Blackwood's Magazine*, CCXXV (May, 1929), 653–60.

Gordan, John D. *George Gissing: 1857–1903* (Catalogue for an exhibition of materials from the Berg Collection of the New York Public Library). New York: New York Public Library, 1954.

Gosse, Edmund. *Leaves and Fruit*. London: W. Heinemann, Ltd., 1927.

Harrison, Austin. *Frederic Harrison: Thoughts and Memories*. London: W. Heinemann, Ltd., 1926.

——. "George Gissing," *Nineteenth Century and After*, LX (September, 1906), 453–63.

James, Henry. *Notes on Novelists with Some Other Notes*. New York: Scribner's, 1914.

Kirk, Russell. "Who Knows George Gissing?" *Western Humanities Review*, IV (Summer, 1950), 213–22.

Korg, Jacob. "George Gissing's Outcast Intellectuals," *American Scholar*, XIX (Spring, 1950), 194–202.

——. "Division of Purpose in George Gissing," *PMLA*, LXX (June, 1955), 323–36.

——. "The Spiritual Theme of George Gissing's *Born in Exile*," in *From Jane Austen to Joseph Conrad*, ed. Robert C. Rathburn and Martin Steinmann. Minneapolis: University of Minnesota Press, 1958.

Leavis, Q. D. "Gissing and the English Novel," *Scrutiny*, VII (June, 1938), 73–81.

Maurois, André. "George Gissing," *Revue de Paris*, LXV (February, 1958), 1–13.

McKay, Ruth Capers. *George Gissing and His Critic Frank Swinnerton*. Philadelphia: University of Pennsylvania, 1933.

More, Paul Elmer. *Shelburne Essays*. 5th Ser. New York: G. P. Putnam's Sons, 1908.

Murry, J. Middleton. "George Gissing," in *Katherine Mansfield and Other Literary Studies*. London: Constable, 1959.

Nicoll, Sir William Robertson. *A Bookman's Letters*. London: Hodder and Stoughton, 1913.

Roberts, Morley. *The Private Life of Henry Maitland*. New and Revised Edition. London: Eveleigh, Nash and Grayson, 1923.

———. "The Letters of George Gissing," *Virginia Quarterly Review*, VII (July, 1931), 409–26.

Shafer, Robert. "Introduction" to *Workers in the Dawn*. New York: Doubleday Doran, 1935.

Sichel, Edith. "Two Philanthropic Novelists: Mr. Walter Besant and Mr. George Gissing," *Murray's Magazine*, III (April, 1888), 506–18.

Steiner, Jacqueline. "George Gissing to His Sister: Letters of George Gissing," *More Books* (Bulletin of the Boston Public Library), XXII (November, December, 1947), 323–36, 376–86.

Swinnerton, Frank. *George Gissing, A Critical Study*. London: M. Secker, 1912.

Times Literary Supplement (London), No. 2,402 (February 14, 1948), p. 92 ("The Permanent Stranger").

———, No. 2,861 (December 28, 1956), p. 780 (Gissing's Heroines").

Weber, Anton. *George Gissing und die Soziale Frage*. (Beiträge zur Englischen Philologie, 20 Heft.) Leipzig: B. Tauchnitz, 1932.

Wells, H. G. "The Novels of Mr. George Gissing," *Contemporary Review*, LXXII (August, 1897), 192–201.

———. "George Gissing, An Impression," *Monthly Review*, XVI (August, 1904), 160–72.

———. *Experiment in Autobiography*. New York: Macmillan, 1934.

Wolff, Joseph J. "Gissing's Revision of *The Unclassed*," *Nineteenth Century Fiction*, VIII (June, 1953), 42–52.

Woolf, Virginia. "George Gissing," in *The Common Reader, Second Series*. London: Hogarth Press, 1932.

Yates, May. *George Gissing, An Appreciation*. (Publications of the University of Manchester, English Series No. XII.) Manchester, Engl.: The University Press, 1922.

Young, Arthur C. "George Gissing's Friendship with Eduard Bertz," *Nineteenth Century Fiction*, XIII (December, 1958), 227–37.

INDEX

307

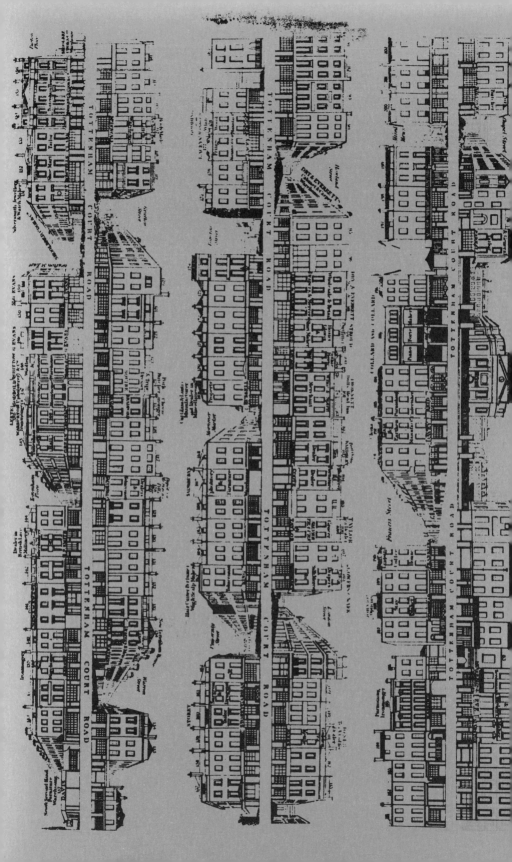